373.7 JOH

D0230934

1998745

LEARNING TO TEACH MATHEMATICS IN THE SECONDARY SCHOOL

University of
South Wales
Prifysgol
De Cymru

Library Services

What is the role of mathematics in the secondary classroom?
What is expected of a would-be maths teacher?
How is mathematics best taught and learnt?

Learning to Teach Mathematics in the Secondary School combines theory and practice to present a broad introduction to the opportunities and challenges of teaching mathematics in modern secondary school classrooms. Written specifically with the new and student teacher in mind, the book covers a wide range of issues related to the teaching of mathematics, including:

- the role of ICT
- Assessment for Learning*NEW*
- using mathematics in context*NEW*
- communicating mathematically
- planning mathematics lessons
- including special-needs pupils
- teaching mathematics post-16
- professional development.

Already a major text for many university teaching courses, this fully revised third edition takes into account new developments in the National Curriculum as well as recent changes to the standards for Qualified Teacher Status. Featuring two brand new chapters, a glossary of useful terms, addresses for resources and organisations, and tasks designed to prompt critical reflection and support thinking and writing at Masters level, this book will help you make the most of school experience, during your training, your NQT year and beyond.

Designed for use as a core textbook, this new edition of *Learning to Teach Mathematics in the Secondary School* provides essential guidance and advice for all trainee and practising teachers of secondary mathematics.

Sue Johnston-Wilder is Associate Professor at the University of Warwick; she works with PGCE students and in-service teachers in the West Midlands. She has previously taught at King's College London and the Open University.

Peter Johnston-Wilder is Associate Professor at the University of Warwick.

David Pimm is Professor of Mathematics Education at the University of Alberta, Edmonton, Canada.

Clare Lee leads the Mathematics PGCE programme at the Open University and works with in-service teachers nationally. She was previously a research fellow for the King's Formative Assessment Project.

LEARNING TO TEACH SUBJECTS IN THE SECONDARY SCHOOL SERIES

Series Editors: Susan Capel, Marilyn Leask and Tony Turner

Designed for all students learning to teach in secondary schools, and particularly those on school-based initial teacher training courses, the books in this series complement *Learning to Teach in the Secondary School* and its companion, *Starting to Teach in the Secondary School*. Each book in the series applies underpinning theory and addresses practical issues to support student teachers in school and in the training institution in learning how to teach a particular subject.

LEARNING TO TEACH MATHEMATICS IN THE SECONDARY SCHOOL

A companion to school experience

3rd Edition

Edited by

Sue Johnston-Wilder, Peter Johnston-Wilder, David Pimm and Clare Lee

University of
South Wales
Prifysgol
De Cymru

Library Services

Routledge
Taylor & Francis Group

LONDON AND NEW YORK

First edition published 1999 by Routledge
Second edition published 2005 by Routledge
Third edition published 2011 by Routledge
2 Park Square, Milton Park, Abingdon, Oxon, OX14 4RN

Simultaneously published in the USA and Canada
by Routledge
711 Third Avenue, New York, NY 10017

Routledge is an imprint of the Taylor & Francis Group, an informa business

© 2011 Sue Johnston-Wilder, Peter Johnston-Wilder, David Pimm and Clare Lee for selection and
editorial material.
Individual chapters © the contributors.

Typeset in Times and Helvetica by FiSH Books, Enfield

All rights reserved. No part of this book may be reprinted,
reproduced or utilised in any form or by any electronic, mechanical
or other means, now known or hereafter invented, including
photocopying and recording, or in any information storage or
retrieval system, without permission in writing from the publishers.

British Library Cataloguing in Publication Data
A catalogue record for this book is available from the British Library

Library of Congress Cataloging-in-Publication Data
Learning to teach mathematics in the secondary school: a companion to school experience /
    edited by Sue Johnston-Wilder...[et al.].
        p. cm.
    Includes bibliographical references and index.
    1. Mathematics—Study and teaching (Secondary)—United States. I. Johnston-Wilder, Sue.
    QA13.L43 2011
    510.71'2—dc22   2010009231

ISBN13: 978-0-415-56559-2 (hbk)
ISBN13: 978-0-415-56558-5 (pbk)
ISBN13: 978-0-203-84412-0 (ebk)

This book is dedicated to our children, the maths students of the next generation:
Robin, Beth, Jaclyn, Daniel, Alex, Alastair, Olivia, Rhiannon and Steve
and is offered in memory of Jill Bruce, Rita Nolder, Christine Shiu and Gill Hatch,
inspirational teacher-researchers who died before their time.

CONTENTS

1   MATHEMATICS EDUCATION: WHO DECIDES?   1

JOHN WESTWELL

■ mathematics and you ■ mathematics and education ■ competing influences on the mathematics curriculum ■ agencies for change

2   MATHEMATICS IN THE NATIONAL CURRICULUM   16

JOHN WESTWELL AND ROBERT WARD-PENNY

■ the scope, prescription and presentation of the curriculum ■ the development and revision of the curriculum ■ performance standards and assessment within the curriculum ■ programmes of study for the curriculum

3   PUPILS LEARNING MATHEMATICS   36

MARIA GOULDING

■ the social context of learning ■ theories of learning and knowledge ■ feelings and motivation ■ the cognitive dimension

4   DIFFERENT TEACHING APPROACHES   54

DAVID PIMM AND SUE JOHNSTON-WILDER

■ teaching as listening, asking and telling ■ forms of classroom organisation ■ resources and ideas for enhancing your teaching

12 GETTING THE WHOLE PICTURE 225

JOHN WESTWELL AND CLARE LEE

■ the whole curriculum ■ the whole person

13 TEACHING MATHEMATICS POST-16 242

GEOFF WAKE

■ background: 14–19 pathways ■ knowledge for teaching ■ qualifications: types and levels ■ mathematics and qualifications post-16 ■ institutions catering for post-16 students ■ the nature of students post-16 ■ teaching styles ■ preparing to teach a topic ■ the use of ICT in post-16 mathematics ■ reflecting on the past: looking to the future?

14 PROFESSIONAL DEVELOPMENT 267

GILL HATCH AND CLARE LEE

■ finding the right post ■ the first year of teaching ■ developing as a teacher ■ developing as a mathematician ■ career development

INTRODUCTION TO THE SERIES

This third edition of *Learning to Teach Mathematics in the Secondary School* is one of a series of books entitled *Learning to Teach Subjects in the Secondary School* covering most subjects in the secondary school curriculum. The books in this series support and complement *Learning to Teach in the Secondary School: A Companion to School Experience*, 5th edition (Capel, Leask and Turner, 2009), which addresses issues relevant to all secondary teachers.

These books are designed for student teachers learning to teach on different types of initial teacher education courses and in different places. However, it is hoped that they will be equally useful to tutors and mentors in their work with student teachers. A complementary book has also been published, entitled *Starting to Teach in the Secondary School: A Companion for the Newly Qualified Teacher*. That second book was designed to support newly qualified teachers in their first post and covers aspects of teaching that are likely to be of concern in the first year of teaching.

The information in the subject books does not repeat that in *Learning to Teach*; rather, the content of that book is adapted and extended to address the needs of student teachers learning to teach a specific subject. In each of the subject books, therefore, reference is made to *Learning to Teach*, where appropriate. It is recommended that you have both books so that you can cross-reference when needed.

The positive feedback on *Learning to Teach*, particularly the way it has supported the learning of student teachers in their development into effective, reflective teachers, has encouraged us to retain the main features of that book in the subject series. Thus, the subject books are designed so that elements of appropriate theory introduce each topic or issue. Recent research into teaching and learning is incorporated into this. This material is interwoven with tasks designed to help you identify key features of the topic or issue and apply these to your own practice.

Although the basic content of each subject book is similar, each book is designed to address the specific nature of each subject. In this book, for example, the reasons why mathematics is regarded as a key subject in the curriculum are discussed, as are different philosophical approaches to mathematics. Mathematics is one of three core subjects for all pupils in secondary school, alongside English and science. There is an argument that an understanding of mathematics is important for all members of our society and is therefore an essential subject in school, as well as being a subject of keen interest to those who will become mathematicians, scientists or engineers.

We, as editors, have found this project to be exciting. We hope that, whatever the type of initial teacher education course you are following, and wherever you may be following that course, you will find that this book is useful and supports your development into an effective, reflective mathematics teacher. Above all, we hope you enjoy teaching mathematics.

Susan Capel, Marilyn Leask and Tony Turner
March 2010

ILLUSTRATIONS

FIGURES

TABLES

TASKS

NOTES ON
CONTRIBUTORS

Ruth Edwards is a highly experienced teacher with many years of experience in secondary schools and post-16 institutions. She now works at the University of Southampton where she is a member of the university's Mathematics and Science Education Research Centre. Her research interests include mathematical subject knowledge for teaching, the transferability of mathematics to outside of the classroom, and applied and practical approaches to learning. She holds consultancy roles on functional skills (and their implementation) with the QCDA and with several examination awarding bodies. (For up-to-date information see: www.crme.soton.ac.uk)

Maria Goulding originally taught secondary mathematics in Liverpool comprehensive schools. She has since taught on PGCE courses at the University of Liverpool and the University of Durham and is currently working at the University of York. Her published work includes research on the process of becoming a teacher of mathematics, student teachers' mathematical subject knowledge, practising teachers' attitudes towards mathematics coursework and their understanding of the Cognitive Acceleration in Mathematics Education (CAME) project. Maria is co-author of several Evidence-Informed Policy and Practice (EPPI) systematic reviews: on confidence and competence in Key Stage 1 mathematics, motivation in mathematics at Key Stage 4, and ICT in mathematics learning.

Gill Hatch worked for many years at the Centre for Mathematics Education, Institute of Education, Manchester Metropolitan University. She was involved in the preparation of very many mathematics resources. She was a longstanding member of ATM and the convenor of a joint working group with the Mathematical Association: Teaching and Learning Undergraduate Mathematics. Sadly, Gill died after the second edition of this book was published.

Peter Johnston-Wilder is Associate Professor at the University of Warwick. After teaching mathematics for several years at an inner-London comprehensive school, he moved to De Montfort University, Bedford, to work in initial teacher education and in-service training for teachers. During this time he was also joint editor of *MicroMath*, a journal of the Association of Teachers of Mathematics, and an examiner of A-Level mathematics and statistics. In 2001, he moved to the Open University to research learners' perceptions of randomness. He joined the Warwick Institute of Education in 2004. His research interests are in statistical education, learners' understanding of probability and randomness, assessment in mathematics education and the impact of new technology on teaching and learning of mathematics and statistics.

Sue Johnston-Wilder (formerly **Sue Burns**) taught secondary mathematics in London comprehensive schools. In addition to her current work with PGCE students and in-service teachers in the West Midlands, Sue has taught at Kings' College London and the Open University. She has been involved with CPD and curriculum development for many years, including the Nuffield Advanced Mathematics Project (precursor to Use of Mathematics), Graded Assessment in Mathematics (precursor to the National Curriculum) and the Bowland Mathematics materials. She has written widely, and her current research interests include mathematical resilience, and teachers using ICT to support learning. (For further information see: www.go.warwick.ac.uk/mathsed)

Keith Jones taught mathematics for more than ten years in a number of multi-ethnic inner-city comprehensive schools, becoming a head of department. He now works at the University of Southampton where he directs the university's Mathematics and Science Education Research Centre. His main research interests are the integration of technology in the teaching and learning of mathematics, and the development of mathematical reasoning and how teachers can promote this. He has published widely. (For up-to-date information see: www.crme.soton.ac.uk)

Clare Lee taught secondary mathematics for over 20 years and subsequently became a local authority adviser. After a few years working at Warwick University, she currently works on the Mathematics PGCE programme at the Open University. She worked on the Formative Assessment Project at King's College London and co-authored *Assessment for Learning: Putting it into Practice* (Black *et al.*, 2003). She has published her own book on *Assessment for Learning*. Her current research interests include the contribution of language to increasing mathematical learning, and pupils' confidence in that learning, and applying these principles to classroom pedagogy.

Candia Morgan was a secondary mathematics teacher and advisory teacher in London schools for 13 years. She currently works at the Institute of Education, University of London, where she contributes to programmes of initial and continuing professional development for mathematics teachers, as well as supervising research students. Her research interests include mathematical language, and curriculum and assessment issues.

David Pimm worked in mathematics education at the Open University for 15 years from 1983 to 1997. After two years working at Michigan State University, he is currently Professor of Mathematics Education at the University of Alberta, Edmonton, Canada. The main area of his work has been in exploring interactions between language and mathematics education, thinking specifically about the issues of spoken language and written notation in mathematics classrooms.

Melissa Rodd was a secondary mathematics teacher in three comprehensive schools in Oxfordshire and became a school teacher mentor for the Oxford University PGCE while teaching at the Cherwell School. She moved into teacher education by becoming a part-time university curriculum tutor for the Oxford PGCE course while teaching at Cherwell, then moved to the University of Cumbria to teach mathematics and develop work in teacher education. After completing a PhD at the Open University, she moved to the Centre for Science and Mathematics Education at the University of Leeds, and is now a member of the mathematics special interest group at the Institute of Education, University of London.

Geoff Wake is a senior lecturer in mathematics education at the University of Manchester where, following a successful career teaching in schools and colleges, he contributes to PGCE and Masters courses. His research and curriculum development work is situated in secondary mathematics, in particular in post-14 teaching, learning and assessment. He worked with the Qualifications and Curriculum Authority to develop freestanding mathematics qualifications and AS Use of Mathematics, and has recently researched students' transitions into the study of mathematics and mathematically related subjects in colleges of higher education. He worked as part of the Evaluating Mathematics Pathways project, researching proposed mathematics curriculum changes for students post-14, and has contributed to a number of European projects seeking to support mathematical modelling and interdisciplinary learning involving mathematics and science.

Robert Ward-Penny has worked as a mathematics teacher and head of department in a Warwickshire secondary school. Currently teaching mathematics education at the Institute of Education, University of Warwick, he works with undergraduate, PGCE and Masters students. His interests include motivating the study of mathematics through the use of authentic contexts and cross-curricular opportunities, and critically appraising the role of mathematics education in the twenty-first century.

John Westwell works for the Training and Development Agency for Schools (TDA), where he is professional lead for CPD strategy. Previously he worked for the General Teaching Council on the Teacher Learning Academy, and Blackburn with Darwen LEA as Learning Communities Co-ordinator. Before this he worked as a KS3 mathematics consultant and advisory teacher for mathematics in Blackburn and the London Borough of Barking and Dagenham. Formerly, he was head of mathematics at a school in Chelmsford, where he was also the mathematics tutor for the Mid-Essex School-centred Initial Teacher Training (SCITT) consortium. He was one of the editors for the Charis Mathematics Project.

ACKNOWLEDGEMENTS

Douglas Butler, for permission to use screenshots from the Oundle School maths site.

John Hibbs, HMI, for permission to use his report of Jill Bruce at work.

Rosie Hunt for providing the handwriting in Figure 7.1.

Helen Osborn, for reading and for friendship.

The QCA, for permission to reproduce Table A3.1, taken from page D7 of the *Mathematics National Curriculum Non-Statutory Guidance* (NCC, 1989).

Yale Babylonian Collection, for permission to use the photograph of Babylonian tablet YBC 7289 in Figure 4.2.

The Open University, for permission to use the transcription of the same tablet, previously published in Fauvel and Gray, *The History of Mathematics: A Reader* (Palgrave Macmillan, 1987).

Sage Publications, for permission to use the 'Categories of knowledge for teaching' diagram (Ball *et al.*, 2008) in Figure 13.1.

NRICH, for permission to use a screenshot from their website in Figure 9.9.

Beth Burns and Olivia Johnston-Wilder, for loving support and help with checking.

INTRODUCTION

Learning to teach mathematics is not something you will do in just a year. This book might have more appropriately been titled *Beginning to Learn to Teach Mathematics in the Secondary School*. For however long you continue to teach mathematics, you will also continue to learn about the extremely complex and challenging profession you have joined. Having said that, the lessons you learn about teaching mathematics as a student teacher will have a significant impact on your future career. This book will guide you through the very important first stage of your formal development as a mathematics teacher.

Start to think of yourself as a mathematics teacher right from the beginning of your course. The career on which you are embarking is multifaceted. Not only will you be developing as a teacher, but you will also be developing as an educational researcher, as a mathematician, as a writer, as a counsellor, as a team worker and as a reflective practitioner. You will find yourself stretched intellectually, physically and emotionally; there may be times when you wonder why you ever decided to teach. However, along with the challenge, there will also be the rewards and satisfaction that come from working with young people and with your colleagues.

MAKING THE MOST OF YOUR SCHOOL EXPERIENCE

There have been some significant changes in the structure of teacher education courses in recent years. As well as there being more central government control over the aims and content of courses, there has also been a considerable increase in the time spent by pupils in schools. Many people see this as a positive development, arguing that it is essential that new teachers learn 'on the job' in the school environment. However, there is a danger that you will not get the maximum benefit from your school experience *unless* you use it as an occasion to reflect on and learn from a full range of experiences. Here is a list of ways that you can learn from and through your school experience.

Reflective journal

It is widely accepted that reflecting on your experiences in a structured way is essential if you are to develop as an effective practitioner. You will be bombarded by experiences during your time in school, so it is important that you make time to reflect. Perhaps the most effective way of supporting this process is by means of writing down your thoughts, as a record that you can look back on. Indeed, the practice of using a reflective journal as a tool for personal development goes back many centuries, and many people now use internet blogging for this purpose. If you establish the habit of keeping a reflective journal during your training, you will be well prepared to continue the practice throughout your career.

Classroom research

During your training, you will spend much of your time in classrooms. For a significant proportion of this time, you will not be primarily responsible for the teaching. Instead, although you may be supporting a teacher, you will have an excellent opportunity to observe and investigate aspects of classroom life in some detail. While student teachers often complain that they have to spend too long just observing, many experienced teachers complain that they have too few chances to observe their colleagues or their pupils. Using this special time effectively to undertake a variety of focused classroom research activities will add significantly to your knowledge and understanding of teaching and learning.

Investigating the school and the department

Given how much time you spend in school, it is important that you are familiar with how both the school and its mathematics department are organised and operate. However, you should go further than just finding out enough to survive. You have the opportunity to develop an understanding of factors that lead to an effective school and department. Comparing your school and department with those of fellow student teachers will also support this process. The teachers in your school will also benefit from the presence of a student teacher who can, on occasion, ask perceptive questions and cause them to reflect on their policies and practices.

Researching the curriculum and resources

Even if you have gone straight from school to university to teacher training, you can still expect the mathematics curriculum to have changed in the intervening years. It is important to understand the structure and content of the curriculum for different phases of schooling and to be familiar with associated qualifications and/or assessment arrangements. There is an abundance of teaching resources available to mathematics teachers. Your period of training is an ideal time to investigate these resources and to evaluate them critically. You may find that your department will also appreciate hearing about the results of such research.

Studying mathematics

As you begin to teach, it is important that you continue to study mathematics. This can include both exploring new areas of mathematics and going deeper into areas you have previously studied. In particular, you need to develop your subject knowledge in those areas of the mathematics curriculum about which you are less confident. However, even with topics with which you have no difficulty, you can enhance your teaching by thinking more deeply about the concepts and connections related to each topic. A further aspect of studying the subject involves learning more about its diverse applications and history.

Interviewing staff and pupils

You will have plenty of opportunity to discuss education informally with both staff and pupils, but it is also valuable to explore issues more formally. At the end of lessons, teachers may well need to prepare for the following lesson or they may want a break. However, arranging to interview staff, even for a short time, will mean that both you and the teacher have a chance to reflect in more depth about her or his thinking and practice and to relate it to your own developing practice. Interviewing pupils in a small group or perhaps in a pair within the wider school environment would allow you to listen to what they really think about some aspect of their education.

Reading about education

With much of your time spent in schools during your course, it is important that you make time to read widely about education. This will contribute towards the development of your personal theoretical base from which you can reflect more effectively on your school experience. It is worth planning to include reading time and visits to your education library during your school experience.

Teaching

Many student teachers consider that taking sole responsibility for teaching mathematics to a class is the main point of their school experience. Obviously, you have to have enough opportunity to learn how to cope with the complex demands that teaching lessons on your own can bring. However, in order to develop your understanding and skills for teaching, you will need to have experiences in which you just focus on particular aspects of teaching or learning. You can do this by teaching just a small group, or pair or individual, by taking responsibility for just part of a lesson or by team teaching with a colleague. Whatever form the teaching takes, be sure that it also includes opportunities for planning, assessment and evaluation.

HOW TO USE THIS BOOK

This book is divided into 14 chapters, each of which addresses an important theme. Every chapter has an introduction, and objectives, which are designed to clarify the key ideas addressed in the chapter. The summary at the end of each chapter highlights the main points made. You might find it helpful to read a chapter prior to addressing the theme in a tutorial (either at school or university). You might also find it helpful to dip in and out of the book when you want to read something to support your reflection on particular school experiences. Obviously, you will need to read more than just this book, so, in order to support your further reading, each chapter ends with some recommendations for relevant reading on the same theme. In addition, the chapters are fully referenced, thereby offering you alternative additional sources of further reading.

An important feature of this book is the tasks, which comprise a key element in each chapter and provide you with many suggestions for making the most of your school experience. There are tasks to support each of the types of learning experience addressed in the previous section and to prompt you to reflect on and evaluate your learning in school. Your course will place various requirements upon you, but there will be opportunities to negotiate with your school mentor the details of how you use your time in school. You may wish to suggest to your mentor some of the tasks from this book as possible elements of your school experience programme. The tasks will be of more value if you can talk them through with your mentors or your fellow student teachers.

At the end of the book, you will find a glossary of useful terms (Appendix 1) and a collection of useful addresses for resources and organisations (Appendix 2). You will likely add to these as you progress through your career.

The training will be hard work; at the end you will emerge as a qualified 'beginning' teacher of mathematics, prepared to inspire and encourage the next generation of young people. You are much needed. Welcome to the challenge.

INTRODUCTION TO THE THIRD EDITION

Teachers now work in a climate of constant change. You can expect change to be a feature of your teaching career; if anything, the pace of change will increase. In this third edition, we continue to reflect the waves of change that have happened since the second edition was published five years ago.

- Assessment for Learning has grown in importance and there have been major changes in summative assessment, placing increased emphasis on the reliability of teacher judgements about their pupils' learning.
- ICT has become more prevalent in schools for both teacher and pupil use and there are increased expectations that it be used. However, in England, mathematics is falling behind other subjects in use of ICT in learning (Ofsted, 2008).
- There was a major inquiry into 14–19 mathematics education in England (Smith, 2004); enquiries into mathematics education continue.
- Functional mathematics has been defined and is now part of Key Stage 3, GCSE and post-16 courses in England.
- GCSE and post-16 assessment methods have changed and continue to change.
- In England, the latest revision of the National Curriculum for mathematics (QCA, 2007a) has an emphasis on key mathematical concepts and processes, making room for greater use of ICT and studying the historical roots of mathematical topics.
- The new curriculum in England places a much greater emphasis on pedagogy, including learning in cross-curricular contexts, interactive approaches and collaborative work.
- Personal learning and thinking skills (PLTS) now feature explicitly in the new curriculum in England.
- In government documentation in England, there is an emphasis on supporting teachers' planning at both medium-term and short-term levels.

In addition, the standards for qualified teacher status (QTS) have been revised, and many PGCE courses now include M-level study. Teaching in England has become a Masters Level profession and you should expect to apply for your status as a Chartered Mathematics Teacher (CMathTeach) within 5 years.

In response to these changes, we have revised all of the chapters and added two new chapters: a chapter on Assessment for Learning that leads into the chapter on summative assessment, and a chapter that explains ideas about using mathematics in context, which complements Chapter 12 on developing the whole pupil. The tasks in each chapter have been revised in order to prompt critical reflection and to support you in developing your thinking and writing at Masters level.

There are other aspects of being a secondary mathematics teacher that do not change over time and so it is right that many aspects of this book have stayed the same. The changes we have made reflect the changed environment in which you are preparing to work.

MATHEMATICS EDUCATION: WHO DECIDES?

John Westwell

INTRODUCTION

The Mathematical Association, one of the professional organisations for mathematics teachers in the UK, published a booklet in 1995 that began with these thoughts:

> To teach Mathematics is a high calling. The truth of mathematics is real and fundamental, and we believe it is right for all pupils to study mathematics throughout all of their compulsory schooling. The questions we address in this booklet are:

> **Why** does mathematics deserve its place in the curriculum?
> **What** mathematics will it be appropriate to learn in the early 2000s?
> **How** can mathematics best be learnt by each individual pupil?

> (MA, 1995: 1)

As you learn to teach mathematics, you will need to seek answers to these key questions, though the second one has at least been addressed in part by the government via the National Curriculum for England (QCA, 2007a). However, you will soon discover that there are no simple answers. You may also be surprised to find that there is often much disagreement about the issues raised, and even whether these are the best questions to explore (see, for example, DfES (2004a)).

Indeed, some people go even further, beyond the issues raised by these questions, and argue that what really needs to be addressed is mathematics itself. The American mathematician Reuben Hersh claims that:

> The issue, then, is not, What is the best way to teach? but, What is mathematics really all about? [...] Controversies about [...] teaching cannot be resolved without confronting problems about the nature of mathematics.

> (Hersh, 1979: 34)

Your time spent as a student teacher can provide opportunities to develop your understanding of the ideas that underlie these controversies. You will then be better prepared to make teaching decisions in the best interests of your pupils.

OBJECTIVES

By the end of this chapter, you should:

■ understand how your experiences of mathematics have shaped your views about mathematics education;

■ be able to articulate clearly your current rationale for mathematics education;

■ be aware of how different groups have influenced the current shape of mathematics education in the UK;

■ be able to respond more confidently to the different expectations that will be placed on you as a mathematics teacher.

MATHEMATICS AND YOU

You are about to begin exploring how to teach mathematics, but in reality you are not a beginner; you already have a wealth of experience of mathematics education upon which to draw. Whether you have studied mathematics at degree level or not, you will have spent many hours of your life engaged in learning and using mathematics. 'The teacher's view of mathematics is shaped to a very large extent by his/her own mathematical experience as a student' (Dörfler and McLone, 1986: 87). Indeed, not only will these experiences inform your views on the nature of mathematics, but they will also influence your personal philosophy about mathematics education. It is a valuable exercise, then, at the beginning of your course, to look back and reflect on where you have come from. Task 1.1 leads you through this process.

Task 1.1 **Mathematics – your story so far**

In this task, consider your experience of mathematics and mathematics education. Read the following passage, 'Mathematical memories', which consists of a substantial number of questions and prompts. Give yourself some undisturbed time, at least thirty minutes, to reflect upon the thoughts stimulated by what you read. Note down ideas and memories as they occur to you in your reflective journal. Read the various bulleted sections slowly and do not worry if your thoughts wander. Be aware of this happening and record what you believe to be important.

Mathematical memories

■ What is your earliest memory of learning mathematics? Call to mind where you are, what you are doing, how old you are. Is it a positive memory?

■ When did you last *do* some mathematics? Think about why you were doing it and how you felt at the time.

■ Have you ever called yourself 'a mathematician'? If you have, think about when this first happened and what it meant to you at the time. If you have not, think about why not, and who you think is entitled to use such a title. Do you expect to meet mathematicians during your school experience?

■ How do you rate your ability in mathematics? Think how this view was formed and whether it has changed over time. Do you believe that your ability is something you were born with or that it is a product of your education to date? Perhaps it is a product of both, or neither? How does your ability compare with those of others? What basis are you using for your comparison?

■ Can you remember a time when you have used mathematics for something important? Think about the type of mathematics that was involved and whether it was something you learnt at school. Would other people share your opinion, do you think, about the importance of the activity? Why?

■ Can you remember a time when you have chosen to do mathematics for pleasure? Think about where you were, who you were with (if anyone) and how long you spent doing it. Do you think other people would derive pleasure from the same task? Why?

■ Try to remember some times when being mathematical has been enjoyable and satisfying. Think about what brought about the enjoyment or satisfaction. Now try to remember other times when mathematics has been boring or frustrating. How do you account for your different responses?

■ Who was your best mathematics teacher? Think what it was about this person that impressed you. Try to remember some particular moments that exemplify all that was good about his/her teaching. What aspects of this person's teaching would you like to emulate?

■ Who was your worst mathematics teacher? Think what it was about this person that led you to such a judgement. Try to remember some specific occasions that exemplify what was poor about his/her teaching. Which aspect of this person's teaching would you wish to avoid replicating in your own practice?

■ Think about all the qualifications that you have in mathematics. Consider all that you have had to do in order to earn those qualifications. Do you think they offer a fair assessment of your mathematical abilities? Are there other ways in which you would have preferred to be judged?

■ Try to remember some times when learning mathematics was difficult and times when it was easy. Why was there a difference? Consider other people with whom you have learnt mathematics. Did they find it easier or harder? Why do you think that was? Do you think you have a preferred way of learning mathematics?

■ Why did you decide you wanted to be a mathematics teacher?

Having looked back over your encounters with mathematics, you are now in a better position to look forward. You will already have hopes for your life as a mathematics teacher, but you may also have some doubts about your decision. To grow and develop as a maths teacher you will need to go on reflecting about mathematics, about education and about your place in relation to both.

Task 1.2 **Your personal vision for mathematics education**

It is important to be clear about your opinions about mathematics and mathematics education, because they will influence your practice. In order to articulate your views clearly, it can be helpful to try writing them down in a concise form. Write a statement outlining your personal vision for mathematics education. This could be kept in your reflective journal and referred to at different times during your course. For instance, you might consider reviewing it prior to any job interview and also at the end of your course. Limit yourself to a maximum of 250 words. Having finished your statement, you might like to ask other student teachers on your course how it compares with their own views. How will the differences among you have an impact on the pupils you teach?

MATHEMATICS AND EDUCATION

While you are learning to teach mathematics, you may feel that you have more important priorities than considering the somewhat abstract issues of the nature of mathematics and the purpose of education. You may quite reasonably wish to focus instead on surviving in a classroom full of pupils. However, it is important to understand at this early stage the way in which these philosophical issues impinge significantly on classroom practice.

The nature of mathematics

Is the nature of mathematics a controversial issue? Surely everyone has a fairly clear idea of what the subject is and, consequently, what should be taught in schools? If you have had a chance to talk to other student teachers about the issues raised in either Task 1.1 or 1.2, you may already have encountered varying perspectives on, if not conflicting views about, what is important about mathematics.

The two quotations that follow, both written by professional mathematicians and published in the same year, illustrate that mathematics can mean different things to different people.

> It is security. Certainty. Truth. Beauty. Insight. Structure. Architecture. I see mathematics, the part of human knowledge that I call mathematics, as one thing – one great glorious thing.
>
> (Halmos, quoted in Albers, 1986: 127)

> Mathematics does have a subject matter, and its statements are meaningful. The meaning, however, is to be found in the shared understanding of human beings, not in an eternal non-human reality. In this respect, mathematics is similar to an ideology, a religion, or an art form; it deals with human meanings, and is intelligible only within the context of culture. In other words, mathematics is a humanistic study. It is one of the humanities.
>
> (Davis and Hersh, 1986: 410)

You might conclude that although the responses of these people are different, they are nonetheless still talking about the same thing. However, there is a significant difference between these two views, and it is rooted in different understandings of 'human knowledge'. For Paul Halmos, mathematics seems to possess a unity as well as a truth and a certainty, uniform characteristics that provide security. For Philip Davis and Reuben Hersh, mathematics is closer to other systems of human meanings, making sense only within a human cultural context. Developing your standpoint on the nature of mathematics is important because it will influence the values about mathematics that you convey to your pupils.

The aims of education

Aims express intentions of individuals or groups; they are not just abstract ideas. It is important, then, in order to understand educational aims fully, to ask *whose* aims are being expressed. As with the nature of mathematics, there is no universal agreement or happy consensus. This is because different groups can and do have different sets of values, values which are, in turn, rooted in different world views or belief systems.

There are, however, some broad categories that help to illuminate the area of educational aims. These are indicated in Table 1.1, which presents a simplified categorisation of the possible purposes for education. Each of these areas of development has, at some time within the history of mathematics education, been the focus of concern for different groups. Considering your aims for education is a further important part of clarifying the values that will inform your mathematics teaching.

■ **Table 1.1** Some aims for education – four different types of development

---

Academic development

Education should help pupils to develop a thorough knowledge and understanding of each subject. At the same time, pupils are encouraged to form appropriate attitudes towards it. The desired outcome is sufficient people inducted into the academic community, including an adequate supply of good teachers at all levels. This is to guarantee each subject's place within our cultural heritage and its future development.

Vocational development

Education should provide pupils with the relevant knowledge and skills that they need in the world of work. The desired outcome is a suitably equipped workforce ready to adapt to the needs of a growing economy.

Personal development

Education should provide opportunity for the all-round development of the individual. The desired outcome is fulfilled and autonomous people who have a well-developed self-awareness and who continue to grow and mature in adult life.

Social development

Education should provide the forum within which pupils can develop socially and find their roles within society. The desired outcome is individuals who will be confident in their interpersonal relationships and in their role as critical citizens.

Further issues

Your perspectives on the nature of mathematics and on the aims of education come together to form your aims for mathematics education. However, having established the purpose of mathematics education – a sense of 'why?' – there remain the further questions, 'what?' and 'how?'. The way you answer these questions will be strongly connected to your aims. Table 1.2 lists questions that follow on from the more philosophical ones you have been considering thus far. You will explore many of these areas in more detail in later chapters of this book. However, you might immediately begin to see how different aims might lead you to answer these questions differently. You are faced with the challenge of developing your own considered responses to these questions, consistent with your aims.

▪ **Table 1.2** Fundamental questions

Area of interest	Questions raised
Philosophy	Why should pupils learn mathematics?
Curriculum	What mathematics should be included in the school curriculum?
	Which pupils should learn which aspects of the subject?
Learning	How do pupils learn mathematics?
Teaching	What teaching methods will best support your aims?
Resources	What resources are most appropriate to the tasks and the learners?
Assessment	How should/could/might pupils' development in mathematics be measured?
Differentiation	What accounts for the diversity of pupil response to mathematics?
	How should/could/might you respond to this diversity?

Task 1.3 **The aims of the mathematics department**

During your school experience you will find out much about how your mathematics department works. It is also useful to find out what aims or vision the department has for mathematics education and how this comes through in its policies. Ask to read the department handbook and, in particular, consider:

▪ what views about the nature of mathematics and education underpin any statement of aims;
▪ how well policies and procedures relate to the department's aims;
▪ the extent to which the official aims are shared by all members of the department;
▪ whether classroom practice supports the achievement of the department's aims.

COMPETING INFLUENCES ON THE MATHEMATICS CURRICULUM

This section includes various aims for mathematics education and some discussion of the implications these could have on your work as a maths teacher in the classroom. Below are descriptions of the mathematical perspectives of four different social groups: the mathematical purists, the industrial pragmatists, the progressive educators and the social reformers. These groups are not real, organised associations of people, but instead represent a categorisation offering a framework for exploring competing influences within mathematics education. No claim is made that all or even any individuals fit neatly into any particular group; indeed, as you read the descriptions, you may find you have certain sympathies with some or even all of the groups and their aims. However, the origins of much current practice in mathematics education have roots within the opinions attributed to one of these four groups. Many of the ideas expressed here are based on the work of Paul Ernest (1991).

Mathematical purists

This group is primarily concerned with the academic and some aspects of personal development of pupils. Its members strongly reject any utilitarian emphasis on work or the applications of mathematics as a justification for this school subject. They also assume that it is obvious that mathematics education has no particular role in the social development of young people.

Members of this group have a long tradition within mathematics, one which can be traced back to Greek philosophy, where mathematics was seen to be educationally valuable in the development of thought rather than for learning about any applications.

> Now that we have mentioned the study of arithmetic, it occurs to me what a subtle and widely used instrument it is for our purpose, if one studies it for the sake of knowledge and not for commercial ends [...] it draws the mind upwards.
>
> (Plato, in Lee, 1987: 332)

The tradition of emphasising the importance of mathematics as a subject for the improvement of the mind continues to be maintained by some today.

The mathematical purists consider mathematics to be an objective form of knowledge, a complex, hierarchical structure of ideas linked together through proof and rational thought. They celebrate its significant contribution to our cultural heritage, identify it more as an art than a science, and believe it to have aesthetic qualities (note this reflects aspects of both the Halmos and the Hersh and Davis quotations given earlier). The Cambridge mathematician G. H. Hardy wrote:

> The mathematician's patterns, like the painter's or the poet's, must be beautiful; the ideas, like the colours or the words, must fit together in a harmonious way. Beauty is the first test: there is no permanent place in the world for ugly mathematics.
>
> (Hardy, 1940: 25)

For more on the connection between mathematics and the aesthetic, see Sinclair *et al.* (2006) and, specifically with regard to school teaching in north America, Sinclair (2006), though these actual authors would not be seen primarily (or exclusively) as mathematical purists.

Mathematical purists see the role of the teacher as enabling the effective transmission of this body of knowledge and encouraging particular qualities in the pupils, such as concern for rigour, elegance and precision. This tends to involve a lecturing and explaining style that makes use of standard texts and traditional mathematical equipment, but makes little use of other resources. Teachers will have an enthusiasm for the subject that will be conveyed to the pupils.

This group supports major competitions for pupils such as Mathematical Olympiads, partly because these help to identify the next generation of mathematicians. Assessment on the whole is not a major concern. However, it is important that qualifications such as A-Level Mathematics preserve their high standards (a discussion very much to the fore in some quarters in 2010). Consequently, members of the group express concern if they think examinations or courses are becoming less demanding. On the whole, there is little consideration given to what form of mathematics education is appropriate for pupils who will not be part of the new mathematical elite: it is just to be accepted that some people are born with a talent for the subject.

Industrial pragmatists

This group is primarily concerned with the vocational development of pupils through mathematics. There is some recognition of the need for social development, but only in so far as it prepares young people for the world of work. Academic development is acknowledged to be relevant for a few, but the dominant focus of mathematics education must be on the great mass of ordinary pupils. Everybody needs an adequate mathematical education so that they can contribute to the development of a productive economy and be successful at finding a productive place within it.

Members of this group are most likely to be found among employers in industry or leaders of technical and scientific professions. There is a tradition of this group trying to influence mathematics education from the start of the last century. At that time, their argument was mainly with the mathematical purists. One strong advocate of this group's views was Professor John Perry, an engineer and former science teacher. At the 1901 meeting of the British Association for the Advancement of Science, Perry said:

> The study of Mathematics began because it was useful, continues because it is useful and is valuable to the world because of the usefulness of its results, while the mathematicians, who determine what the teacher shall do, hold that the subject should be studied for its own sake.
>
> (cited in Griffiths and Howson, 1974: 17)

This group grew considerably in numbers and strength throughout the twentieth century and was arguably the most influential at the end of the twentieth century.

The industrial pragmatists see mathematics as an established collection of very useful techniques and skills that can be applied to a large range of technical and scientific contexts. They recognise that there is a body of knowledge to be learnt, but consider that it is only to be learnt in order to be applied. There is, however, sometimes a tension within this group as to which areas of mathematics are most important. Some advocate a strong emphasis on arithmetic and basic numeracy while others require pupils to learn the mathematics most helpful for them to function in a rapidly changing technological society and so welcome an increased emphasis on the use of calculators and, especially, computers.

Such pragmatists see the role of the teacher as developing pupil skill at *doing* mathematics and motivating pupils by the use of real work contexts. Learning requires thorough practice, and pupils benefit from doing practical and possibly experimental work. At a higher level, pupils should learn the skills required for applied problem-solving and modelling. (See also Chapters 11 and 12 of this book.)

Assessment has a dual function for the industrial pragmatists. On one level, it acts as a simple aid to selection, though this function has also been termed a 'critical filter' (Sells, 1973) with regard to its use as a means of exclusion of various groups from different forms of work, whether intentional or not (with regard to its connection to male and female ability in mathematics, see Sherman, 1982). For instance, unless pupils have a Grade C at GCSE, they will not be considered for a particular job. However, there is also an emphasis on assessment, ensuring that core skills have been developed and verified. Concern is expressed by this group if standards of numeracy are falling. In consequence, vocational qualifications, which include an element of 'the application of number', are welcomed.

Progressive educators

This group is primarily concerned with the personal development of pupils, with the individual child as the focus of attention. It rejects the adult-orientated nature of vocational development and supports social and academic development only to the extent that these encourage and serve the goal of personal development.

Members of this group, like the industrial pragmatists, grew in prominence during the twentieth century, but there is a tradition rooted as far back as the work of Jean-Jacques Rousseau in the eighteenth century. His advice to potential teachers included:

> Your first duty is to be humane. Love childhood. Look with friendly eyes on its games, its pleasures, its amiable dispositions. Which of you does not sometimes look back regretfully on the age when laughter was ever on the lips and the heart free of care? Why steal from the little innocents the enjoyment of a time that passes all too quickly?
>
> (cited in Boyd, 1973: 33)

Here we find a concern to put the child, not the future adult, at the centre of the educational project.

While accepting that mathematics is a body of knowledge, this group is not very concerned about the particular mathematics to be learnt. Instead, its members are much more interested in the process of learning and reject any attempt to impose mathematics on pupils (a challenge when the subject is compulsory in schools around the world). They believe that pupils should be supported in exploring and discovering the subject for themselves. There is also a concern for the child to remain motivated and to have positive feelings and attitudes towards the subject. Learning mathematics should build up children's self-esteem and help them to become confident and autonomous. They are to be encouraged to pursue their own open-ended investigations, to engage in projects related to personal interests and to find their own ways of expressing and communicating their own mathematics.

They see the role of the teacher as coming alongside the pupil and acting as a guide in the individual pupils' journeys of discovery. This means that it is the responsibility of the teacher to create an appropriate learning environment, both in terms of stimulating resources and supportive social dynamics. Mathematical educators with arguable links to the aims of this group have been influential in developing and promoting specialist mathematics equipment, such as Cuisenaire rods and geoboards (due to Caleb Gattegno) or Dienes structural apparatus (due to Zoltan Dienes). Computers and calculators are considered important for offering new environments within which mathematical exploration can happen. There is also an emphasis on developing caring, supportive relationships in the classroom, with children being shielded from significant social conflict.

Children are to be treated as individuals and allowed to learn at different rates. It is important to recognise and celebrate their success, so records of achievement and criteria-based assessment are to be welcomed. External examinations are not considered helpful, as they have the potential for bringing discouragement and disappointment to the child. They are also seen as skewing the curriculum towards short-term goals (a criticism that had been consistently levelled at the SATs, before they were scrapped for the end of Key Stage 3 in July 2009, a decade after they were introduced for this level).

Social reformers

This group is primarily concerned with the social development of pupils, in the sense that education should empower the individual to participate fully and critically in a democratic society. Consequently, aspects of personal development are considered important. Encouraging vocational and academic development is appropriate only through negotiation with the pupil.

Members of this group have only relatively recently begun to influence mathematics education, but the origins of this group within education (also called 'Public Educators') can be traced back to the nineteenth century. Then, the primary concern was education for all. In more recent times, 'social reformers' have had more influence in the emerging education structures of developing countries. For example, President Julius Nyerere expressed the aims of a Tanzanian education programme as being:

> to prepare people for their responsibilities as free workers and citizens in a free and democratic society, albeit a largely rural society. They have to be able to think for themselves, to make judgements on all the issues affecting them; they have to be able to interpret the decisions made through the democratic institutions of our society.
>
> (cited in Ernest, 1991: 202)

The other stimulus to the work of the group of 'social reformers' has been the need to work towards equality of opportunity for all within education. Within mathematics education, significant work has been done in the fields of gender issues, multicultural and antiracist mathematics, as well as ethnomathematics, all of which areas have been informed by the aims and desires of the social reformers (see, for example, Shan and Bailey, 1991; Gates, 2002; Noyes, 2007).

The view of mathematics held by some in this group is also relatively new. Mathematics is seen to be 'a social construction: tentative, growing by means of human creation and decision-making, and connected with other realms of knowledge, culture and social life' (Ernest, 1991: 207–8). This offers a much wider definition of mathematics than is the norm and challenges the mathematical purists' exclusive ownership of 'real mathematics'. Pupils should experience mathematics as relevant to their own lives, as important in addressing wider social issues, as a vehicle for social emancipation and as enabling the development and maintenance of a critical stance towards society.

They see the role of the teacher as facilitating pupils in both posing and solving their own problems. This requires the teacher to set conditions in which pupils can partic- ipate in decisions about their learning and under which they feel able to question their mathematics course and its associated teaching methods. Resources need to be socially relevant and include authentic materials such as newspapers and other sources of real data. Discussion is seen as central to the learning process and conflicting ideas are welcome in promoting greater understanding.

Any form of assessment must be seen to be fair to all pupils and should not disad- vantage any social group. This requires a greater variety of modes of assessment and so project work and the ongoing assessment of coursework is highly valued. The GCSE qualification initially had scope for a large percentage of assessment by coursework and so was welcomed by 'social reformers'. Because of the status that certain mathematical qualifications have within UK society, helping pupils to pass external exams remains crucial, so teachers have to work within the existing assessment system.

AGENCIES FOR CHANGE

Given that there is a range of views about the aims of mathematics education, you may wonder how these competing influences actually bring about change in the school curriculum and teaching approaches. In this final section, you will see how the social groupings discussed above have acted through different, real agencies to bring about the reforms they seek. You will also consider the influence of people who express their expectations at ground level within your school context.

Mathematics teaching associations

The influence of different groups can be seen in the history of the two main UK mathe- matics teaching organisations. The Mathematical Association (MA) was established in 1871 as 'The Association for the Improvement of Geometrical Teaching', with an overt agenda for change. The initial focus was on reforming the teaching of Euclidean geom- etry. The Association of Teachers of Mathematics (ATM), which was originally set up in 1953 as 'The Association for Teaching Aids in Mathematics', was initially a splinter group from the MA and strongly influenced by the ideas and work of Caleb Gattegno. Articles in the early issues of the journal of the newer association (*Mathematics Teaching*) show clearly the dominance of the Progressive Educator group (see Cooper, 1985: 69–90). These two organisations are discussed further in Chapter 14.

In addition to these professional groups, 2009 saw the introduction of the designa- tion of Chartered Mathematics teacher (CMathTeach), awarded under the auspices of the Institute of Mathematics and its Applications (www.ima.org.uk/cmathteach/). This benchmark designation is designed to reflect the substantial professional demands of the role and, while it does not specifically support or reflect the goals of a particular ideo- logical group, it does promote the idea of the mathematics teacher as a pedagogic practitioner. The Registration Authority, which oversees this procedure, has members from the MA, the ATM, the IMA itself and NANAMIC (the National Association for Numeracy and Mathematics in Colleges).

Curriculum development projects

Mathematics education has had its fair share of curriculum projects. Some succeed and have a large impact in schools across the country; others do not extend much beyond the initial project schools and are soon forgotten. In either case, projects will normally have the strong support of one of the four social groups listed above, which recognise that courses and the associated materials are a significant way of influencing the way teachers work. The School Mathematics Project (SMP), first established half-a-century ago, in 1961, was perhaps particularly successful in establishing itself because it was the product of an alliance between 'members' of both the mathematical purists and the industrial pragmatists (Cooper, 1985: 235–66).

More recent curriculum developments in mathematics education in the UK reflect different ideologies at work. The Qualifications and Curriculum Authority (QCA) was established in the 1997 Education Act to 'develop and regulate the National Curriculum, assessments in schools and qualifications'. In 2007, QCA brought in a revised version of the National Curriculum for secondary schools in England (QCA, 2007a), with the introduction of some significant and fundamental changes relative to earlier incarnations. This is discussed in Chapter 2. In 2007, the government set up an independent exams regulator, Ofqual, which has now taken most of QCA's regulatory functions. The Qualifications and Curriculum Development Agency (QCDA) took on the curricular part of the QCA's role until 2010. The Functional Skills qualification in mathematics (as well as in English and ICT) was introduced in 2009 by the QCDA. As this edition is being prepared in early 2010, the AS qualification in 'Use of Mathematics' is being extended to A2. Both of these latter developments are discussed further in Chapter 13, but you should be able to detect the presence of different interest groups behind their promotion.

Official inquiries

Every so often, the climate within education reaches such a level of concern that an official inquiry is commissioned. The reports then produced can become key reference points against which all future proposals are tested. Consequently, many groups wish to influence the findings of these inquiries.

Dr W. H. Cockcroft chaired the most influential inquiry into mathematics teaching in the past 40 years. Its report was entitled *Mathematics Counts* (DES, 1982) and the terms of reference included considering the needs of employment. But perhaps its most famous paragraph (para. 243 – see Chapter 4) is about the need for a broad range of teaching methods in classrooms. It can be interpreted as being supportive of the views of both industrial pragmatists and progressive educators (Ernest, 1991: 220–2).

The post-14 mathematics inquiry, chaired by Professor A. Smith, was set up in 2003, in the light of the shortage of young people studying mathematics-related subjects and to make recommendations on changes to the curriculum, qualifications and pedagogy of post-14 mathematics. The recommendations in its report *Making Mathematics Count* (DfES, 2004a) have implications for the full range of mathematics education.

The QCA has also undertaken various evaluations, such as its study into participation in A-Level mathematics (QCA, 2007b).

Ofsted published a thematic report *Mathematics: Understanding the Score* in 2008. The report surveyed the way mathematics was taught in England but, importantly, discussed what Ofsted understood to be good teaching. The report described what Ofsted saw as the essential components of effective mathematics teaching and gave examples of good practice. The evidence presented suggests that a heavy emphasis on 'teaching to the test' only succeeds

> in preparing pupils to gain the qualifications but [...] not equipping them well enough mathematically for their futures. It is of vital importance to shift from a narrow emphasis on disparate skills towards a focus on pupils' mathematical under-standing. Teachers need encouragement to invest in such approaches to teaching.
>
> (Ofsted, 2008: 4)

The report once again demonstrates the views of at least two of the interest groups.

Joint councils and committees

You have seen that there are many competing voices within the mathematics community. However, there have been attempts to provide ways of bringing together people and organisations with differing perspectives. The Joint Mathematical Council of the United Kingdom (JMC) was set up in 1963 to provide a forum for discussion among a range of mathematical and educational societies. Its aim is to promote the advancement of mathematics and the improvement of mathematics teaching at all levels. Within the Council, it is possible to find people who have sympathies with each of the four orientations discussed earlier in this chapter.

Central government now has a much more significant role in shaping curriculum and teaching policy. Consequently, there is a need for the mathematical community to speak with a more unified voice, if it wishes to influence policy. In 2002, the JMC and the Royal Society established the Advisory Committee on Mathematics Education (ACME). It is an independent body and aims to act as a single voice for the mathematics community and, particularly, to develop an effective and constructive partnership with government. This has largely been successful. In consequence, reports and advice that emerge from the JMC and ACME have a significant impact on government policy. This influence will be seen in the next chapter on mathematics in the English National Curriculum.

Local expectations

Finally, it is important to recognise the influence of much more localised groups on your teaching. Parents, colleagues in the mathematics department and the school's senior management will all have expectations of you as a mathematics teacher. These expectations may coincide with your own views or may be in conflict with them. You will need to learn to negotiate with different individuals and groups if you are to remain in contact with your own values while you are working to meet the legitimate demands of others. In particular, pupils will certainly let you know their own expectations. This theme is addressed in Tasks 1.4 and 1.5.

Task 1.4 **What do pupils want from their mathematics education?**

Pupils are arguably the group that will most regularly express to you their views about maths education – and much else besides. It can be valuable for you to understand what they want from their mathematics education. There is scope for exploring this in every mathematics lesson, but there is not normally the time to consider the issue in depth with individuals.

Design an interview sheet that you could use with pupils to explore their views. The prompts in 'Mathematical memories' (Task 1.1) offer possible questions, but you may also want to add some of your own. If you ask questions about teachers, make sure the pupils understand that you do not want to know names; you just want to know what teaching styles work well for them. If it is possible within your school, ask to interview three Year 7 pupils, three Year 10 pupils and three A-Level pupils. Arrange with your head of department to speak with them for about 15 to 20 minutes. Also check with your head of department that your interview questions are acceptable to the staff. Record the results of your interview and write some notes in your journal, indicating the extent to which you believe you could accommodate the pupils' perspectives within your teaching.

Task 1.5 **Using research to reflect on your experience**

There is an increasing amount of research which incorporates the 'voice' of the pupil in mathematics. One instance is Brown, Brown and Bibby (2008) which summarises the attitudes of a large number of pupils deciding whether or not to study mathematics at Advanced level. Compare your own results from Task 1.4 to those found in this research study. Were there any common features or ideas?

SUMMARY AND KEY POINTS

The role of mathematics education in our society is complex; there is no simple consensus as to which topics in mathematics are important or how mathematics should be taught. Indeed, there is controversy about the nature of mathematics itself. Different social groups have influenced, and will continue to influence, the shape of mathematics education. Mathematics teachers experience the influence of such groups through their teaching associations, curriculum projects, recommendations of official reports and government policy on curriculum and assessment.

The chapter title posed the question 'Mathematics education – who decides?'. Now you must prepare to decide where you stand on the issues raised within it.

FURTHER READING

DES (1982) *Mathematics Counts*. **London: HMSO.**

> This volume, often referred to as 'The Cockcroft Report', remains a key text for mathematics education in this country. It is much referred to, although often quite selectively, and so it is worth being familiar with its full range of contents.

DfES (2004a) *Making Mathematics Count*. **London: HMSO.**

> This report reviews the nature and importance of mathematics, the supply of teachers of mathematics and the effectiveness of current pathways for 14–19-year-olds. It proposes possible actions on the curriculum and possible support for the teaching and learning of mathematics.

Ernest, P. (1991) *The Philosophy of Mathematics Education*. **Basingstoke: Falmer Press.**

> This book is an ambitious work, one that seeks to offer both a new philosophy of mathematics and to examine its impact on mathematics education. The influence of different ideologies on mathematics education is explored in some detail.

Hersh, R. (1998) *What Is Mathematics, Really?* **London: Vintage.**

> This book is an accessible and engaging overview of the range of questions addressed within the philosophy of mathematics. Hersh illuminates much of the field, as well as presenting his own radical 'humanist' viewpoint.

Ofsted (2008) *Mathematics: Understanding the Score*. **London: Ofsted.**

> This report and the accompanying booklet specifically for secondary mathematics teachers (Ofsted, 2009) sets out evidence for a level of concern over the way that mathematics was taught in schools up to 2008. It also exemplifies the approaches that Ofsted would like to see used in order to improve mathematical learning.

Sinclair, N. (2006) *Mathematics and Beauty: Aesthetic Approaches to Teaching Children*. **New York: Teachers College Press.**

> This book makes a strong case for the inclusion of the aesthetic in the teaching and learning of mathematics and illuminates how the materials and approaches used in mathematics classrooms can be enriched for the benefit of all pupils.

MATHEMATICS IN THE NATIONAL CURRICULUM

John Westwell and Robert Ward-Penny

INTRODUCTION

Imagine that the country that you are teaching in did not have a National Curriculum (such as was the case in England prior to 1989) and that each school was free to teach whatever mathematics they wished, however they chose. What might be some of the consequences of this level of freedom for teachers? How might it affect pupils' learning of mathematics?

Your own National Curriculum is a critical document for you to use and understand as a secondary school teacher. Not only does it provide a practical outline of the content that you are legally expected to cover in your mathematics teaching, but it also carries a message about the place of mathematics within the wider school curriculum and deals with some of the philosophical issues discussed in Chapter 1. In particular, it addresses decisive questions such as which mathematical topics are more difficult and how to integrate opportunities for pupils to use and apply their mathematical knowledge. The website for the English National Curriculum proposes that 'there should be real pride in our curriculum: the learning that the nation has decided to set before its young' (QCA, 2007a).

However, whilst each country's National Curriculum influences classroom practice, it is important to recognise that it does not dictate it. In the introduction to his book on mathematics national curricula around the world, the English mathematics educator Geoffrey Howson (1991) wrote:

> It is well known that teachers throughout the world do not slavishly (or even unslavishly) follow their National Curriculum. What is 'intended' by those who draw up national curricula is never 'implemented' in all classrooms. [...] Moreover, what is learned by students may bear little relation to the implemented curriculum. Much that is taught is misunderstood, not understood or not retained. [...] Are national curricula, therefore, so important? (p. 1)

By the end of this chapter, you will be able to address Howson's question critically, by considering just how influential your National Curriculum is in shaping pupils' learning experiences, and how prominent it will be in determining your practice. You will have also developed your knowledge and understanding of the structure and content of your country's National Curriculum, so that it can inform the processes of your planning, assessment and evaluation.

In order to help you interpret some of the issues surrounding a National Curriculum, this chapter will examine in detail the mathematics section of the National Curriculum in England, henceforth referred to as the NC. The latest version of this (QCA, 2007a) is termed the 2008 NC, referring to the year it was introduced in schools; similarly, the previous edition (DfEE, 1999a) is referenced as the 2000 NC. The mathematics curricula for Scotland, Wales and Northern Ireland are all different to varying extents and where these differences help elaborate alternative curriculum models, they are highlighted.

OBJECTIVES

By the end of this chapter you should:

- ■ understand the structure and be more familiar with the specific content of your mathematics National Curriculum;
- ■ be aware of some of the main issues and debates that surround the development of mathematics curricula;
- ■ understand some key aspects of the mathematics programmes of study;
- ■ be aware of alternative curricular models and possibilities for future development.

THE SCOPE, PRESCRIPTION AND PRESENTATION OF THE CURRICULUM

Mathematics curricula can have very different structures, apply to different ranges of pupils and be presented in a variety of forms. When examining any mathematics curriculum, the following questions are worth considering:

- ■ Who is the curriculum for and to what ages of pupils does it apply?
- ■ Is there a common curriculum for *all* pupils in *all* schools?
- ■ Is the curriculum *statutory*, that is with legal requirement, or is it *advisory*, solely offering guidance?
- ■ How much prescription is there in the curriculum and how much freedom is there for teachers?
- ■ What forms of documentation are used to present the curriculum?
- ■ In which ways are teachers expected to interpret the curriculum requirements?
- ■ To what extent are textbooks used to dictate or elaborate the curriculum?

Task 2.1 **Reading the curriculum**

It is essential that you have a personal copy of your mathematics National Curriculum and that you become increasingly familiar with its structure and contents. Begin by skimming the document to establish its structure and to gain a broad sense of its contents. Then, start to read for the details. You may initially wish to concentrate on the secondary curriculum, but do also read about the primary curriculum and look at any measures included to ease transition between phases of schooling. Make notes in your journal so that you can follow up your reading, and:

▪ seek clarification on any aspects of the document that you do not understand;
▪ discuss questions that the document raises for you with others;
▪ resolve any areas of ambiguity within the text;
▪ start to investigate any aspects of the mathematics that seem new or unfamiliar to you.

Scope and prescription

The current version of the mathematics NC (QCA, 2007a) was introduced in schools in September 2008. It is the fifth version of the curriculum since the mathematics NC was first introduced in 1989. This version contains a number of significant changes, the most immediately obvious of which is the fact that the mathematics curriculum is now presented as one part of the larger curriculum document, rather than as a separate publication. This mode of presentation underlines the government's intention for schools to provide a coherent curriculum, one which encourages pupils to make links between subjects and develop a set of skills that transfer between disciplines. This ideology is represented graphically by the change in the NC logo; previously, each subject was shown as a distinct, coloured 'brick', but now the logo consists of the colours that represent each subject weaving together.

Mathematics is one of the three core subjects in the NC, along with English and Science. This means that there are statutory requirements that apply to all pupils in state schools in England from the ages of 5 to 16. Prior to this age, the curriculum that the pupils follow is organised around another statutory document called the Early Years Foundation Stage Profile. The NC is organised into four Key Stages (see Table 2.1), so in secondary schools your main concern will be with KS3 and KS4. The curricula in Wales and Northern Ireland are also organised around Key Stages and again contain legal requirements.

The current version of the mathematics NC is notably both less prescriptive and less descriptive, containing much shorter programmes of study than the previous version (DfEE, 1999a). This has left schools with the power to interpret the curriculum more flexibly and the responsibility to do this for the benefit of their pupils. This flexibility can even extend to changing the structure of the Key Stages, and some schools have adopted, an accelerated, two-year Key Stage 3 (Years 7 and 8). Other schools have, instead, integrated 'flexible curriculum days' or adopted a more ambitious programme such as the Royal Society for the Encouragement of Arts, Manufactures and Commerce (RSA)

■ **Table 2.1** Key Stages in the National Curriculum

Key Stages	Pupil ages	Year groups
Key Stage 1 (KS1)	5–7	1–2
Key Stage 2 (KS2)	7–11	3–6
Key Stage 3 (KS3)	11–14	7–9
Key Stage 4 (KS4)	14–16	10–11

Opening Minds scheme (www.thersa.org/projects/education/opening-minds). It will be both important and interesting for you to see how the schools you visit whilst training have responded to the greater level of freedom they have been afforded.

In Scotland, a new 'Curriculum for Excellence' was implemented in 2010 for ages 3–18 (www.ltscotland.org.uk/curriculumforexcellence/mathematics/index.asp). This non-statutory curriculum replaces the 5–14 *National Guidelines* (SOED, 1991) on the curriculum and on its assessment. These mathematics guidelines are commended to teachers as a basis for mathematics programmes in all Scottish state schools. Both Wales and Northern Ireland have their own statutory National Curricula: The National Curriculum for Wales (DCELLS, 2008) and Northern Ireland Curriculum (CCEA, 2010), respectively.

Task 2.2 **Prescription or guidance?**

The balance between prescription and guidance is a key issue in each revision of the National Curriculum. There is also much variability internationally. Compare your current NC either to the previous edition or to the National Curriculum of another country, such as Spain or Singapore. What similarities do you notice in their construction? What differences are there in their presentation?

Presentation and relationship to other documents

The latest version of the mathematics NC can be found online. As discussed above, the 2010 version sees a significant decrease in the detailed description of the programmes of study for Key Stage 3 and 4, from 44 pages to 16 pages. However, alongside the programmes of study, the Qualifications and Curriculum Development Agency provides an extensive range of materials that offer guidance on how to teach mathematics in context, as well as inform teachers' planning and assessment strategies. This includes content as diverse as commentary on planning for inclusion, and a case study centred on the mathematics of the Battle of Trafalgar. The breadth and depth of material attached to the latest version of the NC is significant and reflects a wider commitment to an integrated curriculum.

In England, additional documents exist that elaborate the curriculum even further. Many of these were produced by the National Strategies, most notably the Key Stage 3 *Framework for Teaching Mathematics: Years 7, 8 and 9* (DfEE, 2001a). Although this is no longer being produced, the document remains a common feature in school mathematics departments. This guidance document went further than the statutory order by including suggested *yearly teaching programmes* with very detailed teaching objectives. There was also a 285-page section, the *Supplement of Examples*, which attempted to illustrate the meaning and level of difficulty of these objectives.

An alternative or supplementary way in which mathematics curricula are presented in some countries is through the use of official textbooks. In the United Kingdom, although publishers produce new textbooks that claim to meet the various mathematics NC requirements, these are not officially recommended texts. By contrast, there are many countries where there is either a required textbook or a range of approved texts. For example, in Cyprus there are various series of textbooks, but they all have to be approved by the Education Ministry. It is worth noting that even when textbooks are not officially approved, as in the UK, they are still strongly influenced by official documents – for instance, many English textbooks follow the teaching programmes originally laid out in the KS3 Framework. These textbooks, in turn, have a strong influence by proxy, shaping teachers' views of the official curriculum.

In whichever way a National Curriculum is presented, there will always remain the issue of how teachers interpret it. In the research study carried out for the School Curriculum and Assessment Authority (SCAA) – a forerunner of QCA – on the implementation of the mathematics NC, the problem of interpretation was examined in relation to 'Using and applying mathematics' (Johnson and Millett, 1996: 99–112). For some teachers, the *title* of this Attainment Target (now called 'Mathematical Processes and Applications' – see later) informed their view more than its actual contents. This led to a restricted view and little stimulus to change. This is an example, then, of a possible gap that can form between the 'intended' and the 'implemented' curriculum that Howson described. You, too, may encounter this problem, both during and after your course. As you read the documents, form your own views on what you think is actually required by them. You need to continue refining your understanding through discussion with teachers and other student teachers.

THE DEVELOPMENT AND REVISION OF THE CURRICULUM

The development of a mathematics curriculum is a complex process. The ways in which this is carried out will have a significant impact on the success of its implementation. When examining how curricula are developed or revised, it is worth considering:

■ who is involved in the development or revision of the curriculum;
■ how teachers are included in the process;
■ the timescale for development, revision and implementation.

The mathematics NC was first introduced in 1989 and was revised in 1991, 1995 and again in 1999. The publication of the latest version of the mathematics NC in 2007 followed a relatively long period of no change. During this decade of stability, the QCA monitored the impact of the curriculum and consulted widely about potential changes, taking into account the opinions of teachers, subject associations and working groups. For example, the work of two Royal Society/Joint Mathematical Council working groups has had a significant influence on curriculum changes. The first of these investigated the teaching and learning of algebra pre-19 (JMC/Royal Society, 1997) and led to clear changes and an expansion of the algebra component in the 1999 edition of the curriculum. The second of these reports, investigating the teaching and learning of geometry pre-19, recommended that:

> the mathematics curriculum be developed in ways which recognise the important position of theorems and proofs within mathematics and use the study of geometry to encourage the development of logical argument appropriate to the age and attainment of the student.

> (JMC/Royal Society, 2001: 10)

Task 2.3 **Proofreading**

Look through the KS3 and KS4 programmes of study in your National Curriculum. Do you feel the curriculum encourages 'the development of logical argument appropriate to the age and attainment of the student'? To what extent is the idea of mathematical proof implicit or explicit within the curriculum?

Some recommendations have had a definite influence – for example, the group recommended that the title of the *Shape, space and measures* strand should be changed to *Geometry*. The new NC titles the strand as *Geometry and measures*. More recently, the Smith report, *Making Mathematics Count* (DfES, 2004a), has influenced the role of functional skills in the latest NC.

The work of these groups demonstrates that the mathematics NC is not an unchanging, uncontroversial domain; instead, you can expect the curriculum to go on being contested and altered during your career as a mathematics teacher.

Task 2.4 **The impact of your National Curriculum**

Your mathematics National Curriculum will have had a significant impact on the work of secondary school mathematics departments. In this task, examine the extent of the impact of your mathematics National Curriculum on the mathematics department within which you work by:

■ reading the departmental handbook to see what reference is made to your mathematics National Curriculum (and/or supporting documents);

■ examining the department's schemes of work to see how your mathematics National Curriculum (and/or supporting documentation) is used within the planning process;

■ investigating what changes have been made to the department's resources following the most recent revisions of your curriculum;

■ discussing with teachers in the department what they believe has been the main impact of your mathematics National Curriculum on their practice;

■ finding out how often and for what purpose teachers in the department refer to your mathematics National Curriculum documentation (and/or supporting documents).

LIB

PERFORMANCE STANDARDS AND ASSESSMENT WITHIN THE CURRICULUM

One intention behind the introduction of national curricula was to raise standards of attainment in schools. A National Curriculum can be used to clarify the performance standards that will be expected of pupils. In order to do this, a range of issues needs to be addressed, including:

■ whether performance standards will be explicitly defined within the curriculum;
■ whether age-specific standards or continual scales will be used;
■ whether there are different performance standards for different types of schools or pupils;
■ the place of national assessment in clarifying and measuring performance standards.

Defining standards

Many countries have decided to define performance standards explicitly. Some have chosen to define *continual scales of levels* that apply to pupils of all ages. The Scottish and English national curricula both use this approach. The terminology used is different, but the structure is similar.

■ **Table 2.2** The structure of attainment standards in English and Scottish curricula

England (ages 5–16) Attainment Targets (ATs)	Scotland (ages 5–14) attainment outcomes
Mathematical processes and applications (AT1) Number and algebra (AT2) Geometry and measures (AT3) Handling data (AT4)	Problem-solving and enquiry Information handling Number, money and measure Shape, position and movement
Levels 1–8 and exceptional performance	Levels A–F

For each Attainment Target in the National Curriculum in England, there is a scale of eight *level descriptions* and a description of exceptional performance. Each of these descriptions outlines the type of skills and performance that pupils working at that level should typically demonstrate. For example, here is the level description for pupils working at level 8 in AT3: 'Pupils understand and use congruence and mathematical similarity. They use sine, cosine and tangent in right-angled triangles when solving problems in two dimensions' (QCA, 2007a: 152).

For each broad *attainment outcome* in the Scottish curriculum, there are a number of *strands*, and for most of the strands there are Attainment Targets at six levels of attainment (A to F). (Note: the term 'Attainment Target' is used in a different way here from the National Curriculum in England.) For example, the level D Attainment Target for the *interpret information* strand in the *handling information* attainment outcome is: 'Pupils should be able to interpret from a range of displays and databases by retrieving information subject to one condition (SOED, 1991: 24–5). The exception to this structure is the *problem-solving and enquiry* strand, for which a range of desirable process strategies is described, along with some indication of how pupils are to improve.

In contrast to the continual scales of levels used in the UK, some countries and states have chosen instead to define *age-specific* performance standards. For example, in the USA (which does not have national curricula; each state determines its own), in the state of Wisconsin, 'performance standards are grade (year group) related and are given for grades 4, 8 and 12 (ages 10, 14 and 18)' (Ruddock, 1998: 9).

Continual scale versus age-specific performance standards

There has been much debate both nationally and internationally as to whether to use continual scales or age-specific standards. Those in favour of age-specific standards believe it is important to make clear the expected minimum standards for all pupils at particular ages, especially in core areas of the curriculum such as arithmetic. They are also concerned that a single scale implies that all pupils have to follow the same path, albeit at different rates, and that for many this will lead to an unsatisfactory experience. They believe that, consequently, there will be little opportunity for pupils to take mathematics courses that have a sense of unity and completeness, as well as being relevant to the pupils' future study.

Those in favour of continual scales believe they offer a clearer progression for pupils throughout their schooling. This, they consider, is particularly helpful in improving continuity for pupils as they move between phases of schooling, such as at primary–secondary transfer. They are also concerned that having age-specific standards will lead to an emphasis on many pupils achieving the minimum standard and so could well result in limitations on the most able or little reward for the least able.

This debate was particularly strong when the National Curriculum was first being introduced in England. The Task Group on Assessment and Testing (DES/WO, 1987) settled on the ten-level model (since revised downwards to eight), but some members had wanted age-specific targets (Johnson and Millett, 1996). Some broad guidance was offered as to expectations of pupils at particular ages. For example, the original non-statutory guidance (NCC, 1989) stated that it was expected that the attainment of the great majority of pupils at the end of KS2 would be in the range level 2–6. Level 4 was generally understood to be a median level for pupils at this age. However, at around the time of the introduction of the Numeracy and Literacy Strategies in primary schools, and with the change of government, a subtle but important change happened. Level 4 was no longer seen as an average level but as an expectation. This was a significant shift towards an age-specific standard. Along with this came targets for the number of pupils now expected to achieve level 4. A similar change has happened at KS3, where level 5 is now seen as a minimum target level for the great majority of pupils.

Assessing pupils against performance standards

If performance standards are established within a curriculum, then it is with the expectation that some assessment of pupils' performance against these standards will take place. The particular requirements for carrying out this assessment vary between different national systems. In all cases, however, there is an expectation that teachers will assess their own pupils against the standards. This is supported in various ways. In some countries, example questions and tasks are provided for teachers to use when they think they are appropriate. Another approach is for teachers to provide annotated examples of pupils' work, indicating which standard or level they demonstrate, and a third method is to use national tests (either optional or compulsory) to assess pupils.

Although assessment by teachers can, arguably, be tailored towards the needs and abilities of individual pupils, it is open to claims of bias. Also, unless the data are collected together, it does not provide any indication of system-wide standards. Concerns such as these led to the introduction in England in the 1990s of externally marked Key Stage National Tests (commonly called SATs) in mathematics for pupils aged 7, 11 and 14. These served to provide pupils, parents and schools with a nationally comparable assessment of the mathematical ability of each learner. However, since each school's results were published publicly, the results of the tests were used not only to assess the pupils but also to assess the performance of the school. This led to claims that the assessment tool was driving classroom practice and putting pressure on young learners. In 2009, the Key Stage 3 National Tests were abolished.

The removal of the external assessment at the end of KS3 in England has been balanced in part by the introduction of Assessing Pupils' Progress, or APP, into schools. It remains a statutory obligation in England for teachers to produce an assessment of their pupils' attainment against the NC levels at the end of KS3. The APP system can produce a record of each pupil's progress in mathematics and can therefore contribute to teachers' assessments of attainment. It draws on a number of ideas about Assessment for Learning (see Chapter 6). The teacher compares each pupil's performance against a list of objectives and makes a judgement as to whether the pupil's work contains sufficient evidence to suggest that the pupil has acquired competence or mastery of that objective. It is recommended that judgements made by individual teachers be moderated within each school to ensure consistency of judgements. This approach is designed to help teachers track pupils' progress over time and to enable assessment to inform curriculum planning. However, APP has the potential to be very time-consuming and many schools may choose to use other approaches.

Whether there will be further changes in the English approach is uncertain, but what is sure is that compulsory tests, the place of assessment by pupils' own teachers and the publication of school-level results will continue to be controversial.

PROGRAMMES OF STUDY FOR THE CURRICULUM

Right at the heart of the debate about mathematics curricula is the question of *what* pupils should be taught. This final section of the chapter addresses a range of issues stimulated by this question, including:

■ the breadth and balance of mathematical topics included in the curriculum;
■ whether certain aspects of mathematics are considered foundational and therefore require special emphasis;
■ how the applications of mathematics and the contexts in which mathematics is used are addressed;
■ the place given to process skills of problem-solving, enquiry and investigation;
■ the value placed on promoting personal qualities and attitudes towards mathematics;
■ the impact of calculators and computers on both the content and teaching of the curriculum.

As discussed above, the new NC places a great emphasis on developing mathematical thinking as a 'habit of mind' (see Chapter 11), on cross-curricular opportunities and on the promotion of thinking skills. Both the KS3 and KS4 programmes of study contain a short introduction, which comments on the importance of mathematics and the wider aims of the National Curriculum, and three of the four main sections focus on process skills and the importance of mathematics within the wider curriculum.

Section 1 of each programme of study details four 'key concepts' said to 'underpin the study of mathematics' (QCA, 2007a: 140). These are: competence; creativity; applications and implications of mathematics; and critical understanding. Section 2 goes on to outline four 'key processes', which pupils are said to require in order to make progress. These are: representing; analysing; interpreting and evaluating; and communicating and reflecting.

The third section of each of the programmes of study details the range and content that should be covered at each Key Stage. This is remarkably brief compared with the previous edition of the English NC, which organised objectives into sections, then further into subsections known as 'strands'. Although there are some explanatory notes provided, and further exemplification could be gleaned from the Attainment Targets provided later on, the actual description of content only occupies two pages for each Key Stage. Another noticeable difference in the 2008 NC is the provision of only one programme of study for Key Stage 4 – the previous edition contained two, labelled 'foundation' and 'higher' (DfEE, 1999a: 43–72).

Finally, section 4 details curriculum opportunities offered by mathematics. These include opportunities to work in a cross-curricular way and problems that facilitate both group and individual approaches to problem-solving. The 2008 NC utilises this four-section structure for every subject, and you might find you gain new insights by comparing the KS3 programme of study for mathematics with that of another subject, such as geography or art.

Mathematical processes and applications

The question of how best to teach the use and application of mathematics has always been a contentious one. Should the skills associated with the posing and solving of problems be taught discretely or alongside skills such as how to find the area of a circle or how to multiply decimals? Is it even possible to unpack mathematical competence into an ordered list of skills that can be presented in the classroom and subsequently assessed?

The presentation and interpretation of this aspect of the mathematics NC has been problematic since it was first introduced. The current NC holds that it should be viewed as both separate, as in the first Attainment Target, *Mathematical processes and applications*, and embedded. One helpful way to think about this embedded relationship is to consider the three dimensions of any use or application of mathematics. The first is the *context* within which mathematics is deployed, the second is the mathematical *processes* that are to be used and the third is the mathematical *content* (concepts, facts and techniques) that is employed. Figure 2.1 illustrates the way these three dimensions can be integrated.

The first dimension in the application of mathematics, the possible context, is variously described in different curricula. In the 2008 mathematics NC, this is outlined in section 4 *Curriculum Opportunities*, where there are references to pupils using and applying mathematics:

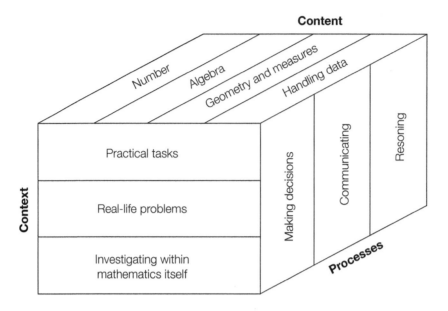

▨ **Figure 2.1** Three dimensions of applying mathematics
Source: adapted from ATM (1993b)

▨ in contexts of varying difficulty and familiarity;
▨ in real and abstract contexts;
▨ in problems that arise in other subjects, and problems that lie outside the school.

As mentioned above, the NC website contains case studies of some of these opportunities. The Scottish curriculum expands slightly on the range of contexts, by including:

▨ real-life and everyday problems;
▨ imaginary or simulated contexts;
▨ problems and investigations where the structure of mathematics itself provides the setting.

The second dimension involves the processes employed when people *use* mathematics. These are diverse and not easy to classify. The 2008 NC draws a distinction between 'Key Concepts' that support the use of mathematics to solve problems, and 'Key Processes', which are the actual skills and processes that pupils may use as part of a problem-solving activity. For instance, developing a convincing argument creatively or recognising the limitations of an abstract mathematical model are instances of 'Key Concepts'. Looking at patterns in data and reasoning inductively are classified as 'Key Processes'. Although there is a clear theoretical distinction between these two categories, there is some overlap in terms of practical output.

The third dimension is the mathematical content, which includes the various mathematical concepts, facts and techniques that are to be taught. The details of these are to be found throughout the programmes of study. A significant change in the 2008 revision

MATHEMATICS IN THE NATIONAL CURRICULUM

of the mathematics NC was the separation of the using and applying processes (the second dimension) from the sections on mathematical content (the third dimension). Although the surrounding text makes it clear that they need to be thought of together, the distinction serves to underline each teacher's challenge to help their pupils develop both a functional mathematics and a wide set of thinking skills.

Task 2.5 **Investigating number chains**

In this task, you will apply your knowledge of mathematics 'within mathematics itself' (the first dimension). You will use a range of processes (second dimension), including structuring your own enquiry, reasoning and communicating, and you may draw on a range of numerical and algebraic knowledge (third dimension). Begin by carrying out this mathematical task.

A number chain is generated by the following rule from any starting number:

■ if the number is even, halve it to generate the next number in the chain;
■ if the number is odd, multiply it by 3 and add 1 to generate the next number in the chain.

Investigate. Keep a record of your work and produce a written report when you have finished investigating.

When you have completed the task, read through the 'key processes' sections of the KS4 programme of study (QCA, 2007a: 142–4) or the equivalent section in your National Curriculum. Which of these skills did you explicitly exhibit in your working? Which skills did you use but not produce evidence of?

Now evaluate your performance against the Attainment Target level descriptors on pages 148–9 or the equivalent Attainment Target/Outcomes in your National Curriculum. At what level would you assess your solution? Finally, return to the original task and improve your work accordingly.

The pedagogical and practical issues of what it means to teach mathematics 'in context' are discussed in more depth in Chapter 11. However, before moving on, it is important to recognise that there is perhaps a fourth dimension that is often largely neglected within national curricula, which has been referred to in the past as 'personal qualities'. This dimension encompasses a pupil's ability to use and apply mathematics as an individual in society. It also includes the wider learning skills that are developed solely through the activity of mathematics. These aspects are discussed in more depth in Chapter 12. The 2008 NC touches on these elements explicitly for the first time, with three ideas that cross between all subjects: *Every Child Matters*, functional skills and *Personal Learning and Thinking Skills*.

The QCA defines personal development as 'the means by which all young people are supported in their spiritual, moral, physical, emotional, cultural and intellectual development according to their needs, and regardless of their social and/or economic backgrounds. It promotes their wellbeing and enables them to develop their potential as healthy, enterprising and responsible citizens in our society' (QCA, 2007a, 'Personal

Development' section). This goal is embodied in the five outcomes of the *Every Child Matters* initiative: Be Healthy, Stay Safe, Enjoy and Achieve, Make a Positive Contribution and Achieve Economic Well-being. These are embedded across the current NC and departmental documentation should, ideally, make reference to them.

Pupils' personal skill sets have also come into focus in the latest NC; these are also required to be embedded throughout the curriculum in all subjects. The first way in which this has been done is through a renewed emphasis on 'functional skills' in all subjects – the 'core elements of English, mathematics and ICT that provide individuals with the skills and abilities they need to operate confidently, effectively and independently in life, their communities and work' (QCA, 2007a, 'Functional Skills' section).

The curriculum also specifies six types of personal learning and thinking skills, or PLTS. These are described as 'the qualities and skills needed for success in learning and life' (QCA, 2007a, 'PLTS' section). The six groups of skills are: independent enquirers, creative thinkers, reflective learners, team workers, self-managers and effective participants. There are clear links here to the 'Key Concepts' and 'Key Processes' sections of the programmes of study described above.

Chapter 12 looks at these skill sets in more detail and considers the mathematics teacher's contribution to the personal development of pupils.

Task 2.6 **Mathematics and society**

Re-read the five outcomes of the *Every Child Matters* initiative listed above. Do you think that mathematics plays an important role in promoting an individual's well-being and developing their potential as a member of society? Justify your answer. You may wish to draw on some of the ideas discussed in Chapter 1, such as those concerning Ernest's (1991) groups of progressive educators and social reformers.

Number

Although the programmes of study for each of the curriculum areas are very brief, they contain a number of important issues that you will need to address as a classroom teacher. For example, within the 'Number and Algebra' section, there is reference to making calculations. Taken as a whole, the curriculum encourages the use of mental methods, estimation and approximation, and the use of calculators, as well as written methods. It is the balance within the curriculum among these different approaches to calculation that is the cause of many debates (see also Chapter 9). The guidance on number in the KS3 Framework for mathematics suggested that:

> All pupils need to continue to learn when it is, and when it is not, appropriate to use a calculator, and their first-line strategy should involve mental calculations. They should have sufficient understanding of the calculation in front of them to be able to decide which method to use – mental, written or calculator, or a combination of these.
>
> (DfEE, 2001a: 12)

Task 2.7 **Pupils' calculation methods**

For this task, you are to interview some of your pupils to investigate how they carry out calculations and their relative confidence with different methods. You will need to arrange to interview six pupils, either individually or in pairs. There are three stages to the interview. Tell the pupils that you are interested in *how* they do calculations. Explain that you will specify whether they should do the calculations mentally, with pen and paper or by using their choice of calculator or pen and paper.

Stage 1
Ask pupils to do the first set of calculations mentally, without the use of pencil and paper. Tell them that you particularly want to know what they do in their heads and what their approach was.

(a) 23 + 48 (b) 82 – 37 (c) 15 × 7 (d) 96 ÷ 4

Record details of their methods as they explain them to you. Also note down any problems they have, whether in doing the calculation or in explaining their approach. Read what you have written back to them and see if they agree.

Stage 2
For the second set of calculations, tell the pupils that they can use pen and paper if they wish to.

(a) 267 + 584 (b) 645 – 178 (c) 23 × 57 (d) 624 ÷ 12

Ask them to talk through their methods, noting down responses and checking with them afterwards as you did in stage 1.

Stage 3
For the final set of calculations, tell the pupils that they may use a calculator or pen and paper if they wish to.

(a) 247 + 345 + 692 + 701 (b) 10,000 – 2,637 (c) 16 × 18 × 20 (d) 325 ÷ 17

If they use the calculator, note which keys they press and in which order. Ask them to explain the reasons behind their choice of method and device.

Having carried out the interviews, analyse the results and consider what implications they have for the way you might teach pupils to calculate. Write a short report of your investigation in your journal.

The importance of mental methods is now widely accepted and there is a growing understanding that this consists of much more than knowledge of arithmetic facts. It is recognised that pupils need to be helped to develop strategies for handling calculations mentally, an area that had, on the whole, been neglected. There is a considerably increased emphasis on mental calculation at KS1 and KS2, as well as an expectation that secondary mathematics teachers will continue to build on this at KS3.

Written methods have long had a place in the number curriculum, but generally pupils would only have been taught how to use a narrow range of standard algorithms. Since the introduction of the mathematics NC, there has continued to be a requirement that pupils are able to carry out standard written methods. Whereas written guidance might suggest what these 'standard' methods are, there is still scope for flexibility by pupils in the methods that they use. This is important, given the reality of how people calculate. Studies of people at work suggest that, despite being taught standard methods, they tend to use *ad hoc* personal approaches dependent on the situation. International studies show that there are, in fact, many different calculation algorithms and written methods, so it is a mistake to believe that the 'standard' methods used in Britain are in some way universal. Psychological studies have gone a step further, exploring how different approaches to mental arithmetic call upon a person's working memory, and how the size of the numbers involved impacts upon the time taken to perform a calculation (Ashcraft, 1995).

Teaching pupils *how* to estimate or approximate answers has also been an under-developed aspect of the mathematics curriculum. Pupils, who often place more value on finding exact solutions, tend to resist. However, these skills become more significant in a calculator age, when the reasonableness of answers needs to be checked. The appro-priate use of the calculator is much discussed. Some would like to see it removed from primary and early secondary school. Others think it can be an invaluable tool for promot-ing understanding of number and so should be used as early as possible. International comparisons lean more towards the former view, especially at primary level (but see Kitchen, 1998); a few countries like Spain welcome the use of any calculating device. Japan offers a further contrast, where teachers are expected to introduce pupils to the use of the *soroban*, the Japanese abacus (see Chapter 9 for more discussion).

Algebra

One of the impacts of the initial introduction of the mathematics NC was to encourage a much broader algebra curriculum than before, which consequently resulted in a reduced emphasis on algebraic manipulation. For example, far more attention was given to exploring patterns and making generalisations. Some of this shift in the algebra curricu-lum had begun with the GCSE. Various teachers at both university and post-16 level soon raised concerns that their students no longer had adequate algebraic skills for higher courses. These criticisms have continued to be made (see, for example, DfES, 2004a).

The Royal Society/Joint Mathematical Council report into the teaching of algebra sought to address these concerns and bring greater coherence to the algebra curriculum. The report identified three important components of school algebra:

▪ *generational activities* – discovering algebraic expressions and equations;
▪ *transformational, rule-based activities* – manipulating and simplifying algebraic expressions, solving equations, studying equivalence and form;
▪ *global, meta-level activities* – ideas of proof, mathematical structure, problem-solving.

(JMC/Royal Society, 1997: 28)

Their concern was that too much emphasis had been placed on the generational activities and pupils had had little opportunity to develop 'symbol sense', where algebraic symbols are seen as meaningful and powerful.

The 1999 revision of the mathematics NC sought to respond to many of the recom-mendations of this report and much greater detail was given in specifying the programmes of study for algebra. However, the 2008 NC offers much less specificity and teachers tend to be led by other documents, such as a textbook series. The three types of activities mentioned above, whilst not named, all have a clear place within the programmes of study. Although they are not explicit in the 'Number and Algebra' section, reading the text of the 'Key Concepts' and 'Key Processes' with a view to teaching algebra readily exposes the relevance of these tasks. If your pupils are to appreciate the meaning and power of algebra, then it will be important that they do genuinely experience a balance among all three types of activities, and develop an understanding of algebra as a tool with which to explore and express generality (Mason *et al.*, 2005).

Generally, within the NC, there is now a much clearer expectation that pupils undertake tasks that require using appropriate ICT. This is very explicit in the references to 'functional skills' as described above. In the case of algebra, this would include use of graphing packages (on computers or calculators) and spreadsheets. It is clear that the use of this technology can enhance the pupils' understanding of central concepts in sequences, functions and graphs (see Chapter 9). However, the existence of symbolic manipulator software or computer algebra systems has, as yet, had little impact on the teaching of algebra pre-16. Some would argue that such technology will call into question the place of much of the algebraic manipulation that currently comprises a significant part of school algebra. Just as the easy availability of numerical calculators has stimulated much debate about the number curriculum, you can also expect the increasing presence of symbolic manipulators to fuel an ongoing debate about the algebra one.

Geometry and measures

This area of the curriculum brings together ideas of shape, location, movement and measure, and is a long way from the traditional geometry curriculum. Aspects of coordinate and transformation geometry have become well-established since the 1960s and have retained a significant place in the 2008 mathematics NC. The 'measures' strand of the curriculum has been shifted around in the course of the various mathematics NC revisions. This is mainly due to it having close links with both number and shape/space. It therefore provides a good instance of a topic where the curriculum cannot be neatly divided into discrete chunks.

One contentious issue in this area of the curriculum is the place of geometrical reasoning. Originally, geometry was taught using the ideas and works of Euclid, following strict definitions and deductive reasoning. Whilst most countries have moved away from this type of geometry curriculum, some countries, such as France, have retained elements of it, principally because it is thought that this form of teaching contributes to the development of reasoning. There have also been some British mathematics educators who consider that traditional approaches to geometry can offer pupils an experience of rigour and proof. The influence of this sort of thinking led to the introduction of an explicit *geometrical reasoning* strand in the 1999 version of the mathematics NC, but this is no longer included in the 2008 version. This is not to say that geometric reasoning is absent and your findings in Task 2.3 should have found it mentioned implicitly via the Key Concepts and Key Processes sections. The aim of the 2008 NC to promote mathematics as a 'habit of mind' is broad in scope, but the lack of specificity has led to some concerns (ACME, 2007, for example) that the new structure does not fully support teachers in planning for progression.

The 2008 revision also omits any explicit mention of pupils being provided with 'hands-on' experience to help develop their understanding of and knowledge about geometry and measures. There is a danger that pupils actually receive a rather restricted curriculum in this area because of the difficulties of organising practical lessons. A useful test of your teaching in this area is to evaluate how much time pupils spend handling, drawing, measuring and constructing 2D/3D shapes.

A new way in which geometry can now be explored involves using specially designed dynamic geometry software (see Chapter 9). Such software gives pupils the opportunity to see ideas demonstrated, explore shape for themselves and develop and test hypotheses. In particular, the software allows pupils to explore some traditional Euclidean topics in a new way.

Examples of the use of dynamic geometry software are included in Johnston-Wilder and Mason (2006). One area of geometry that is still not finding a place in the curriculum, despite the opportunities offered by new technology, is fractal geometry. It can take a long time for important mathematical developments to filter into the school curriculum.

Task 2.8 **Making it visual**

The purpose of this task is to develop some resources to support your teaching of geometry and measures, and then to examine the impact of the use of such resources. For some time, mathematics teachers have used stimulating posters as starting points for work with their groups. However, with the increasing availability of projection facilities in classrooms, it is now possible to draw from a huge stock of geometrical images. Identify one of your classes that is about to cover some aspect of the 'Geometry and measures' programme of study (or its equivalent). Consider what form of visual stimulus related to this topic would engage pupils and provoke their thinking. Then:

- find suitable images through an internet search or take your own digital photographs;
- plan how you will introduce the images and what discussion/questions you want them to provoke;
- talk through your lesson plan with the class teacher, discussing whether you are using the images to full effect;
- try to notice, during the lesson, the impact of the images on the pupils' engagement;
- evaluate the success of the lesson afterwards through discussion with the class teacher and consider how you might use images within your future geometry and measures teaching.

Handling data

The growing emphasis on both statistics and probability within the mathematics curriculum reflects changes in society, which is increasingly influenced by the way data, usually numerical, are handled. Although there have been elements of statistics and probability included in mathematics curricula for some time, the breadth of what is now expected within the mathematics NC is relatively new. Consequently, the place of statistics within the mathematics curriculum is still questioned by some mathematicians and mathematics educators. They consider that it might be better taught in the context of its use in other subjects (e.g. see DfES, 2004a).

The programme of study is now very clearly structured around the idea of the data-handling cycle (see Figure 2.2), which is, in turn, linked to the stages of the Key Processes. This assumes that any meaningful statistics or probability work is carried out using the four stages suggested in the cycle.

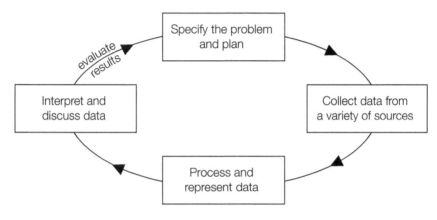

■ **Figure 2.2** The handling data cycle
Source: DfEE, 2001, Section 1: 18

Task 2.9 **Questioning the data**

Watch a main evening news broadcast. Record all occasions where data are used in the reports. After the programme, try to answer the following questions for each piece of data.

■ What was the original reason that the data were collected and who wanted them to be collected?
■ How were the data collected and how reliable do you think the methods were?
■ In what ways have the data been analysed and presented? How appropriate were these methods?
■ How were the data interpreted and what conclusions were drawn from them?

Having worked through this process for yourself, consider what implications this has for the way you might teach pupils to 'handle' data.

It is expected that pupils will have experiences of the full data-handling cycle. This would involve carrying out their own meaningful statistical enquiries, but would also include considering how others may have gone through the cycle in producing statistical claims or results. This should help pupils to be more statistically literate in adult life and connects with the wider aims of the curriculum in preparing pupils for being active participants in society.

The increased emphasis placed on the full cycle is important, given that pupils have often had a narrow experience of calculating statistics or producing diagrams with no reference to genuine contexts. However, it is still important to consider how pupils will acquire the particular knowledge and skills required at the different stages of the cycle. This is not always possible to do within the context of carrying out an enquiry. Some of the issues surrounding the use of the data-handling cycle in the classroom to develop statistical thinking are discussed in more detail in Graham (2006).

The aspects of probability required by the programmes of study are also much broader in scope than was often covered prior to the mathematics NC being introduced. Indeed, many other countries' curricula (including the Scottish one) do not tackle probability until the upper secondary level. In the mathematics NC, there is an emphasis on more than just theoretical probability, encompassing the use of statistical data and experimental results. There is, however, a need to be cautious here: concepts underlying probability are subtle; so there is a danger that, through a superficial treatment of the subject, understanding of key ideas will not be developed.

The teaching of both statistics and probability can be significantly supported by the use of ICT. This is now a requirement for various aspects of the handling data curriculum. ICT should be used to gather data from secondary sources, to generate statistical diagrams and to communicate the results of enquiries using diagrams and related text. The use of ICT has the potential to shift the pupils' efforts away from just processing and representing data and towards spending more time on interpretation and discussion. Also, with the much-easier access to secondary sources of data mediated by ICT, pupils can experience mathematics as topical and rooted in the 'real world'.

SUMMARY AND KEY POINTS

Your mathematics National Curriculum will undoubtedly have an impact on your teaching. The scope and degree of prescription of the curriculum will influence the extent of this impact, and your interpretation of the curriculum will be affected by the manner in which it is presented. The way performance standards are defined will partly shape your practice, particularly how you address the issue of pupils learning at different rates. The programmes of study will not remain static; you will need to continue to refine your understanding of their content and of different possible emphases within them.

You are likely to experience a number of revisions of your National Curriculum during your career as a mathematics teacher. You need to go on thinking about the issues raised in this chapter, if you are to engage with and contribute to the important debate that surrounds the revision process.

FURTHER READING

Foremost, it is important for you to read through a copy of your own mathematics National Curriculum (see Task 2.1). The following readings may also be of interest.

Hoyles, C., Morgan, C. and Woodhouse, G. (eds) (1999) *Rethinking the Mathematics Curriculum.* London: Falmer Press

This edited book brings together chapters on an array of topics looking at mathematics, change and the curriculum. It examines many of the issues considered in the first two chapters of this book and offers a range of perspectives on how school mathematics might continue to develop in the twenty-first century.

JMC/Royal Society (1997) *Teaching and Learning Algebra Pre-19*. London: The Royal Society.
JMC/Royal Society (2001) *Teaching and Learning Geometry 11–19*. London: The Royal Society.

These two reports have had, and will continue to have, a significant impact on the shape of the mathematics curriculum. They offer valuable reading that can help you to understand the way in which such reports are produced in order to influence policy. However, they are equally valuable in the breadth of perspectives that they bring both to the algebra and the geometry and measures curricula.

Ruddock, G. (1998) *Mathematics in the School Curriculum: An International Perspective.* Accessed from INCA website, January 2010: www.inca.org.uk/pdf/maths_no_intro_98.pdf

This paper provides a very helpful overview of mathematics curricula around the world and helps to set our various curricula in Britain into a broader context. By considering 16 countries, it addresses curriculum organisation and structure; assessment arrangements; classroom organisation and teaching methods; use of textbooks and other resources; and teacher specialisation.

PUPILS LEARNING MATHEMATICS

Maria Goulding

INTRODUCTION

As a student teacher, you will probably spend a period of time observing lessons, helping individuals and groups and then gradually move to teaching full classes. You will, therefore, be entering a ready-made social situation and your growing understanding of how pupils learn mathematics will be strongly influenced by the context in which you see this learning take place. For this reason, I approach pupil learning in this chapter by peeling back layers: looking at the social context first, then moving on to feelings before finally looking at pupils' thinking. This is by no means a typical approach.

For some writers, the mathematics being learned, the conditions under which it is learned and the feelings and attitudes that learners bring to the situation are all but ignored. The shared view is that you cannot begin to make sense of what is going on inside a learner's head until these other dimensions are considered. They interact, of course, and the picture is even further complicated by the dynamic relationship between teaching and learning.

The purpose of this chapter is to expose some of the common features of mathematics classrooms, but also to introduce you to some insights from the mathematics education research literature. This will help you to think critically about the circumstances in which learning takes place and the processes it involves. As you try out the accompanying school-based tasks, you should aim to connect what you see in your classroom with the research and theorising offered here. Making such connections will best be done by sharing your observations with teachers and other students and by looking for similarities and differences. It is assumed that this will take place for each of the suggested tasks.

This chapter discusses some contrasting theoretical positions about the learning of mathematics. Some of these arise from research. An important summary of older research in mathematics education is that by Askew and Wiliam (1995). Other collections include Nickson (2004) and Mason and Johnston-Wilder (2004a, b). You will find it useful to have a copy of one of these texts to work with as you read this and some later chapters.

OBJECTIVES

By the end of this chapter you should:

■ appreciate the social, emotional and cognitive dimensions of learning and the importance of context;
■ be aware that pupils are both individuals and members of groups;
■ be making links between reading and what you experience in school;
■ realise how learning and teaching are intertwined.

THE SOCIAL CONTEXT OF LEARNING

You will probably meet pupils first in a mathematics classroom, so you will immediately see them learning within the frame of this social situation. Typically, there will be one teacher with about 30 pupils in the class, with possibly a support teacher to work with pupils with special educational needs (see Chapter 10). If the pupils are in Years 8–11, then the class will probably be a set based on perceptions of ability – and the numbers of pupils in the sets may vary. Lessons will be about an hour long and there will likely be two or three in the week.

Task 3.1 **Classroom organisation**

As you observe a lesson, note how the class is organised.

■ How many teachers are there in the classroom?
■ How many pupils are there in the lesson?
■ How are the pupils grouped into classes for mathematics?
■ How long is the lesson?
■ How is the furniture arranged? Does this correspond to the way the children are working (e.g. are the pupils sitting in groups but working individually)?
■ Do the pupils work as a whole class, in smaller groups or as individuals? Is there a mix of these ways of working? Note how long they work in the different groupings for any one lesson. How are transitions effected?
■ Do pupils all do the same tasks? Is there any choice?
■ Do pupils make comparisons among different methods of doing the mathematics problems or is everyone expected to use the same method?
■ What physical resources are used (e.g. texts, practical equipment, calculators, posters, etc.)?

After the lesson, talk to the teacher about the forms of classroom organisation he or she finds most conducive to learning and why. Which factors influence decisions (e.g. control, the ability of the set, the teacher's own preferred style, etc.)?

Reflect on how the organisation of mathematics lessons in this school compares with the school you went to as a pupil yourself. There may be some interesting similarities and differences within the group, depending on when and where you were educated. Write a paragraph in your journal to summarise this.

You may find very strong views about the forms of organisation found in the classes you observe. Some of these may highlight the importance of the individual child and the difficulty of catering for individual needs within a class.

1   No learner can be expected to think in the same way as his or her teacher.
2   No two learners in a class can be expected to think in the same way as each other (possibly excepting twins).

(Backhouse et al., 1992: 54)

Some teachers may justify the use of setting by referring to such individual differences and explaining how difficult it is to cater for a very wide spread of individual attainment in a mixed-ability class.

In the past, individualised learning schemes such as SMILE were commonly used in primary and secondary schools as a way of accommodating individual differences. In England and Wales, such schemes became less common after the National Numeracy Strategy (DfEE, 1999b) (hereafter called NNS) and the *Key Stage 3 National Strategy: Framework for Teaching Mathematics* (DfEE, 2001a) (hereafter called KS3 NS) were first introduced.

In individualised learning schemes, pupils worked at their own pace through commercially produced materials with periodic tests and reviews to monitor progress. There is a wide range of tasks in such schemes, including the use of games and practical work, as well as those designed to teach skills and concepts. Some examples of such tasks in the case of SMILE can be found as small programs for the TI-73 graphic calculator. Moreover, the class could be taught as a mixed-ability group, thus avoiding the potentially damaging effects of labelling pupils by putting them into sets.

For a new teacher using an individualised learning scheme, keeping track of pupils is very demanding and some find themselves simply coping with issues of administration and reacting to pupils' demands rather than initiating interactions. Another potential problem is that pupils working from the text meet a predetermined sequence of questions, instructions and explanations that places great demands upon their reading comprehension. This involves far more than simply being able to read the words. Pupils have to extract the meanings and make the connections intended by the writer of the materials. Difficulties such as these, however, are not confined to individualised learning schemes, since excessive use of textbooks presents similar problems to the learner.

The National Numeracy Strategy in primary schools and the KS3 National Strategy in secondary schools both encouraged the use of more whole-class teaching, sometimes regardless of the fact that it can be of variable quality. This move to a whole-class focus rather than the individual was prompted by comparisons with teaching methods in other countries. Those countries that appeared to perform significantly better on international tests of mathematical content, if not on tests designed to assess ability to use and apply mathematics (Budge, 1997), were held up as models to teachers in England and Wales. David Reynolds (1996) claimed that the interactive whole-class teaching methods used in Taiwan are based on the assumption that the pupils will move forward together, in contrast to our western focus upon individuality. He argued that, by accommodating difference, we may actually *produce* it, with a long tail of underachievement.

Whole-class teaching, however, can mean different things to different people. In a class selected by ability (a set), the intention may be to produce a homogeneous attainment group. This often entails the class *being taught as if it were an individual.* The teacher may give explanations and demonstrate how to do examples, with the pupils following a sequence that is in the teacher's head. The intention is that pupils master the material at roughly the same rate as each other. If this is the dominant model of teaching/learning, there is very limited opportunity for pupils to be actively involved in learning mathematics or for individual understandings to be explored.

In contrast, whole-class teaching could also mean that the pupils work on accessible starting points, develop their own ideas and strategies with the teacher's help and then share them with the whole class. During this process, these different viewpoints and methods can be evaluated and the class may come to some agreement about which are most useful, efficient and/or worthy of further investigation. Here, difference and diversity are drawn on, exploited by the teacher rather than ironed out, and the class may work as individuals, small groups and as a whole class at different points in the process, even within a single lesson.

These two possibilities actually amount to very different theoretical positions about teaching and learning, but the pupils in both cases are taught as a whole class. 'Theory' here is taken to mean an explicit account that describes how children learn, from which implications of how best to teach effectively can be drawn (see Capel *et al.*, 2009). A learning theory will draw upon evidence and involve interpretation and argument, but it also incorporates a theory of what knowledge is and what kinds of knowledge are most desirable and useful, both to the learner and to society as a whole.

THEORIES OF LEARNING AND KNOWLEDGE

In what follows there are a number of references to different views and theories of learning (including various forms of constructivism, behaviourism and Vygotsky's sociocultural theory). For more information on any one of them, read at least the introduction to Wood (1998) or Unit 5.1 in Capel *et al.* (2009).

As you read this section about theories of learning and knowledge, you will need to relate what you read to your own experiences of learning mathematics and to what you see taking place in lessons in your school. The following task is intended to help you to do this.

Task 3.2 **Relating theory and practice**

1   Think about your own experiences of learning mathematics. Try to identify two contrasting experiences: one where you were expected to work alone and one where you were encouraged to work with other learners.
2   In the lessons you watch in your school, look out for parts of lessons where the pupils are expected to work alone, and times where pupils are encouraged to work with each other in pairs or in small groups.

For each of the cases that you identify in 1 and 2 above, keep them in mind as you read about the theories of learning discussed in this chapter. Keep notes in your journal of your reflections on how the theories relate to those incidents and experiences that you have identified.

The first instance of whole-class teaching outlined above, if adopted in its most extreme form, really amounts to a view of learning as copying. In contrast, Barbara Jaworski (1992) outlines a *social constructivist* perspective:

> In the classrooms which I have studied, I have regarded the students as meaning makers, and teachers as supporters of the process of meaning making by their students. This does not mean that I see teaching as some wishy-washy process of 'letting it happen', the teacher being no more than a facilitator. This is as simplistic a view as the image of teacher as the expert who hands over knowledge and skills. (p. 13)

Jaworski is stressing the active roles of both teacher and learner, and uses two negative comparisons for emphasis. In the first of these ('some wishy-washy process of "letting it happen"'), we have a very simplified but commonly held version of Piaget's constructivism, in which children learn by passing through a sequence of four stages.

With this simplistic interpretation, no amount of direction and teaching can move a child between stages if the child is not 'ready'. According to this view, the child is cast as a lone but active discoverer, motivated to understand the world around her in terms of previous experiences, but constrained by her particular stage of development. (For a helpful discussion of aspects of Piaget's theory in relation to mathematics teaching and learning, read at least Chapter 4, 'Must we wait until pupils are ready?' in Orton, 2004: 48–70.)

No such active role is available for the learner in Jaworski's second example ('teacher as the expert who hands over knowledge and skills'). This image describes learners in behaviourist theory, where the teacher's role is to shape and reinforce pupils' responses positively until they are correct. This theory has its roots in experiments on training animal behaviour and was later applied to human learning. Its effects are still commonly seen in classrooms where the learners' motivation, experience and understanding are not taken into account and 'rote' learning is achieved through copying and practising until perfect. With an externally imposed curriculum, where much hangs on examination performance, however, it can be very tempting to teach in this way, even for teachers who can see the limitations of this approach.

In acknowledging the importance of action and problem-solving in learning, social constructivism has much in common with Piaget's constructivism, but there is a much stronger emphasis on the role of language, communication and instruction. The American psychologist Jerome Bruner is a leading proponent of social constructivism. For him, children do not invent or discover how to adapt their thinking and act intelligently in new situations by themselves. These processes are developed by negotiating and interacting with more mature peers and teachers. In developing this theory, Bruner has been strongly influenced by the Soviet psychologist and sociocultural theorist Lev Vygotsky, for whom social interaction was a necessary condition for learning:

> Indeed [Vygotsky] defined intelligence itself as the capacity to learn through instruction.
>
> (Wood, 1998: 9)

Instruction here, however, is not the one-directional process involved in behaviourism. It is a much more subtle process in which several important ideas are involved.

(i) *The zone of proximal development*
This is the 'gap' between what the learner can achieve on his own and what he can achieve with help from a more knowledgeable adult or peer.

(ii) *Contingent teaching (or scaffolding)*
This is the process by which a more knowledgeable adult or peer can help a child move from her actual performance level to her potential level, giving just enough help to move the child from one to the other.

(iii) *Self-regulation*
In interacting with more knowledgeable peers or teachers, pupils can begin to think about and regulate their own thinking. This could involve questioning their habitual first responses, refining their solutions, asking themselves questions and trying alternative approaches.

Jaworski and Watson (1994) have illustrated some of these constructs at work with specific examples of lessons in secondary classes. Here, negotiation was taking place between skilful teachers and pupils in classes where an investigative approach to mathematics was established and the values behind it were shared. The teachers were inducting their pupils into a particular way of thinking and acting in mathematical situations. They were doing so by making judgements about the degree of challenge offered to pupils, based on sensitive interactions with the pupils as they pursued lines of enquiry in investigative tasks. These interactions often took the form of the teacher acting as a 'mirror' to the pupils' thinking, subtly probing and asking questions that would help them to clarify their position and to see ways forward.

In another study, Mike Askew *et al.* (1995) explored the metaphor of scaffolding. However, in their observations of 105 primary lessons of mathematics, science, and design and technology, they found little evidence of teachers using this strategy intuitively. This they attributed to the very special constraints and circumstances in school settings, which make the notion of scaffolding problematic:

> Perhaps the best way to regard scaffolding is as some form of general orientating metaphor, alerting the teacher to watch out for the extent to which pupils can succeed at tasks on their own, suppressing the desire to step in and help too soon, yet being prepared to work alongside the pupil when a genuine need arises. (p. 56)

Jaworski's (1992) examples of contingent teaching that built on and developed pupils' own thinking took place in mathematics settings where there were largely shared values, together with an external imperative for pupils to work investigatively in preparation for GCSE coursework tasks. These two factors may have been necessary for the teachers to become explicitly aware of opportunities where they could work patiently and sensitively with pupils' present understanding, in order to develop a more sophisticated understanding. Research that takes place in a larger random sample of classrooms will not necessarily uncover this phenomenon, because the teachers may not be working with shared understandings.

Vygotskian theory, coupled with the Piagetian notion of big mathematical ideas (or higher-order thinking), is made explicit in the Cognitive Acceleration in Mathematics Education project (CAME). This project, and its big sister, the Cognitive Acceleration in Science Education (CASE) project, both predate the NNS and the KS3 NS. Pupils participating in CASE and CAME performed significantly better in Year 9 and Year 11 public examinations of Mathematics, Science and also English when compared with pupils in control schools (Shayer, 1999; Shayer *et al.*, 1999). This evidence has proved very attractive to schools aiming to boost the performance of those pupils in the middle of the attainment range (i.e. between the thirtieth and the seventieth percentiles).

The accompanying materials for CAME, *Thinking Maths* (Adhami *et al.*, 2007), include a clearly articulated constructivist theoretical background; lesson plans and analysis; sample lessons; and pupil materials. They are to be taught in Years 7 and 8 as a supplement to 'normal' mathematics lessons. The style is highly interactive and collaborative and teachers are expected to act as mediators in moving pupils from one state of thinking to another. The tasks themselves have been trialled in many schools and are carefully chosen to expose pupils to powerful mathematical ideas requiring pupils to restructure their thinking. These important ideas (e.g. reasoning in ratio and proportion contexts, functionality, modelling) are returned to in increasingly complex and diverse contexts, although all the tasks have accessible starting points. Participating teachers are expected to use the materials as a focus for professional development:

■   with a trainer demonstrating lessons or coaching the teacher within the classroom;
■   in discussions at departmental meetings;
■   in out-of-school in-service training where trainers may introduce elements of theory or encourage participants to share their experiences of teaching in relation to specific tasks.

It is hoped that in such meetings, teachers will begin to reflect on insights and experiences that will draw them together, thereby increasing the likelihood of their developing shared values and expertise. A descriptive case study of a student teacher teaching a CAME lesson is presented in Goulding (2002a); details of how the project was implemented in seven schools and the understanding of 21 participating teachers can be found in Goulding (2002b, 2002c). More recent examples of teachers using CAME can be found on the NCETM website.

Neither the NNS nor the KS3 NS explicitly claimed to have a theoretical basis, although the whole-class teaching in the recommended three-part lessons is intended to be highly interactive, prioritising the use of language as in social constructivism:

A typical mathematics lesson:

■   **An oral and mental starter** (about 5 to 20 minutes):
    whole-class work to rehearse, sharpen and develop mental skills, including recall skills, and visualization, thinking and communication skills.
■   **The main teaching activity** (about 25 to 40 minutes):
    combinations of teaching input and pupil activities;
    work as a whole class, in pairs or groups, or as individuals;
    interventions to identify and sort out misconceptions, clarify points and give immediate feedback.
■   **A final plenary** (to round off the lesson):
    whole-class work to summarise key facts and ideas and what to remember, to identify progress, make links with other work, discuss the next steps, set homework.

(DfEE, 2001c)

The KS3 NS also incorporated teacher development opportunities with numeracy consultants working directly with teachers in schools or during off-site in-service education, but it was a big national initiative and hence it is not surprising that current interpretations and practice are very variable. This, together with a lack of a research basis or theoretical orientation, may account for the findings from the evaluation of the NNS that suggested that while surface features – like the use of the three-part lesson – had been adopted, deep change had been harder to identify (Earl *et al.*, 2003).

Task 3.3 **What does it mean to help a pupil?**

Try to analyse a situation in which a pupil needs help from you, from the teacher or from another pupil.

- How does the pupil signal the difficulty? Ask the pupil to describe the difficulty.
- How is the pupil seeing the problem? Write down the pupil's exact words and actions as soon as possible after the event.
- How was the help given? Write down the words and actions as soon as possible afterwards.

Discuss the incident with the class teacher and later with other student teachers. Was there enough/too much/too little guidance? How did you judge? Did the help move the child on or simply solve the immediate problem? Did you see any evidence of scaffolding, and what form did it take?

It is important to realise that social constructivism *as a theory of learning* could coexist with a view of mathematical knowledge as fixed and objective. However, if you adopt a humanistic view of mathematics (as described, for instance, in Davis and Hersh, 1986), you need to incorporate the idea that unless we negotiate meaning by arguing, discussing and exploring disagreement, we would not be able to communicate with each other. Without this consensus, any one mathematical statement would be as valid as another.

Within this paradigm, the classroom could be regarded as a 'community of practice', one where ideas are explored, discussed, shared and evaluated. Here, the consensual knowledge is a product of social activity. I have already referred to Jaworski's closely observed examples, but you should also read about how this model is illustrated in the research by Jo Boaler (1997, especially pp. 42–5), which features heavily in the next section. Both writers show how teachers were able to work with and around the fixed and seemingly objective body of mathematical knowledge drawn up in syllabuses, by choosing tasks that allowed for a certain amount of originality on the part of pupils. While we are still thinking about the social production of mathematical knowledge, it is appropriate to step outside the mathematics classroom for a moment.

Situated cognition

The industrial pragmatists, mentioned in the first chapter, want pupils to be able to apply the mathematics they learn at school to the workplace, but this notion of 'transfer' may not be as straightforward as it seems. American social anthropologist Jean Lave (1988), for instance, in summarising the research on out-of-school uses of mathematics, concluded that all learning is closely tied to the situation in which it occurs. She is able to explain people's inability to use the mathematics they learn at school, because it is so closely tied to peculiar and unrealistic practices adopted there. In other words, school mathematics may only be useful in school.

This may be a depressing outlook for anyone starting out as a mathematics teacher, particularly if they share some of the aims of the industrial pragmatists. Perhaps this yawning gap is not inevitable. We may find that transfer across contexts is poor, because the common practices of school mathematics need to be questioned, challenged and adapted. 'School' mathematics and 'out-of-school' mathematics may yet have some common ground, not only in the contexts employed, but in *the ways of working* adopted in the classroom.

Jo Boaler (1997) used the idea of situated cognition to compare what she describes as *different forms of knowledge* found in two London schools of very similar intake and circumstance but with radically different approaches to the teaching of mathematics. The first school, which she named Amber Hill, was perhaps typical of many schools in that it adopted a conventional textbook-based approach to teaching and learning mathematics. But despite good relationships between staff and pupils and controlled classroom conditions, many of the pupils:

> appeared to be disadvantaged in the face of new or 'applied' situations. [... They] believed that mathematical success required memory, rather than thought. They had developed a shallow and procedural knowledge that was of limited use in new and demanding situations, and their desire to interpret cues and do the 'right thing' suppressed their ability to interpret situations holistically or mathematically. (p. 143)

The students in the other school, which she called Phoenix Park, performed better in the GCSE examinations set at the time. The teaching approach there was based on open-ended projects lasting two or three weeks, with content and techniques interspersed as necessary. Despite a lack of imposed order, most of the pupils responded well to the amount of choice given and were able to adapt flexibly to new situations:

> When the Phoenix Park students encountered a mathematical problem, they believed that they should consider the different variables present and then develop ideas in relation to the specific setting in which they found themselves. They were not disabled by the need to try and remember relevant algorithms. When the students described their use of mathematics, they talked about the importance of thought, the adaptation of methods they had learned and their interpretation of different situations. (p. 144)

Boaler does not paint a completely rosy picture of Phoenix Park, nor a completely negative picture of Amber Hill, and she is wary of generalisation. But she does question the common practices in mathematics classrooms, which many of us have come through, and in which some, indeed many, of you will find yourselves immersed on teaching practice. Her work requires closer reading because of these controversial questions, not just about teaching approaches but also about ability groupings and gender. It is also important to note that the practice at Phoenix Park was abandoned in the face of an imminent Ofsted inspection, which shows how effective teaching can be constrained by perceptions of what will be judged acceptable by external bodies.

Ability

Our own experience of schools supports evidence (for example, Watson, 1996; Ofsted, 2008) that mathematics teachers use ability, more than teachers of other subjects, as a major organising principle for their teaching. The view that attainment is mainly deter- mined by some innate ability (Lorenz, 1982; Dweck, 2006) and that it is stable over time can be variously seen as defeatist, realistic or damaging. In her study, Boaler argues that the practice of setting disadvantaged some Amber Hill students in the top sets, particu- larly those who felt anxiety under pressure, as well as those in lower sets, some of whom felt that restrictions were placed on their learning opportunities. (See also Nardi and Steward, 2003; Wiliam and Bartholomew, 2004.) Wiliam and Bartholomew's (2004) longitudinal study of 42 classes in six London schools concluded that progress made during Key Stage 4 varied greatly from set to set, with pupils in lower sets progressing more slowly than those in higher sets even when Key Stage 3 test scores were taken into account. An earlier report on the same study (Boaler and Greeno, 2000) claimed that the teachers employed a more restricted range of teaching approaches with 'homegeneous' groups than with mixed-ability groups and this had a strong negative impact upon pupils.

Task 3.4 **Setting or mixed-ability?**

■ Are there any mixed-ability classes in your placement school? Which years are they employed in? How are they managed? What resources are used?

■ Are there any setting arrangements? If so, make a diagram to show the struc- ture of the setting arrangements for the different year groups. Under what circumstances do pupils move between sets?

■ Talk to teachers. Find out about the reasons for the organisation and their own personal preferences. If the classes are setted at your school, compare low sets with high sets for the same teacher. How does she describe differences in practice for these sets?

■ Find a way of asking pupils how they arrived in the set they are in and how they feel about it. Note the actual words they use in describing themselves in rela- tion to the set. Has their self-esteem been affected, and if so, how?

Gender

One aspect of the social dimension of learning mathematics that has received consider- able attention over a long period has been the perceived problem of girls and mathematics, largely because of girls' general apparent underachievement and their low level of participation post-16. Explanations arising from biological differences between the sexes have been inconclusive and also undermined by evidence of negligible sex differences in some countries and changes over time (Hanna, 1989). Many of the initia- tives designed to improve this situation have focused on making mathematics 'girl-friendly', for example by widening the contexts, using non-sexist resources, improving careers advice and raising teachers' expectations of girls. Performance is now very even at age 16, but participation post-16 still remains stubbornly unbalanced.

This framing of girls as disadvantaged is very problematic, however, since there may be very positive reasons why they reject mathematics in favour of other subjects offering more relevance and interest. Interestingly, Boaler found that in the face of the traditional practices at Amber Hill, girls did underachieve and were disaffected, but that neither disaffection nor anxiety was found among the girls in the more open, process-based approach employed at Phoenix Park.

Task 3.5 **Sex differences in performance?**

▪ Find out how your school monitors examination performance in mathematics. Do they look at sex differences? Do they have information on entries at different tiers? Are there any sex differences apparent?
▪ Are there any noticeable differences at Key Stage 3, GCSE or post-16? Are there any differences in other subjects?
▪ Talk to boys and girls about their expectations of success in mathematics. Compare this information with their teachers' predictions.

Much of the research on gender has moved from looking at sex differences in perform-ance to looking at the unwritten social rules in play in mathematics classrooms. This has thrown light upon the way in which membership of a group, not necessarily of the same sex, can affect an individual's experience of learning. This ability to function effectively in a group, so that the learner's potential is realised, may have a great deal to do with feel-ings of belonging, of being safe and of being motivated to learn.

FEELINGS AND MOTIVATION

One of the most striking things to emerge from the Assessment of Performance Unit's (APU) study of attitudes and gender differences, in 1988, was the way in which it connected attitudes with performance. Results showed that feelings ran high when it came to mathematics and that expressions of enjoyment declined after the age of 11, where 250 out of 500 pupils rated it their favourite subject. It is still found that girls' attitude to mathematics tends to be more negative than boys.

Boaler and Greeno (2000) make a link between negative attitudes and mathemati-cal teaching practices that do not emphasise understanding. Johnston-Wilder and Lee (2010) describe an excessive focus on acquisition of skills, solution of routine exercises, preparation for tests and examinations and the need for speed (Ofsted, 2008) as 'cogni-tive abuse', because these factors have been demonstrated to contribute to anxiety about mathematics and subsequent avoidance patterns (see, for example, Ashcraft, 2002). They found that, of a 2008 cohort of students training as primary teachers, 50 per cent had some symptoms of mathematics anxiety, and several experienced severe panic in relation to mathematics.

By asking 14-year-old pupils to recount good and bad experiences of learning, Celia Hoyles (1982) was able to gain insight into pupils' perceptions of their mathemat-ics learning. She found that about one third of the good stories (42 out of 135) and one half of the bad stories (72 out of 146) were about mathematics learning:

> The stories also showed that anxiety, feelings of inadequacy and feelings of shame were quite common features of bad experiences in learning mathematics. (p. 362)

Although there was considerable diversity, with some pupils enjoying challenge and others simply wanting to know what to do, many of the pupils seemed to want their teachers (in Hoyles's words) to 'make it easy' for them or to 'tell them the way':

> Pupils were appreciative of a secure, encouraging environment in their mathematics lessons and liked teachers to provide a structured logical progression in their work, with plenty of patient explanation, encouragement and friendliness. (p. 368)

Task 3.6 **Good and bad stories about mathematics**

Try to replicate some of Hoyles's research; ask pupils to write stories about good and bad learning experiences. Ask them to tell you about the situation in which the event happened, how they felt about it, the reasons why it was good or bad and why they think they reacted the way they did.

Hoyles's comments about the need for security echo Gordon Pask's (1976) distinction between *serialist* and *holist* learning strategies, in which he focuses upon the amount of risk learners are prepared to tolerate. Whereas serialists like to move from certainty to certainty, holists prefer to start working on the whole framework first and then fill in details later. Rosalinde Scott-Hodgetts (1986) used this distinction to account for the apparent discontinuity of girls' performance at primary–secondary transfer, but concluded that:

> children who are predisposed to a serialistic approach are less likely to develop into versatile learners within the mathematics classroom, than those who are inclined to adopt holistic strategies; this situation is held to be directly attributable to teacher behaviour. (p. 70)

Yet another insight into the effect of pupils' preferred learning styles is offered by David Galloway *et al.* (1996), who emphasise that motivational style may be more a product of situation than a feature of the individual. In their study, they identified adaptive and maladaptive styles of motivation. 'Mastery orientation' was considered adaptive because pupils who were faced with the possibility of failure were able to demonstrate perseverance and overcame difficulties. In other words, these pupils were not deterred if they did not always succeed; difficulties were seen as challenges to be overcome rather than insurmountable objects. Dweck (2006) would say that these pupils demonstrated a 'growth mindset', which allowed them to regard challenge as an opportunity for learning. The opposite mindset is 'fixed'. Pupils with a fixed mindset avoid challenge, as any failure can demonstrate that they have reached the ceiling of their available ability; that is, it can show them to be 'unintellegent'. Such pupils often demonstrate 'learned helplessness', as they believe in their lack of ability and, therefore, failure was inevitable. In the light of this, it seems vital to: 'foster a view of ability in mathematics as changeable rather than fixed' (Askew and Wiliam, 1995: 28).

It also appears important to create a classroom climate in which mistakes can be made without shame and where there is clear feedback that students can use to improve their performance. Such a classroom will contribute to what Johnston-Wilder and Lee

(2010) term 'mathematical resilience': 'Mathematical resilience is fostered when pupils face, and succeed in meeting, mathematical challenge' (p. 218).

THE COGNITIVE DIMENSION

Much of the research and writing on pupils' understanding of mathematics has relied on a conventional framework that links facts, skills and conceptual structures – but there is rather less research on pupils' development of problem-solving strategies. For the purposes of this chapter, I will concentrate on research and writing about pupils' understanding of the content areas of the curriculum.

There can be very few people in the UK mathematics education community who have not been influenced in some way by the work of Richard Skemp. His arguments made in 1976 for the development of *relational* rather than solely *instrumental* understanding still have the power to rouse strong emotions and fierce debate.

Relational understanding refers to the rich body of interconnected conceptual understanding that a sophisticated thinker can draw upon flexibly, whereas instrumental understanding refers to a set of rules, algorithms and definitions that can be recalled and used accurately in specific situations. For Skemp, relational understanding includes instrumental understanding, but goes far beyond it. He compares these two forms of understanding by using the analogy of a person lost in a strange town. If the person had a map then there would be a good chance of his finding his destination. If the person could only remember a sequence of instructions (turn right at the crossroads, straight on at the next junction etc.), then a single mistake in the sequence would leave him stranded.

Task 3.7 **Making connections**

While you are observing mathematics lessons, look out for pupils who are:

▨ making connections among different mathematical ideas;
▨ only able to follow a predetermined procedure and are thrown when something slightly unfamiliar occurs;
▨ being taught to make connections;
▨ being taught a mechanical procedure without reference to meanings or reasons.

South African mathematics educator Michael de Villiers (1994) argues that we need to go further and add another desirable category, that of *functional* understanding. This involves: 'understanding the role, function or value of specific mathematical content or of a particular process' (p. 11). An example of these types of understanding working in harmony would be when a pupil has a flexible method for solving an equation like:

$$5/x = 3/4$$

but could also think of a context or situation in which that equation might need solving.

Task 3.8 **Functional understanding**

Can you think of a variety of ways of solving this equation and a context in which it might arise? Find some other examples in the topics you are going to teach, and try to justify their role, function and purpose.

Skemp's distinctions have been identified empirically by his colleagues Eddie Gray and David Tall (1994), who write about a 'proceptual divide', distinguishing pupils who can use the condensed symbolic forms found in mathematics, and adapt them flexibly, from pupils who constantly return to memorised procedures and rules. The latter ended up undertaking more laborious and memory-intensive mathematical procedures while the former could select and retrieve certain facts and procedures from memory, use them to derive new facts and then add these new facts to their memory store. Common arithmetical examples of non-proceptual thinking would be:

■ an over-reliance on counting, for example by counting back from 56 in order to compute $56 - 17$;
■ continued reliance on repeated addition rather than the use of multiplication facts when working on paper or employing repeated addition even when using a calculator.

In contrast, proceptual thinkers see expressions like $3 + 5 = 8$ and $y = x + 5$ as objects in their own right rather than processes to be performed. These learners can manipulate such objects, e.g. when using known number facts to derive new ones, when recognising the relationship between the graphs of $y = x + 5$ and $y = x + n$ and $y = nx$ where n is a natural number.

The difficulty here is moving children on and helping them develop more sophisticated strategies, since we know from other research (such as Hart, 1981; Kerslake, 1986; Johnson, 1989) that pupils will keep using their sometimes restrictive 'own' methods with which they feel comfortable. Other findings from these related studies are that:

■ many pupils have restricted or incomplete views of mathematical entities like fractions or restricted models of operations like multiplication;
■ many pupil errors are quite logical and are derived from faulty premises.

You can use such insights to inform your teaching by:

■ using situations designed to show the limitations of restricted methods, for example by using $6 \div \frac{3}{4}$ to expose the limitations of the sharing model of division;
■ building upon children's own methods and understanding;
■ realising that some mathematical ideas take time to develop, because they are intrinsically complex and difficult;
■ using a wide range of analogies, materials, contexts and language over time;
■ looking out for pupils actively and systematically trying to make sense of their mathematics and using their errors and misconceptions as starting points for future teaching;

▨ encouraging pupils to think about and evaluate their methods; that is, to regulate their own thinking.

Task 3.9 **Thinking about errors**

Collect some apparent errors when observing pupils in school. Try to find out how these pupils have been thinking by talking to them.

Observe the language used by teachers when referring to, say, multiplication or scale transformation. Is a wide range of alternatives used?

Make notes in your journal about the variety of representations and contexts used to embody one mathematical notion (such as fractions).

Discuss this with teachers and other students. Compare with your reading.

It is very useful for the beginning teacher to have some idea of common areas of pupils' difficulties and there are very good collections (e.g. Nickson, 2004) that offer much enlightenment. Some of the research reports included in such collections give figures for the percentage of pupils getting test items right or wrong, or they show how the *facility level* of different items (the percentage of those asked who answer correctly) can be altered radically by the context or presentation of the task.

For example:

▨ The item 'Add one tenth to 2.9' elicited the correct answer from 38 per cent of 11/12-year-olds. (Brown, 1981)
▨ 'What is the distance all the way round this rectangle?'

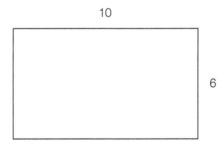

▨ **Figure 3.1** Rectangle task

The correct answer was given by 69 per cent of 13-year-olds whereas 'What is the *perimeter* of the rectangle?' was answered correctly by only 49 per cent of 13-year-olds (cited in Dickson *et al.*, 1984: 343).

In some cases, we have evidence from these big surveys of the ways children may be thinking. For instance, when pupils were asked to ring the decimal with the smallest value from the following list:

0.375   0.25   0.5   0.125   (APU, 1986)

34 per cent of 11-year-olds chose 0.375, 43 per cent chose 0.5 and only 17 per cent chose correctly (0.125).

The first error was identified as 'largest is smallest' (LS), indicating some confusion about the value of digits in the decimal positions. The second error was identified as decimal point ignored (DI) and was more common amongst the lowest 40 per cent of pupils.

Over the intervening years, much effort and money has been spent on strategies to tackle these difficulties in a focused way; but there is no clear evidence of improvement in attainment or engagement in mathematics. Children continue to have considerable difficulties (see, for example, Brown *et al.*, 2008). Teachers in the highest-achieving nations tended to focus on relationships, connections and complexities within mathematics, not reducing everything to technical performance (Askew *et al.*, 1995). However, projects such as Deep Progress in Mathematics (Watson *et al.*, 2003) demonstrate improvements in outcome by focusing on teachers. The Deep Progress project showed that:

> teachers who are free to innovate for themselves are able to improve the attainment, engagement and mathematical thinking of low-achieving students. Their students were not disadvantaged in the short term, their test results compared well to other groups, and there were significant gains in participation, self-esteem and their ability and willingness to engage with extended, unfamiliar and complex tasks.
>
> (Watson *et al.*, 2003: 51)

All this research is of interest, but perhaps the most enlightening work is that which does not just give us results, but also presents a research method available to a student teacher not unlike that used by the skilful teacher in her everyday formative assessment work. One such example is the clinical interview technique described by Herbert Ginsburg (1981), amongst others.

> The clinical interview procedure begins with (a) a *task*, which is (b) *open ended*. The examiner then asks further questions in (c) a *contingent* manner, and requests a good deal of *reflection* on the part of the subject. (p. 6)

Task 3.10 **Clinical interviewing**

Arrange to speak:

- ■ individually with a pupil;
- ■ with a pair of pupils.

Choose an open task from a familiar topic for them to work through. (There are some good examples of open tasks reproduced in Appendix 3.)
Try to probe their understanding without being over-directive. Cued requests like:

- ■ 'Could you explain what this means?'
- ■ 'Would you tell me why you did that?'

may be helpful, but you will need to be sensitive to what the pupils say. Mentally counting to five before 'butting in' can prove another useful strategy.
See if there are any interesting differences that strike you between individual and paired interviews.

It seems to me that not only is this a good research technique, but it could also inform a potential teaching sequence. The choice of task is crucial, but it should give opportunities for thought and exploration; then the contingent questions would be those that probe and acknowledge the ways in which pupils are thinking, perhaps suggesting further ideas that pupils could pursue. The final element, asking pupils to reflect upon what they have done, would be an opportunity for them to hold up a mirror to their own activity, to think about their own thinking and to evaluate their learning, much like the self-regulation described earlier.

With the teacher's support and guidance, this could represent a move towards intelligent rather than mechanical learning. Note that the emphasis here is on the individual or the pair of pupils, so the teacher with a whole class could use this technique while the class is working and she is circulating, but she will clearly be more constrained than a researcher concentrating on one or two children in a non-naturalistic setting. Note, too, how the choice of probing questions depends upon the teacher's expertise and subject knowledge, as well as the response of the pupil linking back to the ideas of contingent teaching discussed earlier.

SUMMARY AND KEY POINTS

Pupils often fail to make sense of the mathematics they are taught at school or develop very insubstantial understanding. They may learn many tricks or routines that are of limited use to them in novel situations. There needs to be a subtle balance of support and challenge in teaching, plentiful interaction between teachers and pupils and among pupils themselves, and explicit consideration of errors and ways of thinking. There are no blueprints. Teaching for learning is a contingent activity.

FURTHER READING

Boaler, J. (1997) *Experiencing School Mathematics: Teaching Styles, Sex and Setting.* **Buckingham: Open University Press.**

This is an important book that draws upon very close-grained research into the mathematics teaching and learning in two schools with different teaching approaches. The author uses the insights of situated cognition, which acknowledges that learning is very closely tied to the conditions in which it takes place and which questions the transfer of school mathematics to out-of-school contexts. Boaler concludes that two different forms of mathematical knowledge were produced in the two schools and that the school that adopted a less structured, project-based approach produced the better GCSE results, as well as pupils who were more able to adapt successfully to unfamiliar mathematical situations.

Dweck, C. (2006) *Mindset: The New Psychology of Success.* **New York: Random House.**

Dweck proposes that everyone has either a fixed mindset or a growth mindset. A fixed mindset causes pupils to view their talents and abilities as incapable of change, they are who they are and there is a ceiling to their intelligence and talents that they cannot go beyond. Consequently, they go through life avoiding challenge and therefore trying to avoid failure. When pupils have a growth mindset, they see themselves as a work in progress; they are prepared to take every opportunity as they know that can result in growth and learning. Dweck shows how pupils can be convinced to remain open to challenge and growth in their learning. Mindsets are not set; at any time, someone can learn to use a growth mindset to achieve success.

Nickson, M. (2004) *Teaching and Learning Mathematics: A Teacher's Guide to Recent Research and Its Application.* **London: Continuum.**

This book brings together the findings of the best of recent research and a detailed analysis of the most important findings. Marilyn Nickson relates this research to practical issues like pupils' progress and differentiation, and inclusion issues such as gender, as well as the nature of assessment and the impact of ICT on the classroom. It is accessible and helpful to classroom teachers.

Orton, A. (2004) *Learning Mathematics: Issues, Theory and Classroom Practice,* **3rd edn. London: Continuum.**

Tony Orton acknowledges that teachers making automatic decisions about mathematics teaching in the classroom are guided, albeit unconsciously, by their theories about learning mathematics. He looks at various schools of thought, some of them conflicting, and draws together some of the large body of research which has informed a considerable body of knowledge about learning mathematics. Although intended as an introduction for higher-degree students, much of the book is appropriate for beginning teachers, and each chapter raises an issue of direct relevance to the classroom.

Watson, A., De Geest, E. and Prestage, S. (2003) *Deep Progress in Mathematics*: *The Improving Attainment in Mathematics Project.*

http://www.atm.org.uk/journal/archive/mt187files/DeepProgressEls.pdf

This is a booklet about a project involving low-attaining pupils improving attainment through the teachers building on the belief that all students can think hard about mathematics.

Wood, D. (1998) *How Children Think and Learn,* **2nd edn. Oxford: Blackwell Publishing.**

This second edition contains new material about children's developmental psychology, but retains the first edition's clarity in synthesising what is known about how children think and learn. It looks at theoretical debates and outlines the position of major twentieth-century figures, but it also looks at the problems that teachers face trying to put theory into practice in the classroom. There is a specific chapter on mathematics.

DIFFERENT TEACHING APPROACHES

David Pimm and
Sue Johnston-Wilder

INTRODUCTION

This chapter takes a direct look at the range of actions, decisions and intentions that constitute teaching. You will see described a range of different ways of being with pupils in mathematics classrooms, both while you are initially learning to teach and as an ongoing practitioner. Your own repertoire will continue to grow, develop and change as you continue to teach, think and read about teaching.

It is worth looking out for all sorts of teaching practices, whether formal or informal – sports 'coaching', musical instrument 'tuition', masterclasses, apprenticeships, individual tutoring – in order to decide what you wish to appropriate from, experiment with, and transform into elements of you as a teacher of mathematics. In the words of actor Michael Caine (talking about acquiring from others), 'Steal, steal, steal – but steal from the best!' The people from whom you decide to lift ideas will considerably shape the sort of teacher you become.

What does it mean to teach? The first section of this chapter looks at the complex interrelation between teaching and telling, teaching and asking and teaching and listening. We have then structured the second part of the chapter around three possible levels of classroom organisation: whole-class, small-group and individual ways of working. We look further at some mathematical tasks that might be most appropriately tackled in one of these three settings. In the third part of the chapter, we look briefly at wider resources and strategies for enriching your teaching, including the use of homework. Finally, arising from all these ingredients, we consider a description of a lesson.

OBJECTIVES

By the end of this chapter you should be able to:

■ start to relate various forms of classroom organisation to particular pedagogic intentions and tasks;

- think more deeply about what constitutes mathematics teaching and the roles of exposition, investigation, questioning, listening and explanation within it;
- engage in the debate around the exclusive merits of different ways of teaching.

TEACHING AS LISTENING, ASKING AND TELLING

There is a sense in which, in our culture, teaching is talking.

(Stubbs, 1983)

Who needs the most practice talking in school? Who gets the most? Exactly. The children need it, the teacher gets it.

(John Holt, 1970)

There is a fundamental truth to the first observation, made by educational linguist Michael Stubbs: a teacher can teach certain things, at certain times and in certain circumstances, simply by talking. But this is *far* from the whole story. A teacher can teach by asking a question, one that perhaps focuses a single pupil's, a group's or a whole-class's attention on something, or encourages a consideration of alternatives. A teacher can also teach by listening and then engaging directly with what has been heard. A teacher can teach by *not* talking; for instance, by withholding what may seem to be an obvious form of help (namely telling a pupil how to do something), by allowing pupils to struggle and think for themselves or by working visually in silence. A teacher can work with pupils' powers of mental imagery or on conjecturing and convincing – the giving of reasons – for it is answering the question 'why?' as much as 'what?' that lies at the heart of mathematics. A teacher can also significantly facilitate mathematical learning by a range of non-verbal actions, such as providing suitable resources, structuring appropriate groupings and offering significant and well-thought-out mathematical tasks.

Notice, crucially, that Stubbs does not say teaching is *telling*, which is a common misinterpretation of the current emphasis on whole-class teaching. There are a number of different forms of, and purposes for, teacher talk, two of which, *exposition* and *explanation*, are distinguished later in this chapter; these forms, at a naïve level, might both be considered *telling*. Before turning to them, however, here are some comments about teaching and listening from a secondary mathematics teacher, Mark. He was being interviewed about how his teaching had changed over the years. Mark commented:

'Listening is part of what I do and I didn't think that it needed to be, other than listening to see if they got it or not. I have to listen more critically now to know what they are saying, to know what they are becoming confused about or what might be an interesting thing to pick up and run with. Before, if I didn't understand what a kid was saying, I needed to help him or her understand what I was saying. Then I could hear the way I was thinking about it come back through him or her – which was really not the way I thought about it, it was the way the book was doing it. Now I would rather hear about how the kid thinks about it.'

Later on in the interview, he added:

> 'I see my job as completely different now. Going in [as a novice teacher], I thought it was telling kids and doing it in an understanding or clear or creative or fun way – that was what my job was to be. My expectation of what I would consider a good classroom is completely different [...] I see my role as finding ways to put kids into situations where they are going to be able to really talk about the material and learn.'
>
> (Gormas, 1998: 93–4)

Teacher talk in mathematics classes has many important functions, including:

■ the giving of instructions and orientation;
■ efficient transmission of information;
■ focusing a pupil's attention or making an observation of potential significance to the whole class;
■ encouraging reflection on what has been done or what could still be done.

However, there are also significant disadvantages to the teacher's voice being the dominant one heard in the classroom every day, as indicated in the quotation from John Holt. Teachers already start out being good at producing and giving mathematical explanations and expositions (it is likely that this is part of the skill you bring to the classroom) and get even better at it as time goes on. How do *pupils* get to acquire such fluency at speaking mathematically? A significant part of learning mathematics involves learning to speak and write *mathematically*: pupils need many opportunities in various sizes of groupings to hear themselves and their peers speak. (This theme is taken up in Chapter 8.)

Task 4.1 **Listening out for listening**

Choose a lesson when you are not directly involved in the teaching and pay attention to the teacher. When do you notice her or him listening to pupils, and to what effect? What is done with the pupil talk? Are the pupils aware of being listened to and do they seem to expect it? Does the teacher encourage them to listen to each other, and if so, how? What do pupils do with what they hear from other pupils? Make notes about your observations in your journal.

One of the more common forms of classroom control is that exercised by the teacher over what is allowed to be said (when, by whom, in what way) and even the manner in which it is to be said. Yet in order to be able to do what Mark is advocating, you have to work on pupils feeling comfortable saying things aloud in class. Achieving this will probably entail you having to give up some of your control of the 'public speech channel' at certain times and in some circumstances, for particular reasons, and with it some sense of control over what is happening, quite simply because you cannot control what pupils will say.

Mathematics educator Mary Boole, writing towards the end of the nineteenth century, coined a term 'teacher-lust' to describe the desire to control classroom activity. In the following passage, Boole compares teacher-lust with sex-lust and alcohol-lust: heady stuff, you might think, particularly bearing in mind the historical context in which she was writing.

The teacher [...] has a desire to make those under him conform themselves to his ideals. Nations could not be built up, nor children preserved from ruin, if some such desire did not exist and exert itself in some degree. But it has its gamut of lusts, very similar to those run down by other faculties. First, the teacher wants to regulate the actions, conduct and thought of other people in a way that does no obvious harm but is quite in excess both of normal rights and practical necessity. Next, he wants to proselytise, convince, control, to arrest the spontaneous action of other minds, to an extent which ultimately defeats its own ends by making the pupils too feeble and automatic to carry on his teaching into the future with any vigour. Lastly, he acquires a sheer automatic lust for telling people to 'don't', for arresting spontaneous action in others in a way which destroys their power even to learn at the time what he is trying to teach them. What is wanted is that we should [...] not go on fogging ourselves with any such foolish notion as that sex-passion is a lust of the flesh and teacher-lust a thing in itself pure and good, which may be legitimately indulged in to the uttermost.

Few teachers now are so conceited as not to know that they have a great deal to learn, and that their methods need revising and improving, but the majority are seeking for improved methods of doing more of what they are already doing a great deal too much of. The improvement which they most need is to [...] see their conduct, their aims, their whole attitude towards their pupils [...] in the light reflected on them from those of the drunkard and the debauchee.

(in Tahta, 1980: 11)

Alternative approaches to your teaching may involve you working on the utterances of your pupils, working with the *form* of what they have said: shaping, correcting, reformulating or offering alternatives, probing for more detail or a clearer way of saying something, checking that others have understood what has been said.

Questioning questioning

All questions are not the same, either in their form or in their purpose, and questions can be one of the most subtle instruments available to a teacher. A question can be asked simply by raising your inflection at the end of a sentence (something that cannot be done in print), or by tagging on a phrase like 'isn't it?' or 'do you?' at the end of a statement (which are then, for obvious reasons, called *tag questions*): 'You think it's going to be four, do you?' Then there are the more direct question forms beginning with what are called interrogatives – words such as *who, what, when, which, where, how* and *why*.

- Who hasn't finished their work?
- What is in common between this example and this one?
- When might you choose to multiply rather than add?
- Which algorithm would be better here?
- Where on the figure is the *vertex* of the triangle?
- How could you explain to someone who isn't here how to do that without pointing or touching?
- Why do you think it is cosine?

There are many other ways as well: the English language provides a terrific set of resources for asking questions.

Task 4.2 **Listening out for questions**

Over the next couple of days, set yourself the task of listening out for the variety of ways in which people ask questions in different circumstances. Try to think about the different purposes for which they are asking. Do this both within lessons and outside, around the school and in your day-to-day life. What forms do people use and how can you tell what they want? Are there any occasions when the responder failed to give the hoped-for response and, if so, what happened next? Record what you find in your journal.

Questions in classrooms are not used just to find things out that the asker does not know (this is perhaps the most common use outside school and, for that reason, such questions are sometimes called *genuine* questions) – in fact, they are perhaps *least* used to that end. In addition, the words alone are seldom sufficient to find out what the asker intended and what the hearer made of them.

One very common classroom purpose is the *testing* question, in which the intent is not to discover something the asker does not know, but to find out whether the person being asked knows something. This need not be carried out in a formal atmosphere of right or wrong, putting pupils on the spot in public. It can also be carried out jointly with a class, more as a form of rehearsal of expected common knowledge present in the class.

Questions can also be used to draw attention to something, to *focus* pupil attention or call their awareness to it. A question can shift the level of a conversation or interaction: 'What might you do next?' (reminding pupils that there is a next, when they are perhaps caught up with this one, as if it were the only one) or 'What am I about to ask you?' (calling attention to the fact that there are regularities in the questions you, as teacher, ask – by inviting pupils to notice this, you tacitly suggest they might take on some of this role of you-as-questioner for themselves).

However, it is also possible to get locked into a series of questions with a pupil and, when they look blank or can't answer, feel you have to offer them a simpler question and a simpler one still. John Holt (1964), writing in *How Children Fail*, tells how he questioned a pupil and got 'I don't know' right up to the simplest one to answer. 'I've been had,' he thought.

This is, of necessity, the briefest of introductions to questioning. More can be found in an article called 'Telling questions' by Janet Ainley (1987), in *Designing and Using Mathematical Tasks* by John Mason and Sue Johnston-Wilder (2004b) and in *Questions and Prompts for Mathematical Thinking* by Anne Watson and John Mason (1998).

Exposition and explanation: two forms of telling

We would like you to consider the difference between *exposition* and *explanation* (for more on this, see Mason and Johnston-Wilder, 2004b). Explaining often inadvertently turns into 'expositing'. It can be valuable to decide which is the more effective strategy for telling in the prevailing circumstances and to be aware that different effects frequently arise from these two modes of telling.

Exposition involves speaking directly to the pupils from your own mathematical understanding. It is likely that, when you are expounding, you are guided by a desire for completeness and coherence of your account of an area or topic. In some sense, you are talking *to* your class. It may not be important for the pupils to grasp all the detail at first hearing, but they can gain a number of things from listening attentively to your exposition. The rest of their bodies will probably be still and passive (can you imagine a situation in which they would not be still?), so it is important to keep your attention on the pupils' degree of attentiveness and not get caught up in the joy of your own mathematical fluency.

One possible gain from exposition is that pupils will hear some technical terms used in a context and in meaningful mathematical sentences, not as vocabulary items encountered in isolation. Another arises from the educational effect of hearing coherent mathematical expressions that they are, as yet, unable to produce for themselves. Exposition could be used to provide an overview of a project, an idea or a procedure. You will probably be able to think of other uses. The point here is that exposition is a valuable tool but one to be used with care: too much exposition can have a rapidly deadening effect on the attention of your class and, you can end up talking to yourself. Even ten minutes unbroken listening may be too much for some pupils.

Explanation, whether to the whole class or small groups and individuals within it, involves taking the pupils' current positions as your starting point and making a substantial attempt to shape and gear what you say to their developing understanding, with their responses providing you with feedback. To explain is to talk *with* members of your class, where their understanding and current position are the strongest influences on what you say. Thus, in explanation, the teacher's words and actions must be subordinated to the pupils' understanding of the situation and the teacher must make continual effort to obtain whatever information is possible about that understanding. In exposition, the pupil's understanding is temporarily subordinated to the teacher's understanding, giving rise to the account he or she is producing. The distinction is between finding a way to enter the learner's world, working with them in it, and speaking from *your* (the teacher's) mathematical world to the pupil *about* it. When working post-16 (see Chapter 13), these two modes are commonly identified with the different forms of action and interaction seen in a typical lecture and tutorial, respectively.

Task 4.3 **Distinguishing exposition from explanation**

Read the following excerpt from a dinner conversation between Lynn (aged 10), her father Larry, and Laurel (aged 16). Identify where explanation starts to become exposition. The recipient could have felt left out and may have lost confidence. Think about why, in this case, this does not seem to happen.

Lynn:	'We're doing algebra in maths. Give me an algebra problem. But don't use those boring letters like x and y.'
Larry:	'OK. Five alpha plus two is seventeen. What is alpha?'
Laurel:	'What's alpha?'
Larry:	'The first Greek letter. It's definitely not boring.'
Lynn [after a pause]:	'Three.'
Larry:	'Wow! How did you figure it out?'
Lynn:	'Well, I tried alpha as one, then two, then as three, and it finally worked.'

Laurel:	'There's an easier way. You have the equation five alpha plus two equals seventeen. So you subtract two from each side and get five alpha equals fifteen. Then you divide both sides by five to get alpha equals three.'
Lynn:	'I don't understand a word you said. [Pause] But I have an idea. What if you subtract two from seventeen to get fifteen and then divide by three. That's just undoing what you did to alpha to get seventeen.'
Laurel:	'That's just what I said.'
Lynn:	'No, it's not. You were talking about equations and doing something to both sides. I didn't understand that.'
	(in Pimm, 1995: 198)

One moral is that teaching is not the same as expounding; be sure to work on explanations with your pupils and develop strategies for eliciting a pupil's existing understanding.

FORMS OF CLASSROOM ORGANISATION

Those who qualify as teachers are expected to:

▨ have a commitment to collaboration and co-operative working (TDA, 2007: Q6);
▨ plan for progression across the age and ability range for which they are trained, designing effective learning sequences within lessons and across a series of lessons and demonstrating secure subject/curriculum knowledge (TDA, 2007: Q22);
▨ use a range of teaching strategies and resources, including e-learning, taking practical account of diversity and promoting equality and inclusion (TDA, 2007: Q25a);
▨ build on prior knowledge, develop concepts and processes, enable learners to apply new knowledge, understanding and skills and meet learning objectives (TDA, 2007: Q25b);
▨ assess the learning needs of those they teach in order to set challenging learning objectives (TDA, 2007: Q26b).

Although not mentioned explicitly in these QTS standards, a substantial part of teaching involves:

▨ deciding on the mathematical tasks to offer your pupils (whether made up yourself, absorbed from another teacher, taken from government material, textbook or other resource – in other words, tasks 'stolen' from the best – tasks involving the pupils' own bodies, physical action, practical materials, work outside school, mental imagery, having them close their eyes to imagine, communicating without saying a word or without pointing or touching, making things, ...);
▨ choosing how you are going to work with your pupils on these selected tasks, whether individually, in pairs, in groups, in two or three large groups or as a whole class;

■   selecting what materials or resources to use, with what focus and with what hoped-
for activity on the part of the pupils.

Importantly, these three key components of mathematics teaching are not independent
of one another. Certain tasks seem to call out for specific forms of working, and,
conversely, certain ways of working in a classroom can enable or hinder particular
educational actions. So when you are planning lessons (discussed in Chapter 5), these
components need to be decided on in concert with one another. When looking at a
lesson, you will see some ways in which these elements interact in positive or negative
ways.

Developing as a mathematics teacher requires developing a repertoire of mathematical ways of being with children in the classroom. It also involves refining your
reasons for choosing one way over another in response to a particular topic and a
particular group, and the known strengths and weaknesses of any particular way of
working. Paragraph 243 of the Cockcroft Report (DES, 1982), although necessarily
incomplete and prepared some 30-plus years ago, has not been bettered as a short
checklist for the developing repertoire of a successful mathematics teacher.

Maths teaching at all levels should include opportunities for:

■   exposition by the teacher;
■   discussion between teacher and pupils and between pupils themselves;
■   appropriate practical work;
■   consolidation and practice of fundamental skills and routines;
■   problem-solving, including the application of mathematics to everyday situations;
■   investigational work.

Notice that although the paragraph is phrased in terms of mathematics *teaching*, it can
be read as an entitlement charter for diversity of *learning* opportunities for pupils
related to mathematics. However, it is not envisaged that all these opportunities could
be available in any one lesson! In this next part of the chapter, we have chosen to focus
on what might happen within one lesson; we have opted for tasks that we feel suit a
variety of ways of working and have tried to explain something of how the interaction
works.

Whole-class ways of working

There is a difference between the *task* you set a class and the *activity* the pupils generate.
The activity is produced as a result of the pupil interpreting the task as given. Remember,
pupils never have any direct access to your intentions. So if you find some of your tasks
going awry, try to listen to what you say, when offering the task, with the ear of someone who does not know either *why* they are being asked to do the task nor *what* that task
is. Pupils always construct their own interpretations and rationale for what they are asked
to do, so you could do worse than ask them from time to time about the sense they are
making of, and the purpose they are seeing in, what you ask them to do. Here is one
description of a whole-class lesson.

I stand by the whiteboard and ask the pupils to be totally silent. I ask them to work inside their own heads. I ask them to watch what I am doing and try to decide what it is. I write on the board:

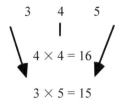

Then I pause and suggest that they think about where I started, what numbers I chose, what I did and what the result is. Then I write:

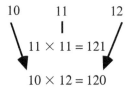

I remind them not to shout out. I suggest that if they think they know what is happening they should construct some similar examples in their heads, or think of a word description of the situation, or think about an algebraic description. Meanwhile I tell them I am going to do another one and they must continue to watch.

(Watson, 1994: 52)

The teacher has described the *task*. As Anne Watson writes, she has no control over what goes on inside each pupil's head, which is the resulting *activity*.

A second example of a whole-class task comes from Pimm (1987), who transcribed a videotape of a lesson in which a teacher set up a task to encourage pupils to develop greater precision in speech about mathematical perceptions.

The pupils (P) are looking at a coloured poster of a great stellated dodecahedron [see Figure 4.1], and are not allowed to point or use their hands. One child is invited to sit in the 'hot seat' (a single chair out front near the poster where the pupil sits to address the class as a whole) and describe something they have seen in this complex picture (T is teacher).

T: Does everyone see it as a three-dimensional object?
P: Yes. [*chorus*]
T: [*Invites Jamie to go to the front*]
J: [*Taking the hot seat*] Well, in the middle, right in the middle, there's a kind of a triangle that kind of points out towards you, and all the fa[ces], the sides of it – there's other triangles that have been kind of broken up from it – say if they was joined to it, and when – by the dark green and the yellow and the light green, the kind of medium green kind of long triangles – and if the ones outside it was moved inwards, they would join the inside one.

(Pimm, 1987: 35)

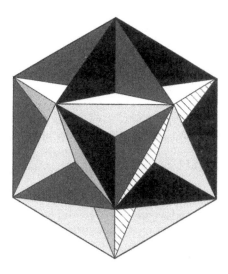

■ **Figure 4.1** Great stellated dodecahedron
Source: Pimm, 1987: 35

The pupils were listening and responding to each other. The structure of such a task encourages focused, active listening in order to see whether the person in the hot seat has successfully communicated to the others. The constraints of 'no pointing and no touch-ing' are there to focus the pupil talking from the hot seat on the use of language to point, and the need for language to be more self-contained in mathematics. A further account of this lesson is provided by Barbara Jaworski (1985) in an article in the ATM journal *Mathematics Teaching*.

Both the previous two passages describe relatively unusual use of whole-class time. More common whole-class ways of working involve the teacher telling the class some-thing or a pupil responding. The most familiar sight in a whole-class situation is that of a pupil responding to a teacher's question and the response then being evaluated in some fashion by the teacher. In whatever way you express this response, and possibly despite your best intentions, it is likely to be heard as evaluative; even if you say nothing, the absence of a comment can be interpreted as a negative evaluation. This more usual pattern of teacher–pupil interaction has been named by Sinclair and Coulthard (1975) as the Initiation–Response–Feedback sequence (see Pimm, 1987, for more details).

Another role for whole-class teaching is that of staging, managing and making use of 'reporting back' after a period of group or individual work. Those who might benefit from the reporting back include:

■ *the pupil(s) doing the reporting*:
   they have the opportunity to develop a range of communication and mathematical skills, including reflection on and distillation of events they were involved in for an audience who were not present;
■ *the other pupils in the class*:
   they hear about others' difficulties and alternative approaches; they may engage in trying to understand a less-polished presentation of mathematical work than they are usually exposed to;

▪ *the teacher*:

he or she has opportunities to make contextually based comments about methods, results and processes, to value publicly the work done by pupils and to broaden the pupils' experience by proxy (other groups working on the same or a similar task).

The teacher's role in reporting back might be one of repeating, re-broadcasting (perhaps with minor editing, for instance by omission) and reinterpreting (reformulating the expression to be more conventionally accurate, providing a different emphasis on what was said, going further to add points of your own, for example, 'While I was watching them working on this, what I noticed was . . .').

You might work with the class on comparison and evaluation of methods. The class may need to discuss difficulties found in ways of working and strategies used for overcoming them. You may need to set an agenda for future work. You will mark certain events or ideas as worthy of the attention of the group. Having allowed the pupils their own voice, you might use an expression such as, 'And what struck *me* about what we've just heard is . . .'.

Task 4.4 **Reporting back to the whole class**

Try to locate a teacher (not necessarily in maths) who uses report-back sessions and watch one of these sessions with the following questions in mind. If you are able, run a report-back session yourself on an investigative or practical task, ideally with an observer who has the following list of questions (if no observer is available, try an audio recorder). Make notes in your journal.

▪ Who might benefit from the reporting-back?
▪ How can you resolve the tension between wanting the pupils to say themselves what they have done and wanting to *use* what they say to illustrate general points and processes?
▪ How can you help the pupils develop the skills of selection of and reflection on what to report?
▪ To whom is the reporter talking?
▪ What justifications can a teacher make for having the pupils' report back?

The importance of both preserving your pupils' voices *and* allowing yourself your own voice to talk about what has been said is considerable. There is a danger in saying, 'What Sally said is . . .', because that might be reinterpretation concealed as repeating. If you assume the pupil is trying to say what you think they are but merely cannot say it right, and you help them by saying it for them, you may also miss out on something novel that the pupil is seeing.

Task 4.5 **Whole-class variety**

Having worked on this subsection of the chapter, draw up, in your journal, a list of ways in which you might see a class working as a whole. Arrange to watch a selection of lessons with whole-class elements, both in other subjects and in your own department. What uses do you observe the teacher making of opportunities to work with the class as a whole? What do you observe the pupils doing?

Small-group ways of working

'How can I be teaching if I am sitting on the radiator?'
'I kept wanting to go round and interrupt them.'

A mixed-ability class of 10–11-year-olds is working with its teacher on a mathematical investigation involving movements with a square grid. He starts the lesson with the whole class by having a three-by-three array of mats on the floor and inviting eight pupils to stand on them, leaving one corner mat free. The pupil who is standing in the diagonally opposite corner to the empty mat is asked to wear a red hat and to see whether, by using only sideways and forward-and-back shuffle moves, which exchange the position of two adjacent pupils at a time, she can end up in the target square. Having seen that it is possible, the pupils are encouraged to pose questions about this situation. One pupil asks, 'What is the minimum number of moves?' and another, 'What happens with grids of different sizes?'.

The pupils then set off to work in groups, employing a variety of apparatus, and develop a range of forms of recording of their explorations, some focusing on the state after each move and others recording the pattern in the moves themselves. Some continue to work on this between lessons and the groups continue in the first part of the second lesson. Later in the second lesson, there is a whole-class report-back session.

The same distinction between exposition and explanation holds here as in the whole-class discussion. The difference is that there is a greater opportunity to listen to pupil exposition and gain some feedback to inform future practice. Group work offers the opportunity for pupils to formulate their own thinking in explaining their ideas to their peers, engaging in exposition and gaining feedback. The pupils listening have an opportunity to reflect upon what they hear and respond critically but constructively by asking questions to seek clarification or by offering suggestions for improving the account. There is clearly a need for the teacher managing these exchanges to be sensitive to pupils' concerns about being open to criticism from their peers.

It is important to remember that there are times when a class does *not* need you as a teacher. In a group, quite often one or more of the pupils will take on some aspects of the teacher's function: for example, keeping the others focused on the task, sharing out the sub-tasks to be done, explaining or mediating between two other pupils who are arguing unproductively or seem caught in an impasse. If you are there, even if you are not actively talking with the group, you may have a perturbing effect on the group functioning as a self-contained group, so be aware of this possibility.

When the small group is working, it may stop functioning as a small group and temporarily become several individuals, each working independently of the others in their own preferred ways to explore different aspects of a problem, before pooling their data for further communal discussion. The fact that a group has separated out in this way does not necessarily indicate that there is a problem with the group's functioning as a group; it could well be simply part of the normal variation in choice about ways of working. Nonetheless, if a group predominantly operates simply as individuals sat at the same table, then you may need to work with this group on developing alternative strategies and perceiving strengths when working collaboratively on a task.

The two quotations at the beginning of this subsection reflect a concern about what to do when the pupils are engaged on a task working in groups. As you go round the class, you may sometimes find that a useful prompt to get pupils to engage with you can be to ask them to tell you what they are doing. However, be aware that this necessarily pulls them away from working where they are and into the very different role of recount, recall and summary, so you need to use this means of intervention with care.

Individual working

While giving attention to the broadening of mathematical classroom activities to include purposeful discussion, peer working and practical activity, it is important to remember that a key element in gaining mathematical fluency involves practice: at times, this will involve the learner working quietly alone with a piece of mathematics.

When you work with an individual pupil, you have an opportunity to tune in more exactly to what that pupil has already understood and thought, as well as to his/her personal preferences. You can look for alternative ways of working, presenting and explaining. However, a simple piece of arithmetic says you can only offer each pupil about one-and-a-half minutes in a 50-minute lesson, were you simply to move from one to the next. Your attention is one of the scarcest resources in the classroom and you need to allocate it efficiently. What would the others be doing for that time that you are working with an individual? This is one reason why pupils need to become habituated into asking each other for assistance first, before coming to you.

The issues around teacher purposes for questioning are particularly acute when working with an individual. You will need to be clear about what your aims are and how your questioning contributes to achieving them. For example, in a task where it is an advantage to have a lot of individual data, you might allocate particular cases to different pupils. You might choose indirectly to differentiate by ability here, by knowing which cases are harder, and allocating them accordingly.

RESOURCES AND IDEAS FOR ENHANCING YOUR TEACHING

This section consists of a large number of possible resources and suggestions for possible use to enhance and diversify mathematics teaching in your classroom.

Textbooks and schemes

Textbooks are an important resource for teaching mathematics in many secondary schools, if only because they are so widespread. Very often the only resource to which all pupils will have access during the lesson, other than the teacher, is a textbook. In many schools, the major determinant of the programme of work taught in mathematics lessons is a commercially produced 'scheme', often consisting of either a sequence of textbooks or a system of photocopiable or printable worksheets. For years, many mathematics teachers have come to rely heavily on published schemes to provide them with an overarching organisation of the day-to-day work in the classroom, and to provide a source of material and tasks.

Schemes are available to help teachers to interpret the current curriculum. The National Strategy produced supplementary resources that have added to the range of materials available. Examples include 'mini-packs': detailed plans and resources to support the teaching of specific topics.

Many textbooks and schemes contain some excellent ideas for classroom tasks. However, not all the ideas in a textbook are equally good and the linear presentation of the idea in printed form is very often not the best way to present the idea to your pupils. It is also worth bearing in mind the importance of the particular knowledge of your pupils that you use in your teaching, knowledge that will not be reflected in a published scheme of work.

The best use of a textbook or scheme is selective, adapting the material to suit the needs of individual pupils and classes and ensuring variety of presentation. There is a risk that the scheme will take over, and class activity such as questioning, debating, exposition and whole-class discussion will disappear. It is your responsibility as the teacher to engage fully in the long-term planning of the curriculum and the detailed planning of how to present a topic or a task, as well as to use the full range of approaches available in a classroom.

Practical apparatus

The provision of practical equipment in secondary mathematics classrooms varies widely. At all ages, mathematical equipment can provide tools to think with. Task 4.6 invites you to consider the provision in your school: ICT tools are left to Chapter 9.

Task 4.6 **Maths equipment**

Consider the list of equipment in Table 4.1 (overleaf). It includes some of the many items that have been used by secondary mathematics teachers to promote learning. Make a copy of the table. Note, in the second column, *whether* the equipment is available in your school, and in the third, *when* you observe it being used.

Discuss with a friend or colleague how each of the items might be used and for which topic. Make a brief note in the final column.

Homework and parents

Those who qualify as teachers are expected to:

> Plan homework or other out-of-class work to sustain learners' progress and to extend and consolidate their learning. (TDA, 2007: Q24)

■ **Table 4.1** List of possible equipment for a maths classroom

Equipment	Available	Used	For use with (topic)
3D kits (or straws)			
abacus			
ATM mats (Pinel, 1986)			
bouncy ball			
card and glue			
coloured pencils			
compasses			
counting sticks			
curtain track or shelf			
decimal number flips			
drawing pins			
dry-wipe boards			
elastic bands			
geoboards/pinboards			
graph paper			
marker pens			
matchsticks			
mirrors			
Multilink™ cubes			
number/fraction fans			
overhead calculator			
overhead dice			
overhead number grids			
paper and pencil			
paper fasteners			
pie chart scales			
playing cards (blank)			
polar graph paper			
polygon stencils			
polyhedral dice			
probability kits			
protractors/angle measurers			
rulers			
scissors			
sellotape™			
set squares			
square paper			
square/isometric dotty paper			
stop clock			
string			
toy cars			
weighing machine			
weights			

A common observation by parents and mathematics teachers is that pupils working on a textbook exercise at the end of a lesson will often be told 'just finish this at home for homework'. However, textbook exercises are usually designed to become progressively harder, so pupils regularly get stuck at home. Since homework commonly involves working alone, often with little support, this does not help the learner's confidence if this is the only homework they are asked to do.

In addition to exercise and practice, pupils can be asked to:

■ find out what words mean;
■ carry out research for the next topic;
■ write *about* the topic in hand;
■ write questions for their peers to work on;
■ write questions whose answers meet certain constraints;
■ generalise from a sequence of exercises;
■ express what is in common between a set of questions or tasks (technique, principle, idea, ...);
■ explain *why* something works the way it does;
■ produce some special cases for a general theorem.

The outside world, a world also inhabited by pupils, can also be a source of ideas, data and materials to be brought back into the classroom for discussion and further work. For instance, when working on symmetry with Year 7 pupils, car wheel hub caps could be sketched or a rubbing of a manhole cover could be taken.

Parents and other carers can be an important but unpredictable resource. Some (perhaps many) will find working mathematically at this level difficult and challenging, even threatening. An important role that parents can play is listening to their children explain what they are doing. This is helpful because acting as a teacher or explainer can enhance the pupil's grasp of what she or he is doing, and may reveal to the pupil some gaps in their own understanding. It can help if the teacher tries to ensure that parents know how important this listening role can be.

Parents and grandparents can assist a project in different ways by providing ideas, materials, past experience, diverse languages and cultures. For example, grandparents may be able to tell your pupils about different arithmetic algorithms and practices from the past or from different places around the world. One teacher reported:

> We had a parents' meeting when the Year 7 pupils were doing some investigative work within the theme of topology, because many parents did not know what it was. After I had spoken about the main ideas, some parents started contributing. One was an electrical engineer who commented that the idea of looking at connections while ignoring the distances between the nodes was fundamental to electrical wiring. A printer spoke about his need to minimise the number of colours necessary and linked this with the pupil's work on the four-colour map theorem.

Your room

It may seem slightly odd to think of your room as a resource, but it is too easy to think of the room as given, rather than something over which you can exercise some influence and control and which can assist you in your task of teaching mathematics. Every room has a 'grammar', a structure that goes towards shaping what can easily take place in it and what cannot. Go into various classrooms in your school. Ask yourself which ones 'feel' welcoming, thoughtful, exciting, open. Identify some of the physical features of the room that contribute to this feeling and atmosphere. It may be the placing of furniture, windows, grouping of desks, or the wall displays, or sometimes things hanging from the ceiling. You can experiment with varying your teaching space (if your mentor agrees) to suit the approach and the task and watch for effects on pupils.

The history of mathematics

Much of mathematics can be taught as if it were timeless and detached from any partic-ular culture. One way of remedying this fallacious view is to make use of the history of mathematics in your teaching. In this way, you can begin to make the study of mathe-matics as much the study of a story of human endeavour as an abstract exercise. As an example, in Task 4.7 you will study an ancient Babylonian method for finding an approx-imation to $\sqrt{2}$.

Task 4.7 **Babylonian mathematics**

The 500 or so mathematical Babylonian tablets so far excavated date from between 3200 BC and 300 BC. The Babylonians approximated $\sqrt{2}$ as 1: 24, 51, 10 written in their base 60 numeration system; they found other roots accurately to several sexagesimal places. (The transcribed notation reads as follows: 1 whole and 24/60 and 51/3600 and 10/216,000.)

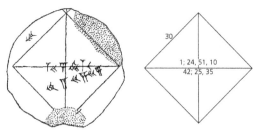

▣ **Figure 4.2** A Babylonian tablet and its transcription
Source: Yale Babylonian Collection and Fauvel and Gray, 1987: 32

First of all, work out the base ten equivalent of 1: 24, 51, 10 and compare it with a calculator value for √2. In which decimal place does the first deviation between the values occur?

The following may inform your understanding of the Babylonian method for finding √2.

√2 is the length of the side of a square with area 2.

Start with a rectangle that you know has area 2, for example, 2 by 1.

Taking a corner of the rectangle as centre, and the smaller side as radius, draw a quadrant of a circle, and mark off the resulting square.

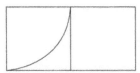

Cut the remaining rectangle (in this example at this stage it is also a square) in half and slide one half under the square, as shown below.

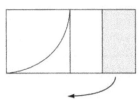

The new shape is a square of side 1.5 with a missing corner.

Use the top of this 'square' as the top of a new rectangle of area 2. The length of the side of the new rectangle is found by dividing the area 2 by the side 1.5, getting the answer 4/3.

The Babylonians had methods for calculating divisions of this kind (see Katz, 2008).

How many times do you have to repeat this process to get an excellent approximation to √2?

You will find Katz (2008) to be a useful source for extending your knowledge of the history of mathematics. In addition, Eagle (1995) provides some suggestions for worksheets and resource sheets to be used with pupils, with background notes.

Role play

You may find that some teacher colleagues in other subjects, in history or RE for example, use role play to great effect, but it is an under-used resource in mathematics teaching.

Task 4.8 **Play time**

Find a colleague in another department with experience of using role play and either talk over the experience or arrange to observe a lesson in which role play is used. Try the following example with a small group of well-motivated Year 7 pupils:

> Ask the pupils to work in pairs: one pupil to take the role of a weather forecaster in the winter and the other a member of the public who does not understand negative numbers well. The task is to create a dialogue that covers adding and subtracting of negative numbers.

After your experiment, think hard about how the use of role play could help to make you a more effective teacher. Remember that some pupils can connect particularly well to mathematical ideas when they can see them embedded in a human setting or when they approach them through the pupils' own strengths.

A second suggestion for a starting point for a role play is Leibniz's argument that the probability of throwing 12 with two dice is the same as that of throwing 11, and half that of 10. He reasoned that there is one way of scoring 12 (6 and 6) and one way of scoring 11 (5 and 6), and there are two ways of scoring 10 (6 and 4 or 5 and 5). Further ideas for role play emerge from an exploration of the history of mathematics or from modern applications.

Simulation

Some real-world situations are very complex and it is sometimes difficult or time-consuming to collect data about them. Simulating a real-world situation means setting up a simpler, easier or safer situation that will produce a similar pattern of data more easily or more quickly. With the increasing power of technology to help, many industries are making increasing use of simulations to solve hitherto intractable problems. For pupils, simulation of a real-world situation can help to bring insight or understanding of how mathematics can be used to model the world. The following examples of classroom simulations illustrate this.

> Prepare a large, transparent plastic jar full of beans, a known number of which have been painted yellow. Each pupil takes a turn to draw a sample of beans from the jar using a small plastic cup. In each case, the number of yellow beans in the sample is recorded and the number of beans altogether. The idea is to obtain from the samples an estimate of the proportion of yellow beans in the whole jar and to use this, together with the known number of yellow beans in the jar, to estimate the total number of beans in the jar. This simulation illustrates how capture–recapture methods are used in biological investigation to estimate the populations of some forms

of wildlife. A sample of the population is captured and marked (like the yellow beans) and then released into the wild. Later, a second sample is captured and the proportion of marked creatures in the population is estimated.

A second example of a classroom simulation is to simulate the flow of traffic at a road junction controlled by traffic lights.

Collect data beforehand about the time interval between changes of a set of traffic lights and about the number of cars arriving per minute on one road at the junction. Arrange the desks and chairs in the classroom to resemble a road junction, so the gaps between the chairs represent the road. The pupils can then pretend to be cars, arriving at times determined by a spinner. In this way, the effect of different timings can be explored.

You can find further examples of simulations to use in the classroom in the professional journals: see, for example, Selkirk (1983a, b).

Video and TV

Video is an under-used resource in mathematics teaching. There are possibilities afforded by both published videos and by taping programmes from the television. Your school may already have some video resources. To start your collection of published videos, contact the London Mathematical Society (see Appendix 2) and ask for their current list of popular lectures. These are aimed at sixth-form pupils.

School libraries

The school librarian is an under-used resource for most maths departments. Librarians are often highly trained professionals who can be of great help to the maths department. There is often a budget for mathematics library resources that is not fully used.

Task 4.9 **Maths library resources**

Visit the school library. Carry out an inventory of the materials that could be used for teaching mathematics. Include encyclopaedias and material with data, such as *Key Data*, an annual publication from the Government Statistical Service (see Appendix 2 for a contact address). The librarian may be able to help you with this task provided you make the effort to go at a convenient time.

■ Make a note of books that pupils would enjoy.
■ What dictionaries are there?
■ Look up 'right angle' and 'algebra' in any available dictionary and reflect on what light is shed on the meaning.
■ Ask the librarian about CDs available in the library. There may be a CD ency-clopaedia at the very least. Check to see what maths there is in it.
■ Plan a homework using the library resources.

Maths clubs

You might be lucky enough to be in a school that has a maths club already, but it is more likely that you are not. So now is the time to collect ideas. A maths club is relatively easy to start but harder to maintain. Some ideas that you might use to sustain a maths club are:

- enlist the help of the pupils;
- conduct surveys;
- collect resources;
- ask colleagues about their own experiences;
- talk to teachers who run other clubs;
- find out whether any parents have relevant expertise and will help;
- use the NRICH website as a source of problems to work on.

A *Micromath* article about one teacher's experience of using this resource is Dadd (1998). A *Mathematics in School* article about the experiences of four teachers who are running maths club is Cocker *et al.* (1996). One possible way to start is with a maths homework club or maths workshop where you provide practical resources and tasks that pupils do not usually see in their maths lessons. You will find ideas for such activities in such catalogues as the one from Tarquin Publications or the ATM (see Appendix 2 for addresses).

Books by Martin Gardner, Ian Stewart, Brian Bolt and other writers can be a rich source of stimulating mathematical ideas for a maths club and copies are often to be found in second-hand bookshops. Why not start your own collection of interesting and enriching books? There are also many useful references on the internet (see Sinclair, 2004, as well as Chapter 9).

Maths trails

Those who qualify as teachers are expected to:

> Establish a purposeful and safe learning environment conducive to learning and identify opportunities for learners to learn in out-of-school contexts.
>
> (TDA, 2007: Q30)

The idea of a mathematics trail is to encourage pupils to see mathematics in the world around them. It is possible to adapt the notion of a maths trail to fit the circumstances and conduct them within the classroom, within part of the school building, outside the school grounds or as part of a more adventurous field trip. Look around the room you are in for a moment. You could either start from a particular topic, such as measurement or shape, or you could take a general approach depending on your objectives. Suggestions for questions include:

- estimate the height of the blue shelf from the ground;
- sketch the window frames;
- find out how many rectangles there are;
- estimate how much paint it would take to paint the ceiling if 1 litre covers 2.5 square metres;
- find a cylinder.

When setting a trail for the town, which could then be used as a homework task, you might ask questions like:

■   How old are the black railings outside the Town Hall, in the cathedral?
■   Find the grave of the Lord Mayor by the east door. How old was he when he died? How long ago did he die?

For the more ambitious, the following idea might be thought-provoking. In a forest in Norfolk is a dinosaur park, where a forest trail leads past life-size tableaux of dinosaurs 'grazing' or hunting. A maths trail here might include questions about scale (estimating heights, lengths and weights) and about time.

Task 4.10 **Devise a maths trail**

Read further about maths trails: for example, you might read Selinger and Baker (1991), Morris (1986) or Blair *et al*. (1983). Devise a maths trail of your own around the school or the school grounds. Try it with a couple of volunteer pupils and ask them for their comments and ideas.

Task 4.11 **Reflecting on a lesson**

Before you move on, consider the following account of a mathematics lesson. This is an unusual lesson in lots of respects. Mathematics teachers go about providing diversity for their pupils in many different ways. What works for one teacher may not work for another. As you read the account, make notes in your journal about:

■   the environment in which the lesson takes place;
■   the ways in which pupils are involved with and given responsibility for their own learning;
■   the role of written dialogue with pupils.

A lesson observed

I got to the room before the class or the teacher. It was furnished simply with groups of tables and chairs informally arranged. A couple of grey filing cabinets stood at the back, their half-open drawers bulging with SMILE cards. The wall displayed pupils' work. One large poster declared the 'Puzzle of the Week', while another invited pupils to contribute their own matchstick puzzles. On one side of the board was pinned a statement on cheating yourself, while on the other was a pupil-composed policy on equal opportunities. Three-dimensional solids hung from the ceiling. Pupils began to arrive, first a trickle, then a rush. Some sat, others stood. A few busied themselves giving out folders. One boy cleaned the board and then wrote his name alongside number 1. Others followed, adding to the list. A girl entered, writing her name next to 15, leaving a large gap in the list. As a pupil approached to ask me whether the teacher was away and was I there to take them, in walked the teacher. I had counted by this time 29 pupils: 15 boys, 14 girls.

'Sorry I am late,' said the teacher, 'thanks for getting yourselves organised.'

'Oh, hello,' she said, turning to me. Turning back to the class she continued, 'I've got your books here. They have all been marked. Now remember, your first job before you do anything else is to read my comments and write at least one or two sentences by way of reply to me on what I've said. OK?'

The books were given out. Pupils opened their exercise books and read the teacher's comments, some reading them out loud to their neighbours. By now they were all sitting in groups. After writing their replies, they all got down to work. I roamed the room to find out what they were doing. One group was designing a board game; another group was working on graphs, taking the British Telecom charge leaflet and trying to turn it into something more easy to understand. Another group seemed to be working on a textbook exercise, whilst yet another was doing some paper folding from a SMILE pack.

The rest of the class appeared to be working individually, mostly from SMILE cards. A few left their places to get cards or equipment from filing cabinet or cupboard. The room hummed with purpose. The teacher joined one group and got into conversation.

'Why the list of names?,' I asked, pointing to the board.

'Oh, that's the help list,' a boy replied. 'You put your name down and she comes around in the order of the list. It stops queue-jumping by shouting out.'

For the first time, I noticed that there was no teacher desk, just a group of cupboards in the corner of the room, stacked with papers.

'Why did Hannah put herself down at 15 when she could have got in at 7?,' I asked.

'Ask her. She's over there.'

So I went to Hannah. Hannah had her head down and was hard at work.

'What's that?,' I asked.

'ShSh! I'm trying to finish it off', she said. 'It's English.'

'Is it homework?', I asked.

'No, I started it off last lesson and I want to finish this bit off before I forget what I want to say.'

I left to disturb others before returning to Hannah. She now appeared to be on her mathematics. I asked her about the list. She explained that she knew that she needed some help with her maths project but had wanted to finish off her English first. She also wanted to have another look at her maths work before the teacher got to her. I asked her about her project and whether she liked maths.

'It's all right,' she told me, but she did not think she was very good at it. The project had been hard initially, but it had got easier after she had 'learnt up about sines, cos and tangents and things'. She got stuck a couple of times, but with the help of the teacher and one or two other pupils she 'chatted up' she had got herself sorted out. She now needed some advice on how to write up her conclusions. I helped her as much as I could. I asked if I could look at her exercise book and I read an interesting dialogue between her and her teacher throughout the book. The teacher was now sitting alongside another pupil and was in no hurry to move on. I asked if I could help and was told to help the next person on the list.

(John Hibbs, HMI, personal communication)

SUMMARY AND KEY POINTS

This chapter has given you lots of principles, ideas and starting points for beginning to teach. You read at the beginning of the chapter about the complex interrelation between teaching and telling. You will need to work out how this interrelationship will operate in practice in your own teaching. There are different possible levels of classroom organisation: individual, group and whole-class; and you have begun to think about how you might take advantage of the differing strengths of these various ways of organising work in a classroom. Furthermore, you have begun to think about a range of resources and about the use of homework to develop and extend the tasks that give rise to pupil activity in the mathematics classroom. Finally, at the end of this chapter you have read and reflected on a description of a lesson in which pupils were given a lot of responsibility for their own mathematics learning.

Your task as a mathematics teacher will require you to use teaching methods that sustain the momentum of your pupils' work and keep them engaged. You should aspire to:

■ ensure that all learners make good progress so that they fully achieve the challenging intended learning outcomes;
■ teach lessons that invariably capture the interest of learners, are inclusive of all learners, and feature debate between learners and between learners and the teacher;
■ have a rapport with learners – high-quality dialogue and questioning, guiding learning, with attention to individuals and groups.

(Ofsted, 2009b: 29)

What you need now is to consider thoughtfully how to weave these ingredients into lessons. This you will work on in Chapter 5.

If teaching and learning is seen only in terms of lessons, you might be tempted to think about what 'the perfect lesson' might be, a lesson that is to be repeated endlessly through time in all its perfection. When looking at issues of balance, diversity and entitlement (which is how we started this chapter), you have to look beyond the constraints of the single lesson and think about the overall experience of the pupils.

Although you will inevitably focus on the lesson as the unit of teaching and planning, you will also need to think of both the larger and the smaller scale. This means, on the one hand, long-term planning of sequences of lessons and schemes of work for larger-scale structure and, on the other, detailed short-term planning of smaller sections within a lesson when different things are happening.

FURTHER READING

Boaler, J. (2009) *The Elephant in the Classroom: Helping Children Learn and Love Maths*. London: Souvenir Press Ltd.
Grounded in Boaler's research in mathematics classrooms, this book offers many suggestions for helping to make mathematics teaching and learning more effective.

Bowland (2008) *Bowland Mathematics*. Blackburn: Bowland Charitable Trust. (Available from: http://www.bowlandmaths.org.uk.)
This collection of materials is designed to stimulate interest in mathematics through provision of

non-routine, substantial problems involving multiple connections. The original pack includes CPD materials and 20 examples.

Katz, V. (2008) *A History of Mathematics*, **3rd edn. New York: HarperCollins.**
A well-written, accessible and comprehensive history of mathematics book, originally written for American teachers. It includes accounts of mathematics and mathematicians from all over the world and provides exercises for pupils to work on both inside and outside the classroom.

Swan, M. (2005) *Improving Learning in Mathematics: Challenges and Strategies.* **London: Department for Education and Skills Standards Unit. Also available from: https://www.ncetm.org.uk/files/224/improving_learning_in_mathematicsi.pdf**
This book was part of a well-respected pack of multimedia resources made available to all schools and colleges in the years after its publication. At the time of writing, there is an area of the NCETM website dedicated to extending this work.

PLANNING FOR MATHEMATICS LEARNING

Keith Jones and Ruth Edwards

INTRODUCTION

Learning how to plan effective mathematics lessons is one of the most important skills you acquire as you learn to become a successful mathematics teacher. Having a good lesson plan is important for a whole host of reasons; primarily in providing a structure within which you can be confident that your pupils are learning the mathematics that you intend them to learn. Not only does effective planning result in lessons that are interesting, challenging and motivating for your pupils, but it is also closely linked to the equally demanding (but often more overt) issue of effective classroom management. A good lesson plan that actively involves your pupils helps to boost your confidence in the classroom and gives you a sound basis for managing the class successfully. It goes a long way towards *preventing* classroom problems.

Learning to plan successful mathematics lessons requires work and effort – and it takes time. This is because planning depends on your knowledge and understanding of a complex set of matters including: how pupils learn mathematics; the nature and format of the mathematics curriculum; the specific mathematical concepts and skills that you are teaching; the prior knowledge of the pupils; methods of teaching mathematics; and how mathematics lessons can be structured for maximum effectiveness. Devoting considerable time to planning is definitely worthwhile; it is a valuable investment for future years that, in the longer term, reduces the demands of paperwork as your preparation becomes quicker and easier as your experience grows.

This chapter addresses what it takes to plan a mathematics lesson, covering the setting of objectives and how to structure an individual lesson. This leads on to how to plan sequences of lessons, including how to take account of your pupils' prior knowledge and varying needs, and how to select and prepare resources, including ICT. Later sections consider the use of different formats for lesson plans in response to other aspects of planning, such as predicting pupil responses, preparing appropriate teacher responses and assessing pupil learning. The chapter concludes by looking at the wider aspects of planning, including planning as part of a team and planning for out-of-school learning. We begin by looking at why planning is important, how it links with other aspects of teaching and how planning individual lessons fits in with other levels of planning.

OBJECTIVES

By the end of this chapter you should be able to:

- understand the relationships among the mathematics curriculum, a scheme of work, the choice of teaching strategies and your individual lesson plans;
- select appropriate teaching strategies and mathematical tasks and resources (including ICT);
- plan mathematics lessons and units of work, identifying clear objectives and content;
- establish appropriate and demanding expectations for pupil learning and plan for inclusion;
- work as part of a team in collaborative planning and planning for out-of-school learning;
- reflect on and improve your practice in planning lessons.

LEARNING FROM TEACHERS PLANNING MATHEMATICS LESSONS

The demands of lesson planning can become frustrating if you are not clear about why lesson planning is necessary and exactly how it can help you in your role as a teacher.

Task 5.1 **Why is planning important?**

Write down five (or more) reasons for planning lessons. Provide one or more reasons why each reason is important.

How might the research by John (2006) or by Zazkis *et al.* (2009) inform your approach to lesson planning?

For your reasons, you may have written down some or all of the following:

Planning:

- makes you articulate what you think will happen in a lesson;
- helps you to ensure that your lessons begin in an interesting way, maintain a good pace throughout and have a satisfying ending;
- enables you to rehearse various aspects;
- makes you more likely to be receptive to the ideas of others;
- provides a basis for post-lesson discussion and evaluation;
- creates a feeling of confidence for you, the teacher;
- provides a history of your thinking and development.

Or you might have written that lesson plans help you to:

- structure your lessons;
- build on previous lessons and learning;
- share the objectives of the lesson with pupils;
- develop effective Assessment for Learning (AfL), so pupils receive feedback that helps them to improve;
- assess pupil achievements so that you can take these into account in future lessons;
- make lessons more inclusive and address a range of needs;
- make explicit the key teaching strategies you are using;
- address the key questions you need to ask;
- highlight key vocabulary;
- focus on targets for raising the level of achievement of pupils in the class;
- set homework;
- work collaboratively with other teachers and education professionals;
- make good use of classroom learning assistants and other in-class support.

What is a lesson?

The conventional unit of *teaching* is the lesson, which, in any given school, might last anywhere from 30 to 70 minutes (or even longer). In contrast, there is no conventional unit of *learning*. Learning can take place at any time, day or night, and does not necessarily occur only in the presence of the teacher. Breaking down mathematical content and offered experience into lesson-size chunks is, in general, necessary for teaching, but this can result in a fragmentation of topics and ideas if teaching is solely thought of in terms of individual lessons. For example, without careful planning, your pupils may never appreciate the connections among fractions, decimals and percentages, particularly if these are treated entirely separately. Another form of fragmentation can happen with investigative and open-ended tasks when these are treated as comprising solely of distinct components such as 'generating results', 'drawing a table' and 'finding a formula'. Effective planning has to be in terms of individual lessons that work well, but it also has to look to the longer term.

Task 5.2 **What are mathematics lessons like?**

The mathematics lessons you observe are likely to differ in format and approach. From your observations of different teachers and different mathematics lessons, record as many different formats as you can. How might the lesson plan (and the lesson planning) be different for different forms of lesson?

Devise a way of categorising all the mathematics lessons that you have observed. How much variety is there in the teaching strategies that are used? How does this variety shift over time and with different classes?

Talk to teachers who use a variety of teaching strategies about how they have come to use those particular strategies in the way they do. Can any piece of mathematics be introduced to pupils in any way you choose? Or can you detect influences that guide teachers' choices of teaching strategy?

There are a number of reasons why the mathematics lessons you observe may differ in format and approach. This may be due partly to the individual teacher, but there can be other underlying reasons. What you should observe is that effective lessons have a structure. Typically, a mathematics lesson might consist of: a starter activity taking about 5–10 minutes (perhaps an oral and mental starter, or perhaps the introduction to a problem that might take at least one lesson to resolve); a major segment of whole-class and/or paired or group work (about 25–40 minutes) combining teaching input and pupil activities; and a final plenary (of 5–15 minutes) to round off the lesson (by summarising key facts and ideas, discussing the next steps, setting homework, etc.).

Of course, other lesson structures are possible. Below are examples of the structures of mathematics lessons from a study of mathematics teaching in the USA and Japan on the topic of the area of triangles (Stigler *et al.*, 1996):

Typical US lesson
teacher reviews concept of perimeter (1 minute);
teacher explains area of rectangle, then pupils do practice examples (8 minutes);
teacher explains area of triangles, then pupils do practice examples (25 minutes);
pupils work individually on an exercise (11 minutes).

Typical Japanese lesson
teacher presents a complex problem (4 minutes);
pupils attempt to solve the problem on their own or groups (15 minutes);
pupils' presentations and class discussion of pupil solutions to the problem, combined with teacher explanations, leading to general solution (21 minutes);
pupils work on practice problems (5 minutes).

Even though lesson structure is not the only influence on pupil achievement, it is worth noting that, in a large-scale international survey of mathematical achievement (TIMSS, the *Trends in International Mathematics and Science Study*), Japanese pupils scored amongst the best in the world in mathematics, whereas pupils in the US (and similarly across the UK) scored somewhat lower (for more on this, see, for example, Jones, 1997; Stigler and Hiebert, 1999). This suggests that what may influence how successful your pupils become in mathematics is both *how* mathematics is taught to them (that is the teaching strategies that are used) *and* what *forms of mathematical knowledge* they encounter through your teaching.

Task 5.3 **How are mathematics lessons structured?**

From your observations of mathematics lessons, what different structures are used? Are the lessons you see more like the typical US lesson or more like the typical Japanese lesson?
    How might the research of Stigler and Hiebert (1999) influence how you might structure some of your own mathematics lessons?

Learning from how experienced teachers plan

Whenever you observe effective teachers of mathematics in classrooms, you observe the result of their planning. Research suggests that, in constructing lessons, experienced teachers draw on a range of experiences and knowledge in an attempt to match the observed (and anticipated) needs of their pupils to a particular lesson or set of lessons (John, 1991, 1993, 2006; Li *et al.*, 2009; Wragg, 1995). According to the DfES (2004c: 2), experienced teachers consider the full range of factors illustrated in Figure 5.1 when designing lessons.

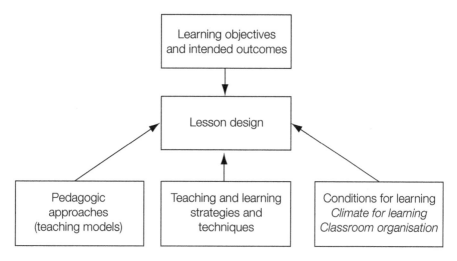

■ **Figure 5.1** Factors affecting lesson design
Source: DfES, 2004c: 2

For experienced teachers, in many instances, lesson *outlines* (perhaps consisting of phrases or illustrative diagrams) are entirely appropriate. While such outlines may be fully meaningful to the teacher concerned, they may not conjure up a complete lesson to someone new to teaching. For the experienced teacher, there are times when a more detailed lesson plan may be appropriate (for instance, when a new or seldom taught topic is scheduled or as a useful basis for dialogue with a teacher colleague such as you), but such detailed plans are not always necessary for them.

This preference of experienced teachers for a more fluid mode of planning can appear to pose a difficulty for you. It can be that the more *skillful* the planning or the more the planning happens at unscheduled times (such as at the teacher's home), the more *difficult it is* for you to understand how successful lesson planning is achieved. What is more, the requirement for you to produce detailed written plans may seem oddly at variance with the practice of established teachers. *Nothing could be further from the truth.* All successful teachers carry out planning, and it remains of critical importance to teaching. It is how planning *changes* as you develop professionally that you should keep in mind.

Task 5.4 **How do experienced teachers plan?**

a) Ask a class teacher if she or he can take you through the process involved in planning a particular lesson. What are the important aspects of this process? What aspects of the plan are recorded? How are they recorded?
b) See if you can observe or take part in the lesson and then discuss with the class teacher how the lesson went in practice. How and why may it have deviated from the lesson as planned?
c) Write some reflections on how you can best learn from the ways in which experienced teachers plan their lessons.

How planning connects to other areas of teacher knowledge and expertise

By now it should be clear that planning is a key professional responsibility and that your own planning is a key means by which you develop and show the high expectations you have of all the pupils you teach. Working with others in planning, and in reflecting on how successful you are in implementing your plans, are also central to developing and showing professional values of the highest level. In order to plan confidently and effectively, you need a high level of subject knowledge and understanding. This enables you to judge how mathematical ideas and concepts can be broken down and sequenced so that they scaffold pupils' learning and, additionally, how you might tackle likely pupil errors and misconceptions. Planning entails ensuring the purposeful use of a range of monitoring and assessment strategies and then using the information gathered to improve your future planning and teaching.

What can support your development is dialogue about your planning with teacher colleagues, and the reflective writing you do about your lesson plans as you use them. You will find that appropriately detailed written plans should give you the confidence to begin teaching well. As your confidence grows, and as you make progress with your classes, you might begin to adjust the amount of detail you include in your plans. A lesson plan should not be thought of as 'use once only'. When you have taught a lesson, reflect on those parts which went well and what could be improved. Your lesson plan can then be edited and augmented by your notes for use in the future, perhaps through adaptation for a different class.

Levels of planning

Planning can be thought of as operating at three levels.

LONG-TERM PLANNING

This occurs at the level of the mathematics department and is informed by school-wide policies and procedures. Such long-term planning demonstrates, amongst other things, how the required (perhaps statutory) components of the mathematics curriculum are to be covered. It also captures how much time is allocated to mathematics teaching and shows how coverage of the mathematics curriculum is structured for different age groups of pupils.

MEDIUM-TERM PLANNING

This considers a block of teaching time, perhaps five to ten weeks in length (or longer). Such planning is often specified within what is sometimes called a departmental *scheme of work*. In England, the *Framework for Secondary Mathematics* continues to inform medium-term planning in many school mathematics departments. In planning mathematics for pupils aged 14–19, subject 'specifications' (implemented through the Examination Awarding Organisations) play a major role.

SHORT-TERM PLANNING

This can include weekly, daily or individual lesson plans. The planning of individual lessons, and how this leads to planning sequences of lessons, is covered in detail below.

Task 5.5 **What is a scheme of work?**

Examine a scheme of work in a school mathematics department and see to what extent it:

■ provides the framework for classroom practice;
■ lays out the mathematical knowledge, skills and processes to be taught during specified blocks of time (anything from five to ten weeks, or longer);
■ gives guidance about the range of teaching strategies to be used.

Choose a topic or an area of work from the scheme of work in the school in which you are learning to teach. Find out what the topic is designed to achieve, what the pupils were taught before and what they will do next, what length of time is devoted to the topic, what resources (including ICT) are suggested and how pupil learning is to be assessed.

The structure of national (or local) curriculum documents needs to be taken into account when learning to plan. For example, for England, the mathematics NC has, as currently specified, two structural aspects that inform lesson planning: the *programme of study* and the *level descriptors for the Attainment Targets*. One way to think about the relationship between these two aspects is to consider the programme of study as indicating *what* should be taught, while the level descriptors allow you to judge *what your pupils have learned*. What happens during your lessons provides the link between the two. Another important use for the level descriptors is to provide some indication of what you can expect from pupils. For those teaching in England, this can be especially helpful in planning mathematics lessons.

Task 5.6 **How can the specification of the mathematics curriculum aid planning?**

Choose some statements from the curriculum documents with which you need to work and examine how these statements link to the scheme of work in the mathematics department in your school. As an example, if you are teaching in England, you can focus on the *National Curriculum Programme of Study for Mathematics* (QCA, 2007a) and see how this is reflected in the level descriptors. How might the specification of the programmes of study and the level descriptors aid you in your lesson planning?

Write some reflections on how your use of the curriculum documents can inform the targets you might have for developing your skills in lesson planning. Focus your reflections on the impact on your planning of how relevant curriculum documents set out what mathematics is to be taught and what pupils should know as a result of being taught.

It is probably worth noting at this point that the structure of any curriculum document – such as the current version of the National Curriculum for Mathematics in England – is only one vision of how a mathematics curriculum can be specified. Rather than arranging the curriculum in terms of content, such as 'number and algebra', 'geometry' and so on, another concept might be to arrange the curriculum around what are sometimes referred to as the 'big ideas' in mathematics. These 'big ideas' might include such notions as place value, variable, function, invariance, symmetry, proof, etc. The resulting curriculum might well appear very different from the documentation that informs your teaching and, as a consequence, might perhaps be taught in a different way.

This illustrates the idea of the *curricular shaping of teaching*; that is how the specification of the curriculum directly, and indirectly, influences the teaching strategies used. This is partly because it is not only mathematical skills and techniques that need to be taught and developed; the ways in which pupils communicate mathematically and how they represent, analyse and interpret mathematical situations are an essential part of their mathematical understanding and development. In the current curriculum documents in England, these latter elements are termed 'mathematical applications and processes'.

PLANNING A LESSON, PLANNING COLLABORATIVELY

A good place to begin your first steps in lesson planning might be with a reasonably self-contained part of a lesson – something you plan collaboratively with the class teacher. The reasonably self-contained part of a lesson could be one or more of the following:

- a lesson starter (perhaps a piece of oral or mental mathematics);
- an agreed segment of the main part of a lesson (this could be introducing a specific mathematical idea or way of tackling a mathematics problem);
- the concluding part of a lesson (probably some form of plenary).

While all first steps need to be negotiated and agreed with the class teacher, each one noted above is designed to boost your confidence with speaking to a whole class (and may also help you to get to know the pupils' names). Planning for these first steps might well involve specifying precisely what you say, based on the class teacher's lesson outline (or scheme of work). Zazkis *et al.* (2009) liken scripting a specific part of a lesson to writing a play in which you imagine (and write down as for a play) the classroom dialogue between you and the class. From the research evidence to date, it can be worth trying this form of scripting of specific lesson segments.

In addition to scripting specific lesson segments that you are to teach, it is worth practising the use of presentation aids such as presentation software and interactive whiteboards – see the Further Reading section at the end of this chapter for some suggestions of useful guides to using presentation software and interactive whiteboards.

Task 5.7 **Planning and presenting parts of lessons**

a) Negotiate to take a reasonably self-contained part of a lesson. Be clear on what you need to do and discuss your plan for the lesson segment with the class teacher. What aspects of the lesson segment would you like feedback on? Discuss how the element went in practice. Write some reflective notes on the aspects of your lesson presentation skills that you need to work on.

b) Negotiate to plan a complete lesson *with* the class teacher – one that the teacher will take. During the lesson, make notes on the opening, middle and closing segments of the lesson, the timing of each segment and any deviations from the set plan. Discuss with the teacher how each segment went and the reason that the teacher decided to make any adjustments to the plan *during the course of the lesson*.

c) Negotiate with the class teacher to plan further whole lessons of which you will take agreed elements. For example, you could start the lesson, introduce the main part or take the concluding part. Discuss the extent to which the learning outcomes were achieved. It is important to build in formative assessment opportunities and use the outcomes to inform your future planning (see Chapter 6 for ways of doing this).

d) Write some reflections about how working with an experienced teacher in this way can inform targets you might have for developing your skills in lesson planning.

In addition to planning collaboratively with a class teacher, as a beginning teacher you might be paired with another beginning teacher. This provides for many opportunities for collaborative planning. For more information on collaborative planning with another beginning teacher, see, for example, Smith (2004); Sorensen *et al.* (2006); Wilson and Edwards (2009).

Planning your own first whole lesson

As you will have found out from beginning to work collaboratively with an experienced teacher (or with a peer beginning teacher), planning a whole lesson entails specifying, as a minimum, at least the following (while taking into account the teaching time for the lesson):

- the objectives and activities for the starter activity (perhaps a piece of oral and mental mathematics);
- the objectives to be addressed within the main teaching activities, probably with objectives adjusted as appropriate for higher- and lower-attaining pupils in the class;
- the key teaching points and activities for the lesson, matched to the lesson objectives (with suggestions for how the activities can be developed, including extensions for the more able or simplifications for those pupils requiring additional support);
- the timing of each segment of the lesson;
- key mathematical terms, notation and specialised vocabulary to be introduced and used;
- the resources needed, including ICT (with references to any departmental resources, relevant parts of textbooks, software, web-based material etc.);
- ideas to be drawn out in the plenary (or mini-plenary segments), including some key questions, plus homework tasks (if appropriate);
- opportunities for assessing (usually formatively) how successfully the pupils are learning the key ideas in the lesson.

As with planning a reasonably self-contained part of a lesson, it is worth thinking about scripting specific lesson segments of whole lessons. It is also worth continuing with practising the use of presentation aids such as presentation software and interactive whiteboards.

Planning more whole lessons

As you become more experienced, your lesson plans can become more developed and might also include:

- potential difficulties or misconceptions that pupils may have, and suggestions to preempt or rectify them;
- how best to deploy any available support staff (such as teaching assistants);
- assessment strategies and what adjustments to future plans might be needed as a result;
- connections with other mathematical topics and other subjects.

One way to approach the planning of whole lessons is to use *lesson pro forma*. Such pro forma usually contain space to record some or all of the following:

- practical details such as date, class, time, room;
- references to curriculum documents or the scheme of work;
- learning objectives and learning outcomes (or success criteria);
- teacher and pupil activity;
- indicative timings for each segment of the lesson;
- homework.

Task 5.8 **Using lesson planning pro forma**

a) Review some *lesson pro forma* that you have seen or have been given (examples are provided in John, 1993). How suitable are they for the lessons you teach or are likely to teach? How might using such pro forma aid your planning of lessons? In what ways might using such pro forma restrict what you do with your classes?

b) An alternative to using pre-printed pro forma is to design your own or modify one that you already have. How could you vary the design of lesson pro forma according to the format and/or learning intentions of the lesson?

c) How might the research by John (2006) inform your approach to using lesson pro forma?

When you are working on a lesson plan, an important aspect that needs careful consideration concerns the various stages of a lesson. It is certainly likely that some segments of the lesson might take longer, when it comes to teaching, than you might have anticipated, while other segments may take considerably less time. Clearly, you need to adjust your plan as you teach each lesson in order to account for both eventualities. This involves working flexibly with your lesson plan and having more ideas at hand in case you need them. Whatever happens to the length of the various segments of a lesson, it is always worth ensuring that you finish on time and avoid rushing any elements that might be taking longer than you expect. If the main activity needs more time than you allocated in your plan, it is usually better to cut out part of it and have a proper finish than have the lesson end abruptly.

Working with learning objectives

In any discussion of learning objectives, it is important to remember that an objective is *not* which set of mathematics questions the class are to do, nor that your pupils are going to draw a graph, nor even that there is going to be a class discussion about how to solve a particular mathematical problem. Such things are the *activities* used to *promote* learning. Objectives specify *what is to be learnt*. It is known that a major pitfall in learning to plan is to neglect objectives and to see planning as simply organising activities. There is much more to it than that.

As John (1991, 1993, 2006) reveals, it is very common for guidance on lesson planning to stress the importance of specifying suitable learning objectives. This reflects the view that the way to introduce beginning teachers to the complexities of lesson planning is to use a framework based around the 'rational planning model' first outlined by Tyler (1949). This model asserts that planning a lesson, or a sequence of lessons, involves:

- specifying objectives;
- selecting and sequencing learning activities;
- evaluating the outcomes.

There are, of course, advantages to specifying objectives clearly. These include that such objectives are likely to be measurable, easily communicated and make planning, assessment and evaluation more transparent. While it is undoubtedly important to be clear about what pupils are to learn during a lesson, there are disadvantages associated with *starting* the process of lesson planning with specifying the learning objectives. These disadvantages can include:

▨   planning can become more rigid;
▨   opportunistic learning may be inhibited;
▨   learning may be trivialised to what is 'easily' communicated and measured;
▨   teaching is viewed more (or even solely) as a technical matter, rather than also being a creative activity.

Consequently many teachers opt for the term *learning intentions* (in place of objectives), in order to emphasise that these are to be used flexibly and creatively in response to what a particular class needs to learn (or shows an interest in) and not rigidly adhered to in spite of opportunities that present themselves during a lesson.

In terms of learning objectives (or intentions), one approach is to work with an objective for the overall topic being taught and, in light of this, look to specifying suitable *objectives* (or intentions) for individual lessons. Selecting such lesson objectives involves separating a topic into distinct elements (or aspects) and designing a sequence through these elements. Research suggests that this is the most demanding aspect for a beginning teacher (see, for example, John, 2006). Deciding how to select objectives in a way that satisfactorily meets the needs of your pupils is something that demands good subject knowledge and awareness of pupil needs.

When thinking about individual lessons, and especially when using lesson pro forma (whether pre-printed or designed – or modified – by you), you certainly need to learn how to work creatively with objectives. Unless you do so, research evidence (such as that reviewed by John, 2006) suggests that there is a real risk that your planning becomes overly rigid, thereby inhibiting learning opportunities that can arise during any lesson. Working creatively with objectives can mean, among other things, looking for worthwhile learning activities and deciding how these match with what you are teaching (rather than necessarily always starting with the objective and trying to find tasks or activities that match).

Task 5.9 **What's involved in specifying objectives?**

Review some of the successful lessons you have seen. How easy is it to specify the objectives for each one? Are some sorts of objectives easier to specify than others? How can you tell to what extent objectives have been met?

Write some reflections on how research evidence (such as that reviewed by John, 2006) helps you to guard against inflexibility in your lesson plans and to look to learning opportunities than can arise during any lesson.

Learning objectives and learning outcomes

Specifying objectives (and the associated learning outcomes or success criteria) concentrates attention on both *what* is to be taught and on *how* pupils' learning is to be judged.

What also needs to be addressed is the equally important issue of how pupils will be provided with learning opportunities. Where possible, learning outcomes should be precise, assessable and achievable and, as such, provide a way to assess pupil learning (rather than being about what the pupils are doing as they complete a task or an activity). In this way, used appropriately, learning outcomes should help to frame the lesson (or a short series of lessons) and aid the articulation of 'key' questions that help inform how you might script a lesson introduction or conclusion.

Learning outcomes can also be framed as assessment criteria and, where appropriate, provide different learning outcomes for different groups of pupils. These ideas are developed in more detail in Chapter 6 of this volume where you can find ideas using phrases that begin 'By the end of the lesson, pupils will...'.

All this means that having clear learning objectives (and outcomes) for lessons is important. Yet what is of similar importance is developing a way of planning that means that you are working creatively with setting objectives and outcomes for particular lessons. This entails, amongst other things, seeking out learning activities that engage your classes and deciding how these activities match with what you want your pupils to learn.

Working with existing lesson plans

A potentially very useful way of approaching planning whole lessons is to work with existing lesson plans. By modifying an existing plan, such as the one provided in Table 5.1, you can match the lesson to the particular circumstances of the class that you are teaching. Modifying existing plans is an important skill. Some of the questions to ask when modifying existing lesson plans include the following: will my pupils find this lesson engaging and motivating? Does the context need adjusting? Is the timing of the various segments suitable? And so on.

Task 5.10 **Modifying existing lesson plans**

Find some existing lesson plans that are suitable for a mathematics topic that you are planning and try modifying these for the pupils you are teaching. The Teacher Resource Exchange (http://tre.ngfl.gov.uk/) is one example of a database of resources and activities where teachers can share ideas for lessons. Once you have accumulated some existing plans (or lesson ideas), ask yourself what aspects of these existing plans (or ideas) can you retain for your lesson planning? What needs adjusting to match the needs of your pupils? How might you take ideas from several plans and shape these into a single coherent lesson or a short series of coherent lessons?

Reflecting on lessons

Through reflecting on all the points raised in this section, you should have the basis for sound evaluation of your work and of your progress as a developing teacher. For individual lessons, you are likely to concentrate on some or more of the following issues.

■ **Table 5.1** A sample lesson plan

Class: 7c (middle set)   Year Group: 7   School: _____   Date: _____
Number in class: 30   Male: 17   Female: 13   SEN: 1 / dyslexic   Time: 10.00–11.00

<table>
<tr>
<td colspan="2">Lesson (title and summary)
Topic: Fractions
Reference: KS3 Framework
2.3 Fractions, decimals, percentages, ratio and proportion</td>
<td colspan="2">Prior learning
Work on shading fractions of shapes.
Terminology; numerator, denominator
Cutting activity on fractions of amounts</td>
</tr>
<tr>
<td colspan="4">Curriculum references and links to other aspects of NC:
National Curriculum reference: Ma2, 2.3 (KS3 PoS) levels 3–5</td>
</tr>
<tr>
<td colspan="2">Main learning objective(s)
Use simple fractions and recognise when two fractions are equivalent
Work out a simple fraction of an amount
Cancel down fractions to their lowest form</td>
<td colspan="2">Learning outcomes (concepts, skills, attitudes)
Pupils will be able to represent two digits as a proper fraction
Pupils will be able to calculate simple fractions of 60 and represent them on a number line
Pupils will be able to associate equivalent fractions</td>
</tr>
<tr>
<td>Resources
Large sheets of paper with 60 cm line drawn
Dice
Whiteboards and pens</td>
<td colspan="2">Use of ICT
Virtual image fractions</td>
<td>Vocabulary
Numerator, denominator, equivalent fractions, proper fraction</td>
</tr>
<tr>
<td>Time
10.00</td>
<td colspan="2">Introduction/Starter
Develop mental methods to find fractions of amounts
Use whiteboards
Quick 10 on PowerPoint. Questions such as: 18 ÷ 3, 20 ÷ 5, 1/4 of 80, 1/10 of 70, 2/3 of 24, 4/5 of 40
Discuss methods.</td>
<td>Key questions
Which words do we use to talk about division?
Which symbols can we use in maths to show division?
What do the words Numerator, Denominator mean?
What methods can we use to work out fractions of amounts?
How can we tell if two fractions represent the same proportion?</td>
</tr>
<tr>
<td>Time
10.10

10.15

10.25

10.30</td>
<td colspan="2">Main teaching activities (development, extension, differentiation)
• Model the activity they are to do in pairs using a 60 cm line on the board. Throw 2 dice. Make a proper fraction. Plot the fraction on the line. Repeat several times.
• Pupils work in pairs. Using 2 dice pupils create random proper fractions and mark them underneath their number line
• Ask pairs to put in any other fractions with denominators 2,3,4,5,6 (without rolling the dice) …
• … then to add tenths
Extension work
Plot sevenths, eighths and ninths as well on the line.</td>
<td>Organisation, discussion, possible pupil response, teacher intervention
Teacher demonstration of activity. Ask two pupils to roll the dice.
Discussion about how we could arrange the two values as a fraction. Why is the smaller number on the top?
What is a proper fraction?
How do we record it if we get the same fraction again?
What if the numbers on the dice are the same?
Can you think of any fractions that you haven't rolled yet?
How many fractions will there be altogether?
What if the dice had 10 sides? Which fractions could you make?
What if it had 7, 8 or 9 sides?</td>
</tr>
<tr>
<td>10.45</td>
<td colspan="2">Plenary (review, consolidate, extend)
Did you find any equivalent fractions?
Look at results
Virtual image equivalent fraction activity</td>
<td>Key questions
Which fractions are equivalent?
How can you tell?
Is there a quick way to find out if two fractions are equivalent?
Which is larger, 2/5 or 1/3? 3/4 or 4/5? 2/3 or 7/10?
Which pair of fractions has the bigger difference: 3/5 and 4/6, or 4/5 and 5/6?</td>
</tr>
<tr>
<td colspan="4">Assessment opportunities
Class discussion, individual pupil responses – all linked to key questions (above)</td>
</tr>
</table>

■ What were the elements of the lesson that worked best?
■ What did I enjoy most? What did the pupils enjoy most?
■ How did the pupils react to the lesson? Why?
■ Was the lesson pitched at the appropriate mathematical level?
■ What would I change about the lesson if I did it again?
■ At what points in the lesson could I have engaged the pupils more? How?
■ Were the pupils able to do what I wanted them to do? Why/why not?
■ What did the pupils learn? How do I know what they learned?
■ Did the pupils reach the learning objective for the lesson? Why/why not?
■ Do I need to teach the pupils anything more on this topic before moving on to the next?

Reflecting on individual lessons should help you to develop your planning skills so that you become ready to plan sequences of lessons.

PLANNING SEQUENCES OF LESSONS

Being confident about planning and teaching individual lessons is a good start. Building on this so that you can plan and teach a series of lessons confronts you with a range of issues associated with having to divide mathematics learning into lesson-sized chunks – where the danger is that mathematics can seem fragmented and incoherent to your pupils. In this section, the focus is on how you can ensure that there is continuity and progression of pupil learning with your classes such that, over time, you can be confident that your pupils are learning the mathematics you intend.

In this context, a topic of work is a coherent series of lessons on a mathematical topic (such as adding simple fractions or solving simultaneous equations), a 'big idea' in mathematics such as invariance or symmetry, or a piece of project work such as a mathematical investigation or open-ended problem. The scheme of work in your school department may well specify quite precisely what each lesson within a topic of work should comprise. Alternatively, the scheme of work may provide no more than a title and a list of suggested resources. No matter what you have in your current situation, there are inevitably going to be times when you need to plan, in detail, a topic of work.

Given that mathematics is not merely a group of isolated learning objectives but an interconnected web of ideas and concepts, it is the connections between these ideas and concepts that may not be all that obvious to your pupils. Good planning entails trying to ensure that mathematical ideas and concepts are presented in an interrelated way. This means planning, as far as possible, so that you are:

■ presenting each topic as a whole, for example by showing pupils that decimals and percentages are particular forms of fractions;
■ bringing together related ideas across strands, for example by linking ratio and proportion (in number) to rates of change (in algebra), to enlargement and similarity (in geometry) and to proportional thinking in statistics and probability;
■ helping your pupils to appreciate that important mathematical ideas permeate different aspects of the subject, for example linking the concepts of inverse and order in the four number operations to the transformation of algebraic expressions and the geometrical transformations of reflection, rotation and translation;
■ using opportunities for generalisation, proof and problem-solving to help your pupils to appreciate mathematics as a unified subject.

Your plan for a topic should include:

▓ the key learning objectives for the topic as a whole (these will be mainly mathematical in nature but may also include cross-curricular and personal development objectives such as improving collaborative learning etc.);

▓ an indication of what topics should come before, and what might come after, the topic being considered, the links to other topics and other school subjects (such links could be detailed in the departmental scheme of work);

▓ lesson plans for each lesson, detailing possible objectives for each individual lesson, outline starter activities, how the work is to be developed in the main part of the lessons through teaching input and pupil activities, how each lesson is to be rounded off, suggestions of what homework should be set;

▓ details of relevant resources, such as textbooks, worksheets, ICT resources, web-based material etc.

When selecting learning activities it is a good idea to reflect on what makes an interesting, motivating and challenging activity for your pupils, so that you provide some variety across the lessons that make up the topic of work. Consideration here includes deciding about:

▓ the context (whether 'real-world' or 'pure' mathematics);

▓ the form of result of the activities (for example, whether it is an individual graphical presentation, a group-devised animation using dynamic geometry, a poster explaining the result, some written exercises or other written work – or whether the pupils might choose what they consider the result might be, and so on);

▓ possible ways of working (whether teacher exposition, discussion in small groups or with the whole class, problem-solving, investigating, and so on).

One way to begin to plan a topic is to rely on established practice (for example, the scheme of work in the school, a textbook scheme, or local or national guidance material, or equivalent).

An example of working within a scheme of work

In England, the national *Framework for Secondary Mathematics* (see the *Essential Documents* listing below) provides guidance on meeting the National Curriculum requirements for mathematics for pupils aged 11–16. The Framework lays out progression within each of five strands (mathematical processes and applications, number, algebra, geometry and measures, and statistics) and identifies yearly learning objectives across the secondary school years for pupils aged 11–16.

Using the framework as a backdrop, a scheme of work in a particular school can comprise related teaching objectives grouped together to give a long-term overview of the progress that is expected of pupils across a number of school years (say, age 11–14, and then age 14–16). Such a scheme of work can consist of a number of components:

▓ a 'curriculum map' – a logical sequence of sets of teaching objectives to be addressed within each academic year;

▓ a teaching 'calendar' – a sequence of teaching objectives organised to fit the school calendar and incorporating other school dates and events;

■ a number of teaching 'units' (or topics), each consisting of a cluster of objectives describing the mathematics that specific groups of pupils are to learn across several lessons.

Individual lessons are then planned within teaching units (or topics) that fall within a teaching calendar that itself is informed by a curriculum map. Full guidance about working in this way is provided via a 'Secondary mathematics planning toolkit' covering the elements laid out in Figure 5.2.

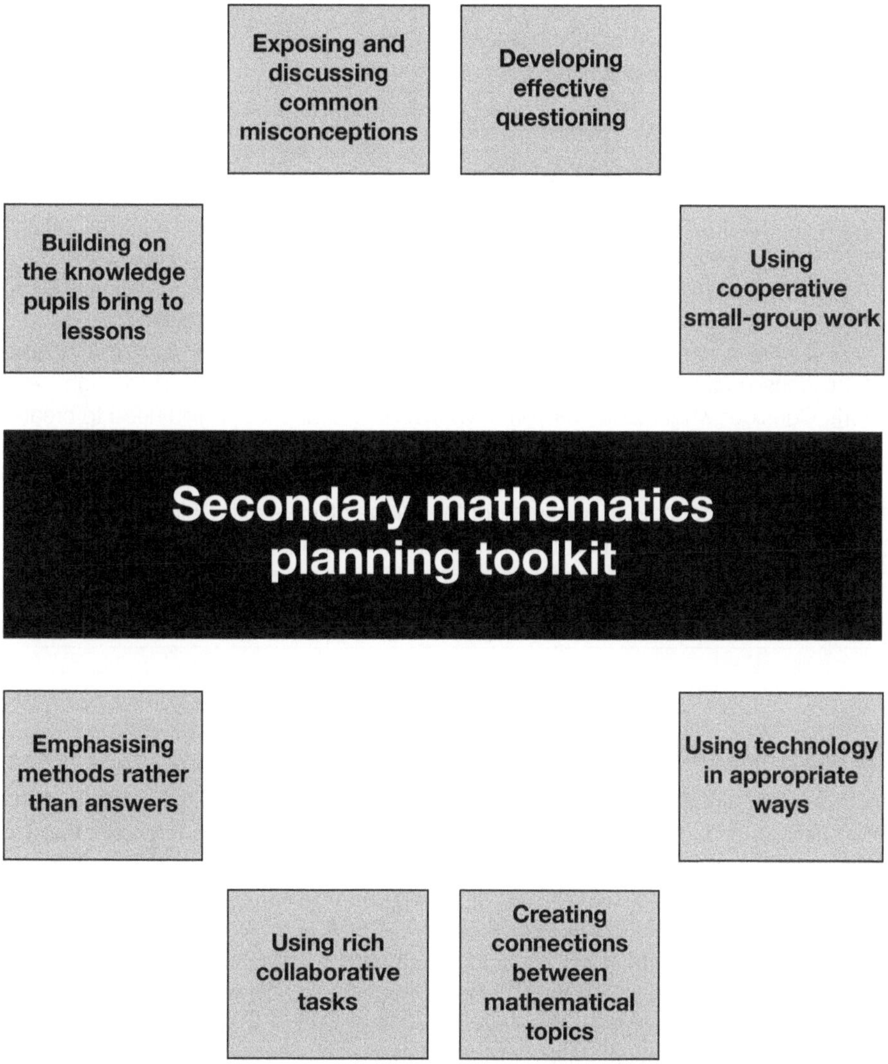

■ **Figure 5.2** Components of a secondary mathematics planning toolkit (DCSF, 2008)

Planning for assessment

Planning assessment opportunities is very important in terms of monitoring the progress of your pupils. Here it is worth asking yourself if such assessment opportunities are to be formal (and probably summative – through a test, say) or informal (and most probably formative). If the latter, formative assessment certainly entails you being *active and purposeful in the classroom* (not just waiting for pupils to ask for help) and involves you observing, questioning, checking, and so on. Planning for assessment involves including AfL strategies (Assessment for Learning, the topic of the next chapter) into your plans with a view to reinforcing the learning being developed, and helping pupils to reflect on what they already know and to set targets for their own future learning (see the *Further Reading* section at the end of this chapter for some suggestions of useful guides to planning for assessment in mathematics).

Task 5.11 **Planning a topic**

When planning a new topic, consider which aspects of mathematics your pupils need to have understood before they can progress further. These aspects of mathematics may come from other mathematical topics that your pupils have studied previously or possibly from the experience of another curriculum subject.

For a topic you are beginning to plan, make a list of the mathematics that needs to be consolidated and a list of the mathematics to be developed through new work. Consider what resources you have available and whether you need to create any yourself. Think about the types of activities your pupils find interesting. Plan to include a range of activities (including open-ended work, group work and individual work) and consider how to accommodate a range of ways of learning. How will you plan for differentiation? What misconceptions might pupils have about this topic? What assessment opportunities can you build in to your planning and how will you record pupil achievement and progress in the topic?

Planning for inclusion, equity and differentiation

The promotion and realisation of equity of opportunity for your pupils to learn mathematics need to be integral to your planning. This entails taking care to ensure that your pupils' experiences of mathematics do not reinforce, but, rather, wherever possible, positively counteract stereotypical thinking. It means you providing the best for *every* pupil, irrespective of gender, social class or ethnicity.

Differentiation is not solely about helping pupils who are encountering difficulties with mathematics or stretching those who show mathematical talent. Differentiation is about *all* pupils. In this context, *diversity* refers to the range of individual aptitudes, while *differentiation* is the planned process of intervention in the classroom to maximise potential based on individual abilities and aptitudes (see, for example, Kerry, 2002). Individual pupil aptitudes can vary in terms of attainment, motivation, interest, skills etc., and you take these into account in how you differentiate. For example, you can *differentiate* in a number of ways:

in planning   – by employing an appropriate variety of tasks;
                            – by identifying outcomes of tasks;
                            – by ensuring elements of pupil choice.
in task design   – through type and design of tasks (text, worksheet, poster, audio, video, computer-based etc.);
                            – through ease of use (for example, reading level).
in providing support   – from you as teacher;
                            – from other adults and/or pupils;
                            – in terms of materials or technology.
in expected response   – by having accessible objectives and outcomes;
                            – by making assessment criteria explicit.

Task 5.12 **Planning for inclusion and diversity**

Review some of the successful mathematics lessons you have seen. How has the variety of pupils in the classes been included in the classroom activity? How do teachers differentiate their teaching to try to ensure all their pupils are achieving their best?

Collaborative planning and working as part of a team

While, as a classroom teacher, you have specific responsibility for the learning of the pupils that you are teaching, there are a number of ways in which you can be involved in collaborative planning and working as part of a team. For example, you may share responsibility for a class with another trainee teacher and/or you might be involved in planning at a departmental or cross-curricular level, or you may plan work for specific pupils in collaboration with a learning support assistant. John (2006) suggests that joint planning can help you, as a beginning teacher, to gain access to the expert knowledge of experienced teachers. Research by Matthews *et al*. (2009) reports beginning teachers (who have experienced planning lessons as part of a group) saying that, 'Collaboration is very helpful. People see different things in different ways and [this] can help give another way a student might perceive something' (p. 508).

   One form of collaborative planning that you may experience is some form of 'lesson study', an idea inspired by practice in countries like Japan. In general, 'lesson study' consists of a highly structured process of teacher collaboration, involving lesson planning, observation, reflection and further planning. Interestingly, 'lesson study' is not primarily aimed at producing a set of tried-and-tested lesson plans. Rather, it is more concerned with the professional development potential of involving teachers in the collaborative process of planning, teaching, observing, discussing and reflecting upon their lessons. For more on 'lesson study', see, for example, Isoda *et al*. (2007).

   When working with another adult in the classroom, such as a teaching assistant, the ways of working can be open to some negotiation or can be quite clearly prescribed – the latter is often particularly true for assistants working with pupils with identified special educational needs (SEN), especially if the pupils are 'statemented' (see Chapter 10). It is good practice to try to liaise in advance with such an assistant in order to help ensure lesson planning is consistent and makes best use of her/his presence in the classroom.

Task 5.13 **Planning as part of a team**

Find out about the best ways of planning when you have other adults in a class you are teaching. How might you involve them in your planning or brief them about what you plan to do in a lesson? How can your planning make sure that they are clear about their role in the lesson? How might you learn from their expertise?

PLANNING FOR OUT-OF-SCHOOL LEARNING

When planned appropriately, homework experiences may provide a valuable supplement to classroom activities (Sharp *et al.*, 2001). For example, you can use homework to reinforce and consolidate classroom learning or to gather information that you will then use in classroom activities. Homework is one way in which parents come to know about what their child does in your lessons. Among the things you can investigate are the use of home–school contracts and how mathematics departments, in particular, and schools, more generally, involve parents in supporting pupil learning.

One particular issue to consider in your planning is whether you can use homework as an opportunity to practise mathematical skills or for widening the perceptions of mathematics – or perhaps you can aim to do both over time.

Planning for other out-of-school learning

Valuable pupil learning can take place in a wide range of out-of-school contexts. Such opportunities are known to have positive effects on the achievement of lower-achieving pupils in mathematics (Masingila and de Silva, 2001). Such out-of-school learning can involve liasing with pupils' learning mentors and seeking the assistance of various educational partners such as museums, hands-on science centres, galleries, libraries, sports clubs, theatres etc.

Task 5.14 **Planning for out-of-school learning**

Find out about what is involved in planning for out-of-school learning. For example, what are some good ways of using homework, either to consolidate classroom learning or to gather information that you will then use in the classroom? What are the benefits of home–school contracts and how might you involve parents in supporting pupil learning?

What are some other ways in which you can plan for pupils to learn in out-of-school contexts?

SUMMARY AND KEY POINTS

Your success in teaching depends, crucially, on the effectiveness of your planning and how well you put your plans into action. Your planning needs to be explicit and detailed, particularly in the early stages of taking over classes. This takes good organisation and time. Developing a range of lesson structures and matching these to what you want to achieve in your lessons is vital. It is wise to invest some time in getting to know the structure of the curriculum and the departmental scheme of work so that you can begin to work creatively within local and national frameworks. It also pays to practise your presentation skills, both verbal and non-verbal. If you plan to use ICT, you can make sure that the software you plan to use works in the classroom and you can practise using and writing on whiteboards and interactive whiteboards (see also Chapter 9). Getting to know what your classes can do and what motivates them is a good idea, as is building up a collection of tried-and-tested classroom tasks that you are confident can engage the attention of pupils. Review and evaluate your work and both seek out, and act on, advice. Always expect a high standard of work.

Successful planning entails preparing a rich mathematical diet for your pupils. Your efforts will be rewarded with the quality of pupil learning you engender.

ESSENTIAL DOCUMENTS

Framework for Secondary Mathematics:
> http://nationalstrategies.standards.dcsf.gov.uk/secondary/secondaryframeworks/mathematics framework

Planning Using the Framework for Secondary Mathematics:
> http://nationalstrategies.standards.dcsf.gov.uk/node/16072

Secondary Mathematics Planning Toolkit:
> http://nationalstrategies.standards.dcsf.gov.uk/node/175489

FURTHER READING

General guides to lesson planning

Butt, G. (2008) *Lesson Planning,* 3rd edn. London: Continuum.

Haynes, A. (2007) *100 Ideas for Lesson Planning.* London: Continuum.

John, P. (1993) *Lesson Planning for Teachers.* London: Cassell.
> Though the last title is out of print (and hence may only be available through a library), these practical guides to the general issues involved in planning lessons contain a range of useful ideas.

Guides to presenting and presentation software

Finkelstein, E. and Samsonov, P. (2007) *PowerPoint for Teachers: Dynamic Presentations and Interactive Classroom Projects.* San Francisco, CA: Jossey Bass.

Gage, J. (2005) *How to Use an Interactive Whiteboard Really Effectively in Your Secondary Classroom.* London: David Fulton.

Harris, J. (1995) *Presentation Skills for Teachers.* London: Routledge.
> These practical guides contain a range of useful ideas about presenting lessons and using presentation software and equipment (note that the last title, though dated, remains in print and is still useful).

Guides to aspects of mathematics teaching

Foster, C. (2008) *Variety in Mathematics Lessons*. Derby: Association of Teachers of Mathematics.

Gammon, A. (2002) *Key Stage 3 Mathematics: A Guide for Teachers*. London: Beam.

Oldknow, A., Taylor, R. and Tetlow, L. (2010) *Teaching Mathematics Using ICT*, 3rd edn. London: Continuum.

Prestage, S. and Perks, P. (2001) *Adapting and Extending Secondary Mathematics Activities*. London: David Fulton.

All these books provide examples and guidance on aspects of mathematics teaching that can inform lesson planning.

Guides to planning for assessment in mathematics

French, D. (2006) *Resource Pack for Assessment for Learning in Mathematics*. Leicester: The Mathematical Association.

Hodgen, J. and Wiliam, D. (2006) *Mathematics: Inside the Black Box*. Slough: NFER-Nelson.

These practical guides provide a range of useful ideas to inform how you might plan for assessment in mathematics.

6 ASSESSMENT FOR LEARNING

Clare Lee

INTRODUCTION

I start this chapter by considering what I mean when using the phrase Assessment for Learning. The definition that I prefer is the one used by the King's Medway Oxfordshire Formative Assessment Project Team in 2003:

> Assessment for Learning is any assessment for which the first priority in its design is to serve the purpose of promoting pupils' learning. It thus differs from assessment designed to primarily serve the purposes of accountability, or of ranking or of certifying competence. An assessment activity can help learning if it provides information to be used as feedback, by teachers, and by their students in assessing themselves, to modify the teaching and learning activities in which they are engaged. Such assessment becomes 'formative assessment' when the evidence is actually used to adapt the teaching work to meet learning needs.
>
> (Black *et al.*, 2003: 1)

Assessment for Learning (AfL) can encompass tests and quizzes in class, but also homework, questions, activities and presentations – in fact, anything that will reveal to teachers, and preferably to the pupils themselves, how well the pupils are learning. Observation of the pupils working will be an important assessment tool, as will carefully designed questions and tasks that reveal the extent of the pupils' understanding. As the definition says, both the 'design' and 'purpose' are important. Are you asking ten quick questions to explore facets of the pupils' understanding of a topic? That can be Assessment for Learning. Are you asking ten quick questions to wake the class up and get their brains working? Although this can still be a valuable exercise, this is unlikely to give rise to Assessment for Learning. Its *purpose* is different.

You may have noticed that I have said, 'this can be AfL' and, 'this is unlikely to be AfL' rather than definitively this 'is' or 'is not'. I have done this because there is a further criterion to consider before a decision can be made about whether an assessment opportunity is Assessment for Learning or not. It is only when the information gained is actually used by either the teacher or the pupils themselves 'to modify the teaching and learning activities in which they are engaged' that the assessment opportunity becomes Assessment for Learning. It is only when action is taken to remedy any lack of understanding or to meet the pupils' learning needs that the questions can generate Assessment for Learning.

OBJECTIVES

By the end of this chapter you should:

- ■ understand the terms *Assessment for Learning*, *formative assessment* and *summative assessment*;
- ■ be able to articulate when and how an assessment opportunity can be seen as formative;
- ■ be aware of the roles of learning intentions, success criteria, feedback, questioning and peer and self-assessment in formative assessment;
- ■ be able to incorporate Assessment for Learning effectively into your mathematics lessons.

The terms 'Assessment for Learning' and 'formative assessment' are frequently used interchangeably and often there is no actual difference. However, formative assessment is a more precise term, indicating that the assessment is to be used to 'form' or add to a person's current understanding. It is often used in contrast to 'summative assessment', which is assessment used to 'sum up' an episode of learning, or to rank or certify a person's attainment. I have seen the term 'Assessment for Learning' used to mean several things that are not formative, such as the progress checks that are often made at school. Filling in grades on a sheet and checking to see that the grades are higher than they were last time, or not, may serve to ascertain whether the pupils' overall experience has allowed them to make progress.

However, filling in these grade sheets is not, in itself, formative assessment. Progress checks only have an indirect effect on the pupils' learning. They may indicate that something is amiss but not *what* is amiss or *how* to remedy any revealed problem.

With formative assessment, the teacher and the pupil use assessment to indicate where there are learning needs and then the teacher's expertise is drawn on to provide ways for the pupil to go about advancing his or her learning. There is a necessary immediacy about this activity which will normally include involving the pupils themselves. In some ways, it would be easier to use the term 'formative assessment' solely for the concept that I am discussing in this chapter. However, that would be disingenuous, when the term 'Assessment for Learning' is used so widely in education. Consequently, when I use 'Assessment for Learning', I do so to mean formative assessment only.

A requirement of Assessment for Learning is an acknowledgment that the pupils are the ones that have to do the learning; the teacher cannot learn for them. Pupils who know what they are learning and what is needed for a successful outcome will be more involved in the whole process and can begin to be able to take appropriate responsibility. In Assessment for Learning, the pupils themselves often make decisions, guided by their teacher, about how the learning process will proceed. This makes Assessment for Learning complicated because it involves:

- ■ a dialogue between at least two people – a learner and the person who is guiding his or her learning;
- ■ a clarification of where the learner currently is in the learning process and where they want to be, often called 'the gap' (Sadler, 1989);

■ the person guiding the learning knowing how the learner might go about closing that gap;

■ communicating that knowledge to the learner, so that learners can act to close the gap themselves.

Assessment for Learning has been shown to have a significant effect on pupil results (Black *et al.*, 2003), not only because it demands that pupils take responsibility for their own learning, but also because it supports them in taking on this responsibility. It requires teachers to use their professionalism to synchronise more closely the learning tasks offered with the learning needs of the pupils and, additionally, it requires that pupils and teachers work together to facilitate the best learning outcome possible. Assessment for Learning not only increases attainment, but it also educates pupils to be good learners, a skill they will need throughout their lives.

> 'It's much more extending this idea of them telling me what they need to learn [...] I think it helps that you are not telling them what you think they got wrong and they need to go over; they are telling you what things they can't do. I no longer have to guess.'
>
> (Ceri, Two Bishops School) (in Black *et al.*, 2003: 82)

> 'The influence has shifted from "What am I going to teach and what are the pupils going to do?" to "What are the pupils going to learn and how am I going to help them do that?"'
>
> (Susan, Waterford School) (in Black *et al.*, 2002: 19)

There are four main areas to think about when discussing Assessment for Learning:

■ learning intentions and success criteria;
■ feedback;
■ questioning;
■ peer and self-assessment.

I will deal with each of these areas separately in the next four sections, but it is impor- tant to realise at the outset that each of these areas intertwines with the others to enable pupils to learn mathematics effectively.

LEARNING INTENTIONS AND SUCCESS CRITERIA (LISC)

> Pupils do not know how to take control of their own learning and have to be taught to learn [...] They do not know how to extract from everything they do that which they are supposed to know and understand. We, at least I, have never disentangled all this for the pupils. Most of them learn by experience something of what is required of them. For many pupils, this experience is hard and dispiriting. Some of them, usually the weakest, never do learn.
>
> (Fairbrother, 1995: 110–11)

I am using the phrase 'learning intention', which was used by Clarke (e.g. 2005), rather than other phrases that are common in school (e.g. 'learning objective'), because lessons start with the intention that the pupils will learn what the teacher has planned, but the learning tasks may reveal that the pupils need to learn something else, either the basis of the ideas themselves or something more challenging. The term 'learning intention' indicates that teachers should not be constrained but should help their pupils learn what they need to learn. The idea behind using learning intentions and success criteria (LISC) is to begin to untangle for the pupils what they are supposed to learn from what they are supposed to do in order to learn what they are supposed to. Therefore learning intentions should be about learning, not about what the pupils are supposed to do.

Experience has shown me that using learning intentions and success criteria is quite hard for mathematics teachers for several reasons. For example:

▨ Many mathematics teachers tend to teach disconnected procedures; for example, how to solve quadratic equations, how to subtract two-digit numbers. Therefore what the pupils are 'learning' and what they are 'doing' feels like it is one and the same thing. This can be resolved by using something like 'how quadratic equations work' or 'what quadratics do and what they don't do' as a learning intention. Then the success criteria for a given lesson would include the processes involved in becoming fluent at solving quadratic equations. Such learning intentions also provide scope to explore quadratics and to allow and encourage pupils to understand what they are doing when they go through the complicated processes involved in solving quadratics.

▨ When pupils are presented with a problem to solve or investigate, setting out specific learning intentions can constrain the lesson. What if you intend your pupils to learn about the angles in triangles and they notice a relationship between the lengths of lines in right-angled triangles. Are you going to say that they have failed to achieve the learning intention? More than this, if you state at the start that you want the pupils to use a dynamic geometry programme to learn that there is a relationship between the angles in a triangle, will that constrain them from looking for other relationships? It is possible, therefore, to say to the pupils on occasion that you do have learning intentions for this lesson and they should think about what they are and that the discussion at the end of the lesson will be about what they were.

Learning intentions and success criteria (LISC) must work together:

▨ to make clear what is important to know and what is part of the learning process;
▨ to enable the pupils to be able to talk about what exactly they are learning and how they are learning it;
▨ to indicate the *quality* of work that is to be produced;
▨ to open up and clarify the learning, not constrain it.

Framing learning intentions

Learning intentions can feel hard to phrase; they will not be the same as teaching objectives from a scheme of work which are normally directed at teachers. Learning intentions will grow out of teaching objectives, but they will be framed specifically for the pupils. Learning intentions can be the same over a series of lessons, because that may be how long it takes to learn as much as is appropriate about the concepts. It is also appropriate that learning intentions might be similar in Year 7 and Year 8 or even Year 11; for example, when do we stop learning about drawing graphs? However, it would not be appropriate if the success criteria for this learning intention were the same for each of those year groups. The success criteria explain exactly what we are supposed to be learning about graphing *today*.

Learning intentions could be framed as:

By the end of this lesson you will:

- know that ... (*knowledge*)
  e.g. Know that $a^2 + b^2 = c^2$, know how to multiply fractions and why, know more about the properties of quadrilaterals
- develop/be able to ... (*skills*)
  e.g. develop your skill in using Pythagoras's theorem, be able to draw a graph for any linear equation, be able to represent data accurately in various charts, develop your ability to interpret graphical representations
- understand how/why ... (*understanding*)
  e.g. understand how to use Pythagoras's theorem in 3D. Understand more about linear graphs, including why if a linear graph goes through the origin then the constant term of the corresponding linear equation has to be zero; understand how rationalising surds works to clear roots from the denominator
- develop/become aware of ... (*attitudes and values*)
  e.g. become aware of the reasons you might use one measure of average rather than another, develop an awareness of what you can do when you get stuck on a problem, become aware of ways that data can be misused, become aware of what you are calculating when you integrate.

Task 6.1 **Framing learning intentions**

Take some time now to use the sentence starters above to frame learning intentions in your journal for at least two lessons, either lessons that you have seen taught recently or that you will teach soon. Frame these learning intentions to enable the pupils to know what they will *learn* in those lessons rather than what they will *do*.

Framing success criteria

Success criteria are sometimes called learning outcomes; they are intended to guide pupils and to help them know that they have made specific progress with their learning. In mathematics, there are several ways that success criteria can be stated in order to fulfil these purposes:

1   Success criteria can lay out the route for going through a mathematical process or method successfully. By setting out criteria in this way, pupils are introduced to the language they may need to ask for help if they get stuck, to talk themselves through any difficulties they encounter (either in this lesson or subsequent ones) or to help one another in the lesson. Success criteria written in this way could, for example, be:

Remember to:

- use a pencil and a ruler;
- label your axes carefully allowing equal spaces between the numbers;

  ▪ create a table to put your values of x in and work out the corresponding value
      of y;
  ▪ use a spread of values for x;
  ▪ plot the points on the grid and draw in the graph using a ruler – extend your
      line beyond the plotted points.

2 Success criteria for the process of learning can guide the pupils through the various
   stages of the lesson, enabling them to: assess for themselves the stage they are at;
   time themselves to reach as far as they can; challenge themselves to go through all
   the stages; and at all times help them to know where they are and where to go next.
   Success criteria set out in this way may be the most frequently used in mathematics. They could be:

   In this lesson, you will:

   ▪ draw three of the graphs whose equations are given on the right-hand side of
       the whiteboard on the same set of axes using *Autograph*;
   ▪ state what effect the number multiplying the x has on the graph;
   ▪ draw three of the graphs given on the left-hand side of the whiteboard on one
       new set of axes;
   ▪ state what effect the number at the end of the equation has on the graph;
   ▪ write a set of three linear equations that all go through the same point on the
       y-axis but have different gradients and then check that they do;
   ▪ draw two different straight-line graphs that go through a point that you have
       chosen and state their equations. Check your work with a friend.

3 Assessment criteria – sometimes success criteria will indicate how a piece of work
   will be assessed and therefore could be better termed 'assessment criteria'. This is
   likely to happen when pupils are set a longer piece to complete. For example: research
   the contribution women have made to the development of mathematical ideas; investigate 'growing cubes'; find the best mobile phone tariff for your needs; complete an
   examination paper. The success or assessment criteria will unpick the various stages
   that the pupils will go through in completing their assigned task and give details of
   what an assessor is looking for. In all of the above examples, an understanding of the
   assessment criteria will help the pupils know what to include and what not to include,
   give them an idea of the number of examples needed or the areas of mathematics that
   they might look at and how the results of their thinking, reasoning and exploration
   should be reported. In that sense, once again, the success criteria will guide their learning. In many of the above examples, the success criteria can be gathered from the
   pupils. Teachers could ask: 'What would constitute a reasonable number of women to
   investigate and why?'; 'Is it OK to print off what a website says and just include it?';
   'What is OK then?' and quickly get a list of what the pupils should do to answer the
   task brief. This list of success criteria can be used by the pupils to assess their work as
   they progress through the stages of completing their task.

There will be many variations on these basic forms of success criteria and, as with everything else to do with Assessment for Learning, it is the principle and purposes behind the
way a teacher acts that are important. Success criteria should be designed to help pupils
understand what they have to do in order to make progress with the learning intention.

The criteria are there to guide pupils through the lesson, to help them know where they are and what to do next, and to enable the pupils to see themselves as successful learners. If the criteria that are set out fulfil these principles, then they are good success criteria whatever they look like. Success criteria will also help pupils know what is expected of them and enable them to act more independently during lessons. Pupils can be involved to the extent that they set out the success criteria for themselves. Once the pupils have become used to the ideas of using success criteria, it is often useful to have a class discussion that results in 'our success criteria for today'. If the outcome of today's lesson is to be a poster describing the properties of different quadrilaterals, then asking the class to set out the criteria for a 'good poster' can quickly get over problems such as not everyone contributing or a well-coloured title but no content. If they tell you what they are going to do, they are more likely to get involved and do a good job.

Different pupils can also negotiate different success criteria. The pupils who say, 'We really like this, can we go on further with it?' can record what will count as success for them. Those pupils who have not yet met an idea in the detail that others have, could negotiate further practice or more exploration of the ideas behind the concept and rephrase their success criteria accordingly.

■ **Table 6.1** Common myths about learning intentions and success criteria (LISC)

Myth	Comment
They must be written in the pupils' books.	If the pupils are to know what they are learning and to use success criteria to guide their learning, they must be able to see them. Sometimes they will be written on the board at the front of the class, sometimes a few copies will be printed out, say one between four, and then put where they can be referred to. Occasionally, the pupils will write them down but this tends to waste time when pupils want to get on with an exciting lesson. Therefore, there must be a reason that they write the LISC down – e.g. that they are going outside and need them to refer to – but even then, a resourceful teacher might give them stickers containing the LISC to put in their books.
	If the learning intention and the success criteria are written on the front page of a PowerPoint presentation and flashed up but never seen again, they will not serve their purpose. The discussion during the lesson should be about how the pupils are getting on with meeting the success criteria and learning the learning intention; therefore, they should be where both the pupils and their teacher can see and refer to them, mentally or physically tick them off and use them to frame questions about understanding.
They can be taken from the scheme of work.	Clearly, there will be a link between the LISC used with a class and those in a scheme of work or teaching framework designed for teacher use; but they will not automatically be the same. LISC should be designed for a particular class and take account of the stages the pupils are at in their learning. In some schools, the emphasis is on 'covering' the curriculum and this can be at the expense of pupils understanding the ideas that they are trying to 'cover'. When a school focuses on 'coverage', then they may divide up the learning intentions and dictate which are to be taught in which week. However, if the school places understanding above 'coverage', then the LISC will be very different from class to class and from year to year.

■ **Table 6.1** Common myths continued

Myth	Comment
They must be in 'pupil-friendly language'.	LISC are intended to be shared, understood and used by the pupils. Therefore, they are usually couched in pupil-friendly language. However, particularly in the later school years, it becomes important that the pupils understand the phraseology that is used to assess their competence as mathematicians. Therefore success criteria are sometimes offered in 'exam-board' language and the lesson is about helping pupils understand what the words and phrases mean in relation to the way that they must demonstrate their learning.
	Often, LISC will use unfamiliar words and phrases because the way that mathematics is expressed has to be learned alongside the concepts that the words encapsulate. The golden rule here is that the learners can use the language themselves to express their mathematical ideas and LISC often provide a model to help the pupils articulate what they know. (See Chapter 8 on aspects of mathematical language.)
They must always be about mathematics.	LISC must be about what the pupils need to learn in a mathematics lesson and how they will show that they have been successful at learning it. There are many recent publications (e.g. Standards Unit, 2005) that emphasise the value of working collaboratively in mathematics lessons. Sometimes, you will have to help pupils learn how to work collaboratively or how you want class discussion to work or how to explore some mathematical environment that you have provided. Therefore, sometimes, the learning intentions will be about learning to use classroom tools rather than about mathematics itself.
They must take just one lesson to complete.	Learning intentions will almost always take more than one lesson to complete and often a series of lessons. Each lesson will tend to have different success criteria, but often they will run from lesson to lesson. The criteria that the class did not get to in one lesson may become the starter for the next lesson; or the criteria that the teacher had planned for the next lesson may be used in this one, because of the particular trajectory the learning takes.
	Therefore it is a good idea to plan both where you think the class will start with a learning intention and the associated success criteria, but then think both backwards (what might need to precede this piece of learning?) and forwards (where will the learning go next?) so that you can support and challenge your learners.

■ **Table 6.1** Common myths continued

Myth	Comment
They should contain the level that the work is at in the National Curriculum.	The National Curriculum is statutory up to age 16 in state schools in England and, therefore, when teaching in an English school, a teacher will need to know where a learning intention fits into the levels associated with the National Curriculum and to choose a learning intention at a suitably challenging level for their class. Therefore, the levels of the National Curriculum will be taken into account when setting the learning intentions for a lesson. That, however, is where a teacher's statutory duty ends. There is reason to believe that discussion of NC levels with pupils can be detrimental to good learning; this belief will be discussed in detail later in this chapter. Although adding a number to a learning intention is unlikely to have any great impact, it could get in the way of discussing the detail of where pupils are in their learning and how they are going to improve.
	The NC levels have been designed so that an average pupil will take about 18 months to complete one level. This makes statements such as 'if you just do this, you will be working at the next level' quite hard to understand. Is the change of level permanent? Is this the last piece of the jigsaw that needed to be put in place, so that the pupil is now at the next level? Does it matter that tomorrow the pupil goes 'down' a level because they have not yet experienced the next idea at the level at which they are working today? Teenagers are unlikely to understand the complex answers to these questions and therefore will either be confused or daunted by references to levels or ignore them completely. I would not advocate that a teacher does something that confuses or demoralises pupils or that the pupils need to ignore.
They must be stated at the start of the lesson and referred to at the end.	As I have said above, there is a golden rule that every lesson has a learning intention; after all, why would you plan a lesson that the pupils will not learn from? However, there is no corresponding golden rule that you have to state it at the outset of the lesson. Because of the nature of mathematics, you may set out to explore a situation and only know what you have learned from it after some concentrated work. In these cases, the learning may not be known until the end of the lesson.
	Similarly, it is important not to wait until the end of the lesson to discuss how the pupils are getting on with completing the success criteria. Mini plenaries throughout the lesson are one way to find out if some pupils need more input or if they are racing through the work and are about to test your ingenuity in coming up with what to do next. Such mini plenaries provide an opportunity for the pupils to talk about their ideas, to model good practice and to consolidate ideas for others. They entail that the language of mathematics is used by the pupils themselves, giving them a tool to control the ideas now and to conjure the ideas later.
	So although in most lessons the learning intentions will be discussed at the start, during the lesson and at the end, this will not always be the case. Equally, although normally you will want to know how far the pupils progressed with the success criteria during the lesson by discussing them at the end, if this is the only time they are discussed they are not being used as effectively as they might be.

Task 6.2 **Putting together learning intentions and success criteria**

Devise success criteria for the learning intentions that you framed in Task 6.1.

Consider whether your success criteria focus on the process of using a mathematical method or the process of learning in these two lessons.

Now consider and make notes on how you would ensure that your pupils understand and make use of your success criteria to help them monitor their own work in these two lessons.

FEEDBACK

Feedback is an essential component of Assessment for Learning. When information is revealed through an assessment opportunity, it is feedback that enables the learner to align their learning effort more productively. Feedback happens in several ways. For example:

▨ teachers give feedback through marking books;
▨ teachers give feedback orally;
▨ pupils give feedback to one another by means of peer assessment;
▨ pupils get feedback for themselves by comparing their work with success criteria;
▨ pupils gain feedback on their work when assessing others' work.

However, feedback is not the same as formative assessment, although it is a first step. Only when the information that the learner gains through feedback is used to improve learning can the feedback be said to be formative. Feedback that cannot be used by pupils in improving their performance is not formative. This has implications both for the qualities of the feedback itself and for the timing of that feedback. Formative feedback must be phrased in such a way that learners can use it to improve their learning, and it must be given at a time when pupils can use it. Therefore, the common practice of marking at the end of a learning episode does not enable formative feedback to be given to pupils.

Many of the important qualities of effective feedback can be gathered from research conducted by Kluger and DeNisi (1996). They reviewed many studies in both educational and workplace settings and found that, on average, feedback did improve performance. However, they also found significant differences among the studies. In about 40 per cent of the studies, the feedback given had a negative impact on performance. In these studies, the feedback that people were given made their performance worse than if they were given no feedback at all. The researchers found that feedback makes performance worse when it is focused on self-esteem or self-image, which is the case with both grades and praise. They found that using praise can increase motivation, but then it becomes necessary to use praise all the time. It is very difficult to maintain genuine and sincere praise at a sufficient level to maintain motivation over time; hence, the motivation engendered by praise alone will drop away. In contrast, feedback that is focused on what needs to be done to improve, and gives specific and achievable details about how to make that improvement, is clearly shown to improve performance.

Butler (1988) showed that certain ways of marking are significantly more likely to improve learning than others. She experimented with pupils from 12 classes in four schools. Each class received the same teaching, using the same aims by the same teachers, and they were given the same classwork. In addition, each class received one of the following types of feedback: grades, comments or grades and comments. The outcomes are shown in Table 6.2. A quick glance will show you that giving comments is by far the best way to boost performance. However, if that comment is given alongside a grade, level or other numerical or coded mark, the effect on performance of the comment will be negated. Perhaps even more persuasively, those pupils given grades in their feedback based their interest in the subject on the grade that they received. Those pupils who needed to work hardest to improve their work did not have the motivation to do so if they were given a grade. By contrast, those given comments all expressed an interest in continuing to work at the subject.

This research leads to the conclusion that grades and levels have no place in the learning environment. Grades and levels are designed for use in summative assessment, summing up a period of learning and what the learner has achieved. When they are used as part of the learning process, they cause pupils to lose focus on improving their learning because of their effect on self-esteem or self-image. This can also be true for high-achieving pupils who may become complacent. Why should they continue to work hard if they are already performing much better than their peers? If maximum learning is required, and it usually is in schools, then the focus should be on improving learning, and the distractions of grades or levels should be minimised.

■ **Table 6.2** Outcomes from feedback

Feedback received	Gain in learning	Interest in subject
Grades	None	Those with high grades – positive Those with low grades – negative
Comments	30 per cent	All pupils showed positive interest in subject.
Both grades and comments	None	Those with high grades – positive Those with low grades – negative

Source: Butler, 1988

Task 6.3 **Reflecting on feedback**

Think about some written feedback that you have been given on work that you have completed. Note in your journal the aspects of that feedback that were helpful to you. Consider also which aspects of that feedback you might have used to help improve your subsequent work. Now, before you read the next section, reflect and make notes on how you might change the written feedback that you give to your pupils to make it more effective in helping them to improve.

Now compare your notes with the ideas on the next page.

Effective feedback – that is feedback that will enable pupils to continue to improve their learning – should:

▪ be focused on learning intentions not the pupil;
▪ be clear about what the pupil has achieved and what still needs further work to improve;
▪ be about the learning that should be going on, not only about presentation;
▪ ask for a response from the pupil;
▪ be phrased so that the pupil can understand how he/she should respond;
▪ be given at a time when the response from the pupil will help them improve their learning.

These principles are true whether the feedback is written or oral. Feedback given following these principles can be totally honest. These principles are not about bolstering fragile self-esteem but about building good work habits and they stem from a sincere belief that everyone can improve. Feedback given in this way treats everyone equally; everyone has to take the appropriate next step in their learning, starting from wherever they are at the present time. Everyone can take that next step; everyone can improve.

When you have written feedback in pupils' books or have spent time giving feedback orally, it is important that pupils act on the feedback given. The usual situation in schools seems to be that teachers spend a great deal of time writing in pupils' books and the pupils glance at it and then do nothing else with the feedback. This is tantamount to ignoring their teachers, and pupils should never be allowed to do that! When a teacher has spent, say, three minutes writing a comment in a pupil's book, the pupil should spend at least ten to 15 minutes responding to it; otherwise the balance of work is wrong. In order to establish this system, feedback must be given at a time when pupils can use it to improve their learning. Time in the lesson must be given over to reading the comments, asking questions about what they mean and, at the very least, starting to work on the improvement advice given.

QUESTIONING

Being able to ask good questions is a very important skill for teachers using Assessment for Learning. Questioning is the way teachers find out what their pupils know, what they do not know and to what extent they have understood. However, questions only result in high-quality information if they are good questions, and many questions that are asked in classrooms only reveal what pupils can quickly recall and do not explore understanding. Wragg and Brown (2001) found that, when asking questions, teachers commonly made the following errors. They:

▪ ask too many questions at once;
▪ ask a question and answer it themselves;
▪ ask questions only of the brightest or most likeable;
▪ ask a difficult question too early;
▪ ask irrelevant questions;
▪ always ask the same type of questions;
▪ ask questions in a threatening way;
▪ fail to indicate a change in the type of question;

- do not give pupils the time to think;
- do not correct wrong answers;
- ignore answers;
- fail to see the implications of answers;
- fail to build on answers.

■ **Table 6.3** Common myths about feedback

Myth	Comment
You have to give a level; Ofsted says so.	The Ofsted inspection framework indicates that inspectors should check that pupils know where they currently are in their learning and that they know how to improve. It does not say that pupils should know their 'level', although the phase has been interpreted to mean that. By all means use levels or grades to sum up episodes of learning, but grades and levels have been shown to be detrimental to the learning process and therefore it is inappropriate for them to be included during the learning process. Therefore, if teachers intend to give formative feedback that will help their pupils to improve their learning, they should not include either grades or levels.
It is impossible to give truly formative feedback; there simply isn't enough time in the week.	It is certainly time-consuming to give formative feedback. Therefore, it is important to consider when spending that time will be of most help to pupils. Some departments decide on certain key tasks that will receive formative feedback and space them out so that they do not all fall in one week. It is important that learners at all times know how well they are doing and whether they have got the right idea. This can be achieved by: • marking every three weeks, but doing it well when you do it; • marking routine work in class and only spending teacher time on key tasks that explore the learning that has been going on; • marking work with the pupil present and commenting orally; • using peer and self-assessment.
Praise is all that pupils need.	As has been stated above, praise can be counter-productive and, if praise is the only feedback that pupils receive, the feedback will not help them improve their learning. Pupils do need to know what they have done well, primarily because it would be a good idea for them to keep on doing those things. But the feedback that helps pupils improve is detailed advice on how to make that improvement.

Task 6.4 **Checking up on questioning**

Ask a sympathetic colleague to observe you teaching a mathematics lesson and record how often these 'errors' occur; alternatively make a video recording of yourself teaching and note for yourself how often these 'errors' occur. Reflect on your use of questioning in this lesson. How can you avoid making these errors?

Being aware of the possibility that teachers ignore answers, ask the same type of question, answer their own questions or fail to build on answers can help improve questioning sessions. However, possibly the most important 'error' in questioning is the failure to give pupils time to think.

Rowe (1974) analysed 300 tape recordings of teachers asking questions over a period of six years. She found that the mean wait time, which is the time between a teacher asking a question and expecting an answer, giving a clue or answering the question him- or herself was 0.9 seconds. If the wait time is less than a second, then pupils only have the time to react, they cannot consider, reason or think.

The teachers in this experiment were then trained so that they increased the wait time they left after asking a question to between three and five seconds. This increase resulted in:

▦   an increased length of pupil response;
▦   an increased number of unsolicited, but appropriate, replies;
▦   a decreased failure to respond;
▦   an increased confidence of response;
▦   an increase in the incidence of pupils comparing their answers to those from another pupil;
▦   the number of alternative explanations offered multiplying.

These are really important changes in pupil behaviour, obtained by giving the pupils time to think. However, there are other things to consider when providing the pupils with enough time to think. First and foremost, are the questions that are asked worth thinking about? In Assessment for Learning, the questions that teachers ask must be planned if they are to explore pupils' understanding and not just to ask for instant recall.

The classroom ethos must also encourage all pupils to respond and give answers that are long enough to reveal understanding, and to feel that it is appropriate to comment or build on one another's answers. There are two aspects to this: what the pupils do and what the teacher does. I will discuss these in turn.

What the pupils do

It is important during questioning sessions that all pupils are engaged in thinking about answering questions. There are a few approaches that can be used to help make sure this happens.

NO HANDS UP

When a question has been asked, it is common for pupils in classrooms across the world to put their hands up in order to volunteer an answer and it is also common for the teacher to ask a pupil who has not put her or his hand up. Neither of these practices is particularly helpful in developing a classroom ethos where pupils think and discuss answers until they understand. Once several hands have been raised, most pupils will think it is safe to stop thinking about the answer. It is also true to say that those pupils who raise their hands stop thinking about the question as well; they concentrate on remembering what they want to say rather than listening to others' answers and challenging their own conceptions. Hence, asking for 'hands up' limits thinking in the classroom. Asking a pupil who has not volunteered to answer is also detrimental to the ethos of sharing and discussion that best generates learning. They did not volunteer and, in their minds, they probably think they are being punished for not knowing the right answer.

By saying 'no hands up', you are signalling that everyone should be ready to express their thoughts and opinions, and that these will be treated as thoughts and opinions that can add to a growing understanding of a concept. An important part of the 'no hands up' contract is that answers that reveal misconceptions still allow for learning to be generated. It is also important that pupils listen to one another, so that they can think about and comment on one another's answers.

THINK, PAIR, SHARE

When a question has been asked that is worth thinking about, then the pupils will want time to think. Some of these questions will need more than 3–5 seconds of thinking time. A useful idea is to ask pupils to think about the questions on their own for a few seconds and then to discuss what they have thought about with the person sitting next to them. They should then be ready to share their ideas with the rest of the class. Teachers can use the 'pair-talk' time to 'eavesdrop' or assess what the pupils are thinking about, and think about how best to orchestrate the 'share' time to develop understanding.

'SHOW ME' BOARDS

Using mini-whiteboards is an important tool in asking the pupils to think, discuss, make mistakes and correct them. The pupils can quickly display answers to closed requests such as 'show me two fractions that add to one', 'now show me a different pair,' and so on, and help the teacher assess whether pupils can add fractions or perform other important mathematical skills (see Standards Unit, 2005, for more ideas). However, mini-whiteboards can also be used to record thinking, display ideas so far, make a spider-diagram of all the ideas that might help, and so on. By displaying these ideas they can be made public, and those ideas can be shared and used to help build everyone's understanding.

Teachers sometimes worry about pupils 'copying' answers when they use mini-whiteboards. If the pupils know that they will be asked to talk about what they have put on their whiteboard in order to add to the learning discussion, they will stop worrying about the 'right' answer and start recording what they really think. Hence, pupils will be likely to change what they have put on their whiteboards as they record what they learn during discussions, so that they end up with some useful ideas to use in subsequent learning activities. In such sessions, teachers are assessing whether the answers are building to a full understanding or whether they need to intervene to redirect the discussion. Pupils can assess their own understanding against what others are thinking and make changes for themselves. Consequently, Assessment for Learning is deeply embedded in effective questioning and discussion.

What the teacher does

Not surprisingly, what the teacher does during questioning sessions is very important. Teachers who are expert at conducting learning discussions think about where they position themselves, where the pupils are positioned and, very importantly, how they respond to the pupils.

WHERE THE TEACHER IS POSITIONED

Many teachers position themselves out of the direct eye-line of pupils during question-ing sessions. They may want the pupils to look at, think about or respond to a diagram or picture on the board, or what another pupil is saying. If the teacher is directly in the pupils' eye-line, the attention tends to be on the teacher, because that is what pupils are used to, rather than where the teacher wants it to be. I know experienced teachers who move to the back of the room so that the pupils have to talk to each other, and so that they, too, can listen to other pupils' ideas as well as consider the next learning experience they will provide. However, just moving well to the side will give a teacher a good view of what is actually going on in the class but still allow the pupils' attention to be where it should be.

WHERE THE PUPILS ARE POSITIONED

If a teacher wants pupils to talk and respond to one another, then it is a good idea if they can see and hear one another. Moving the desks into a 'U' shape can help make this possi-ble, as can actually moving the pupils to perch on desks during the discussion phase of a lesson. If a pupil is giving an answer, remember it is the other pupils who need to hear the answer so that they can respond to it, and not only the teacher. If a teacher has to 'echo' or 're-broadcast' the answer so that it becomes audible for the entire class, then the answer becomes the teacher's answer and takes on a different status. Teachers also often unconsciously rephrase the answer when they 'echo' it, making it a completely different answer. Effective discussion is best achieved when the pupils can easily see and hear one another so that the discussion moves naturally between those that have a point to make. The teacher then listens and assesses the understanding that is being built and intervenes only when their professional knowledge is needed.

HOW THE TEACHER RESPONDS TO THE PUPILS

In her research, Rowe (1974) found that if a teacher made sanctioning comments, or even rewarding comments such as 'well done', this negatively affected the verbal performance of the pupils even with lengthened wait times. It seems that if teachers want pupils to discuss, then they have to act as part of the discussion not as 'receiver and passer on' or as 'judge and evaluator' of the comments. It is important that the teacher models 'good' answers such as, 'I found ... interesting in your answer but I am not sure about ... could you explain more?' (Or, 'Does anyone else have something to add that might help?'). This is quite different from saying 'good' or 'interesting'. Listening and responding to answers shows how much value is placed on pupils' answers, and this is an effective reward. Task persistence will be greatest where verbal rewards are fewer, but that is not to say absent.

PEER AND SELF-ASSESSMENT

Being able to assess the areas that someone is able to do well honestly, those where more work is needed, and to have strategies to improve what needs to be improved is one of the most useful skills that we can offer pupils. In an age where lifelong learning seems to be becoming the norm, learning to self-assess effectively at school will enable today's

■ **Table 6.4** Common myths about questioning

Myth	Comment
Questioning can give you information about what all pupils understand.	Effective questioning will give you a good idea about what the pupils in your class understand and what they do not. It is true that, if one person in your class reveals a misconception, it is quite likely that others have that same misconception as well, so it is worth paying attention to it. However, if questioning is the only way that teachers assess the understanding of their class, then it is likely that some pupils will be missed, and that is particularly true if short, quiz-type questions are used with mini-whiteboards. Questioning is a vital skill for teachers and reveals all sorts of ideas that they will need to use their professionalism to address. But sometimes a response from the whole class will be needed in order to be sure that every pupil's learning is moving forward well.
It is important that the teacher comments on all answers.	It is important that correct ideas are acknowledged and wrong answers are corrected, and it is the teacher's role to monitor that this is done – but not necessarily always to do it him- or herself. Part of Assessment for Learning is enabling pupils to become independent learners. If the teacher always takes the role of judging whether answers are right or wrong, then he or she is not teaching pupils how they can find that out for themselves, nor teaching pupils to become self-reliant and to evaluate whether they are being successful thinkers and learners.
If an answer is wrong, this should be glossed over.	I do not think I have ever heard this myth actually articulated, but I have seen it occur in many lessons and it does seem to be what many teachers believe. Teachers seem to hear the right answer and 'miss' the wrong ones. Teachers take an answer and echo it, but the answer they repeat 'magically' becomes correct. Wrong answers are inherently interesting; giving a wrong answer is a learning opportunity and therefore nothing to be ashamed of. If a pupil gives a wrong answer, then a teacher might say something like, 'let's explore that'. Misconceptions must not be ignored, but rather thought about and explored so that the pupils understand all the ideas and are able to build their learning further.
If I keep going, I will get the right answer.	Some teachers seem to keep asking questions and giving clues until they get the right answer. This is sometimes called 'fishing' for the answers. This can be detrimental in that it indicates that there is one right answer and that is the one in a teacher's head. The answers may indicate a lack of understanding or the pupils may not know how to express the ideas that they have in the way that is wanted by the teacher. Either way, if the answer required is not given fairly quickly, a modification in the lesson is needed. The pupils could do some research or the teacher could make some links or connections for the pupils, but definitely no more fishing!

teenagers to be effective and successful learners in the future. The evidence shows that pupils learn to assess themselves by engaging in peer assessment.

The power of self-assessment in mathematics is demonstrated by some research conducted by Fontana and Fernandes (1994). Twenty-five Portuguese teachers took part in a 20-week training course in using self-assessment. Their classes formed the experimental group. There were eight- and nine-year-old pupils, and 11- to 14-year-old pupils in the project. They used a pre-test, post-test design with control groups. Over the duration of the project, the teachers helped their classes to understand the learning intentions that they used and the criteria that would be employed to assess their work. Their pupils were given the opportunity to choose their learning tasks based on their assessment of their own needs. The tasks that the pupils used to learn from always gave the pupils scope to assess the outcomes of their learning activity. The younger experimental groups showed *twice* the learning gain of the control group. The researchers believe that the older group showed similar gains, but the post-test was not challenging enough for these pupils to show how well they could do.

There are several points that this piece of research raises, apart from how well pupils can achieve when they are actively involved in their own learning. The first I would like to raise is that becoming good at self-assessment does not happen overnight. Both teachers and pupils in the research needed time to become used to this way of working. The teachers needed to work out how best to organise the class; the pupils needed to be trained in how to use assessment criteria to assess effectively, to be able to recognise what they had done well and to be able to assess what they needed to do next in order to continue to learn. A further point is that once these pupils had discovered for themselves what they needed to do, they had a choice of tasks that would help them improve their learning. Following an assessment, the learning activity changed and the pupils themselves were actively involved in decisions about those changes.

Task 6.5 **Reviewing research on peer and self-assessment**

Review the points outlined above that were raised by research about peer and self-assessment. Make a note of these in your journal.

Find another piece of research on peer and self-assessment and consider whether the same points were raised. You could use, for example: http://www.ltscotland.org.uk/assess/sharingpractice/as/selfpeer/barrheadasg.asp. Again make notes in your journal.

Which of the ideas raised do you consider the most important when thinking about this type of assessment, and why? Which convinces you that it is important to help pupils use peer and self-assessment, and why? Which would be the hardest aspect of research to put into practice, and why?

Note in your journal the arguments that convince you of the importance of using peer and self-assessment and think about the reasons for these.

Peer assessment helps pupils learn because they assess work of the same type and addressed to the same task as their own, and, therefore, in their exploration of others' work, pupils will encounter different ways of tackling the same tasks, thereby extending their own repertoire of ways to proceed. Certainly, the work that they assess will contain a wide range of imperfections and misconceptions, but when pupils try to explain why they consider that the work has met some criteria but not others, they can become more conscious of what they are trying to understand and achieve for themselves. Therefore peer assessment may help in the learning of new and more efficient strategies to tackle tasks. When a cooperative environment is established, peer assessment can help pupils to achieve an objectivity that they can use in their own work and, therefore, it helps to develop the essential skills of self-assessment. It is easier to develop this objectivity with work to which you are less emotionally tied.

Do not assume that peer and self-assessment has to take a large amount of time out of lessons. Many teachers find that, by using quick peer or self-assessment approaches frequently, their pupils develop those skills most effectively. If you are using well-thought-out success criteria, then every mini plenary during a lesson will involve reflection on those criteria and how well the pupils are succeeding with them – in other words, peer or self-assessment. If, after each reflective assessment, the pupils' next learning activity is changed in some way as a result of what the teacher and the pupils have found out, then this is Assessment for Learning embedded in the lesson and the pupils will progress well.

Peer and self-assessment approaches include the following:

- Peer assessing short pieces of work, e.g. homework, against their associated success criteria and deciding on the next task as a result of the advice given.
- Using traffic lights (green means 'I understand', amber means 'I am not quite sure', red means 'I do not understand') frequently during a lesson, so that the work can be changed if the class 'starts to go a bit red'.
- Looking at, assessing and commenting on the quality of a piece of work that could come from a previous year or be another class member's work. This is about coming to an understanding of exactly what the success criteria mean. For example, what does it mean to give examples? As many as possible or a few well chosen ones? What does systematic exploration mean?
- Involving the pupils in setting criteria for the learning intention and using those criteria to assess it. This works well once pupils are used to using criteria and have been shown examples.
- Marking work in groups. The teacher provides a set of model answers and the pupils look at their own answers and consider: where they are correct and have used the same process, where they have used another way to get the answer that is also correct, where they have gone wrong, and where or why they were just lucky and got the answer right. This works very well with older pupils when they are tackling complex problems.

Peer assessment is important but there are many things to put in place first. The pupils need to become used to the idea of using success criteria to guide their work before they can use them to assess one another's work. They also need to know that the more they are involved in the process of learning, the better they will achieve. This is completely new to some pupils, who are so used to the teacher telling them what to do, and when, that they seem to think that the teacher can do the learning for them. By using the principles of effective feedback discussed earlier, pupils can become convinced that they have to consider success criteria and use them to guide their work. The teacher will comment on how well they have achieved against those criteria and they will be required to improve on any that need it. Pupils can then be slowly introduced to the idea that they have to take responsibility for informing the teacher of any difficulties they have, but they also have to work hard themselves to overcome those difficulties. This will take time with most groups, but it is time well spent. Remember, they are being taught skills that will be important to them throughout their lives.

▪ **Table 6.5** Common myths about peer and self-assessment

Myth	Comment
Peer and self-assessment only works with high-ability groups.	In my experience, good learners, who tend to be in higher sets, easily recognise how helpful peer and self-assessment can be in their learning and take to it 'like a duck to water'. Lower sets do find the skills of peer and self-assessment harder to learn. This is because the pupils in lower sets have rarely developed the learning skills that those in higher sets already possess. Therefore, they have more to learn in order to be able to benefit from peer and self-assessment. Research (e.g. Fredikson and White, 1997) shows that where teachers take the trouble to teach the skills of peer and self-assessment to their pupils, the attainment of pupils who previously found learning difficult is significantly improved, with some out-performing previously high-attaining pupils.
Self-assessment is writing the answers on the board or reading them out.	Although pupils' marking their own work is self-assessment, it is not formative assessment. Assessment for Learning requires that the pupils think about what they have done well, have strategies to improve areas that they do not understand and implement those strategies. Putting a tick against one answer and a cross against another or, more likely, replacing the wrong answer with the right one, is therefore not Assessment for Learning. It is possible to enhance these actions into Assessment for Learning: for example, by reading out the answers two-thirds of the way through the lesson and then asking what issues or problems pupils found with answering the questions. The rest of the lesson would then be spent finding ways to overcome those issues. If we are serious about improving learning, it is not the answers that were correct that we are interested in; it is where the problems are and how pupils can improve their understanding.
Pupils do not like to use peer assessment.	When I ask pupils in school whether they find peer assessment useful, I get mixed results. Some say that it is very useful to get advice from their peers and that often they can understand it more easily because the language used is at their level. Other pupils say that they do not 'like' it and that, if the person does not like you, then they will give you a bad 'mark', and anyway it is the teacher's job to mark their work as she or he is the only one who really knows. On further exploration, I usually find that those who 'don't like it' are being asked to peer assess at the end of a piece of work, where the assessment is summative and not formative. They have to mark a piece of work, add comments and then nothing happens as a result of their work. No wonder they do not like it; they appear to be doing the teacher's job for them and they are poorly qualified to do so. If peer assessment is used at a time when the pupils can act on the advice that they are given to improve their work *prior to it being summatively assessed*, then they will quickly see the usefulness of this way of working.

SUMMARY AND KEY POINTS

In this chapter, I have talked about Assessment for Learning and tried to explain why it is powerful, and how to use that power effectively. I have treated the main facets of Assessment for Learning separately, despite the fact that they all work together for the learner. Good feedback cannot be given without knowing the success criteria; it is both easier and more fruitful to give feedback on questions and activities that require exploration of an area of mathematics; the more that pupils are involved in the process of obtaining feedback and modifying the subsequent work, the more they will learn to be successful.

Ideally, every teacher would both find out about and give feedback on how well every pupil is learning in every lesson, but this is not usually possible. When questions are asked, there is usually only time for a few to answer, otherwise the lesson would drag. When groups present the ideas they have worked on, it may represent the whole group's ideas but also it may not. No teacher has time to mark the pupils' books after every lesson and even once a week may be too time-consuming. Therefore, other ideas have to be employed. For example, if mini-whiteboards were used during the lesson, then the pupils could be asked to write something new they have learned this lesson and something they would like to learn. The whiteboards could then be collected, and while you are cleaning them, you can be planning the next lesson based on comments from everyone in the lesson.

Do not be afraid to divide the class up into groups so that the particular learning needs that you have discovered can be attended to; for example, giving a teaching assistant some apparatus to use with a group that is finding it hard to visualise in 3D, while you stretch the pupils who are ready to use Pythagoras' Theorem in 3D. Or you could ask the pupils to self-select from three or four different learning activities, according to their confidence in their understanding.

As you build your experience as a teacher, you will be able to change the course of the lesson or regroup the pupils when you see that such actions are needed. However, in this chapter, I have tried to discuss approaches that will work for new teachers as they gain such experience. One of the many principles of Assessment for Learning is to build on what pupils already know. It is therefore a good idea to prepare a question or an activity that will reveal from where the pupils' learning should start. However, if a teacher uses that activity at the start of a lesson, it may be that the rest of the lesson plan has to change to accommodate what was found. A new teacher would find this very hard. Therefore, new teachers should use such activities at the end of a lesson, so that the next lesson can be planned in the light of this information.

Using Assessment for Learning demands the use of tasks that allow pupils to show which mathematical ideas they understand and which they do not. It demands flexible, knowledgeable, professional teachers who are able and willing to respond to what they find out. If new teachers start their careers by taking steps in each lesson to find out about what their pupils understand, and to change their learning experiences accordingly, then their pupils will learn mathematics more confidently and become better mathematicians. The pupils will also experience good learning approaches and become able to take charge of their own learning, an important education for successful learning throughout their lives.

FURTHER READING

AAIA (2009) *Managing Assessment for Learning*. Association for Achievement and Improvment through Assessment (order copies from the membership secretary, via the AAIA website).

This booklet gives a broad vision of how all people in school can use Assessment for Learning and easily accessible advice on monitoring the extent to which Assessment for Learning has been put into practice. It outlines indicators of good practice for all stages of implementation, from the role that pupils can be expected to play to expectations of management teams.

Black, P., Harrison, C., Lee, C., Marshall, B. and Wiliam, D. (2002) *Working inside the Black Box*. London: NfER-Nelson.

This is a short, sharp resumé of the important findings from the research project discussed in greater detail in the book above. Using the teachers' own words the book shows how the power of Assessment for Learning can be used in every classroom.

Black, P., Harrison, C., Lee, C., Marshall, B. and Wiliam, D. (2003) *Assessment for Learning: Putting It into Practice*. Maidenhead: Open University Press.

This book is probably the most important for understanding Assessment for Learning. It details the hard evidence that development of formative assessment raises pupils' test scores and provides teachers with ideas and advice for improving the use of formative assessment in the classroom. It gives valuable insights into Assessment for Learning as teachers describe how they turned ideas into practical action in their schools.

Lee, C. (2006) *Language for Learning Mathematics: Assessment for Learning in Practice*. Maidenhead: Open University Press.

As well as discussing how using oral and written language in mathematics classrooms can support both learning and assessment, this book provides a range of practical approaches to developing richer language in the classroom.

The Standards Unit (2005) *Improving Learning in Mathematics*. (Available from QIA: http://tlp.excellencegateway.org.uk/teachingandlearning/downloads/default.aspx# math_learning.

This multimedia resource builds on existing successful practice and explores approaches that encourage a more active way of learning through the use of group work, discussion and open questioning. Learners are encouraged to 'have a go', become more independent and reflective about their mathematics, learn to think mathematically rather than simply learning rules and, most importantly, enjoy their mathematics.

ASSESSMENT AND PUBLIC EXAMINATIONS

Peter Johnston-Wilder

INTRODUCTION

Every teacher needs to make judgements about pupil attainment in order to confirm that pupils are progressing, evaluate the effectiveness of their teaching and inform their planning. In mathematics, it is particularly important to assess what pupils already know because, to an extent, mathematical understanding is hierarchical. It is always possible that some pupils will have already acquired deep-rooted misconceptions about, or difficulties with, certain mathematical ideas. Such misconceptions can have serious implications for the pupils' ability to comprehend new topics. So teachers assess:

* to inform their planning;
* to help diagnose the sources of pupils' difficulties;
* to help pupils become effective independent learners by including them in the process of learning mathematics.

In addition, teachers assess:

* to provide a basis for reporting progress to pupils themselves and their parents;
* to meet the requirements of external statutory requirements and public assessments.

Each of these varied purposes for assessment may require a different approach.

This chapter is in two parts: the first is focused on ongoing assessment and the second on public and summative assessments. These are dealt with separately, as the purposes of these assessments are quite distinct. The first is designed to help pupils learn, and track that learning, to ensure good progress and that any interventions are appropriate. The second aspect is a statutory duty for teachers in England and a requirement for most teachers in all countries. Your first tasks in this chapter will be to consider more closely how you can develop your ability to assess pupils during the school year in your lessons. You will be asked to consider the different methods of assessment that are available to you and the resources for assessment that you will probably find in your school. You will also need to consider how to interpret and make use of the information forwarded to you about your Year 7 pupils' attainment in the end-of-Key Stage 2 assessments.

After this, you need to make yourself aware of the elements that make up public assessment of mathematics beyond age 14. These will include GCSE, A-Level and 14–19 Diplomas. An important part of the professional work of a teacher is to be aware of the requirements of public examinations, as they have important implications for the mathematics curriculum as well as for what you teach and how you teach it.

Throughout this chapter, the assessment requirements of the National Curriculum for Mathematics in England are considered as an example of how a national system affects your practice as a classroom teacher.

OBJECTIVES

By the end of this chapter you should:

▨ have used a range of different methods of assessment in mathematics and considered when they are appropriate;
▨ have considered the manageability of assessment in your everyday classroom practice;
▨ be aware of the importance of a departmental assessment policy;
▨ be aware of the requirements of public assessment in mathematics at Key Stages 3 and 4.

IN-CLASS ASSESSMENT

In-class or ongoing assessment might include gathering evidence, in various ways, of what pupils can do and understand. Sometimes the evidence you obtain is in a permanent form that can be reviewed again later, such as written work recorded in the pupil's exercise book. However, the evidence can often be ephemeral, such as when you observe a pupil choosing to use a ruler to measure appropriately or when you overhear one pupil explain her reasoning to another. The list below summarises some forms of evidence that are important in the in-class assessment of mathematics:

▨ marking exercises;
▨ class tests and quizzes (aural and mental maths end-of-unit, end-of-module or end-of-year);
▨ open and extended activities and ICT work;
▨ questioning (both open and closed questions);
▨ observation.

In the core book in this series (Capel *et al.*, 2009), you were introduced to various purposes of assessment, particularly the difference between formative and summative purposes. Formative assessment (see Chapter 6) has the purpose of informing and causing the modification of plans for teaching and learning experiences for individual pupils. In contrast to this, the purpose of summative assessment is to summarise the pupil's attainment at the end of a stage of learning or at the end of a module or course of study. The outcome of summative assessment is often for public consumption and is used to inform other stakeholders, such as parents and school governors, or to select and order individuals, whereas formative assessment is intended to help learners to learn.

A useful list of characteristics of assessment that promotes learning has been given by the Assessment Reform Group (ARG, 1999), a group of researchers from the British Educational Research Association (BERA) who work on policy issues in relation to educational assessment. Such assessment:

■ is embedded in a view of teaching and learning of which it is an essential part;
■ involves sharing learning goals with pupils;
■ aims to help pupils to know and to recognise the standards they are aiming for;
■ involves pupils in self-assessment;
■ provides feedback that leads to pupils recognising their next steps and how to take them;
■ is underpinned by confidence that every student can improve;
■ involves both teacher and pupils reviewing and reflecting on assessment data.

(ARG, 1999: 7)

The distinction between formative and summative purposes may not always seem clear-cut. For example, class test results can be used to inform teacher decisions about what individual pupils need to learn next (this would become formative assessment when the plans are put into action), but also may be taken home to inform parents about current attainment (summative). Information from tests, such as Optional National Curriculum tests and assessments used in Assessing Pupils' Progress (APP), can also be used formatively by both teacher and pupils.

At the time of the Cockcroft Report (DES, 1982) in England, public assessment in mathematics was entirely 'norm-referenced', as was almost all assessment by teachers within their classes. This means that each pupil's achievement was assessed by how it compared with that of other pupils in the same age cohort or, in the case of in-class assessment, by comparison with other pupils in the class. In recent years, there has been a greater emphasis on 'criterion-referenced' assessment, where pupils' achievement is assessed against specific curricular criteria. Criterion-referenced assessment is now acknowledged as an essential feature of good assessment practice in the classroom. However, norm-referencing still features within public assessment, particularly in some aspects of GCSE and A-Level.

Task 7.1 **Taking in pupils' books**

Find a class that has carried out two contrasting tasks: for example, an exercise and an open-ended task. Collect the mathematics workbooks from a group of about six pupils. Look closely at their work on these two contrasting tasks and consider carefully what the evidence recorded in the pupils' books tells you about:

■ what the pupils know and can do;
■ what the task allows and encourages the pupils to show of their ability and hence what information the task does not give you about the pupils' abilities;
■ what the pupils need to do next to follow up the work you have looked at;
■ what the teacher might do next.

Try to be very precise in your responses to each of the points above. You may find it helpful to identify particular aspects of pupil attainment from your National Curriculum assessment framework (in England and Wales, this will be the level description for each Attainment Target or the assessment criteria from the Assessing Pupils' Progress website).

When you observe teachers at work in your school you will see many approaches to assessment used in practice in classrooms. Written tests and exercises have been commonplace assessment practices in mathematics classrooms for generations. However, these alone will not tell you all that you need to know about the present under-standing and abilities of your pupils and their potential to go further. The assessment method needs to fit the purpose of the assessment. For example, if you are assessing the pupils' ability to 'show understanding of situations by describing them mathematically using symbols, words and diagram' (National Curriculum Using and Applying Mathematics Level 5, QCA, 2007a), then you will be looking for the pupils' ability to discuss what they are doing and to explain it and why they are doing it. For this purpose, there would be no point in setting a test consisting only of short-answer questions that can only carry right or wrong answers.

Content and process

The *content* of the mathematics National Curriculum in England is broadly what is spec-ified in Attainment Targets 2, 3 and 4; on the other hand, *process* is specified in mathematics Attainment Target 1, variously called 'Mathematical Processes and Applications' or 'Using and Applying Mathematics' (APP, http://nationalstrategies. standards.dcsf.gov.uk/app). In mathematics, assessment of content can require assess-ment methods different from those required for the assessment of process. The content of mathematics has been described as consisting of facts, skills and concepts (see, for exam-ple, the Cockcroft Report or the range and content of Mathematics Key Stage 3, QCA, 2007a: 145). This classification of content was discussed in Chapter 5 and it can be help-ful when considering how to teach or assess a particular topic. Learning facts involves memory and the assessment of this will be a test of 'recall'. Mathematical skill often involves the ability to perform algorithms quickly and efficiently, which might require regular practice and might also sometimes be assessed by some form of aural quiz or written test.

By contrast, Attainment Target 1, Ma1: Mathematical processes and applications in the National Curriculum (QCA, 2007a: 148) or Using and Applying Mathematics in the APP specify the processes involved in working and thinking mathematically. These involve applying mathematical knowledge and understanding in unfamiliar contexts or making decisions about what mathematical techniques will be helpful or appropriate to solve a particular problem. Processes such as these cannot be effectively assessed through short exercises where the pupil knows what skills or concepts are required. On the contrary, they require the pupil to engage with a problem or a task at a deeper level and over a longer period.

Extended work in mathematics

To appreciate fully what your pupils can achieve in using the processes of thinking mathematically (Attainment Target 1 in the National Curriculum in England), it is important that you include opportunities for the pupils to engage with open-ended and investigational tasks from time to time and that these are allowed to extend over several lessons. Extended work is also a very important learning experience: it is where pupils learn to take responsibility themselves for working mathematically and to make decisions about how to use their mathematical skills to work productively on unfamiliar problems (see Chapter 11 for ideas on how to work in this way).

Assessment of extended work can be very different from the assessment of exercises and tests. Mathematics teachers usually assess extended work by outcome. This involves judging the pupil's level of achievement by the work attempted and by what specific examples and generalisations the pupil has discussed. Higher-level attainment will include some explanation, justification and perhaps proof of the generalisations made. If your school uses the APP materials, which can be found on the Standards Site (DCSF, 2008), then you will be required to judge your pupils' attainment in 'Using and Applying Mathematics' against a series of criteria set out in the APP assessment criteria for Attainment Levels 1–8. The example in Task 7.2 is intended to illustrate very briefly how different pupil responses to the same task might be indicative of differing levels of understanding and attainment.

Task 7.2 **Assessing extended tasks**

Example: A class is set the following task:

> If the answer is 10, what could the question be?
> Show as much different mathematics as you can.

Look at the following extracts from two pupils' responses to this task and consider what each pupil has demonstrated that they know and can do. You might try to assess these two outcomes against the APP criteria or your own National Curriculum assessment framework.

A $3 + 7 = 10$, $13 - 3 = 10$
B $2^3 + 2 = 10$, $\sqrt{9} + \sqrt{49} = 10$

When you have considered the extracts, discuss your ideas with your mentor in school. With the help of your mentor, find a Key Stage 3 class that has completed an open-ended task. Arrange to discuss the work of about six pupils from this class on their extended task. Spend some time working for yourself on the extended task completed by the pupils and identify the content areas of the curriculum that might reasonably be addressed by a pupil working on the task. Assess the work done by each pupil in the various content areas of the curriculum. For each pupil, you should aim to identify the highest level demonstrated in each content area of the curriculum.

Reading what pupils write in their books can tell you a lot about their understanding and their progress, but it does not tell you all that you need to know in order to promote their learning. The more that those pupils are engaged in the task of assessing their progress and promoting their own learning, the more manageable and effective it will be. In the next section, you will be asked to think about what can result from involving pupils in assessing their learning.

Involving pupils in in-class assessment

In-class assessment will always have the purpose of promoting pupil learning and will normally follow the principles of Assessment for Learning (see Chapter 6). Therefore, in-class assessment will usually exemplify the following three important aspects of teachers' practice that help to make assessment effective in improving learning:

▣   involving pupils in understanding the learning objectives and outcomes and recognising when these are achieved;
▣   using questions to find out yourself and to help pupils recognise what they know, understand and can do;
▣   marking pupils' work and giving useful feedback.

These three aspects will be considered in turn in Tasks 7.3–7.5.

Involving pupils through self- and peer assessment

Black and Wiliam (1998), Black *et al*. (2003) and Lee (2006) all point out that learners are more likely to achieve a learning objective if they understand what that objective is and are able to recognise what they need to do to reach it. These authors see teaching pupils to engage in self-assessment as an essential element in ensuring that they develop this understanding. Self-assessment involves pupils learning to make reflective judgements about their own work. In order to engage in meaningful self-assessment, pupils need to develop understanding of three elements: the learning objective, their own position in relation to that objective, and how to close the gap between the two (Sadler, 1989). A device that has been used in some schools to develop the practice of pupil self-assessment is 'traffic lights' (QCA, 2001) and this is developed in Task 7.3.

Task 7.3 **Traffic lights**

You can carry out this task with a class you are teaching yourself or, with the permission of the teacher, with a class that you are observing.

At the start of a topic, tell the pupils what you hope they will have learned by the end of the sequence of lessons. Give them a list of learning outcomes or success criteria (see Chapter 6 for the relation between learning objectives and success criteria) for reference.

Towards the end of the topic or unit of work, give each pupil another copy of the learning outcomes for the topic. Ask pupils to look through their work and consider what they have understood. Ask them to use the following traffic-light code to record their understanding of each learning goal:

▣   green spot (I feel confident that I have fully understood this – I am sure I can do this);

■ yellow spot (not sure – I still have some worries or difficulties about this);
■ red spot (I don't understand this at all).

Collect in each pupil's self-assessment and consider what these tell you about the pupils' learning. Reflect on how you would plan the next learning activity to respond to what you have discovered. Either put those ideas into practice or discuss your ideas with the teacher of the class.

Why is it important not to leave such an activity until the end of the time allotted to a topic?

As pupils become familiar with the process of self-assessment, they gain in confidence and learn to make more sophisticated judgements about their learning. Carefully structured peer assessment activities can also help pupils to develop their judgement. Pupils can first be asked to carry out a piece of work for themselves, such as writing a report on a piece of extended work, explaining how they arrived at a generalisation and possibly offering a justification for it. Then they can be asked to read someone else's report and consider questions such as: 'Does this explanation make sense?', 'Is there a clear generalisation?', 'Is it clear how the generalisation arose?'. Such activity can help pupils to recognise possible approaches to adopt in their own work or to identify pitfalls to avoid.

Another essential aspect of including pupils in assessing their own progress in learning is to ensure that you communicate the intended learning outcomes, success or assessment criteria for each learning episode to the learners in an accessible manner. Finding ways to tell pupils how they are going to assess their learning before they have embarked on that learning, in such a way that they will be able to judge for themselves what they have learned, is no easy task. You will need to practise and you will need to learn from your pupils' reactions.

Oral assessment, questioning and observing

The use of effective oral questioning is the second aspect of effective in-class assessment. Some questions are more effective than others at giving you opportunities for assessment. Through questioning you can find out what pupils know, understand and can do; you can also explore pupils' misconceptions and help them to learn to ask effective questions of themselves.

When you ask a question, it is important that you allow the pupils thinking time to consider the question before you seek an answer. This thinking time often needs to be significantly longer than many teachers allow. If you do not allow enough thinking time, you will find pupils will not answer and you will be reduced to asking lower-level questions. When teachers do not allow at least three to five seconds before expecting an answer, low-level questions that require little thought soon predominate. In these circumstances, most pupils become unwilling to answer, knowing that there is no point in trying as 'the answer or another question will come along in a few seconds'. It is important to allow pupils more time to respond and it is often helpful to encourage them to discuss their ideas in pairs or small groups before you elicit responses from around the class. As you begin to elicit answers, your goal is to encourage a thoughtful and reflective discussion that allows all pupils to participate. A more detailed discussion of this issue may be found in Chapter 6.

In the course of classroom discussion, or when you encourage pupils to present their work to the class, you will sometimes see examples of classic pupil errors and misunderstandings. The following are examples taken from classroom interaction:

- during an exercise on expansion of brackets, a pupil claims that $(x + y)^2 = x^2 + y^2$;
- in solving the equation $2x = x + 2$, a pupil suggests taking away 2 from each side to give $x = x$;
- in an exercise on solving equations, a pupil faced with $\frac{(4x + 2)}{6x} = x$ suggests taking away the x from the numerator and denominator to give $\frac{4 + 2}{6} = x$ and, hence, $x = 1$;

Each of these examples shows that the pupil has not understood something or perhaps the pupil knows that there is a rule that can help, but has not understood when this rule applies. In the third example, the problem is compounded by the fact that the pupil's incorrect reasoning has led to a proposed solution, $x = 1$, which just happens to be a solution to the original equation.

In such situations, the teacher needs to assess the situation and adapt the teaching accordingly. An important method for making a more realistic assessment of the pupil's difficulty in such situations is to use carefully targeted open questions.

Task 7.4 **Assessing for understanding**

In each of the examples above, consider what the pupil has understood and what misconceptions he or she may have. Decide how you would follow up the situation described. What questions could you ask the pupils to help you to diagnose the nature of the pupil's problem? What action might you take to help develop the pupil's understanding in each situation?

Discuss your ideas with your mentor in your school. Look out for examples of teachers using questioning to find out about pupil understanding. Try to identify some general principles about questioning pupils to diagnose the sources of their difficulties.

The examples above were taken from a situation in which the teacher was observing the pupil working on a task, listening to the pupil explaining their work or asking questions in a whole-class question-and-answer session. These are important aspects of in-class assessment. Such methods are part of the teacher's basic skills to focus the teaching on improving each pupil's understanding.

What the pupil most likely needs is *not* to hear a repeat of some explanation she has heard before but to have new explanations and experiences to help see why the rule, as he or she has learned it, does not apply in these cases. The teacher's task is to encourage and enable the pupil to modify her or his existing conceptions in particular respects. Recognise in yourself, and guard against, the tendency just to repeat the answer if it was not understood straightaway.

As a teacher, you need to pay careful attention to the questioning strategies you adopt to elicit a pupil's existing conceptions and explanations. When a pupil gives a wrong answer, it may be quite unhelpful to the pupil if you simply say, 'No, that's wrong', and then give the 'right' answer. It may be much more helpful to ask the pupil to explain how he or she arrived at the wrong answer. When required to do this, the pupil will often see errors in reasoning for him- or herself and correct them.

However, from the pupil's explanation, you may be able to infer much more about what he or she has understood and about the source of the misunderstanding. Pupils' existing conceptions have been adopted because they work in some instances. Therefore, a pupil may be able to give an answer that seems correct, but may have arrived at this answer through incorrect or limited reasoning. The questions you ask to encourage the pupil to explain the reasoning that led to the wrong answer can help you to uncover problems of this kind and can sometimes help the pupil to recognise and correct the problems.

Providing appropriate feedback for pupils

When you mark a pupil's work, you need to consider what to tell them about how they have done and how to present the information. It is helpful to think about what types of feedback are available and when each might be appropriate. Consider under what circumstances it would be appropriate simply to give 9 out of 10 as the feedback on a pupil's work. Where mistakes were made, that will tell you nothing about the pupil's understanding, and if no mistakes were made then it is possible that the pupil was insufficiently challenged. Pupils need informative comments about how to improve and what to pay attention to so that they can be involved in the process of learning themselves; this requires time and careful consideration on your part. A more detailed discussion of the idea of feedback for pupils appears in Chapter 6.

Sometimes it is effective to provide brief written comments to the individual pupil at the end of the exercise and then provide lesson time for the pupil to follow up on your comment. However, if the pupil has a substantial difficulty, or if you are not sure what is the source of the pupil's difficulty, it may be better to ask to speak to him/her during the following lesson. If there are several pupils with the same or similar difficulties, it will be a more efficient use of your time to speak to the group in the next lesson, or to take some time to give a new explanation to the whole class.

Task 7.5 **Providing constructive feedback**

A class of Year 11 pupils preparing for GCSE was given an exercise on multiplying out brackets. One pupil's attempt at the exercise is shown in Figure 7.1 below.

$$a + b = 3 \checkmark$$
$$a - b = 1 \checkmark$$
$$2a + b = 5 \checkmark$$
$$2a - b = 3 \checkmark$$
$$3a + b = 7 \checkmark$$

$$2a + 3b = 8 \times$$
$$2b - 3b = -1 \checkmark$$
$$3a + b = 5 \times$$
$$3b + a = 6 \times$$
$$ab + 4 = 7 \times$$

$$4b - 2a = 9 \times$$
$$2a - 3b = 8 \times$$
$$7ab - 4a = 16 \times$$
$$6(a-b) = 7 \times$$
$$6(a+b) - 7ab = -1 \times$$

$$\left(\frac{6}{15} \right)$$

■ **Figure 7.1** Pupil script

Discuss in your journal the merits of each of the following forms of feedback.

A   6/15
B   You have made a systematic error in questions 8 to 15. Look at your work again and see if you can identify the error. If you have difficulty, you might discuss this with other people in the class. See me after the next lesson to discuss what you have found out.
C   In an algebraic expression, 3*a* means 3 × *a*.

You might consider that none of the suggestions above is ideal or that some combination of more than one of them would be suitable. What do you think is the most appropriate feedback to give to this pupil? Consider which factors would help you to decide how best to respond. Do not forget that you may have 30 other pupils' scripts for this exercise to mark, just from the one class. Think back to Task 7.3 and consider how the pupils might become more involved in providing their own constructive feedback. You will need to be aware not only of the demands on your time but also of the ultimate time saving in the lesson when you give appropriately focused feedback to enable pupils to correct their own misunderstandings.

OTHER ASPECTS OF IN-CLASS ASSESSMENT

Tests and quizzes

In order to help pupils become fluent in using some aspects of mathematical learning, teachers often use aural assessment or quizzes and tests. In such tests, pupils are given spoken instructions and questions and are usually required to interpret the problems posed without further written information. Such questions are therefore a test of pupils' abilities to interpret and process information mentally, something that will often be of help to them outside the mathematics classroom. Success with such questions requires careful concentration and pupils often enjoy the task for short periods at the beginning or end of a lesson, particularly if you use ICT creatively at times (e.g. *Countdown* music to indicate the time they have or voting systems to answer the questions).

Research (for example, Ashcraft, 2002) has shown that it is very important not to cause stress when using this type of assessment; pupils need to aim to become 'more speedy than they were before', rather than be made to feel a failure when they just cannot think as quickly as others. Many pupils dread this kind of questioning and disengage from other mathematical thinking because of the difficulties they have with providing 'speedy' answers. Use speed tests with caution!

In setting tests of this kind or tests for end of unit, end of module or end of year, teachers need to be creative and try to find different ways of testing. If all your tests look the same and are predictable, there is a danger that pupils will learn to perform well without necessarily improving their understanding. As well as providing assessment information, assessment activities (including tests) can, if used carefully, motivate pupils and direct their attention towards those ideas, skills and practices that you want them to develop. Pupils can be asked to find different ways of solving a problem or to explain their reasoning. Setting effective testing activities, which will engage your pupils and motivate them, takes persistent practice and requires careful preparation.

Recording and reporting

It is important that you develop systems to record the results of your assessments of pupils. Your records may be required for several different purposes and it is important that they are kept up to date and in a form that can be understood by other professionals. Some of the purposes to which your assessment records might be put are:

■ consideration of whether each pupil is making appropriate progress or if there are inconsistencies that could be explored;

■ passing relevant information on to subsequent teachers at the end of a school year or when the pupil moves to another class or another school during the year;

■ passing relevant information on to parents through regular reports or at parent consultations;

■ informing your teacher assessment of each pupil's attainment in relation to each Attainment Target at the end of each year, especially at the end of Key Stage 3 (Year 9);

■ informing special assessments of particular pupils such as the assessment for special educational needs.

In the following paragraphs, you will first consider some contrasting systems for record keeping and then some of the different purposes for which your records might be used.

Recording progress

Teachers are required to keep records of each pupil's progress. In England, teachers are required to make an assessment of the National Curriculum (NC) level that their pupils have attained at the end of each Key Stage. Many schools ask their teachers to make interim assessments during the Key Stage in order to keep track of pupil progress. Therefore, teachers may be asked to make an assessment of the NC Level that each of their pupils has attained. Often, the level will be accompanied by a code that indicates if the pupil attainment is high, secure or low at the reported level. Since pupils who are making good progress are expected to master the knowledge, understanding and skills in one level every 18 months to two years, the gradations in the levels are considered important in order to demonstrate that pupils are progressing across the school terms.

You will need to find out precisely what records of pupils' progress will be expected of you within your school. At the time of writing, it is likely that schools in England will use a version of the APP materials, discussed below, as a basis for their recording system in Key Stage 3 and a system based on GCSE grades in Key Stage 4. It is important to note that, whilst it is a statutory duty in England for teachers to make and report an assessment of the NC level that their pupils attain at the end of Key Stage 3, the APP system itself is only advisory. If the school has developed its own system for assessing and monitoring pupil progress, one that allows its teachers to make consistent judgements in line with national standards, then they are at liberty to use it. Many schools see the APP materials as cumbersome and time-consuming, so it is likely that there will be a certain amount of revision of the materials over time.

Many commercial teaching schemes in mathematics have their own assessment and recording system tailored to the scheme. These often relate very closely to the NC levels and to banks of questions and other assessment materials published with the scheme. It is worth obtaining information about some of these from the publishers and comparing them with the APP or other system used in your own school.

Assessing pupils' progress (APP) in mathematics

The Qualifications and Curriculum Development Agency (QCDA) and the National Strategies produced materials (DCSF, 2008) called Assessing Pupils' Progress. These materials were intended to support both day-to-day and periodic assessment in mathematics and, in particular, to enable teachers to demonstrate where their pupils are making progress in mathematics and how well they are making progress in relation to national standards.

The APP materials consist of tables of assessment criteria set out from the National Curriculum attainment targets for each level, and a variety of publications exemplifying the standard of work expected at each level. Since the materials are based on the level descriptions that underpin National Curriculum assessment, the approach aims to improve the quality and reliability of teacher assessment. Together, these materials provide a structured approach to assessing mathematics so that teachers can:

■ track pupils' progress in mathematics throughout Key Stage 3;
■ obtain information about their pupils' strengths and weaknesses.

The APP materials include a teachers' handbook, which explains how to use the resources and how to implement this approach to assessment in school, and assessment guidelines for use with pupils' ongoing work in mathematics. At the time of writing, 'Standards Files' are being developed that contain collections of ongoing work from pupils, assessed and annotated to exemplify the APP approach and national standards.

The APP approach suggests that teachers review pupils' work using the APP assessment grids, in order to build a profile of pupils' attainment. This should be done at regular intervals, which are planned to fit in with school assessment policy. A bank of APP assessment tasks is provided to provide additional evidence of pupil attainment. The information gained from the process allows teachers to analyse the relative strengths and weaknesses of each pupil and to assign each pupil an overall National Curriculum level for mathematics by using a 'best fit' approach. A 'best-fit' approach means that a level is decided by looking over the pupil's attainment as a whole. For example, a secure level 5 could be awarded if a pupil has been assessed as having attained *all* of the level 4 criteria across the attainment targets, *many* of the level 5 criteria and *a few* of the level 6 criteria. This information can be used to set curricular targets in order to strengthen pupils' learning and to inform future teaching.

There are several advantages to using the APP materials. APP enables the combination of both in-class and summative assessments in making judgements about pupils, making it possible to gather together various types of evidence to inform reporting on pupil progress. Used sensitively, the APP materials can contribute to the professional development of all teachers, particularly for you as a less-experienced teacher. The APP materials are also designed to support teachers in aligning their judgements systematically with national standards, thereby increasing the consistency and reliability of teacher assessment and better informing the process of transfer and transition between classes and schools.

However, in some ways the APP is a backwards step. The way in which the mathematics National Curriculum in England evolved from a detailed list of criteria in the 1989 and 1991 versions (DES/WO, 1989, 1991) to the more general level descriptions that we see in the 2007 version (QCA, 2007a) meant that many schools adopted a recording system that took the form of very detailed tables of each pupil's achievement of each identifiable item in the National Curriculum level descriptions. These detailed recording systems sometimes became difficult to manage and some teachers found themselves perpetually ticking boxes. Whilst some detail is clearly desirable to provide a systematic basis for planning, as well as to provide the basis for effective reporting to other teachers, governors and parents, it is very important that the method of recording assessment is manageable and does not take up too much valuable teaching time.

Task 7.6 **Recording assessments**

Try to obtain some examples of assessment recording systems from one or two of the major published mathematics teaching schemes for Years 7–11. This will usually involve a good look at the files and folders on the shelves in the mathematics department office or storage cupboard. Some examples are:

■ *SMP Interact*, published by Cambridge University Press;
■ *Level Up Maths*, published by Heinemann;
■ *Key Maths*, published by Nelson Thornes.

Try also to obtain copies of some other recording systems used in nearby schools.

Arrange a meeting with your mentor to discuss the departmental recording system in your school. Compare the recording system in your school with the APP, published systems and with any other school systems that you have obtained. In particular, try to identify explicitly what are the distinct aspects of performance in mathematics that need to be reported separately, and see to what extent the various assessment schemes succeed in achieving this.

Reporting to parents

Parents are often particularly concerned about how their child is progressing in mathematics. Your school and your mathematics department will have established practices for producing regular reports to parents. This will usually include a programme of parental consultations in which parents have the opportunity to meet teachers, as well as regular written reports on each school subject. These practices will often be formalised as part of the school and departmental policies for assessment, recording and reporting. It is important that you learn to use the established framework to communicate effectively with parents.

In writing comments on both day-to-day learning in books and on formal reports, you can aim to encourage dialogue among parent/guardian, pupil and yourself about the pupil's learning. There are many ways in which parents can be encouraged to contribute to their child's progress in mathematics. However, because the school mathematics curriculum has changed significantly during the last 20 years, many parents rely on the advice of their child's teacher to know how best they can help. The report to parents and the parental consultations can each play a part in this by giving suggestions to parents about ways in which they can help their child to learn.

Transfer from Key Stage 2 to Key Stage 3

All local education systems involve transitions from one phase of education to another. In some areas, schooling is organised into three stages: lower, middle and upper, whilst in others it is in two stages: primary and secondary with transition at age 11. If transition from primary schools or middle schools to secondary or upper schools is not managed well, then pupils can lose up to a year of useful progress in mathematics.

One of the reasons that APP has been introduced across both primary and secondary schools is to smooth transitions between school phases. If every school uses the same system to record progress in mathematics, and uses the advocated system of moderation to ensure that judgements are consistent both across and between schools, then there should not be the same 'stall' in progress that is often seen.

In this section, you will consider the value and use of information from the Key Stage 2 assessments at the transfer between Key Stage 2 and Key Stage 3. This information can support the planning and teaching in Year 7. In secondary schools, where the end of Key Stage 2 is also the transfer from primary to secondary school, this is particularly significant information. In middle schools, the issues are slightly different, but the Key Stage 2 results may still provide an important basis for the information passed from middle schools to upper schools.

In Task 7.7, you will look more closely at the Key Stage 2 curriculum and at the nature of the information available at the end of the Key Stage.

Task 7.7 **Interpreting Key Stage 2 levels**

For this task, you need the National Curriculum programme of study for Key Stage 2, the APP criteria for Key Stage 2 and some Key Stage 2 national tests. Your school may be able to show you some KS2 national tests or you may be able to borrow some from a neighbouring primary school. Some major bookshops are selling books of past questions for KS2. Otherwise, QCA has produced a Digital Test Bank containing thousands of questions from past QCA papers at Key Stages 1, 2 and 3. This is available from NFER-Nelson at the address given in Appendix 2.

Look at the mathematics National Curriculum for Key Stage 2 (age 7–11) and at the level descriptions that describe the likely attainment at age 11 (levels 1–6 in England). In each curriculum area (Attainment Target), reflect on what you would expect a pupil to know, understand and be able to do for each level of attainment at age 11.

Look at some Key Stage 2 national tests for mathematics. Levels in the national tests are awarded according to the total number of marks gained in the test. Reflect on what you can expect to learn from knowing the level achieved by an individual pupil in the KS2 national tests. Consider whether the APP materials would provide you with more useful information.

Talk with teachers in the department about how they make use of the data that comes to them from the feeder schools.

PUBLIC ASSESSMENTS AND EXAMINATIONS

The results of public assessment of school mathematics were the subject of considerable attention in the UK during the late 1980s and 1990s. Some of this attention centred on a concern that the standards of mathematics achieved by young people in schools in the UK were not as high as those achieved in other countries. This debate was fuelled by the publication of results from the Third International Mathematics and Science Study (TIMSS) in 1996 (Keys *et al.*, 1996), and more recently the OECD Program for International Student Assessment (OECD, 2007), which assesses the performance of students near the end of compulsory education on a common framework of skills and understanding in science, mathematics and reading every three years. The latest PISA survey was conducted in 2009 and the results will be released in December 2010. The results from such studies as these appeared to show that results from England and Wales were not as good as those from competitor nations. The level of concern and attention given to standards in school mathematics led to some significant changes and developments in the methods used in the public assessment of mathematics.

There has been a move since the Cockcroft Report (DES, 1982) to introduce criterion referencing into public assessment. This was very noticeable within the early assessment framework for the National Curriculum in England and Wales (DES/WO, 1989a and 1991), where the assessment criteria were tightly specified statements of what a pupil would be able to do. The revisions in 1999 and 2007 of the mathematics National Curriculum in England (DfEE, 1999a; QCA, 2007a) have broader level descriptions, which give, for each level, a description of the kinds of achievement that a child might be expected to show.

In the next subsection, you will look closely at the mathematics teacher assessments required in England at the end of Key Stage 3; in a later section you will look at the GCSE.

Key Stage 3 teacher assessment

Teachers in England are required to make an assessment of their pupils at the end of Key Stage 3. Teachers have to make an assessment of each pupil on each of the Attainment Targets and therefore the APP discussed earlier can be useful. This assessment is made in the final term of Year 9, based on work done in class across the Key Stage. Each school may have a different approach to this requirement, but one approach is to build a portfolio of the pupil's best work, providing written evidence of attainment and recording the judgements against level criteria such as those provided by the APP materials. Some of the work in the portfolio needs to be extended work to provide evidence of achievement in Attainment Target 1.

At the time of writing, the National Tests at the end of Key Stage 3 have only recently been abolished. Schools had become habituated to using these tests to confirm assessments of their pupils and, consequently, many schools carried on using the tests that they could still obtain at no cost from the QCA. Of course, at the end of Key Stage 3, the pupils are moving into Key Stage 4 or what are often called their examination years. Making an assessment of how well their pupils are able to show their mathematical abilities in an examination seems appropriate to many schools at this point of transition. However, it must be remembered that this is not the same as making the kind of assessment required by the APP materials, which requires a holistic judgement of the knowledge, understanding and skills that the pupils have demonstrated over the Key Stage. Tests provide, at best, a snapshot or sample; teacher assessment requires a long look at all the evidence.

Teachers develop their own practice for identifying the level achieved in a piece of extended work. One possible approach is to look first at the relevant Attainment Target. For example, looking at Attainment Target 1 in the National Curriculum in England (Ma1 Using and applying mathematics), start at, say, level 3 and work up the levels, looking for evidence at each level. When you have identified the level whose description is the best fit to the evidence in the piece of work, look at the description for the next level up to identify what is missing from this piece of work that makes it miss the next level. Then look at the description for the level below to identify what is the evidence in this piece of work that marks it out as better than that. In this way, you can rigorously check the evidence of achievement. Then look at the content Attainment Targets that are relevant to the work done and note where there is evidence of any content at levels surrounding the level identified for Ma1.

Task 7.8 **Using level descriptions**

Arrange to carry out an extended task with a Key Stage 3 class, preferably in Year 9. You need to choose a task that will provide opportunities for the most able in the class to be challenged, but will also be accessible to the least able, so that every pupil will be able to achieve something. You may wish to consult your mentor for advice about a suitable task to use. Some ideas about open activities are given in Appendix 3. You will need to allow the pupils at least one whole lesson and you may wish to give them a homework and perhaps another lesson as well to complete their report on their work.

When you have collected in the pupils' work, use the criteria in the APP or another suitable source of level descriptors to assess the work done by each pupil. Look first particularly for evidence of attainment in Ma1 (Using and Applying, or Mathematical processes and applications). Then revisit the scripts to look for evidence of achievement in the content Attainment Targets. Discuss the results of your work with your mentor.

GCSE ASSESSMENT

Key Stage 4 of the National Curriculum in England, Wales and Northern Ireland is assessed through GCSE (the General Certificate of Secondary Education). GCSE is not used in Scotland. The assessment arrangements for GCSE are administered by independent awarding bodies and are overseen by the regulatory authorities in each country: the Office of the Qualifications and Examinations Regulator (Ofqual) in England; the Department for Children, Education, Lifelong Learning and Skills (DCELLS) in Wales; the Northern Ireland Council for the Curriculum, Examinations and Assessment (CCEA).

GCSE mathematics syllabuses are designed to assess Key Stage 4 of the National Curriculum in mathematics, but some are also designed to meet the needs of post-16 students and mature adult learners. Some GCSE syllabuses are written specifically for use with a particular teaching scheme. Within your school, you may find that all pupils are entered for the same mathematics syllabus or it may be that different syllabuses are used with different groups of pupils or with different year groups. It is quite common for a school to use a different syllabus for sixth-form students who want to retake GCSE mathematics to improve their grade.

Awarding bodies for GCSE

In recent years, there has been a reduction in the number of awarding bodies for GCSE and A-Level. There are now three GCSE awarding bodies in England, and one in each of Wales and Northern Ireland:

▓ Assessment and Qualifications Alliance (AQA) (www.aqa.org.uk);
▓ Edexcel (www.edexcel.org.uk);
▓ Oxford, Cambridge and RSA (OCR) (www.ocr.org.uk);
▓ Welsh Joint Examination Committee (WJEC) (www.wjec.co.uk);
▓ Northern Ireland Council for the Curriculum, Examinations and Assessment (CCEA) (www.ccea.org.uk).

GCSE criteria for mathematics

Each awarding body may have two or even three syllabuses for mathematics, so there is still some choice available to schools. However, all syllabuses are required to adhere to the GCSE criteria for mathematics published by the relevant national authority (Ofqual in England, DCELLS in Wales and CCEA in Northern Ireland), which specify the assessment objectives, constrain the assessment techniques and weightings of the assessment objectives and include indicative grade descriptions for grades A, C and F.

The grade descriptions provide a general indication of the standards of achievement represented by these grades and are used by the awarding body in arriving at candidates' grades. The awarding body syllabus documents include the grade descriptions, which can assist schools in deciding which is the appropriate tier of entry for particular pupils. The grade C description current at the time of writing is shown in the quotation below.

> Candidates use a range of mathematical techniques, terminology, diagrams and symbols consistently, appropriately and accurately. Candidates are able to use different representations effectively and they recognise some equivalent representations; for example numerical, graphical and algebraic representations of linear functions; percentages, fractions and decimals. Their numerical skills are sound and they use a calculator accurately. They apply ideas of proportionality to numerical problems and use geometric properties of angles, lines and shapes.
>
> Candidates identify relevant information, select appropriate representations and apply appropriate methods and knowledge. They are able to move from one representation to another, in order to make sense of a situation. Candidates use different methods of mathematical communication.
>
> Candidates tackle problems that bring aspects of mathematics together. They identify evidence that supports or refutes conjectures and hypotheses. They understand the limitations of evidence and sampling, and the difference between a mathematical argument and conclusions based on experimental evidence.

They identify strategies to solve problems involving a limited number of variables. They communicate their chosen strategy, making changes as necessary. They construct a mathematical argument and identify inconsistencies in a given argument or exceptions to a generalisation.

Source: Ofqual (2009) GCSE Subject Criteria for Mathematics
(http://www.ofqual.gov.uk/743.aspx)

The GCSE criteria for mathematics are changed from time to time. At present, the criteria specify the weightings that should be given to the assessment of each of three Assessment Objectives, both through externally set and marked examinations, and through coursework, which may be set and marked by the school. The present weightings are set out in Table 7.1.

▨ **Table 7.1** GCSE assessment objectives and weightings

Assessment objectives		Weighting
AO1	Recall and use their knowledge of the prescribed content	45–55%
AO2	Select and apply mathematical methods in a range of contexts	25–35%
AO3	Interpret and analyse problems and generate strategies to solve them	15–25%

Source: Ofqual, 2009, GCSE Subject Criteria for Mathematics (http://www.ofqual.gov.uk/743.aspx)

All GCSE assessment in mathematics is required to be external; that is, there is no provision for coursework or school-based assessment, or for controlled assessments, which are allowed in some other subjects. Furthermore, each scheme of assessment must allocate a minimum weighting of 25%, and a maximum weighting of 50%, to assessment without a calculator. Question papers are targeted at either the Foundation tier or the Higher tier.

All GCSE mathematics syllabuses are required to have a common structure of two overlapping tiers of assessment, Foundation and Higher, with different content specified for each tier. A proportion of the assessment at each tier must be allocated to the functional elements of mathematics; on the Higher tier this should be 20–30 per cent and on the Foundation tier it should be 30–40 per cent. The intention of the different tiers is to provide a fair assessment for pupils of different abilities. The tiers of entry allow achievement at different grades as shown in Table 7.2.

▨ **Table 7.2** Tiers of entry for GCSE

Tier	Grades attainable	Weighting of functional mathematics
Foundation	G F E D C	30–40%
Higher	D C B A A*	20–30%

Schools have to decide which tier of papers is appropriate for each pupil. This decision is sometimes made in Year 9 and certainly by Year 10. Most schools teach mathematics in ability groups during the GCSE years and prepare whole ability groups for one tier of entry. Some schools are able to keep the decision flexible and will allow pupils to be moved from one group to another during Years 10 and 11, but the flexibility to move a pupil to a higher group inevitably reduces during Year 11. Clearly, the decision about which tier of entry a pupil should be prepared for is an important one, with serious consequences for the pupil, and it must be made with care.

Task 7.9 **Comparing different syllabuses**

In this task, you will find out which GCSE mathematics syllabuses are used in your school and which awarding bodies are used. You will consider the syllabuses, their content and the different methods of assessment, and the reasons for choosing a particular syllabus.

1   Ask your mentor if the school can give you a copy of each of the syllabuses available for mathematics. (If necessary, contact the awarding body used in your school to obtain copies of the mathematics syllabuses.) Study these carefully in order to identify what are the similarities and differences between the requirements. Look particularly at the elements that make up the assessment package: module tests, mental or aural tests, coursework, end-of-Key Stage examinations.

As an extension of this part, so as to enrich your own awareness of the range of options available, you might like to contact each of the GCSE awarding bodies to ask for a copy of each of the GCSE mathematics syllabuses they offer.

2   Arrange to talk to the head of mathematics in your school about the GCSE syllabuses used. Discuss the reasons for choosing the awarding body and the syllabus. Try to identify how the departmental work in Years 10 and 11 is affected by the chosen syllabus.

3   What awarding bodies do other subjects use? Ask some other heads of department in your school how they choose between exam boards and syllabuses. Try to find out some of the reasons behind the choices they make.

The final preparation for public examinations brings a different set of priorities. Revision for examinations and the development of exam technique are important aspects of your work with GCSE groups in the final months of Year 11. Pupils need help to maximise their performance in the examination. They need to be totally familiar with what is expected of them in the exam, with the style of questions and with precisely what is in the syllabus. The teacher is clearly responsible for ensuring that the pupils have covered the whole syllabus, but in the final weeks it is appropriate to focus closely: to show pupils the syllabus; to study past papers; to look at past exam questions that address particular syllabus topics.

With the abolition of coursework in recent years, Ma1 Using and applying mathematics is now intended to be assessed as part of the GCSE examination, and questions asking pupils to use and apply their mathematical knowledge are integrated into the papers. Many see this as unsatisfactory, but the widespread availability of coursework solutions via the internet has made coursework and extended assessment tasks much more difficult to manage.

Functional mathematics is now to be assessed within the new GCSE specification, which is to be taught from 2010 and examined from 2012. However, functional mathematics is also an essential requirement within the 14–19 diplomas.

Task 7.10 **Assessing functional mathematics**

Look back at the GCSE syllabus you considered in Task 7.9. Look at how 'functional mathematics' is assessed within this syllabus.

Find out what other assessments of functional mathematics are offered by the awarding body responsible for this syllabus and compare them with the functional mathematics elements within the GCSE examination. Consider whether they are different and why this might be or might not be the case.

Entry policies

Pupils with special educational needs – whether those with specific learning difficulties or the exceptionally gifted – may need special treatment in assessment, especially in public assessment such as GCSE. There are a small proportion of pupils amongst the most able and the least able whose needs are not met by the standard National Curriculum assessment arrangements. Some schools have policies for early GCSE entry of high attainers in mathematics. This can have the benefit of ensuring that able pupils are challenged, but it can also be divisive and sometimes leads to an environment in which pupils are encouraged to enter early for the GCSE when it may not be desirable.

In recent years, increasing numbers of schools have adopted early-entry policies for GCSE mathematics, entering their top sets or even whole year groups for GCSE mathematics in Year 10. Some claim that there are benefits in enabling large numbers of pupils to gain a grade C at GCSE a year early. However, there is a significant danger with such policies that pupils are encouraged to think that they do need to continue to study mathematics beyond GCSE once they have gained a grade C. All pupils should be encouraged to achieve the highest grade in mathematics of which they are capable, and very few can do so by entering early.

The tiers of entry in GCSE can have a similar result at different levels of ability, as pupils who may be best entered for the Foundation level of entry experience pressure from peers, parents or teachers to enter the Higher tier. Remember that the intention of GCSE is to optimise attainment and to enable pupils to experience success. When pupils are entered inappropriately for higher levels, they are likely to experience failure, which can be demotivating or even debilitating. The converse is also true. Entering able pupils for the Foundation tier because all they need is a C can be counter-productive. Ploughing through undemanding questions can mean that pupils lose concentration when faced with the questions that will make the difference between a D and a C. Consequently, deciding which pupil to enter for which GCSE tier will require careful consideration and discussion.

In many schools, pupils who are not entered for GCSE at age 16 follow courses leading to other qualifications that form part of a curriculum for ages 14–19. Amongst these are entry-level qualifications offered by the awarding bodies (OCR, AQA and Edexcel). Some schools also offer courses leading to 14–19 diplomas at levels 1 and 2 alongside the GCSE courses; 14–19 diplomas are discussed in Chapter 13.

Task 7.11 **Departmental entry policy at age 16**

Talk to the head of mathematics in your school about the policy for assessment of mathematics at age 16.

▨ What levels of entry in the assessment are pupils entered for?
▨ How does the department decide, for each pupil, which is the appropriate level of entry?
▨ What assessment arrangements are made for pupils at the extremes: those who will struggle with the lowest level of entry at GCSE and those for whom GCSE is too easy?

Issues of fairness

Within any system of selection and grading in a school, it is very important that every care is taken to ensure that no individual is disadvantaged for any reason. Unfortunately, this high ideal is often challenged in unexpected ways, so it is important that teachers remain alert to the possibility of inequity in their classrooms. In mathematics, pupils for whom English is an additional language may experience difficulties with understanding what is required of them in assessed tasks because of their difficulties in understanding English.

Schools often have a significant role in deciding which tier of GCSE mathematics a pupil will be entered for and this decision is sometimes made several years before the GCSE examination. The basis for these decisions is often assessments made by the mathematics teachers during Key Stage 3. Hence, even assessments made in the classroom during Key Stage 3 need to be monitored to ensure that they are being made fairly and equitably.

Preparing to take examinations

Examination results are very important to schools due their use in league tables and the fact that Ofsted use them to decide whether a school is serving its pupils well. A school with poor examination results can find itself put 'in a category', indicating that Ofsted inspectors have decided that the school needs to improve its provision.

Alongside these considerations is also the fact that GCSE examinations are very important for the pupils themselves: for example, you cannot be considered to train as a teacher for any subject unless you have a grade C or above in mathematics at GCSE or equivalent. Under these circumstances, it is not surprising that many schools focus all their efforts on making sure that as many pupils as possible achieve a C, or above, in GCSE mathematics.

However, many schools interpret preparing for examinations with 'teaching to the test'. Ofsted has been highly critical of 'teaching to the test' as:

> a heavy emphasis on 'teaching to the test' succeed[s] in preparing pupils to gain the qualifications but […] not [in] equipping them well enough mathematically for their futures.
>
> (Ofsted, 2008: 4)

It is not necessary to 'teach to the test' in order to ensure that pupils achieve good examination grades. Evidence from Nardi and Steward (2003) and Boaler (2009) suggests that, rather than boring pupils with repetitive examination questions, teachers should be using the engaging and interesting approaches to mathematics teaching described in all the chapters of this book. Pupils who are interested in mathematics and feel confident to apply their knowledge in novel situations will be in a position to take examinations in their stride.

However, pupils still need opportunities to be prepared before taking examinations, and this can be done in many interesting and engaging ways. Rather than ploughing through paper after paper, pupils can be introduced to examination questions and techniques during Years 10 and 11 as just one of the many ways that they engage with mathematics. For example, they could:

▨ look at an interesting example of what might be asked of them in an examination question on a particular topic and make up a similar question for homework;

▨ read through an examination paper (without answering the questions) and select one or two questions that they think could be difficult, then complete just those questions;

▨ study a mark scheme in order to produce a set of rules for achieving highly in examinations;

▨ read through an examination paper and 'traffic-light' the questions, before finding out how to answer the questions they have labelled 'red';

▨ work together in a group to ensure that they can *all* do *every* question on an examination paper and obtain *every* mark available;

▨ look at an examination question on the use of statistics and make up a more interesting question that demonstrates the same statistical skills, complete with its own mark scheme.

Each of the above ideas fits into the normal varied diet for pupils in mathematics lessons; a balance of these challenges would gradually introduce pupils to the knowledge necessary to apply their mathematical knowledge confidently in an examination environment.

Teachers will probably use the last few weeks of an examination course to ask pupils to get used to completing a whole paper, but even this can be a collaborative activity, one in which pupils are encouraged to explain and justify answers. It is very important for you to ensure that no pupil gets bored with answering exam questions repeatedly and that no pupil is allowed quietly to panic on their own.

SUMMARY AND KEY POINTS

In this chapter, you have considered assessment as part of your everyday classroom practice. You have also considered the summative assessments that your pupils will face up to aged 16, as well as your role in helping your pupils to prepare for these.

A particularly relevant issue for you, as a future mathematics teacher, is how to manage your time effectively. Assessing pupils' work in mathematics can become a full-time job on its own, should you attempt to mark and correct in detail every piece of mathematical work ever done by a pupil. On the other hand, inadequate marking often leads to poor planning of lessons, poor motivation on the part of pupils and under-achievement. It is therefore very important that you learn how to decide which pieces of work to assess and in how much detail. This means that you need to be clear about your purposes in assessing and tailor the feedback you provide to meet your purposes. However, you do need to be able to discuss a pupil's mathematical work and progress with parents and with other teachers, as well as justify your judgements about pupils' attainment at the end of a Key Stage, so you need to keep reliable and manageable records.

FURTHER READING

Black, P. and Wiliam, D. (1998) *Inside the Black Box*. London: King's College London (reissued by NFER-Nelson).

This 20-page booklet provides a clear and succinct account of research evidence indicating how formative assessment can be used effectively in the classroom and how it can lead to gains in learning.

Black, P., Harrison, C., Lee, C., Marshal, B. and Wiliam, D. (2002) *Working Inside the Black Box: Assessment for Learning in the Classroom*. London: King's College.

This booklet presents the findings of a research programme in English schools where teachers implemented ideas from *Inside the Black Box*. The report identifies high-level questioning, feedback through marking, self-assessment and peer assessment as key practices by means of which learning can be improved.

Lee, C. (2006) *Language for Learning Mathematics: Assessment for Learning*. Buckingham: Open University Press.

This readable book gives an introduction to Assessment for Learning in the context of Mathematics.

QCA (2001) *Using Assessment to Raise Achievement in Mathematics*: Key Stages 1, 2 and 3. London: QCA (available from the QCA website: www.qca.org.uk/ages3-14/afl/)

QCA produced this report in response to the issues raised in the documents *Inside the black box* (Black and Wiliam, 1998) and *Assessment for Learning: Beyond the Black Box* (ARG, 1999). It places Assessment for Learning as an idea firmly within the governmental drive to raise standards.

COMMUNICATING MATHEMATICALLY

Candia Morgan

INTRODUCTION

Most of the activities involved in the teaching and learning of mathematics involve some form of communication: between teacher and pupil(s); between pupils; between pupil and text; between pupil and computer. There is oral communication (speaking and listening) and written communication (reading and writing). Much the same might be said of teaching and learning in many other subject areas, but there are special features of mathematics classrooms and mathematical language that make communication a particularly significant issue for mathematics teachers. While all teachers have a responsibility for enhancing pupils' general use of spoken and written language, as a mathematics teacher you have a particular responsibility to help pupils learn to speak and write *mathematically*.

Many beginning teachers see an ability to explain mathematical concepts and procedures clearly as the most important quality of a teacher. Being able to make good use of language yourself is, of course, an essential skill. It is important, however, to remember that you cannot assume that when you tell a child something, however clearly, they will necessarily hear and understand what you intended to communicate. Similarly, it is always useful to bear in mind that a child may not find it easy to communicate their state of mathematical understanding to you.

Learning mathematics is sometimes compared with learning a foreign language. Certainly, it can be mystifying for those who are unfamiliar with its vocabulary and grammar, while becoming fluent at speaking and writing as well as listening and reading can open up new possibilities for creating and communicating mathematical ideas.

OBJECTIVES

By the end of this chapter you should:

- have considered the special nature of mathematical communication and the ways in which the use of language in the classroom may help or hinder the learning of mathematics;
- be aware of some similarities and differences between speech and writing in relation to the mathematics classroom;

■   be able to think about the special nature of the language that is used to talk, write and think about mathematics;

■   have encountered some ways in which children may be helped to learn to communicate effectively about mathematics.

THE NATURE OF MATHEMATICAL LANGUAGE

Task 8.1 **Reflecting on experiences of mathematical language**

Think back to your own experiences as a learner of mathematics. Try to remember some of the different ways in which you were involved in communication – listening, speaking, reading and writing.

■   What was particularly mathematical about the language used?
■   When you first encountered new terms or forms of language, how did you feel?
■   What did you find difficult or challenging?

Like other specialised areas of human activity, mathematics has special forms and ways of using language that make it possible to communicate specifically mathematical ideas. As mathematics has developed through history, mathematicians have developed new words (or new meanings for old words), new notations and conventional styles of argument with which to think and communicate about new mathematical ideas and ways of thinking. This process of linguistic creation is still continuing; *fractal* (a newly invented word) and *fuzzy logic* (a new application or extension of old words) are but two relatively recent examples. Learning to understand and use this mathematical language is an essential part of learning mathematics. For those of us who have succeeded in becoming competent mathematicians, it is often difficult to realise how unfamiliar and confusing this special language can seem to those who are still struggling to learn how to use it. Reflecting on the nature of mathematical language can provide you with some insight into the problems it may cause your pupils. It is therefore worth taking a look at some of its characteristics and at its relationship with the everyday knowledge of language that pupils bring with them into the classroom.

Mathematical English

One of the most obvious places to start is with the *vocabulary* of mathematics. The National Numeracy Strategy provided a booklet, listing the mathematical words that primary school children are expected to learn and be able to use (DfES, 2000)[1] and the Secondary Strategy also set out lists of key vocabulary as part of their exemplification of objectives for Key Stage 3 Mathematics.[2] While some of these words will already be

---

1   Available as a download from http://nationalstrategies.standards.dcsf.gov.uk/node/88462
2   Examples for each learning objective may be found at:
    http://nationalstrategies.standards.dcsf.gov.uk/node/110233

familiar to many children from other contexts, others are unique to mathematics. Mathematics educator David Pimm (1987) distinguishes between words that are unlikely to be encountered outside the mathematics classroom (e.g. *quadrilateral, parallelogram, hypotenuse*) and those which have been 'borrowed' from everyday English (e.g. *face, power, product, rational*). Unfamiliar words may cause difficulties for learners simply because of their unfamiliarity; moreover, they are often long, polysyllabic and difficult to pronounce and spell. Few pupils (or teachers?) nowadays have the familiarity with the Latin or Greek roots of many of these words that might help in constructing and remembering their meanings (e.g. *isosceles* from Greek *iso* – equal and *skelos* – leg; *tangent* from Latin *tangere* – to touch).

Borrowed 'everyday' words, while apparently more familiar, can bring with them their own problems simply because their mathematical meanings are subtly different from their everyday meanings. In some cases, pupils' ability to come to terms with specialist mathematical uses of language may be further complicated by the emotional charges associated with words such as *odd, vulgar, improper, irrational*. The negative (!) connotations of such terms can prevent a pupil from attending to their 'pure' mathematical meanings.

To give a common example of the ways in which everyday meanings may interfere with precise mathematical usage, many secondary pupils will understand *straight* lines to be those that are drawn straight up and down or straight across the page (i.e. vertical or horizontal). For such pupils, *straight* may be seen to be opposed to *diagonal*. This can lead to further problems when dealing with the *diagonals* of polygons. Thus, Pimm (1987: 84–5) describes the work of a girl who saw one rectangle as having no diagonals while claiming that another had four (Figure 8.1).

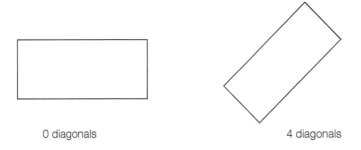

0 diagonals   4 diagonals

▨ **Figure 8.1** How many diagonals?

It is not only less able learners who have such difficulties with mathematical language; a study of 16 high-attaining Year 9 pupils, working on a problem about the diagonals of polygons (Morgan, 1988), revealed that, between them, they interpreted the word *diagonal* in at least six different ways, only one of which was the conventional mathematical meaning.

A particular area of potential difficulty is in the precise ways in which mathematical logic uses 'little' words like *and, or, some, all* or *any*. For example, when faced with a problem like:

show that the sum of any two odd numbers is an even number

some pupils will believe that they have answered satisfactorily if they give an example, such as $3 + 5 = 8$. This may indicate that the pupil, giving such an answer, believes that a single example is enough to prove a general statement. On the other hand, it may be that they have understood the problem to be to provide *any* example that confirms the statement. In mathematical discourse, the convention is that *any* is used to indicate generality, whereas in everyday discourse it tends to indicate mere arbitrariness (e.g. 'any old one will do').

When evaluating pupils' work, it is important for you to consider how they may have understood the question. In this case, you cannot know (without further investigation) whether the problem lies in the pupil's understanding of the nature of mathematical proof or in her or his understanding of the conventions of mathematical language.

Task 8.2 **Identifying mathematical language**

Take a chapter in a textbook or a set of worksheets on a topic that you will be teaching to one of your classes in the near future and consider the following questions:

▨ What specialist mathematical vocabulary or special uses of familiar words are employed in the text?

▨ How much of this terminology would you expect all pupils in the class to be familiar with before starting the topic? What specialist vocabulary and uses of language would you expect to be new or unfamiliar to the pupils? (Check this, using the list of vocabulary in the National Framework for Mathematics if the class is in Key Stage 3.) What sort of problems in understanding might this cause for your pupils? How important is it to their learning of this topic at this stage that they should learn this new language?

▨ How does the textbook or worksheet introduce new language to the pupils? How might you help pupils to develop the necessary language when you are teaching this topic?

Non-verbal forms of written communication

As well as the specialised use of verbal language discussed above, much written mathematical communication is characterised by its use of symbolism and graphic components such as diagrams and graphs. While such forms of communication are very powerful for expressing mathematical ideas, they can also be obscure or confusing for learners who are not familiar with the conventions of the system.

Algebraic symbolism

It is not possible here to give a detailed analysis of the characteristics of the mathematical symbol system or of the difficulties for learners that it may cause. Such an analysis may be found in Pimm (1987). I will, however, highlight a few of the issues that mathematics teachers need to be aware of.

1   Reading text that includes mathematical symbols involves different skills from those needed for ordinary verbal texts (Shuard and Rothery, 1984). Whereas ordinary English text can be read, in order, from left to right, some arrangements of symbols require the reader to attend to the components in a non-linear way. For example:

$$\left(\frac{3}{4} + 5\right)^2 \quad \text{or} \quad \int_1^6 \frac{1}{x^2} dx \quad \text{or} \quad \frac{6x + 4}{7x^2 - 3}$$

2   It is also important to remember that some learners will find it difficult to cope with symbols if they do not have any way of articulating them – reading them aloud to themselves or to others. The introduction of Greek letters (e.g. α, θ, Σ) should not, therefore, be seen as a simple extension of pupils' existing familiarity with algebraic symbolism. It may be necessary to pay attention to helping pupils to develop ways of talking and thinking with these symbols.

3   The commonly used 'metaphor' that algebraic symbols are 'shorthand' (e.g. a stands for apples, b for bananas) does not provide a sound conceptual base for the idea of letters as variables, and may contribute to some of the common difficulties that pupils have with algebra (Nolder, 1991).

Ways of working in the classroom to develop pupils' use of symbolism will be discussed later in this chapter. The National Framework for Mathematics at Key Stage 3 also includes some useful guidance about the early stages of use of algebraic symbolism, stressing the importance of developing algebra as a generalisation of arithmetic.

Task 8.3 **Reading symbols in words**

To add to pupils' difficulties with symbolic expressions, there is not always even a single 'correct' way to say them aloud. Ask some pupils and teachers to read these expressions aloud to you and listen carefully to the words each of them uses:

$$2(x+3), \quad \frac{(3x - 4)}{2}, \quad (A \cap B) \cup C, \quad \sin^2 2x$$

What implications might such diversity have for learners, and how might you deal with it in the classroom?

Graphs and diagrams

Although many other kinds of texts include graphical elements, in most cases these are used to supplement or illustrate information contained in verbal form elsewhere in the text. In mathematics, however, graphs, tables and diagrams are often used independently to communicate information that may not be available in any other form. Again, we cannot assume that pupils will naturally pick up the skills needed to make sense of such diagrammatic forms.

Indeed, there is considerable evidence that many secondary pupils do not read graphs in a conventional mathematical way. For example, the CSMS (Concepts in Secondary Mathematics and Science – see Hart, 1981) study found a substantial proportion of 13–15-year-olds who read time–distance graphs as if they were pictures of a journey. Thus, the journey shown by the graph in Figure 8.2 was described as 'climbing a mountain' or 'going up, going down, then up again' (Kerslake, 1981). As well as learning to read and interpret the values of separate points on a graph, pupils also need to learn how to interpret its overall shape.

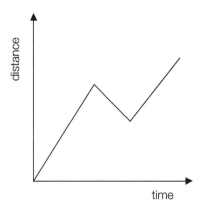

■ **Figure 8.2** A distance–time graph

Mathematical diagrams, too, need to be read in specialised ways. Remember the girl who saw one rectangle as having no diagonals while another had four. For her, the different orientation of the diagram seemed to mean that the two rectangles are different kinds of objects with different properties. The conventional mathematical way of reading such diagrams, however, assumes that, unless otherwise specified, orientation, size (and often other characteristics such as angle) are irrelevant. The reader is supposed to attend to only a subset of the physical properties of the diagram – it is not a picture of a concrete object but a representation of an abstract idea. Again, pupils need to be helped to learn how to make sense of mathematical diagrams. Using dynamic geometry software such as *The Geometer's Sketchpad* or *Cabri-Géomètre* (discussed in Chapter 9) brings new possibilities for making sense of diagrams – possibilities that mathematics educators are only beginning to understand.

Task 8.4 **Analysing diagrams**

Find a geometric diagram in a textbook you are using (e.g. a diagram illustrating a circle theorem).

Which characteristics of this diagram are essential and which are irrelevant, i.e. could be changed without affecting the mathematics?

How might you help pupils to see the diagram the same way that you do?

In some ways, it seems as if the specialised nature of mathematical language, symbols and visual representations forms a barrier to learning mathematics. However, there are some very strong arguments that the nature of mathematical thinking itself is intricately connected with the means used to communicate about it to others and to oneself. Anna Sfard (2008) goes so far as to claim that thinking and communicating mathematically are essentially the same. Taking a rather different approach, Bill Barton (2008) develops some fascinating alternative forms of mathematics that emerge from the structures of non-European languages. This raises questions about the worldwide dominance of the European tradition of mathematics that go beyond the scope of this chapter. Nevertheless, we must conclude that, if pupils are to have access to the school curriculum and to further mathematical studies, they must learn to use the specialised forms of communication that have been developed over the centuries by mathematicians.

Talking mathematics

A lot of talking goes on in many mathematics lessons, as in lessons of other subjects. It is important to ask, however, how much of this talking is likely to be productive for pupils' learning of mathematics and mathematical language. Much of the talking is done by teachers. As we have seen, there are many areas in which it is possible for teachers' talk to be misunderstood, so we should look at how teachers may try to ensure that pupils do understand and improve their knowledge of spoken mathematical language. It is also relevant to consider ways in which pupils may themselves be involved actively in speaking mathematically, through conversation or discussion with the teacher or other pupils.

One of the main ways in which many teachers try to ensure that pupils are listening actively and making sense of what is being said is through the use of questioning or interactive teacher–pupil discussion, expecting pupils to contribute to the joint construction of the exposition of a topic. It is widely recognised that discussion can play an important part in the mathematics classroom. Over 25 years ago, the Cockcroft Report (DES, 1982) included 'discussion' as one of the ways of working that all pupils should experience, seeing it as a means of developing the precision needed for communicating mathematical ideas:

> The ability to 'say what you mean and mean what you say' should be one of the outcomes of good mathematics teaching. This ability develops as a result of opportunities to talk about mathematics, to explain and discuss results that have been obtained, and to test hypotheses. (para. 246)

Moreover, discussion between pupils or between pupils and teacher can be a good way of exploring and developing pupils' concepts and their awareness of relationships among different areas of mathematics.

At the same time, however, there is not a clear consensus among teachers about what it might mean to 'discuss' in the mathematics classroom. Some seem to interpret *any* verbal interaction as discussion, including conventional question-and-answer sequences. Sometimes, however, the pupils' side of such interaction consists only of 'guessing what is in the teacher's mind' and can be little more than 'filling in the gap' left by the teacher. This may be useful for the teacher to check that pupils are following the lesson and may be effective for reinforcing the use of correct vocabulary. It is less likely, however, to involve pupils in higher-level thinking or to encourage them to use and develop other aspects of the language needed to express more complex mathematical ideas and reasoning. Evaluation of the National Strategy for Key Stage 3 carried out by inspectors identified the best mathematics lessons as those in which teachers' questioning elicited thoughtful responses from pupils (Ofsted, 2003). (See also the discussion of forms of teacher questioning in Chapter 6.)

For such purposes, the questioning teacher needs to create opportunities for pupils to think and to formulate contributions in their own words. This means asking more searching questions that demand higher-level thinking rather than straightforward recall (for example, questions that ask for observations, comparisons, explanations). Anne Watson and John Mason have collected together and categorised questions that can be used to prompt mathematical thinking in their useful book (Watson and Mason, 1998). These kinds of questions can occur at many points during a lesson but may be particularly useful during a plenary discussion after pupils have been engaged in an individual or small-group activity, encouraging them to generalise and to reflect on what they have been doing.

Higher-level questioning also means allowing pupils time to think about their answers. If an answer is not volunteered straight away, the silence that ensues can seem threatening to both teacher and pupils and it can often then be tempting to make the question less demanding or to provide one's own answer. More searching questions, however, need to be thought about before an answer is given, not only to work out what needs to be said but also to decide upon the very words with which to say it. One way of dealing with this is to develop a culture in your classroom that values thinking before talking. One teacher, described by Jaworski (1992), achieved this by introducing the idea of a 'hands-down think' after such a question has been posed; the pupils knew that they were then expected to think seriously about the question and that their contributions would be valued.

Task 8.5 **Observing and reflecting on classroom language**

Arrange to observe another mathematics teacher's lesson. Focus on the ways in which they use questioning. Note how they use questions:

■ to assess pupils' understanding or knowledge;
■ to prompt exploration of an idea or problem;
■ to prompt generalisation or reflection.

What sort of responses are expected of pupils? How long does the teacher give pupils to formulate their responses? What opportunities do they get to develop and practise their use of mathematical language?

Observe other teachers, including some of other subjects, with the same questions. You might also record a lesson of your own and then 'examine' it in the same way.

Reflect on these observations. What similarities and differences are there between teachers in the ways they use questioning? Why might this be? How might the different forms of questioning affect pupils' opportunities for learning?

Communication between teacher and pupil, while an essential component of every class-room, is not always the best way to develop pupils' use of precise mathematical language. The pupil usually feels that the teacher has a good idea of what they are trying to say and the teacher usually works quite hard to understand what the pupil is saying, drawing on expectations of mathematical correctness and past experience. A joint under-standing of what is being said may thus be constructed *without* the pupil having to produce a complete and exact verbal statement.

In order to develop more complete verbal communication skills, it can be helpful to create situations in the classroom where the pupil is trying to communicate with some-one (often another pupil) who does not have this sort of prior knowledge of what is being communicated. For example, when working with three-dimensional shapes, one pupil may be asked to construct an object using eight interlocking cubes and then describe it (without showing it) to a partner who must construct the same object from the verbal description alone. This task includes its own automatic feedback: the partner can ask for further clarification, if necessary, and the match or mismatch between the two objects will reveal whether or not the communication has been successful.

The poster lesson using a poster of the great stellated dodecahedron, which was described and discussed in Chapter 4, is a whole-class task requiring the same sort of precision of language.

Task 8.6 **Discussion to develop use of language**

Plan a lesson for a small group of pupils that will involve them in discussion with you or with each other and that will require them to use mathematical language correctly and with precision (some useful suggestions may be found in the Mathematical Association publication *Maths Talk* (MA, 1987)).

You will need to consider:

- what the topic of discussion will be;
- what sorts of things the pupils might be expected to say;
- the social context of the discussion – what is the purpose for the pupils of communicating with each other or with you?
- providing a *context* that requires correctness and precision in order to commu-nicate (not just as an arbitrary requirement on the teacher's part).

After the lesson, reflect on the extent to which the tasks you designed succeeded in encouraging the pupils to use mathematical language effectively.

WRITING MATHEMATICALLY

Some teachers and pupils think of mathematics as an area of the curriculum in which little or no writing is needed. If mathematics were just about carrying out procedures and manipulating symbols, this could be true. This, however, is a very limited view of math-ematical activity, and certainly does not reflect either the way in which mathematicians actually work or the requirements of the National Curriculum. Most importantly, doing mathematics also involves conjecturing, explaining, justifying, proving and, in general, communicating one's thinking to others. While all of these may be done orally, there are some important advantages to using writing. The most obvious advantage is that writing produces a durable record that can be revisited:

a) by the writer:
  - ▓ as a reminder of earlier thinking, perhaps in order to pick up a problem that had been partially solved in a previous lesson or to aid revision for a test or examination;
  - ▓ as a source of reflection on their thinking in order to revise, refine and improve it – for example, to consider whether a justification is sufficient and to change it or add to it.
b) by others:
  - ▓ so that pupils can share their thinking – for example, comparing alternative solutions or explanations side-by-side;
  - ▓ so that teachers can gain fuller access to their pupils' thinking, supplementing the insights gained during oral interactions.

A further characteristic of writing that may aid mathematics learning is that it demands greater completeness and explicitness than is generally necessary for oral communication. When we talk, we are usually able to assume that our audience shares a lot of common experience and knowledge of the immediate context – this then remains unsaid or alluded to in vague terms or by 'hand-waving'. For example, Rowland (1992) documents how pronouns such as 'it' are extensively used in mathematical talk to refer to complex ideas. This is not a problem, as it allows pupils to work with and develop their emergent ideas. In order to crystallise these ideas and build on them, however, it is eventually necessary to name them more explicitly and precisely. Writing the ideas down brings with it the need to be explicit as well as allowing the writer time to think about what words to use and how to express their ideas more precisely.

In addition to the benefits that writing offers to mathematics learning, engaging in literacy activities in mathematics supports pupils' more general development of language skills. There is an expectation that all teachers should contribute to the development of literacy in and through their subject. The National Strategy has provided some suggestions for activities to support writing and other language skills in mathematics (DfES, 2004b).[3]

Many pupils find even short pieces of writing difficult or distasteful; even some of those who are otherwise very successful in mathematics may have problems writing about their mathematical activity. Writing explanations and justifications is particularly challenging for many pupils, including those who might well be able to construct an adequate explanation in a verbal dialogue with their teacher or another pupil. The analysis of pupils' answers to the 2000 Key Stage 3 tests (QCA, 2001) reported that, when asked for explanations, a significant proportion of pupils showed some understanding but appeared unable to communicate their explanations adequately. While explanation and justification may be difficult in themselves, the requirement to write them seems to make the task even harder. In this section, some of the more troublesome characteristics of mathematical writing will be outlined, together with some discussion of ways of supporting pupils as they learn to write mathematically.

---

3 *Literacy in Mathematics* is also available to download from:
   http://nationalstrategies.standards.dcsf.gov.uk/node/96655

Task 8.7 **Writing mathematically**

Here are some suggestions of different kinds of starting points for writing. Try some of them for yourself and, when you have done so, reflect on:

▪ how this mathematical writing is different from other kinds of writing you do;
▪ the mathematical thinking you had to do in order to write effectively;
▪ how these starting points might be adapted for use with pupils in the classroom.

1   Write interesting statements starting 'Circles . . .'
2   Factorise the expression $7x^2 - 62x + 48$. Explain how you did this. Describe your general strategies for factorising quadratic expressions efficiently.
3   'The mean is the most useful measure of central tendency.' Discuss.
4   Explain why the sum of three consecutive integers is always divisible by 3.

If you can work with another mathematics student teacher, read each other's pieces of writing, identify similarities and differences and consider how your writing might be improved by redrafting. Alternatively, a colleague in your school might help.

It is sometimes argued that it is the English teacher's job to teach pupils to write – mathematics teachers have neither the time nor the expertise. It might be convenient to believe this; however, it is clear that English teachers do not, on the whole, have the expertise themselves to teach pupils how to write mathematically (nor the time to devote to the specialised needs of every area of the school curriculum). The forms of language needed to construct a concise and precise mathematical definition or a rigorous justification are quite different from those required in everyday or literary writing or in other subject disciplines. Moreover, it is not possible to judge the complete effectiveness of a written definition or justification without the sort of mathematical content knowledge that belongs to the mathematics teacher's expertise. This is not to say that the English teacher has nothing to offer. Indeed, collaboration with language specialists can be a very valuable experience, both for the pupils and for the teachers involved. See, for example, Lawson and Lee's (1995) description of the support provided by an English teacher during a mathematical investigation and the account of partnership teaching by a mathematics teacher and a language support teacher given in the Association of Teachers of Mathematics booklet *Talking Maths, Talking Languages* (ATM, 1993a).

An example of the way in which learning about the forms of language needed to express definitions can happen alongside learning about the concept being defined is offered by American mathematics educator Raffaella Borasi (1992), in her book *Learning Mathematics through Inquiry*. She collected definitions of the concept *circle* from her pupils, getting typical responses like:

> *All the possible series of points equidistant from a single point*
> πr^2 *area formula, = radius, an exact centre, 360°*
> *Round – 3.14 – shape of an orange, coin, earth – pi*
> *Circle = something whose area is = to πr^2*
> *A closed, continuous, rounded line*

The pupils were then asked to discuss and produce a critique of the written definitions, identifying which were precise enough to make a distinction between circles and non-circles. The discussion with the teacher also addressed the difference between a definition and a list of properties. One outcome of such discussion can be an agreed, revised definition that is acceptable to all the pupils as well as to the teacher. Because all the pupils have been involved in the writing and rewriting of this definition (rather than merely reading or copying a definition given by their textbook or teacher), they are not only more likely to understand and remember the concept itself but are also likely to have learnt something about the ways in which mathematical definitions ought to be written. You cannot assume that children will learn to write mathematically merely by engaging in writing. There is an important difference between assigning a task that involves writing and teaching about that writing. Talking together with other pupils and/or with a teacher, and drafting and redrafting in a group, can provide much needed support and feedback and increase awareness of the requirements of effective communication.

Communicating using algebraic notation

If you ask adults who have not been successful at learning mathematics about their experiences and feelings in the mathematics classroom, you will often get a response that refers to xs and ys as a major source of mystification. In some cases, the introduction of algebraic notation early in the secondary school is felt to have been the turning point at which an otherwise academically successful pupil started to fail in mathematics. To many people, symbols appear to have little meaning and attempting to work with them may be a frustrating and anxiety-inducing activity.

At the same time, however, algebraic symbolism is enormously important in mathematics, not only as a means of expressing generalisation but also as a means of thinking about and manipulating problems that might otherwise prove intractable. It is, therefore, important to help pupils to develop meaning for symbols and to see them as useful means of communicating mathematical ideas.

One way of demystifying symbolism is to introduce it as a natural development of pupils' own attempts to record their generalisations of patterns. James and Mason (1982) described the process by which some children's verbal explanations of how to build square 'picture frames' out of interlocking cubes were converted via the introduction of a 'thinks cloud' standing for the variable size of the picture, into a more conventional algebraic expression (Figure 8.3).

The teacher's role is crucial here in introducing appropriate forms of notation at a time when the pupils can appreciate a need for them. Through having struggled to produce their own means of recording and to interpret others' attempts, pupils are more likely to see the usefulness of a standard notation. In this case, an obvious further benefit that the pupils would be able to see is the possibility of comparing different ways of building the picture-frames through the use of a common descriptive notation. Such an introduction, building on pupils' own patterning and generalising, should enable pupils to attach meaning to algebraic symbols and to see them as a useful addition to their repertoire of means of communicating mathematical ideas.

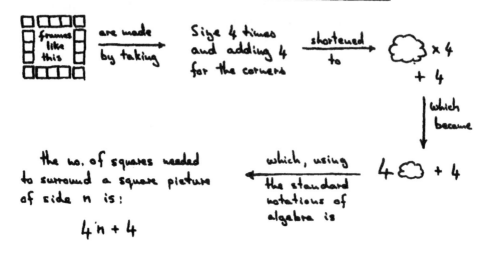

For Susan's Group the recording process looked like:

are made by taking → Size 4 times and adding 4 for the corners → shortened to → ☁ × 4 + 4

which became ↓

4 ☁ + 4

← which, using the standard notations of algebra is

the no. of squares needed to surround a square picture of side n is:

$$4n + 4$$

▨ **Figure 8.3** Progression towards conventional recording
Source: James and Mason, 1982: 257

Communication as the key to assessment

One very important type of communication that goes on in classrooms is that involved in assessing pupils' understanding. Most of a teacher's knowledge about pupils' achievement is gathered through listening to them talk and reading their written work. Much of the recent work discussed in Chapter 6 on developing aspects of formative assessment has emphasised the importance of increasing opportunities for pupils to talk and write (e.g. Lee, 2006). When the classroom is full of pupils talking and/or writing about mathematics, one major benefit is the opportunities provided for teachers to listen and read and hence to gain some access to the pupils' understanding of the mathematics. (This is another reason for not spending too much time talking yourself!)

Miller (1992) suggests that the use of short 'writing prompts', getting pupils to write briefly about a specified topic, can not only encourage the pupils to reflect on and, hence, reinforce what they have learnt, but can also provide the teacher with valuable insight into what pupils have learnt and where they may still have difficulties. For example, you might ask pupils:

▨ to explain *how* (to add fractions, factorise an algebraic expression, ...);
▨ to write *what* they know about a topic (triangles, equations, ...);
▨ to explain *why* (a quick way of multiplying a decimal number by 10 is to 'move the point', 50 ÷ 2 is not the same as 2 ÷ 50, ...).

You must, however, be cautious about relying too much on written forms of communication in order to assess pupils' understanding. Children's written work may not always fully represent what they can do, not only because they lack familiarity with the necessary forms of language, but also because they may be unsure of what aspects of their work and their thinking need to be recorded.

MacNamara and Roper (1992) describe how they listened in as a pair of children discussed how they should write about their work on a problem. They found that the children decided to omit some of their findings because they realised that others in the class had also found the same results and felt that they were therefore no longer interesting enough to be communicated. If the teacher had not been near the pair at the crucial moment, their moment of insight into the problem would never have been noticed. It may happen by chance that the teacher is present and listening at such a moment, but think how many conversations between pupils take place out of the teacher's hearing and, in consequence, how many such decisions may be taken unnoticed. It is probably useful, therefore, for the teacher to plan deliberately to talk with small groups of pupils about their ongoing work and to provide them with some help in making better decisions about what should be recorded in writing.

Task 8.8 **Attending to pupils' attempts to communicate**

Listening to pupils
Plan to work for one lesson with a pair or small group of pupils tackling a problem or investigation (e.g. 'How many different shapes can you make with five cubes?'). Give the pupils some time at the end of the lesson to write about what they have done. If possible, record the lesson or take notes about what the pupils say.

After the lesson, listen to the recording and compare this with the pupils' written records. To what extent does their writing give you a full picture of what the pupils achieved during the lesson?

Reading pupils' writing
At the end of a lesson or sequence of lessons, ask pupils to write a few sentences about what they have learnt and what questions they still have about the topic.

What do their responses reveal about (a) their understanding of the topic, and (b) their grasp of mathematical forms of language?

SUMMARY AND KEY POINTS

In this chapter, you have been asked to think about the special nature of the language that is used to talk, write and think about mathematics. It is necessary to be aware of the difficulties that mathematical language may cause to learners in the classroom as they struggle to understand their teacher's speech and to read and make sense of the written materials they are expected to respond to during a lesson. As you plan your lessons, one of the factors that should be considered is the language demands on the pupils: how familiar or comfortable are they likely to be with the language they will encounter and how will you help them to become more fluent in understanding and using it themselves.

The conciseness and precision of mathematical notation, vocabulary, definition and argument are not merely conventional; they play important roles in mathematical thinking. You have been introduced to some ways of working with pupils in the classroom to help them to develop mathematical ways of speaking and writing and to appreciate the reasons that mathematical language has developed in these ways.

There is, however, a tension between the wish to introduce pupils to conventional mathematical means of communicating and the need to avoid the mystification and consequent anxiety or dislike of the subject that can be induced by using language that pupils are unfamiliar with. It is this tension that you are asked to reflect on in the final task for this chapter.

Task 8.9 **Your reflections on the use of 'correct' language**

Should we insist that children use 'correct' mathematical language? Make a list of the reasons why it is important that pupils should learn to use mathematical language. Make a second list of reasons why it might be better to allow pupils to use non-mathematical language in some circumstances. What are instances of such circumstances?

Compare your lists and discuss with a student teacher or a practising mathematics teacher.

FURTHER READING

Connolly, P. and Vilardi, T. (eds) (1989) *Writing to Learn Mathematics and Science.* **New York: Teachers College Press.**

This is a collection of papers written by teachers (mostly in the United States) who have introduced writing into their mathematics (or science) classrooms. There are lots of ideas of writing activities to use and some useful discussion of ways in which pupils may be helped to write more effectively.

Pimm, D. (1987) *Speaking Mathematically: Communication in Mathematics Classrooms.* **London: Routledge and Kegan Paul.**

This comprehensive book provides a thorough analysis of mathematical language and discusses the many ways in which spoken and written language are used in mathematics classrooms and the ways in which this may affect pupils' learning of mathematics.

Lee, C. (2006) *Language for Learning Mathematics: Assessment for Learning in Practice.* **Maidenhead: Open University Press.**

As well as discussing how using oral and written language in mathematics classrooms can support both learning and assessment, this book provides a range of practical approaches to developing richer language in the classroom.

MA (1987) *Maths Talk.* **Cheltenham: Stanley Thornes.**

Although originally aimed at primary teachers, most of this book is equally relevant to mathematics teachers at secondary level. It discusses developing spoken language skills, including issues related to classroom organisation, and offers ideas for starting mathematical discussions.

ATM (1993) *Talking Maths, Talking Languages.* **Derby: Association of Teachers of Mathematics.**

This book looks at issues involved for mathematics teachers working in multilingual classrooms. It contains discussion, classroom ideas, case studies and a useful resource list. Although there is a focus on the needs of multilingual learners, there is much here that is equally relevant for all those involved in learning to communicate mathematically.

DfES (2000) *The National Numeracy Strategy: Mathematical Vocabulary*. London: Department for Education and Skills.
As well as a list of mathematical vocabulary needed by pupils in each year of the primary school, this booklet contains advice about introducing new mathematical language and encouraging pupils to use it, much of which is equally relevant for secondary teachers and pupils.

USING INFORMATION AND COMMUNICATION TECHNOLOGY (ICT)

Sue Johnston-Wilder and David Pimm

INTRODUCTION

A new teacher, interested in the possibilities afforded by emerging technology, made no headway until she had a computer of her own at home. She was later loaned a graphic calculator, but it sat in the cupboard until she attended an inspiring workshop; the workshop gave her a vision of possibilities and enabled her to overcome the initial complication of starting with a portable, but less friendly, piece of technology.

Personal access is a major advantage in allowing teachers the time and space to make good progress in the use of technology. As well as access, you need inspiration to see possibilities for yourself and your class, before you can start to make progress along what can be, at times, a frustrating road. Happily, access is relatively easy these days and there are inspirational leaders and strong resources to help you along the way.

In this chapter, you will consider the role of new technologies in the mathematics curriculum. Important resources, whose role you will consider, include: calculators, spreadsheets, graph plotters, graphic calculators, dynamic geometry packages, programming languages such as Logo, small teaching programs and the internet. Throughout the chapter, you will be invited to look at some important general features of working mathematically with computers:

- learning from feedback;
- observing patterns;
- seeing connections;
- working with dynamic images;
- exploring data;
- teaching the computer.

(Becta, 2009)

As in Chapter 4, you will consider different organisational structures for working with ICT in the classroom, such as whole-class, small-group or individual ways of working, whether structured or exploratory. You will be asked to compare and contrast different kinds of software use, some appropriate and some inappropriate, in relation to your pedagogic goals. Some research evidence will also be presented, in order to support the development of your critical thinking.

As you read the chapter, and experiment with ICT, do not allow more experienced users to put you off. ICT is only easy when you know how and you have the right to take time to learn.

> An experienced ICT presenter went to run an INSET session and the computers were not logged on. She found the computer specialist and asked him to log on for her. 'Oh, that's easy,' he replied. Nevertheless, she asked him to come and do it for her. It turned out that a secret password was needed and he had forgotten he was the only person available who knew what it was!

OBJECTIVES

By the end of the chapter, you should be able to:

■ understand and discuss thoughtfully the contribution that ICT (including calculators and computers) can make to learning and teaching mathematics;

■ provide an appropriate environment (including tasks) that will enable pupils to learn from feedback, observe patterns, see connections, work with dynamic images, explore data and 'teach' the computer;

■ develop your knowledge of particular software to enhance your mathematics teaching, including getting access to available resources and support for using ICT in the maths classroom.

SOME BACKGROUND

ICT plays an increasing role in many of today's classrooms. Evidence that ICT makes an effective contribution to learning has been available for many years. The evidence claims back in 1994 (NCET, 1994) were that use of IT resulted in:

■ flexibility to meet individual needs;
■ more enthusiasm and confidence, safe and non-threatening;
■ encouragement for those who otherwise do not enjoy or worse fail;
■ reduction in the risk of failure;
■ encouragement of reflection and modification of responses;
■ a shift in focus from technique to interpretation;
■ access to information;
■ access to ideas through alternative presentations;
■ interactivity, motivation, stimulation;
■ trying out ideas, risk-taking, development of autonomy;
■ different approaches and different kinds of thought;
■ a special role helping pupils with SEN to achieve more.

In 1994, the main hurdle to taking advantage of ICT was access to hardware – since that time there has been an enormous investment in school ICT hardware, but a reduction in the impact of ICT on learning in mathematics (Ofsted, 2008). As well as access to hardware and software, we need to consider the role of teachers.

The same NCET (National Council for Educational Technology) report identified that teachers need to be able to design meaningful tasks in the context of ICT, requiring pupils to work more independently of teachers in the classroom, both individually and in groups, in order to take full advantage of what ICT has to offer. In particular, teachers need to learn to recognise when to intervene and when to allow pupils to continue. This dilemma is not confined to ICT and is discussed further in Chapters 6 and 11. Good ICT use is about allowing all pupils to reach for understanding and engage in truly 'deep' relational learning. Implicit in the concept of deep learning is that learning must be an active process, where learners search for patterns and principles while using evidence and logic (Entwistle, 2000).

The National Curriculum for England (QCA, 2007a) takes account of this 'active approach' in embedding ICT as involving tools, access to which is taken for granted. The Curriculum document requires that:

> Pupils should be familiar with a range of resources and tools, including graphic calculators, dynamic geometry and spreadsheets, which can be used to work on mathematics. Pupils are expected to select appropriate mathematical tools and methods, including ICT. They are required to select mathematical information, methods and tools to use. They are to consider the elegance and efficiency of alternative solutions, including ICT. They are to become familiar with a range of resources, including ICT, so that they can select appropriately. This includes using practical resources and ICT, such as spreadsheets, dynamic geometry, graphing software and calculators, to develop mathematical ideas. They are to work with and without ICT, using ICT where appropriate.
>
> (QCA, 2007a: 142–7)

Consequently, mathematics teachers are expected to consider what ICT adds to the learning of mathematics and when it is appropriate to use ICT.

To help with this process of identifying the benefits of ICT, the Becta (2009) leaflet *Entitlement to ICT in Secondary Mathematics* gives a framework of six major ways in which ICT can provide opportunities for pupils learning mathematics (see Table 9.1). By the end of this chapter, you should be able to bring to mind examples from your own use of ICT that illustrate these six 'entitlements'. We hope you will also see some examples in your schools of pupils using ICT to learn from feedback, observe patterns, see connections, work with dynamic images, explore data and 'teach' the computer how to do something.

Task 9.1 **ICT audit**

Look at the audit chart in Table 9.2. There are nine different technological tools, each of which will be covered to some extent in this chapter. For each tool, there are columns for five levels of experience. These levels have been designed to help you audit your present experience and identify where you need to broaden/deepen your experience of technology in your mathematics teaching. If any of these tools is completely new to you (level 0), there is an introductory description in Appendix 4.

■ **Table 9.1** A pupil's entitlement to ICT in secondary mathematics classes

1. Learning from feedback
The computer often provides fast and reliable feedback, which is non-judgemental and impartial. This can encourage pupils to make their own conjectures and to test out and modify their ideas.

2. Observing patterns
The speed of computers and calculators enables pupils to produce many examples when exploring mathematical problems. This supports their observation of patterns and the making and justifying of generalisations.

3. Seeing connections
The computer enables formulae, tables of numbers and graphs to be linked readily. Changing one representation and seeing changes in the others helps pupils to understand the connections between them.

4. Working with dynamic images
Pupils can use computers to manipulate diagrams dynamically. This encourages them to visualise the geometry as they generate their own mental images.

5. Exploring data
Computers enable pupils to work with real data, which can be represented in a variety of ways. This supports interpretation and analysis.

6. Teaching the computer
When pupils design an algorithm (a set of instructions) to make a computer achieve a particular result, they are compelled to express their commands unambiguously and in the correct order. They make their thinking explicit as they refine their ideas.

Source: Becta, 2009

Level 1, 'Acquainted', represents having met and used the tool enough to know what it is. This is the level assumed in this chapter.

Level 2, the 'Personal user' level, describes individuals who have used the tool to explore some mathematics for themselves and who are aware of some of the processes involved.

Level 3, the 'Classroom user', describes someone who has ideas for appropriate use of the tool with pupils learning mathematics at school level, and who has had the opportunity to work through and reflect on a variety of tasks designed to explore the power of the tool for enhancing the teaching and learning of mathematics.

Finally, level 4, the 'Critical user', refers to someone who feels able to identify some pitfalls and problems that may arise when using the tool with pupils and who has some knowledge of educational research findings related to the tool.

This chapter and your background reading will help you to consider some of the important issues that the use of each tool raises. These range from specific curriculum issues to questions about teaching and learning styles and issues of equality of opportunity.

Make a copy of the audit chart in Table 9.2. Use it to record your current level of experience with each of the tools shown. You should return to the table and review your progress at intervals during the year.

▪ **Table 9.2** ICT self-audit chart

	Level 0 Novice: never touched one of these before[1]	Level 1 Acquainted: have used and know what it is	Level 2 Personal user: have used reflectively for own maths	Level 3 Classroom user: have ideas for use with pupils	Level 4 Critical user: have critical awareness of research issues related to use
Calculator					
Spreadsheet					
Graph plotter					
Graphic calculator					
Dynamic geometry package					
Programming language (e.g. Logo)					
Small teaching programs					
Internet					

1 Please read the appropriate part of Appendix 4 if Level 0 applies

CALCULATING DEVICES

Throughout history, various invented devices (such as mathematical tables, abaci, slide rules and mechanical or electronic calculators) have been devised to assist with the performing of calculations. With each one, there are practices and conventions to be learned concerned with how to *use* the device to implement an algorithm (such as when and how to move beads or change rows, how to read off from the cursor or which buttons to press and in which order).

In addition, with each device there are questions about what service it may be in *learning* mathematics directly (rather than merely helping mathematics to be done). What images are offered implicit in the way numbers are represented? What understanding about operations or the numeration system does each device support, in becoming more fluent users? What sort of devices are they? One might reflect on the usefulness of the 'borrow and pay back' story recounted at the start of this chapter for a way of undertaking written subtraction. To what extent does the device promote understanding of the process?

'Slide of hand'

We start with neither an account of the abacus nor the electronic calculator, but with a brief look at the slide rule. Costel Harnasz (1993) has produced a clear and illuminating account of its educational history, entitled 'Do you need to know how it works?', and relates his discussion to current concerns about the use of electronic calculators in schools. In particular, he quotes Richard Delamain (1630):

> For no one to know the use of a Mathematical Instrument, except he knows the cause of its operation, is somewhat too strict, which would keep many from affecting the Art, because they see nothing but obscure propositions, and perplex and intricated demonstrations before their eyes.
>
> (Harnasz, 1993: 142)

Harnasz contrasts Delamain's view with seventeenth-century contemporary William Oughtred's concern that certain teachers' pupils were 'only doers of tricks and, as it were, jugglers'. As Delamain made technical instruments, he had a vested economic interest in not restricting the allowed audience. The issue is practice over understanding. Being able to 'affect the Art' is precisely at the core of the ongoing debate over calculators: the fear of apparent sophistication of performance unrooted in understanding, and the perennial desire of teachers to be able to say a pupil has understood when they exhibit successful practice (the latter having the advantage of being observable, unlike 'thinking'). Conversely, it is not clear that 'understanding' necessarily makes you a better or more proficient user.

On the abacus

Historically, abacuses were widely used (and in some countries, for example Russia and Japan, still are), as were counting boards. These historical counting devices and their associated practices provide a mental image of a computation.

In an article on the Japanese abacus – the *soroban* – Catherine Hoare (1990) remarks how, after gaining remarkable facility with the soroban in performing computations, the Japanese schoolchildren she saw (aged 8–11) were given mental arithmetic (six-digit) additions and subtractions.

> The pupils sat with their eyes shut or half-closed running their fingers an inch above the desk top as if the soroban were still there! At the end of each question just under half of the pupils had the correct answer, but all had attempted questions which would have been unthinkable within our conception of mental arithmetic. Their method consists of mentally visualising a soroban and working through the problem using standard techniques. (pp. 13–14)

This account raises many questions. What range of images do pupils have when carrying out mental computations and what support do these images offer? Are images of Dienes apparatus, for example, available to pupils who have worked intensively with it – are there physical motions in muscle memory (where the hands are doing the thinking) available to be drawn on? Hoare adds: 'Through mechanisation of operation, therefore, the soroban becomes as automatic to the Japanese as the calculator has to the younger generation of English'. Yet, as with the differences between specific numeration systems, the structural differences between these two devices are relevant to mathematics education.

On the calculator

Modern electronic calculators are nowhere near as 'transparent' with regard to their functioning and therefore do not offer much imagistic support. Numbers are entered from right to left as when written down, which acts to 'move' the digit across each 'place'. It is an interesting and open question whether this relative absence of associated imagery with a calculator is a potential weakness (the mechanisms are opaque and therefore offer very little support) or a potential strength (leaving pupils free to form their own imagery) with regard to using such devices to help gain either numerical fluency or understanding.

But what about numerical operations? With most calculators, there is no difference between any of the four arithmetic operations and taking powers or square roots (except possibly a slight time difference in operation). All are carried out by pressing a single operation key. With the soroban, the algorithm is far more accessible to view, implemented by the user, and can be internalised through repetition of hand movements. With the calculator, everything is inaccessible, invisible.

The calculator has single buttons that perform an increasing variety of mathematical functions. But with a calculator you lose the sense of an algorithm for these operations, as there is no evidence of intermediate steps. Such single buttons become *primitives* in the sense that no further interrogation of how they are being carried out is possible – they become inaccessible. What is different between a set of square-root tables and the square-root button on a calculator? Written tables may not provide many clues as to their genesis, but each table is a single object open to inspection and analysis, complete with interpolation rules.

The debate about the use of calculators still rages and has done since the 1970s. The *Second International Mathematics Survey* (Cresswell and Gubb, 1987) claimed to show that numeracy has declined since the first study in 1967. This coincided with a general availability of relatively cheap calculators and an association was conjectured, understandably. However, the classroom teachers in the study claimed they were not allowing the use of calculators.

Following the publication of the *Third International Mathematics and Science Study* (TIMSS) (Keys *et al.*, 1996), there was more debate about calculators. Ann Kitchen (1998) explored further the issue of teachers' reported use of calculators in different countries in TIMSS; she showed that in nearly every country for which data was available children aged 9 who were encouraged to use calculators in their maths lessons performed better than those who were not. At age 14, of the four categories of frequency of calculator use, those who used calculators nearly every day performed best in 16 of the 35 countries. The issue is clearly much more complex than some commentators have suggested.

It is possible to draw the conclusion that the reduction in numeracy is due to the general reduction in the use of number skills. For example, most shops use electronic tills, and other developments in new technology have reduced the level of mental arithmetic skills required to function in everyday life. In various studies, there are reports that calculators are not being used as much as critics are assuming (see, for example, DES, 1982, para. 376).

In recent years, the attention of teachers has tended to be drawn away from the very important question of how calculators can be used to best effect in the teaching of mathematics, because they were caught up in the political argument about whether to allow pupils to use calculators. One major exception to this was the Calculator Aware Number

(CAN) project from the early 1980s, in which primary school teachers were encouraged to look with open minds at what might constitute good practice in teaching with calculators. Now it is statutory in England that 'Pupils should be able to calculate accurately, selecting mental methods or calculating devices as appropriate' (QCA, 2007a: 143). It is worth noting here that in the sixteenth century, Johannes Kepler was rebuked by his mentor for using the latest new idea to facilitate his calculations; he used logarithms. According to Michael Mästlin, he should have done the calculations 'properly'.

Becta gave the following advice in a Key Stage 3 in-service pack:

> As with numeracy, the appropriate use of calculators is a whole-school matter. All subjects need to adopt a similar approach and agree when, how and for what purpose calculators are to be used.
>
> Before Year 5, the calculator's main role in mathematics is not as a calculating tool, since pupils are still developing the mental calculation skills and written methods that they will need in later years. But it does offer a unique way of learning about mathematical ideas throughout all Key Stages. For example, pupils might use a calculator to [help them] find two consecutive numbers with a given product and then discuss their methods.
>
> If pupils are to use the basic facilities of a calculator constructively and efficiently for calculating purposes, you will need to teach them in Key Stage 3 the technical skills that they will require. For example, during Key Stage 3 they need to learn:

> ■ how to select from the display the number of figures appropriate to the context of the calculation;
> ■ how to enter numbers and interpret the display when the numbers represent money, metric measurements, units of time or fractions;
> ■ the order in which to use the keys for calculations involving more than one step;
> ■ how to use facilities such as the memory, brackets, the square root and cube root keys, the sign change key, the fraction key, the constant facility, and so on.

> By the end of Key Stage 3, pupils should have the knowledge and skills to use a calculator to work out expressions such as:

> $$3250 \times 1.05^2 \text{ or } \sqrt{(7.82^2 - 2.91^2)}$$

> All pupils need to continue to learn when it is and when it is not appropriate to use a calculator, and their first-line strategy should involve mental calculations.
>
> (Becta, 2003: 1)

Task 9.2 **What are calculators good for?**

The following three calculator tasks are presented as exemplars. Some of them are better than others. Consider which of them can best promote the intelligent use of calculators as tools for learning and why.

Calculator task 1

Enter any three-digit number less than 900 into a calculator. Now try to reduce the number to zero in, at most, five steps, using any of the four functions with a single digit for each step.

For example, start with 435. Then press – 3 ÷ 6 ÷ 6 ÷ 9 – 8.

(Williams and Stephens, 1992: 233)

When you have tried this first calculator task, consider what work you did in your head. Think about how pupils at different age levels might tackle this task.

Calculators offer the possibility of producing rapid, accurate feedback for the pupil. Pupils can try many different strategies in a relatively short time, without having their progress impeded by their own difficulties with performing algorithms quickly and accurately.

Calculator task 2

Imagine your calculator is broken.
Find the total of 738 + 872 without using the '7' or the '8' keys.
How many different methods can you find for doing this?

(Haylock, 1982: 15)

When you have tried this task, consider what problem-solving strategies you used. Again, you could consider how various pupils might tackle the problem.

Calculator task 3

Choose ten grocery items from a supermarket catalogue or a newspaper advert. Estimate their combined value. Use the calculator to calculate the actual value.

Try the calculator tasks suggested above with pupils that you teach.

Calculators, in general, offer opportunities for pupils to:

■ learn from feedback, for example, by estimating then checking the answer;
■ observe patterns, for example by adding 5 repeatedly, or exploring dividing by 7;
■ explore data, for example to explore the effect on the mean of adding a fixed number to each data point.

Ask some children what they use calculators for and invite them to show you how they work with one. How do they talk about what they are doing? Which, if any, of the three entitlements do you observe being available in practice?

Consider what makes a good calculator task?

Find about your school's departmental policy on calculators.

In your journal, summarise your findings and your reflections on the role of calculators.

There is a general perception that calculators damage children's mathematics. In this section we have tried to place the use of calculators in a historic and pedagogic context, to show that calculators have a role as a tool in the teaching and learning of mathematics and to suggest that their negative impact may have been exaggerated. Nevertheless, the fact remains that it is certainly possible to use calculators badly.

I have seen one lesson in which pupils were working with Pythagoras' theorem to find the third side of a right-angled triangle, and one pupil estimated her answer out loud. She was told it was not possible to find square roots without a calculator, despite the fact that her estimate was useful. It would have been better practice to encourage the estimation, both as a way of checking the answer and a way of reinforcing a sense of number.

It is very important to be aware of the danger of inadvertently reducing pupils' mental arithmetic practice by allowing pupils, particularly slower pupils, to use the calculator as a crutch. You need consciously and explicitly to acknowledge the roles of estimation and mental arithmetic when using a calculator with pupils.

SPREADSHEETS

The National Curriculum 2007 (Mathematics) in England explicitly mentions data from other subjects and data from simulations using ICT to represent a probability experiment. It is expected that pupils will 'explore the effects of varying values and look for invariance and covariance' and use a variety of methods for collecting primary and secondary data; spreadsheets are mentioned explicitly as one of the tools. The standard method for sharing data, for example via the internet, is using spreadsheet format, for example, the data from the rapidly growing Census at School website (http://www.censusatschool.org.uk/).

Although much of the power of a spreadsheet derives from using the algebraic potential of linking values in one column to those of another by means of formulae, on the surface it is a tool for operating on tables of numbers. Thinking of a spreadsheet as an animated or dynamic table might help you to conceive of this superficially simple but mathematically sophisticated tool in a more accessible way.

An initial reason for wanting to incorporate a powerful spreadsheet into the school mathematics curriculum might be that it enables teachers and pupils to have access to large data sets, such as world-record data for track and field events. Its role as an algebraic environment warrants further consideration. A spreadsheet is also a powerful tool for modelling, widely used in industry and commerce, so once you have access to this powerful resource, it is worth discovering what else it can be used for in the mathematics curriculum. It may take you (and some of your pupils) some considerable time to get sufficiently acquainted with a spreadsheet package to feel confident with it, so, within reason, you may find you want to make as much use of it as possible, to make it worth the effort.

Spreadsheet tasks can be thought of as being of two distinct kinds: sometimes it is appropriate to give the pupils a spreadsheet document that has been already created and invite them to work with it. At other times, it may be better for the pupils to create their own spreadsheet documents from scratch.

One of the big ideas about a spreadsheet is the difference between relative and absolute referencing. Task 9.3 will help you to explore this.

Task 9.3 **Multiplication table**

Using a spreadsheet, and starting from cell A2, put the numbers 1 to 12 in column A. Starting from cell B1, put the numbers 1 to 12 in row 1. Now in cell B2 enter the formula A2 * B1. (In Excel, a formula will start with =; other spreadsheets do it differently.)

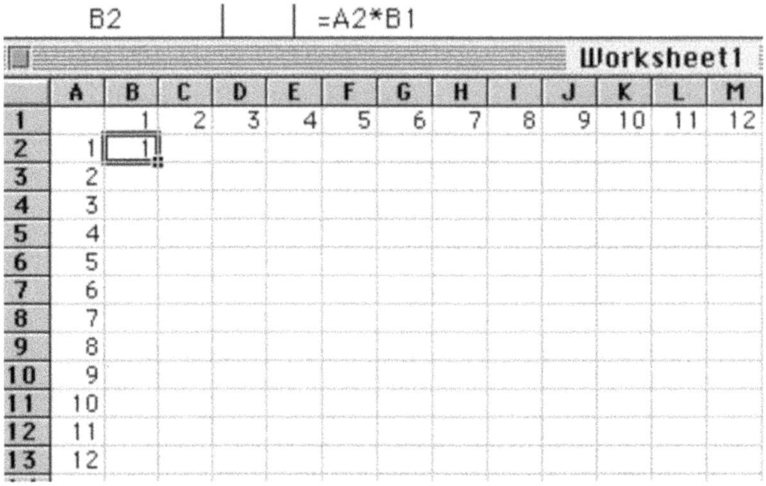

■ **Figure 9.1** Starting to build a multiplication table

Note what happens when you fill this formula down from cell B2 to B13, and then fill right from column B to column M.

Look at the formula in each of the cells.

Now carry out the task again using the formula A2*B1 in cell B2. (A2 is known as an *absolute* reference.)

Look at the resulting formulae now.

Think about the effect of the absolute referencing.

You might like to try also the formula A$2*B2 in the cell B2, before you fill down and fill right as above. Again, look at the resulting formula, and think about the effect of putting in the dollar sign ($).

Now create a multiplication table up to 12 times 12.

Researchers, publishers and others are making available sets of data that may be of interest to pupils of different ages. In addition, many large data sets are now accessible on the internet; for example, a website Census at School, containing a database of children's data from many different countries, can be found at the address given above.

Task 9.4 **Big data sets**

Explore the Census at School website (http://www.censusatschool.org.uk/). Read the guide for new teachers. Download some of the resources and consider how you would need to change them to use in your local school. Download a random dataset and think about how you might use such data with pupils. Consider the advantages and disadvantages of getting involved with the project.

The use of logical functions in a spreadsheet can provide a simple introduction to programming. One particularly useful example is 'if-then-else'. The 'if–then–else' structure is a powerful idea in its own right and it can enable you and your pupils to explore some interesting new ideas. Suppose, for example, you want to set up a simulation that involves a probability of 0.3. You can use a formula to enter a random number between 0 and 1 in cell A1. Then in cell B1 you can have 'IF cell A1 is greater than 0.7, THEN make B1 take the value 1, ELSE make B1 take the value 0'. (The syntax for this in Excel would be =IF (A1>0.7, 1, 0).)

Task 9.5 **Rolling spreadsheets**

Teach your spreadsheet to emulate rolling a die. In Figure 9.2, taken from an Excel worksheet, the cell B1 is highlighted and contains a formula to generate a random integer from the list 1, 2, 3, 4, 5, 6. The images of the faces of the die are created by spreadsheet commands based on the logical function IF, THEN, ELSE.

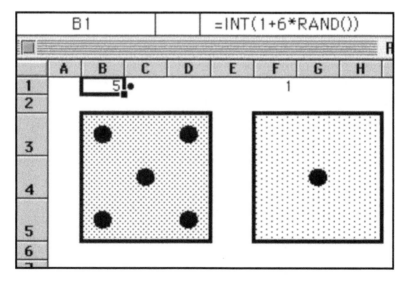

■ **Figure 9.2** A spreadsheet to emulate two dice

You can read more about the role of spreadsheets in articles and resources available on the website of the Association of Teachers of Mathematics. These include 'Algebra for a Purpose' (Ainley *et al.*, 2005) and downloadable 'Spreadsheet Files'. Put 'spreadsheet' into the search engine on the site to download the latest examples. Look also at the Nuffield FSMQ website (http://www.fsmq.org), in particular in the resources section. Make a note of all the resources that make use of spreadsheets.

When using spreadsheets with an interactive whiteboard, you will find it helpful to incorporate scrollbars or slider bars. (See www.tsm-resources.com/useful-files.html for an interactive demonstration of a slider bar.)

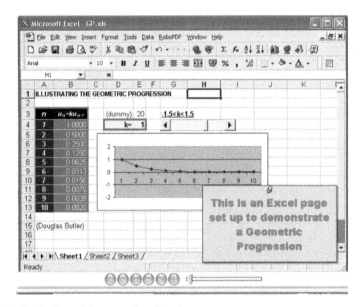

▪ **Figure 9.3** Illustration of the use of a slider bar

Task 9.6 **Entitlement through spreadsheets**

In this section, you have seen examples of using a spreadsheet to:

▪ learn from feedback;
▪ observe patterns;
▪ explore data;
▪ teach the computer.

Now observe how teachers use a spreadsheet to teach mathematics. What entitlements do you observe being available in practice?

GRAPH PLOTTERS

The notion of a graphing environment, in which the user can zoom in and out and investigate intersections and local gradients has been around for a long time, thanks largely to the pioneering work of David Tall. Tall developed his computer graph approach to teaching calculus very early in the 1980s. The Graphic Calculus software he developed for the early BBC computers was the first of its kind. The software enabled pupils to zoom in on a graph over a tiny range of values and build a concept of the derivative function as the gradient of the locally straight graph. Tall's work can be found on his personal website (http://www.davidtall.com/).

There are now many graphing packages that offer the zooming feature. Some examples are: *Omnigraph*, *Autograph*, a website-published function plotter such as *maths online function plotter* (accessed from: www.univie.ac.at/future.media/moe/onlinewerkzeuge.html) or an integrated mathematics package such as *TI Interactive!*

Task 9.7 **Entitlement through graph plotters**

Using either the school graph plotting software or the 'maths online function plotter', experiment with drawing graphs. Plot families of graphs such as $y = mx + c$ for different m and c. Notice how you think as you use the software for something familiar.

Now plot graphs of the form $a\sin x + b\cos x$ for different values of a and b. Notice any similarities and any differences in your approach.

Look at the graphs section of *MathsNet* (www.mathsnet.net/graphs.html).

Ask a teacher in the mathematics department how they use a graph plotter to teach mathematics.

What entitlements do you notice in each case?

GRAPHIC CALCULATORS

The most accessible tool in physical terms for using ICT is the graphic calculator. Graphic calculators can be seen as the point where computers and calculators converge, an interim technology. Kenneth Ruthven (1990) began the first major UK research and development project using graphic calculators in 1986.

Their most striking feature is their accessibility; having access to one means that powerful technology can be available as and when it is needed, even in examinations. For several years they represented a major force for change in mathematics teaching and learning. This force is generally outside the control of the educational establishment in the sense that, although there is some contact between educators and manufacturers, graphic calculator development is very much market-led.

So, pupils can buy – and are buying – hand-held machines with the power to do much of the routine work that forms the basis for advanced-level courses. This is in addition to most pupils having access to personal computers and freely available graphing software. There is therefore a very real need for educators to think carefully about what needs to be learned in mathematics when people have access to graphing tools.

Some research has shown that, if teachers have access to graphic calculators in their lessons, they tend to ask more higher-level questions than they otherwise do. For example, Rich (1993) studied two teachers to investigate how the introduction of the graphic calculator can affect the teacher's questioning strategies, presentation methods and beliefs about mathematics. She observed that the teacher who used graphic calculators:

- used more exploration and encouraged conjecturing;
- asked more higher-level questions, used examples differently and stressed the importance of graphs and approximation in problem-solving;
- used more graphs and showed the connection between algebra and geometry in other classes.

Whilst this research was originally conducted with older pupils, with the increased prevalence of ICT there is an equivalent challenge to be met in the education of younger secondary pupils.

Task 9.8 **Graphic proficiency**

Find a pupil or colleague who is proficient with a graphic calculator. Observe which model is being used. Invite the pupil or colleague to spend some time showing you what she or he uses the calculator for.

Ask him or her to draw two graphs that intersect, then zoom in on one point of intersection and find the coordinates as accurately as possible. Ask her or him to draw a non-linear graph and find the coordinates of the maximum or minimum as accurately as possible.

Invite a consideration of how an understanding of topics changes with access to the graphing facility. Allow this to be a discussion between two people with different expertise.

In Task 9.8 you saw how to use the basic facilities of a graphic calculator to explore graphs and to find solutions of equations graphically. In order to optimise the use of the graphic calculator, you will also need to learn how to produce a table of values for a function on your calculator. Then you can begin to use in your teaching the three different representations of a function the graphic calculator offers: graphic, algebraic and numeric.

Task 9.9 offers you some open tasks to try with pupils to see what mathematics is used.

Task 9.9 **Tasks to try with pupils**

a) Make your calculator screen look like this:

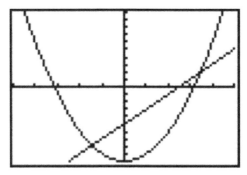

■ **Figure 9.4** A graphic calculator screen

b) Create a picture of a face on the screen of your calculator; you should use a function, shading and lines from the 'draw' menu, and coordinate plots from the 'statistics' menu.

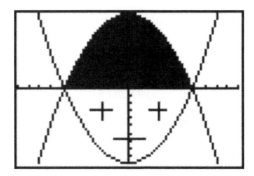

■ **Figure 9.5** A pirate
Source: Graham, 1996: 15

c) Draw a line graph $y = 3x$. Investigate what happens when you change the number 3.

Which of the six entitlements:

■ learning from feedback;
■ observing patterns;
■ seeing connections;
■ working with dynamic images;
■ exploring data;
■ teaching the computer;

have your pupils encountered by carrying out these tasks?

Initially, most resources to support the use of graphic calculators were written for post-16, primarily because of the price of the calculators and the sophistication of the mathematics available. However, younger learners benefit from the large screen, which displays both question and answer as well as graphs. You can find further ideas for using graphic calculators with pupils in resources such as the Open E-Challenge (http://mct.open.ac.uk/802571E800564966/(httpPages)/619AA34EC834F039802572ED 004A30D2?OpenDocument&unid1=619AA34EC834F039802572ED004A30D2&subje ct=maths_ed), in a set of books published by A+B books (for example, Galpin and Graham, 2005) and in Appendix 4.

New developments in calculator technology are appearing every year, so you will need to keep an eye on the maths education press and websites for news. Calculators are available that can be connected by a cable to a computer and can receive data and programs downloaded from the internet. Remote data capture devices can collect data about motion, light or temperature etc. and this can be loaded immediately into a calculator. Some graphic calculators are able to download programs from the internet.

DYNAMIC GEOMETRY PACKAGES

Imagine you are trying to convince a pupil that the angle A remains the same even if the point moves round the circle (see Figure 9.6). You trace round the circle as you speak. If only the diagram would move too.

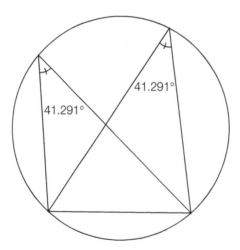

▬ **Figure 9.6** A demonstration of equal angles subtended by the same chord

There are several implementations of the idea of a dynamic diagram using dynamic geometry software. *Cabri-Géomètre* and *The Geometer's Sketchpad* are the two principal alternatives. These two software packages are fairly similar. One difference between them that you will probably notice immediately is that using *Cabri* you select a tool and then the objects to which it is to be applied, whereas using *The Geometer's Sketchpad* you select the objects first and then the tool that you wish to use.

Task 9.10 **Using dynamic geometry software**

1   Using your geometry package, create an equilateral triangle, as described in Appendix 4.

As you do this, record in your journal how your thinking develops and what problem-solving processes you use.

2   The diagram in Figure 9.7 represents a construction of a line segment x given $x^2 = ab$.

Recreate this construction in your dynamic geometry package so that a and b can be varied. Put in the measurements of a, b and x and move the figure around to convince yourself that x is indeed $\sqrt{ab}$.

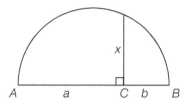

■ **Figure 9.7** Constructing a square root geometrically

Can you explain why $x^2 = ab$? Consider whether and how the dynamic geometry package helps you to construct a convincing explanation.

Issues of the role of dynamic geometry software in the mental construction of proof and explanation are explored in many articles. Jones *et al.* (2000) refer to a range of evidence that, by working with dynamic geometry software, pupils gain access to more theoretical mathematics.

Task 9.11 **Solving quadratics**

This activity for dynamic geometry software is based on methods used by mathematicians in ancient Greece to construct geometric solutions for quadratic problems. The task comes from Bold (1982).

According to Bold, to construct the roots of the quadratic equation $x^2 - 4x + 2 = 0$, you construct the points B (0, 1) and D (4, 2), then you create a circle with BD as the diameter. Then the points where the circle cuts the x-axis represent the roots of the equation.

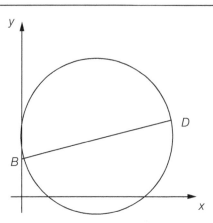

▨ **Figure 9.8** Solving quadratic equations using a circle

Try this. Make a conjecture about where the coordinates of D come from. Test the conjecture for different cases. What happens if you vary the *y* coordinate of B? Keep a note of how you get on.

Consider what processes you went through, then how these activities may be made suitable for pupils and what they might learn from working on them.

Further examples of the use of dynamic geoemtry can be found in a book called *Developing Thinking in Geometry* (Johnston-Wilder and Mason, 2006). Traditional books about geometry may give you further ideas for exploration: some examples are Coxeter (1961) *Introduction to Geometry*; Wells (1991) *The Penguin Dictionary of Curious and Interesting Geometry*; and Bold (1982) *Famous Problems of Geometry and How to Solve Them*. There is also a useful book chapter on geometry packages (Mackrell and Johnston-Wilder, 2004).

Issues to think about

Dynamic geometry software of this kind has explicit applications in the mathematics National Curriculum for England. For example, at Key Stage 3, pupils are expected to:

▨ explore the effects of varying values and look for invariance and covariance;
▨ make accurate mathematical diagrams, graphs and constructions on paper and on screen.

(QCA, 2007a: 142–3)

However, there are also less obvious applications. For example, recent versions of *Cabri-Géomètre* and of *The Geometer's Sketchpad* offer far more: in addition to offering tools for transformation geometry, they provide an underlying grid and a Cartesian coordinate system with which the user can explore and display equations of lines, circles and conic sections. This provides a means, starting from geometrical figures, to make extensive connections with algebraic representations. They also offer tools with which to explore transformation geometry.

What are the entry points?

Experience with other media and other geometrical experiences are important foundations for work with dynamic geometry software. Experiments with folding paper or making shapes with geostrips and elastic bands on geoboards may all be valuable pupil activity.

It is also possible to create stimulating images using overlaid acetates of lines and circles on an overhead projector. These can be linked together using pins to illustrate the ideas of construction, constraints and possibilities. The acetates and geostrips can also be used to demonstrate the idea of action at a distance, which seems to be part of the fascination with playing with constructions. Plenty of time is needed for this kind of experience.

What are the big ideas for dynamic geometry software?

Perhaps one of the key ideas to get hold of in using dynamic geometry software is the distinction between *drawing* and *construction*. A shape on the screen may have been *drawn* to look like a square, but when you move the points in the diagram using the mouse, it changes into a rectangle or perhaps into something that is not even a quadrilateral. On the other hand, a shape *constructed* as a square may rotate or enlarge, but will always remain square.

The distinction between drawing and construction appears to be a significant sticking point for teachers and pupils alike when they first use the software. Associated with the idea of construction is the idea of *invariance*; that some features of a figure will remain invariant as parts of the figure are 'dragged' around the screen. The idea of 'messing up' (Healy *et al.*, 1994) – getting pupils to make a drawing or design of their own choosing, and then encouraging them to try to 'mess it up' – has been used with some success to provide pupils with some motivation for constructing their figures rather than just drawing them. The hope was that the challenge of trying to preserve a design from the threat of being 'messed up' would encourage pupils to think about the construction.

The challenge of constructing particular shapes – for example, to construct a figure that will remain a rhombus whatever you drag – may also lead to some valuable ideas. Finzer and Bennett (1995) suggest that pupils may go through various stages in tackling such a problem.

- *drawing*: dragging a drawing of a quadrilateral to look approximately like a rhombus;
- *under-constraint*: where perhaps the opposite sides are constrained by construction to be parallel, but all sides are not constructed to be equal;
- *over-constraint*: where not only is the shape constrained to be a rhombus but also the angles are constrained to, say, 60° and 120°;
- *appropriate constraint*: where the relationships used are minimal to define the figure.

Another important distinction to understand is that between dynamic coincidence and general property. The distinction is clearly associated with the idea of construction. A general property can be seen as being like a feature of a construction that cannot be 'messed up'. For a deeper understanding of a general property, it seems that the pupil needs to seek for an explanation.

Using dynamic geometry software with pupils

As with spreadsheets, different teaching approaches are possible when using dynamic geometry software with pupils. One approach is to ask pupils to make a construction starting from a blank worksheet. This kind of task may be demanding of the pupil's prior knowledge and understanding of some of the fundamental concepts behind the tools deployed in dynamic geometry software (such as using a circle to construct equal lengths). An alternative approach that has been favoured by some teachers is to use the software to create a dynamic worksheet for the pupils to explore (see, for example, Johnston-Wilder and Mason, 2006). Dynamic geometry software is particularly suited to use with an interactive whiteboard (IWB), discussed briefly at the very end of this chapter.

Task 9.12 **Creating an interactive worksheet**

Create an interactive worksheet to teach a topic of your choice.

Try your worksheet with an appropriate group of pupils.

Observe the pupils' response to the task and consider how you might improve your worksheet for future use.

Look at the interactive geometry pages on *MathsNet* for some examples: www.mathsnet.net/dynamic/index.html

Based on your experience so far, which of the entitlements might pupils encounter using dynamic geometry software? Make notes in your journal about your ideas.

PROGRAMMING LANGUAGES – LOGO

Logo was developed by mathematics educator Seymour Papert; it is a programming language developed as an educational tool. Although you can think of using a spreadsheet or a dynamic geometry package as being like teaching the computer to do new tasks, the metaphor has a clearer link with reality when you are programming using Logo. The turtle graphics screen shows an idealised turtle, which you guide around the screen using commands such as Left 45, Right 60, Forward 20. The turtle can leave a trail behind it. If you have not yet used Logo yourself, ask your mentor in school to introduce you to it.

Seymour Papert's book, *Mindstorms – Children, Computers and Powerful Ideas* (1980), will give you some background about the origins of Logo; it also contains some interesting ideas to explore. Although Logo is seen by many as being 'only' an educational language, it is in fact a very sophisticated computer language and can be used as a vehicle for exploring deep mathematical ideas (Abelson and di Sessa, 1980). More recent developments include NetLogo, used to explore complex systems and emergent behaviour (http://ccl.northwestern.edu/netlogo/).

Task 9.13 **Working with Logo**

1   Make the turtle draw a square, then an equilateral triangle, then a polygon. Now create a procedure to make a square of variable size. Use your procedure to make a two-by-two square the same size as your original square.

2   Explore the following procedure, which is an example of a recursive procedure: that is a procedure that calls itself.

```
TO INSPI (:SIDE, :ANGLE, :INC)
FORWARD :SIDE
RIGHT :ANGLE
INSPI (:SIDE, :ANGLE + :INC, :INC)
```

3   Read Pumfrey and Beardon's (2002) description of using Logo to explore tessellations. The article shows some interesting examples of tessellations generated using Logo procedures. Devise your own tessellation using Logo. What did you learn about tessellations?

Entry points and big ideas

A useful introduction to using Logo in your teaching is the First Forward series available from the NRICH website. This is supplemented by Logo Challenge tasks suitable for a wide range of different pupils.

   One tried-and-tested way of introducing Logo is to get the pupils to 'play turtle' and follow simple instructions such as Forward 10 literally. This gives them some concrete experience on which to hang their developing understanding. (For very young children, teachers have used an electronic turtle or a Pip or Roamer which moves around the floor.) Pupils need to learn to be precise and explicit in their instructions to the turtle and learn to debug procedures. Some teachers begin by asking pupils to write their name using Logo. Initially, the pupils work in direct mode, but they soon realise the need for procedures if they are to save their work. Variables can be introduced as a mechanism for altering the size of their pictures. Pupils learn to build procedures from sub-procedures. For example:

To Man		**To Tree**
Head		Arrowhead 50
Body		Arrowhead 30
Leg	or	Arrowhead 15
Leg		Arrowhead 5
Arm		End
Arm		
End		

Such procedures often need debugging, for example when the arms appear in the wrong place. This immediate feedback, and the possibility of correction with further feedback, is an obvious benefit to the learner.

183 ■

Some pupils enjoy creating and exploring patterns, such as:

To Pattern
Repeat 20 [Square Right 18]
End

Task 9.14 **Using Logo with pupils**

Try some Logo tasks of your own with a small group of pupils. Make a note in your journal of what mathematics the pupils use and which entitlements they encounter.

Logo as a metaphor and as an experience brings some changes to the way pupils experience mathematics. One example of this is in the study of external angles of a polygon; the theorem that external angles add up to 360 degrees is replaced by the 'Total Turtle Trip' theorem. The ATM website has an archive of *Micromath* articles about Logo, and you will find some further ideas there.

SMALL TEACHING PROGRAMS

Many small teaching programs for mathematics were developed on BBC computers during the 1980s; they still have much to offer in teaching mathematics and they are now to be found in the form of applets, small programs usually written in Java. Such programs are designed to be easy to use and to cover a small piece of syllabus. Some of them are investigative in style. One example of collection of small teaching programs is a publication called *An Applet for the Teacher* (Graham and Duke, 2010). In addition, many companies produce electronic games – these are mixed in quality, but some have been found to help with various aspects of teaching and learning mathematics. One source of such games, combined with teaching notes, is Bowland Mathematics (http://www.bowlandmaths.org.uk/).

There is an old, excellent example of a well-thought-out, text-based mathematical adventure game, *L – a Mathemagical Adventure Game*, available from ATM. If you cannot find it in school, it is worth buying a copy for yourself.

Task 9.15 **Small teaching programs**

Find out what small teaching programs are in your school. Spend some time exploring some of the small software you find. In particular, look at the Bowland resources that use ICT.

Think about which of the entitlements are available to the pupils. Find examples of:

■ learning from feedback;
■ observing patterns;
■ seeing connections;
■ working with dynamic images.

THE INTERNET AND CD-ROMS

Many parents, who have computers at home, are accessing the internet or buying books with CD-ROMs for mathematics. The problem is that many of the examples available at present are not very good, either because they do not use the possibilities offered by the technology or because they do not communicate the mathematics very well.

There is a very useful collection of available materials, together with teacher reviews, on the website TEEM (Teachers Evaluating Educational Media) at www.teem.org.uk/. You will find the collection and many of these reviews very helpful.

One example of a CD-ROM that we think is worth looking at now is based on the work of the artist M. C. Escher. The Escher interactive CD-ROM (*Exploring the Art of the Infinite*) is available from Tarquin Publications (see Appendix 2). Another is *The Code Book* on CD-ROM, available from Virtual Image (see Appendix 2), which offers simulations of a variety of coding machines including the Enigma Machine. Review carefully any materials you find in the light of what you have learned about good practice and, in particular, with an eye on the nature of the feedback given to the learner.

Task 9.16 **Mathematics and the internet**

The internet is a rapidly growing resource. The main problem is that it can absorb a lot of time as you search from one list of sites to another. Start with *NRich*, a page of which is shown below. It is a well-organised site, relatively quick to load and includes some useful resources. The address is:

nrich.maths.org/

A second good site is the St Andrews History of Mathematics site, which is a rich resource of historical material. The address is:

www-groups.dcs.st-and.ac.uk/~history/

Try conducting a search for references to a maths topic such as 'Pythagoras' using a search engine such as the Yahoo Mathematics site or Google. The addresses are:

www.yahoo.com/Science/Mathematics/ and www.google.co.uk

Try also using Yahooligans, which is designed for pupils to use. The address is:

www.yahooligans.com/

Visit the following website, follow the links and make a note of each site to which it links:

www.westnet.com/~rickd/Kids/Math.html#Puzzles

Further sites are to be found in Appendix 2. Douglas Butler maintains a website of very useful links at: www.tsm-resources.com/mlink.html (Note, when you visit internet sites in the US, that grades K (Kindergarten) to 12 are equivalent to our school years 1–13.)

■ **Figure 9.9** NRich internet page

SUMMARY AND KEY POINTS

ICT is changing rapidly. Although there is a much potential for improved learning of mathematics, there is also the possibility of wasting a great deal of time and resources.

When using ICT in the classroom, remember that some pupils will know more than you, and amongst the pupils there may be wide ranges of fluency and comfort with ICT and access to machines. Be prepared to use the expertise, interest and energy that is present. One teacher of a Year 9 class discovered that one of her pupils was experienced in using a spreadsheet. Whenever members of the class working on a spreadsheet got stuck technically, she called on his expertise to help solve the problem. Another uses different pupils to 'drive' the class graphic calculator or the computer linked to a data projector.

While you are not necessarily expert in the technology, be prepared to be confident mathematically in dealing with whatever the technology offers. For example, debugging programs is a mathematical activity and it is possible to be helpful to a pupil by having them explain to you what they are trying to do. It is not uncommon for a pupil, half-way through her or his explanation of the problem, to say, 'Oh, that's what's wrong, thank you'. They then go off leaving you unsure precisely what you have achieved, but they are clearly forging ahead with their project. The fallback position is, 'I don't now, let's find out'.

Sometimes it is enough for you to make process observations about how your pupils are going about tackling their task, as pupils of this age may be immersed in technical detail and therefore not paying sufficient attention to higher-level strategic issues.

Task 9.17 **Re-audit**

Check back to your initial ICT audit and note how much progress you have made.

As a final note, interactive whiteboards (IWBs) are changing the nature of pedagogy in schools. As a complement to the six Becta entitlements, Alison Clark-Jeavons (2004) itemised four different modes of IWB use:

1 Flipchart mode
Used in this way, the screen acts as an electronic flipchart, with the facility to save or print any notes or diagrams.

2 Pointer mode
In this mode, the software is being driven at the interactive whiteboard without the need to use the computer keyboard and mouse.

3 Annotator mode
This mode of use enables written notes to be made over the top of another piece of software.

4 Recorder mode
With some interactive whiteboards, it is possible to record all of the actions that have taken place at the board.

However, the focus in this chapter has been on pupils learning with ICT tools. ICT provides a strong motivation to young people to study mathematics. It is important that you develop confidence to allow pupil use through your own exploration and in-service training.

FURTHER READING

Butler, D. http://www.tsm-resources.com/mlink.html
  This web page gives links to software pages mentioned in this chapter and more besides.

Clark-Jeavons, A. (2005) *Exciting ICT in Mathematics*. Stafford: Network Educational Press.
  This book contains practical ICT-based activities and tips, together with a CD-ROM containing resources, software and links to further information.

Graham, A. and Duke, R. (2010) *An Applet for the Teacher: Maths for the Imagination*. St Albans: Tarquin Publications.
  This book provides access to a selection of these applets, with advice and suggestions about how you can use them effectively with learners.

Johnston-Wilder, S. and Pimm, D. (eds) (2004) *Teaching Secondary Mathematics with ICT*. **Buckingham: Open University Press.**

This book will enable readers to develop their own reflective practice and support them in implementation of ICT for effective learning tasks. Several chapters include case studies and practical examples, as well as discussing more general themes and issues. The book is supported by references to research and by access to demonstration copies of software and sample files, via a website.

MTi

This online ATM journal is designed to support and encourage the use of ICT in mathematics teaching and has some very useful articles for beginning teachers, as well as supporting use throughout your developing career. Although the full journal is offered only to ATM members, some articles are available to the wider public.

Oldknow, A. and Taylor, R. (2004) *Teaching Mathematics with ICT*. **London: Continuum.**

The emphasis in this book is on how the use of ICT can contribute to reaching learning objectives, not on using technology for its own sake. The book deals with the use of a range of media, including the internet and CD-ROMs. The book comes with a CD-ROM.

INCLUSION IN PRACTICE: SPECIAL NEEDS PUPILS IN MAINSTREAM MATHEMATICS

Melissa Rodd

INTRODUCTION

This chapter is concerned with teaching mathematics to children and young people within mainstream schools who have a special educational need (SEN) or a disability. In previous generations, pupils with disabilities or an SEN were not generally educated with their peers, but changing social attitudes, coupled with legislation like the Disability Discrimination Act (1995), affected educational policy. Nowadays, for the vast majority of learners with an SEN or disability, their community mainstream school will be expected to meet their special educational needs. In this sense, teaching is to be 'inclusive'; pupils with special educational needs (SEN) should be enabled to reach their full potential within the mainstream environment, given appropriate support. The Special Educational Needs Code of Practice (DfES, 2001) gives the details of the policies that schools must implement.

Such inclusive mathematics teaching is driven by policy, yet is also based on values and professional attitudes. The Professional Standards for Teachers (TDA, 2007) express professional attitudes. For example, a professional standard about relationships with pupils includes 'commitment to ensuring that [pupils] can achieve their full educational potential' (QTS C1). Mainstream schools today are considered the most favourable environment for all pupils to achieve their 'full educational potential', so all teachers should expect to teach learners with special needs and disabilities. Furthermore, under the section on Achievement and Diversity, Standard C19 reads:

> Know how to make effective personalised provision for those they teach, including those for whom English is an additional language or who have special educational needs or disabilities, and how to take practical account of diversity and promote equality and inclusion in their teaching. (p. 17)

This chapter is organised as follows: it starts with an example of 'inclusive mathematics teaching' written by a teacher in training, then section 2 addresses general issues about 'special needs'. Section 3 provides tasks designed to facilitate orientation to SEN.

Section 4 classifies some SEN, and Section 5 looks at a team approach to teaching mathematics to learners with SEN.

Before proceeding, here is an example of inclusive teaching by a mathematics PGCE student, Lesley Thorpe, in 2003. She wrote this about her lesson:

> In the logic puzzle 'Farmer, Fox, Chicken, Corn' the pupils have to use their logical thinking and problem-solving strategies to find the combination of moves that could be undertaken to transport all the characters across the river given certain restrictions.
>
> My idea for the class was to work in groups, some pupils taking roles of the characters and other members of the groups acting in an advisory capacity. For this I used certain props from the drama department. These were all visual aids and would not be suitable for Mary the blind pupil. I had the task of enabling Mary to access and imagine the problem, give her the ability to employ trial-and-error strategies to find a solution and be able to communicate her ideas with confidence.
>
> In collaboration with the visual impairment department, I devised an A4 board using coverings of different materials to indicate fields and a river with counters of differing sizes and different coverings for the characters. This would enable Mary to work as part of a group in an advisory capacity. She would be able to access the problem and move counters to solve the problem, as the pupils in role would move in her group. Therefore, she would be able to participate fully in the lesson. We decided that the characters would be plain counters with the character name indicated in Braille. This would make the counters more easy to identify and also easier to move about the board.
>
> I was surprised how plain the board was when it was actually produced. Instead of using coverings the support staff had the idea of using a vacuum to shape the board using strategically placed shavings. This created an area with a very 'gritty' texture for the grass and a very smooth finish for the river. To help further with identifying these textures the board was also labelled in Braille. The brightly coloured, many-textured fabrics that I had first envisaged had developed into something very plain. I realised that even though I had designed something usable for Mary, I had imagined the coloured pieces making up the board. The teaching material created had to be accessible to Mary, and my view had been 'tainted' by sight. This insight had a great effect on my planning and materials for the class in subsequent lessons.
>
> When using the materials, I found that the group worked collaboratively and openly. Mary was able to follow the moves well and make additions to the strategies used to solve the problem. When the pupils reached a dead end in their current strategy, Mary was able to restart the problem with a new approach just as easily as the pupils who were in role. In fact, Mary was the only pupil in the group who considered the problem as a set of combinations, which were or were not possible and deduced the solution to the puzzle on this basis.

OBJECTIVES

By the end of this chapter you should:

■ know some conditions or behaviours that constitute special educational needs or disabilities and how to take account of diversity and promote equality and inclusion in your teaching (see Professional Standard for Teachers C19, TDA, 2007);

■ be able to recognise several special needs that you may meet in learners in your mathematics classroom;

■ know where to look if you need to know more about mathematical special needs (Professional Standards for Teachers C20 and C21 (TDA, 2007);

■ be aware of the frustration experienced by many children with special needs;

■ have started to understand the complexities of working with other adults concerned with pupils with special needs.

INCLUSION AND DIVERSITY, DISABILITY AND SPECIAL NEEDS

The term 'inclusion' recognises means that diverse populations and communities contribute to society; the intention of its use is that neither race, nor class, nor gender, nor disability should inhibit participation. In particular, ways of understanding disability are changing with the increasing awareness that a disability is very often primarily relative to an environmental or social constraint. By lowering pavements for wheelchairs, training guide dogs, providing text or signing etc., we can give more people opportunities for full participation in society. Dyson and Millward's (2000) case studies of schools implementing inclusive policies give an insight into the challenges and rewards involved in practice.

Special educational needs is a legally defined term in England. A child has special educational needs if he or she has a learning difficulty for which a special educational provision is to be made. Frederickson and Cline (2002), in their comprehensive textbook on special needs, emphasise the difference between the statutory concept of SEN and the looser notion of special needs (p. 37). For example, a child who does not speak English at home may have special needs relative to a particular school environment, but does not have Special Educational Needs.

The Professional Standards for Qualified Teacher Status (QTS) (TDA, 2007: 6–12) require new teachers to understand their responsibilities under the SEN Code of Practice (DfES, 2001) and the role of their specialist colleagues in providing for learners with special needs.

ORIENTING TO SPECIAL NEEDS

This section on 'orientation' is designed to help you to think about learners whose life experiences or capacities are likely to differ substantially from yours. Because the aim is to stimulate thinking through experience, most of this section is in the form of tasks.

Observing

Developing the skill of observing without making judgements or jumping to conclusions is a lifelong endeavour. The following task is designed to help you to develop your observation techniques and immerse you in pupils' worlds, which are not likely to be familiar from your own education.

> ### Task 10.1 **On observation**
>
> *Being alongside*
> Work regularly with one or two pupils with below age-expected attainment in mathematics throughout the time you are placed at your school. Try to get to know them as people, finding out about their interests and how they see themselves. Use your journal to keep a log of interesting or surprising things these pupils do or don't do; be as factual as possible when recording your observations. Also keep a record of your successes with them; for example, a turn of phrase you used or a resource you offered that has enabled them to progress.
>
> As you work with the same pupils for some weeks you will understand them increasingly. It takes time.
>
> *Reflection*
> Using your log and records, write a reflective commentary interpreting the behaviours that you have observed and the successes you have had with them:
> ■ Why do you think the pupil did a particular thing?
> ■ Why do you think a particular way of teaching 'worked'?
>
> *Comparison*
> Compare your own school experiences with those of the pupils that you have been working with. In particular, track the affective side of the experiences of learning mathematics: what opportunities for pleasure, challenge, reward, tension, anxiety, satisfaction and other motivating or discouraging feelings did you find that your pupils experienced and how do these compare with your own memories of learning mathematics?

Thinking about mathematical ability

Are you good at maths? 'Good at maths' is a phrase that some people identify with and others recoil from. Various terms are used to signal being good at mathematics; for example, having 'ability', being 'bright' or 'gifted and/or talented'. The following task is intended to help you to interrogate your understanding of the term 'ability' and related notions, and to relate the views you hold to the core professional values that you are developing as a trainee teacher.

Task 10.2 **On ability**

Views of ability
Read Sally Brown's (2003) three-page retrospective on 'ability', available from the book website, and record your answers to these questions in your journal:

- What views can you articulate about 'mathematical ability'?
- Which of these views are similar to your views and which are different?
- In what ways do you think views change?
- Do you have an example from your own experience related to 'ability'?
- Which of the views about ability do you see as your core values that guide you in your professional aspirations?

Taking everything into account, do you think that some pupils are just 'bad at maths'?

Multifaceted mathematics
There is a commonly held view that some people are 'bad at maths'. Research has shown that although learners have difficulties with specific aspects of mathematics, there is no such thing as being 'globally bad at maths' (Dowker, 2005).

Read the section of Ann Dowker's 2004 research report that deals with examples of differences in children's arithmetical abilities (pp. 2–15). This report is downloadable from the internet: http://www.dcsf.gov.uk/research/data/uploadfiles/RR554.pdf

Reflect on which differences in arithmetical abilities contained in this report you can discern in pupils that you have taught or observed.

CLASSIFICATION AND CHARACTERISATION OF SPECIAL EDUCATIONAL NEEDS

There are many specific special educational needs that manifest themselves as special needs in the secondary mathematics classroom. The following categories of SEN have been highlighted by the government in the Code of Practice (DfES, 2001: 86–8):

1   communication and interaction;
2   cognition and learning;
3   behaviour, emotional and social development;
4   sensory and/or physical needs.

However, another way to classify special needs is to consider their cause. The following classification is intended to raise awareness of when and why some pupils may have special needs or SEN:

- physical conditions – e.g. sight or hearing impairment, severe mobility impairment, pregnancy;
- medical conditions – e.g. heart defects, epilepsy, muscular dystrophy, cerebral palsy, diabetes, asthma, eczema, cystic fibrosis, arthritis, allergies, mental health problems;

■ developmental conditions – e.g. dyslexia, dyspraxia, attention deficit/hyperactivity disorder (ADHD), autistic spectrum disorder, Down syndrome;

■ social conditions – e.g. poverty, abuse, trauma, bereavement, migration, English as an Additional Language (EAL).

Which of these classification systems is most useful to you will depend upon whether the pupil has been diagnosed, in which case you can look up how to address the particular needs related to the diagnosis or whether you are noticing symptoms in a pupil without a diagnosis.

PARTICULAR SPECIAL NEEDS AND LEARNING DISABILITIES

In the next subsections, you will be provided with details about particular special needs and learning disabilities, so that you can consider and reflect on the differences that pupils in your mathematics classes may exhibit and how they can be included in mathematical learning.

Specific learning difficulties

A pupil with a 'specific learning difficulty' has a difficulty with a specific area of learning. Specific learning difficulties may be detected in educational settings and practice, when a pupil exhibits an uneven developmental profile. For example, Simon's profile at eight years old was precociously verbal, excellent at art but unable to read even words that he had written himself, suggesting the specific learning difficulty of dyslexia. Despite being diagnosed from an uneven profile, dyslexia and also dyspraxia – coordination impairment – have physical causes. People with dyslexia have a weakness in processing language-based information and people with dyspraxia have an immaturity (or damage) of parts of the motor cortex in the brain that prevents messages from being properly transmitted to the body. Dyscalculia, having difficulties with number, is also a specific learning difficulty.

Task 10.3 **Taking account of differences**

Read the following vignette and then answer the questions in your journal:

> It was the beginning of the new school year. I was teaching mathematics to a mixed-ability Year 9 class. The pupils and I were all new to the school. On my first meeting with the class we did number puzzles in groups and worked orally, and I started forming impressions of individual pupils' capabilities by their verbal responses. On the next day, I gave a written worksheet-based activity. One boy, Andrew, who had participated enthusiastically and independently in oral communication of mathematics in the first lesson, was relying on his neighbour, Tim, to tell him what he had to do during the second lesson.

■ Why might Andrew be relying on Tim on the second day, but not on the first?
■ What might you do to find out whether Andrew had a particular special need?
■ What might you do next to ensure that Andrew had access to the mathematics curriculum?

Dyslexia

A short conversation with the Special Needs Coordinator (SENCO) at the school and a check on his records revealed that Andrew was an intelligent pupil, who was suspected to have dyslexia, although at that time it was undiagnosed. His mental mathematics was good but any written work seemed to present him with problems. The mathematical attainment of people who display the symptoms of dyslexia varies widely, but some people with dyslexia have made substantial and original contributions in mathematics. Logic and structures of patterns are deeply mathematical and are often accessible to people with dyslexia, who may still find it difficult to communicate this understanding, particularly in writing.

In mathematics a dyslexic pupil may have difficulties with processing written symbolic material and with rote learning, and they may display short-term memory defects. They may be good at tasks involving spatial awareness or strategy, but find difficulty in pairing a symbol, either spoken or written, with its meaning. For example, a person with dyslexia might write sequential numbers as 11, 21, 31, 41, and read these as 'eleven, twelve, thirteen, fourteen'. In cases like this, problems with the symbolic aspects of language may mask a keen perception of structure within patterns.

Because people with dyslexia can often achieve highly on spatial or strategic tasks, employing a multisensory approach to teaching may be effective. Geometric imagery can often help dyslexic pupils to 'plant' a concept and can overcome short-term memory problems, which are a common symptom of dyslexia. For example, Andrew (mentioned in Task 10.3) was not able to set out a 'long multiplication' as he could not get the columns right, even though he could calculate some two-digit by two-digit multiplications in his head. When his teacher represented multiplications as areas, he was much more successful. Specific teaching strategies for helping pupils with dyslexia include using bold visual presentations, giving opportunities for discussion and giving plenty of time for writing. As with many interventions included initially for special needs pupils, these strategies will be helpful for the majority of pupils. As with all vulnerable children, building confidence is also a crucial part of their mathematics curriculum.

Dyspraxia

Pupils with dyspraxia may have particular difficulties in accessing parts of the mathematics curriculum. Generally, limitations with physical manipulation that pupils with dyspraxia experience can inhibit understanding of sequencing, which is important in the development of mathematical concepts (Portwood, 1997). More specifically, standard mathematical instruments cannot be used easily. For example, Peter was not able to place a protractor correctly, even though he could read off the angle when some one else placed it. Planning for practical work in mathematics needs to include the needs and attitudes of pupils with dyspraxia. Tasks that develop coordination skills are to be encouraged, but the pupil with dyspraxia may have a negative attitude to tasks that could 'show them up'.

Dyscalculia

At the time of writing, the term 'dyscalculia' is used in various different ways. One specialist use of the term considers a person to be 'dyscalculic' if he or she has a rare neurological disorder that prevents them being able to retain knowledge or understanding of even the simplest mathematics. Another use of the term defines it normatively: a person is dyscalculic if her or his performance on an assessment is in the bottom 5 per cent relative to a population. The term is in general use and the definition given on Teachernet is very open indeed:

> Dyscalculia – pupils with dyscalculia have difficulty in acquiring mathematical skills. Pupils may have difficulty understanding simple number concepts, lack an intuitive grasp of numbers and have problems learning number facts and procedures.
>
> (http://www.teachernet.gov.uk/wholeschool/sen/datatypes/Cognitionlearningneeds/)

Dyscalculia normally describes people who have significant problems with numbers, but still have a normal or above-normal abilities in other areas. Nevertheless, longitudinal studies have shown that the most positive intervention strategy for 'dyscalculic' pupils was targeted support, which is the same strategy as for pupils having 'mathematical difficulties' as discussed in the 'orientation' section above.

Autistic spectrum

'Autism' is an umbrella term for a developmental disability arising from an impaired capacity for social interaction. The term 'Asperger's Syndrome' is sometimes used for 'high-functioning' autistic people and reference to the 'autistic spectrum' signals the wide variation in diagnosed individuals. This disability leads to problems with language and communication. Learning in a school classroom is especially difficult for those autistic pupils who exhibit challenging behaviour.

Autistic individuals vary 'from withdrawn individuals to those who are "active but odd"' (Jordan and Powell, 1995: 4). Some people with autism or Asperger's are exceptionally mathematically talented, yet still are unable to deal with social situations. The novel *The Curious Incident of the Dog in the Night-Time* (Haddon, 2003), written in the voice of a mathematically gifted autistic teenager, gives insight into the condition.

For pupils with autism or Asperger's, 'relevant' mathematics can be even more of a mystery than pure mathematics. An emphasis on 'real-life' mathematics can obscure the logic of the subject, because of the confusing social and linguistic details, rather than motivating it by placing it in a relevant context. For example, money is often used to help children understand decimals; for an autistic or Asperger's pupil, decimals, once understood, can be used to explain the currency.

Pupils on the autistic spectrum may be able to be successful in mathematics if language and social interaction are recognised as a significant hurdle and they are taught the mathematics first. Such pupils are often comfortable with numbers and many are also good at the geometric aspects of the curriculum, which does not demand so much productive language. As one teacher put it, they 'challenge the teacher to conceive of a kind of mathematical thinking which does not use internalised language but visual representations' (Inglese, 1997: 18). A cognitive perspective on the way in which autistic people think, as well as some strategies to help teachers help their autistic pupils learn, is offered by Jordan and Powell (1995).

Emotional and behavioural difficulties (EBD)

This is a very wide term, which you may feel would incorporate many pupils at times in their school career, but includes the specific diagnosed condition of attention deficit/

hyperactivity disorder (ADHD). Indeed, many behavioural problems mask learning difficulties. Capel *et al.* (1995) offered some 'points to consider' when working with EBD pupils:

■ appropriate school and teacher responses make a difference;
■ behaviour may improve if pupils' self-esteem is enhanced;
■ the teacher needs to be constructive and positive as well as specific about what is and is not acceptable;
■ parental involvement is to be encouraged;
■ stages 1–3 of the SEN Code of Practice (England and Wales) describe school based strategies which can help;
■ pupils should be given short-term goals which stretch but do not overwhelm them;
■ the curriculum should be relevant;
■ sanctions should not include educational activities as punishment.

(p. 206)

Research by Daniels *et al.* (1999) reiterates the importance of suitable intellectual challenges for these pupils. While they also report the importance of a coherent school disciplinary code, the management style used in your classroom will have a strong influence on the mathematics curriculum. For example, if you take a 'hard' approach, you may find the consequence of separating, quietening and reprimanding the pupils is that you deliver an individualised curriculum. This is likely to consist of short tasks, such as a page of 'sums' that does not require full engagement to complete and hence fails to stimulate or provide opportunities for satisfaction.

On the other hand, you may take an approach that focuses on the relationships within the class, through working with mathematical games, projects in small groups and discussion. This will need careful planning (and advice from the usual teacher). A first step could be to take a group of, say, four pupils to work cooperatively around a table on a mathematical game. The pupils' self-esteem can be raised, though their achievement in mathematics expressed in terms of words and actions rather than formal symbols.

SPEECH, LANGUAGE AND COMMUNICATION AND EAL

Speech, language and communication

Some of the ways in which language affects learning in mathematics were discussed in Chapter 8. Linguistic competence supports thinking as well as communication. It also requires and develops an understanding of symbols – letters, words, punctuation, for example. These skills are needed for understanding, manipulating and reading of mathematical notation. Poor memory, difficulty with reading or interpretation of meanings can hamper progress in many areas of the curriculum, including mathematics. In the latest National Curriculum, one of the key processes is concerned with communicating mathematical ideas (QCA, 2007a). This emphasis on a more language-aware school mathematics department could benefit pupils with speech, language and communication difficulties.

English as an additional language

Children who have English as an additional language (EAL) may have their mathematical potential thwarted by their special need relative to the English language environment. During the Early Years Foundation Stage at school, language-support teachers encourage bilingual development of concepts in number, shape and measure. This bilingual (or multilingual) approach encourages mental flexibility, as well as developing the pupil's self-esteem.

In the secondary classroom, skilled multilingual mathematical support is not often available for EAL pupils, and classroom materials become more important. Appropriate classroom materials do not have to be solely text-based: practical work, visual representations and technological advances can both cut through the language barrier and serve as media for inducting the EAL pupil into using English.

Task 10.4 **Mental maths in another language**

If you are essentially monolingual, this task will help you to appreciate the difficulties experienced by many pupils with English as an additional language (EAL) in mathematics lessons.

When you were at school you may have studied a modern foreign language (MFL). Find someone else, who studied this language to the same standard as you, and give each other a mental arithmetic test in the foreign language.

This activity can be fun, but it can also help you to feel how brilliant your mathematical understanding is compared to your ability to respond to the questions. Another language-awareness activity is to ask someone fluent in a language you understand a little to explain a mathematical concept to you. You may experience a cognitive-linguistic gap similar to that which EAL pupils feel in every class.

Moderate learning difficulties

Pupils whose attainment is well below age-related expectations are generally educated in mainstream schools and are likely to be the largest group of pupils with a particular SEN you will meet. As research into learning disabilities continues, we might very well find diagnoses for some of these pupils that could help teachers to understand their difficulties better. These pupils tend to cluster in low-attaining mathematics sets. In such classes, it is important to develop a positive attitude to learning mathematics, by utilising your patience, imagination and humour.

Pupils with weak reasoning skills, poor memories and difficult behaviour require stimulating mathematics. The Improving Attainment in Mathematics Project (Watson *et al.*, 2003) contains details of the ways that teachers worked to improve the attainment of previously low-attaining pupils. Ahmed also developed tasks for these pupils that emphasised 'experimenting, questioning, reflecting, discovering, inventing and discussing' (Ahmed, 1987: 17). This emphasis can reduce memory requirements and give opportunities for experiences that prompt and exercise a variety of thinking skills. In particular, concentration can be developed by tasks that capture the pupils' imaginations, involve a practical or experiential aspect, or appropriate and accessible use of ICT, and are very well planned so that pupils are not confused. Designing tasks that favour kinaesthetic or visual learning styles will give these pupils opportunities for successful participation.

Much information can be gleaned from studying pupils' work; their strategies, errors and their representations. The following task aims to build up your capacity to learn from pupils' work.

Task 10.5 **Learning from pupils' work**

This task is intended to help you to:

1   Perceive evidence of mathematical thinking in work of pupils whose achieve-ment is below age-related expectations.
2   Discern different aspects of mathematics achievement, for example in different areas such as: the spatial, the numeric, the structural, the representational and the logical.

Download and read a copy of Carla Finesilver's paper from the link below. It presents details of pupils' work on a 'Cartesian product' problem called *Holiday clothes* .

■   Consider how you could adapt the methodology to your school context. Discuss with your mentor how you can plan to use this activity with a few pupils.
■   As they use the activities, look out for all the mathematical successes that they show in their work.
■   Write up your findings to discuss with colleagues.

(Finesilver, C. (2009) http://www.educatejournal.org/index.php?journal=educate&page=article&op=viewFile&path[]=216&path[]=206)

SENSORY/PHYSICAL IMPAIRMENTS

Deafness and hearing impairment

Pupils with a hearing impairment will be taught in mainstream schools. However, they are frequently found to be chronologically behind their hearing peers in mathematics attainment. Therefore, being hearing impaired puts children's mathematical attainment at risk, but it is not itself a cause of their lower attainment. This is the conclusion of Nuñes and Moreno's (1997) research on deaf children's understanding of number.

Some ideas for teaching hearing impaired children are given in Capel *et al*. (2009). Their advice includes:

> give visual cues to topics being discussed;
> make sure the pupil is watching your face when you speak and sitting within three metres of you.

(pp. 206–7).

Computers have enormous potential in helping hearing impaired children (Barham and Bishop, 1991), as their capacity to work dynamically and visually can help these pupils develop mathematical concepts without overly relying on detailed spoken language.

Physical impairment

Children in wheelchairs, with hearing aids or with limited vision are integrated, whenever possible, into mainstream schooling. They are, however, likely to have a statement of SEN and so you will have professional advice to turn to for specific teaching strategies tailored to their individual needs. Children with profound physical impairments will have classroom assistants to help them in their ordinary classroom work. For non-subject-specific advice, see John Cornwall's (1997) practical guide for mainstream teachers of pupils with physical disabilities.

Although physical disabilities vary a great deal, mathematics can be a school subject in which physically disabled pupils have equality of access. A mathematics teacher (Callinan, 1992), who works with children with severe physical disabilities, has designed a curriculum for teaching mathematics that tries to minimise the particular problems these pupils face with spatial awareness, emotional frustration, limitations of social experience and restricted language, so that they can experience mathematical achievement in the same way as able-bodied children.

Visual impairment

As the teaching episode recounted by Lesley Thorpe in the introduction to this chapter illustrates, blind or visually impaired pupils can excel at mathematics. For blind pupils, all aspects of learning about location and space need to be experienced kinaesthetically and reinforced aurally. Precision with diction ('10 per cent of' and '10 per cent off' can sound very similar, for example) and awareness of homophones within the mathematics register (e.g. 'sign' and 'sine') are important for a teacher of these pupils. As with physically impaired pupils, much advice will be available from the special needs department in a mainstream school.

RESOURCES FOR LEARNING

While you may be able to design some specific materials for pupils with SEN, as in the example of inclusive teaching given at the beginning of this chapter, many excellent resources are available via the internet. Two wide-ranging sets of resources are the 'Wave 3' primary strategy materials (DCSF, 2008) (available for download from http://nationalstrategies.standards.dcsf.gov.uk/primary/publications/inclusion/wave3pack accessed 26/1/10) and the Standards Unit's *Improving Learning in Mathematics* materials (available from https://www.ncetm.org.uk/files/224/improving_learning_in_mathematicsi.pdf accessed 26/1/10). Your school is likely to have a copy of each of these extensive resources. The Standards Unit's box of materials contains examples of ways of working that will be relevant to all secondary school pupils. The Wave 3 materials will be more suitable for younger pupils. There are also links from the TDA site: (http://www.tda.gov.uk/teachers/sen/resources.aspx)

As an example, a useful page from the Wave 3 is reproduced below that offers advice relevant to secondary pupils as well as those in the primary years:

ONE OF A TEAM

Learning about teaching mathematics to pupils with special needs includes understanding:

Year 6 key objective Carry out column addition and subtraction of numbers involving decimals (NNS *Framework for teaching mathematics*, Supplement of Examples, Section 6, pages 49, 51)

Associated knowledge and skills	Errors and misconceptions	Questions to identify errors and misconceptions	Teaching to address the errors and misconceptions	Next steps in moving towards the key objective
Apply knowledge of the number system to enable efficient counting of a large number of objects.		Imagine you have a money box containing 2p and 1p coins. What do you think would be a good way to count these quickly to find out how much money there is? What is 60 + 20? ... 60 + 30? ... 60 + 40?	Practical opportunities to develop efficient counting strategies for a range of objects, for example coins, cubes, conkers, collectable cards, stickers.	Carry out simple calculations that involve crossing the boundary from hundreds to one thousand and vice versa, supported by an
Add and subtract multiples of ten, a hundred and a thousand. **1 Y6**	Has inefficient counting strategies and/or insecure understanding of the number system. **1 Y6 +/–**	What changed when you found 60 + 40? What is 40 + 40? ... 400 + 400? Which answer is the larger? How is the calculation 40 + 400 + 4000 different from the others? What is 60 – 20? ... 600 – 200? ... 6000 – 2000? Explain how you worked these out. What is 6000 – 200? ... 6000 – 20?	Count forwards and backwards in tens, hundreds and thousands from different starting points, including starting numbers that are not multiples of ten or a hundred. Use an empty number line to support this development. Order multiples of a hundred and a thousand.	empty number line and extending this to a visualised image to develop mental calculation.
Give an estimate by rounding, to determine whether the answer to a calculation is sensible. **2 Y6**	Rounding inaccurately, particularly when decimals are involved, and having little sense of the size of the numbers involved. **2 Y6 +/–**	Is 26 nearer to 20 or 30? Is 271 nearer 270 or 280? Is 1.8 nearer to 1 or 2? Draw a sketch to illustrate your answer and explain how you know.	Use number squares and/or number lines to consider the order and comparative value of numbers to support rounding.	Consider pairs of items from a catalogue and ask child to estimate whether a £10 (or £20, etc.) note would be enough to buy both the items?

■ **Figure 10.1** Wave 3 Appendix 1: Tracking children's learning chart – addition and subtraction, p. 31

- the SEN Code of Practice, as mentioned above;
- the role and functioning of the special needs department in your school;
- the relationships between individual pupils and their key workers;
- how to work with pupil support assistants.

The school's statutory responsibilities for pupils with SEN are translated into school policy by the Special Educational Needs Coordinator and other staff. All teachers will have some SEN pupils, therefore all teachers are part of the special needs team. The following features have been identified as contributing to successful teaching of pupils with SEN within the mainstream classroom:

- clear specification of roles and responsibilities;
- detailed record keeping;
- careful organisation of resources;
- regular meetings to plan and evaluate;
- flexibility.

(cited in Daniels and Anghileri, 1995: 134–135)

One of the roles of the SENCO is to ensure that everyone who should know about a particular pupils special need is (a) aware of the need and (b) ready to help with that need. For example, everyone who teaches a pupil who has epilepsy should be aware of the possibility that he or she may have a fit, and should be able to cope while someone else goes for more specialist help.

Task 10.6 **Talking with teachers at school**

This task is designed to help you to:

1 learn the discourse through which mainstream teachers discuss pupils with special needs.
2 differentiate between polite talk, compassionate talk, talk that aligns with the official government DCFS discourses and other categories of talk you can discern.

When you are at your placement school, you will hear conversations that are relevant to children with additional or special needs.

- Make a point of joining such a discussion and take note of the terms that are used, particularly ordinary words or phrases that are used in special ways. For example, you might hear the word 'in/appropriate' used. What is being referred to? What is the tone?
- If you know the child who is being discussed, do you have a sense of whether the words signal a restriction of challenge (for example, 'I can't use practical maths when he's in the room, it wouldn't be appropriate, he just breaks everything he touches') or just mean 'bad', or some other meaning.
- Look out for the use of stock phrases like 'raising standards' or 'tracking progress'. How are these terms applied to learners with special needs?

If possible, arrange to have conversations with:

1   a mathematics teacher at your school, such as your mentor or head of depart-
    ment;
2   the school's Special Educational Needs Coordinator (SENCO).

Ask each of them for examples of the range of special needs in mathematics in the
school. To encourage them to speak freely, you might ask each of them: 'Who are
the two most different children who have special needs in mathematics lessons?'
Teachers often respond more readily to an invitation to describe specific pupils than
to a request for a more abstract description.

   Reflect on how teachers' informal discussion of pupils with special needs differs
from the language used in the more formal discussions with the head of department
or SENCO. Which differences seem to you to matter?

Working with another adult in your classroom

Various terms are used to describe the 'learning support' or 'inclusion staff' employed to
help children with special needs. Find out which term is used in your placement school.

   Trainee teachers often find the management of learning support assistants difficult.
The more that such people know what the lesson is about, and the way you intend teaching the lesson, the more help they can be. However, it can be difficult to find opportunities
to communicate with them. Many of these assistants are attached to pupils with special
needs to provide them with the in-class support they may need in order to take as full a
part as possible in your lesson. Some learning support workers are not at ease with mathematics and may themselves need guidance to provide appropriate support to the pupils.
Increasingly, advice is available to learning support workers through government agencies' websites. In particular, the Wave 3 materials, mentioned previously, offer advice for
inclusion staff giving one-to-one numeracy intervention. It is important that learning assistants are helped to work in the way that you, as the mathematics expert, think mathematics
should be presented. For example, a Year 9 class was working on multiplication by ten.
The classroom assistant was working with Conrad and had told him to multiply by 10 by
'adding a nought'. The next day (when the assistant was not there) he did literally add
zero, having not understood the reasoning behind the instruction.

   Working in a classroom with a classroom assistant can be a tremendous opportunity. At times, it is like team-teaching the lesson, where you take the lead and the
classroom assistant provides support. Your lesson is more likely to be successful if you
are able to involve the assistant in your planning before the lesson and to plan not only
what you will do but also how the assistant is to assist. For a student teacher, or a newly
qualified teacher who is still a young adult, working with someone of a different generation can, on occasion, be socially awkward. However, a collaborative model of teaching
offers a positive approach, which respects the contributions of both teacher and assistant
for SEN pupils. As an example, in the earlier section on emotional and behavioural difficulties, I reported that pupils who find mathematics difficult often generalise initially by
verbalising their findings, rather than writing them symbolically. A useful collaborative
role that the assistant could play would be to help pupils verbalise their findings, prior to
encouraging them to write.

SUMMARY AND KEY POINTS

If there is anything common to all special needs pupils, it is the greater probability of them being frustrated within a mainstream class. Imagine not being able to quite see or quite hear. Imagine being always given unchallenging work because it was felt that something 'straightforward' would keep you occupied and quiet. Imagine having to do exercise after exercise of some mathematics that is obvious to you and you understood immediately years ago. Imagine never understanding any teacher explanation and always having to hope for a manageable task and a helper to guide you through it.

Task 10.7 **School-based planning with pupil feedback**

Plan to teach a mathematical topic to an individual pupil or a small group of pupils with a specific special need.

■ First, try to imagine what school mathematics is like from their point of view and make notes of your ideas.
■ Interview the pupils in order to find out what they think helps them in their learning and what minimises any frustration they feel. Compare this with your initial notes.
■ Then prepare materials for the topic taking on board their views and frustrations.
■ Evaluate the lesson yourself and, if possible, ask for the pupils' evaluation.

What can a class teacher do to minimise frustration due to the pupils' special needs? This does not mean the teacher should minimise the pupil's struggle or effort! On the contrary, those of us who have studied mathematics have experienced both the 'frustration' of working on a problem that does not yield and the satisfaction when it does. Learning to apply mental effort to solve mathematical problems is a major achievement for children of all capabilities; part of a secondary mathematics teacher's job is to help children develop their mental 'muscles'. The frustration arising from a special need is essentially different from 'mathematical struggle' or mental effort.

As a mathematics teacher, you will aim to maximise effectiveness of struggle or effort while minimising frustration. In doing so, you have to work within the constraint of the special need and the mathematics curriculum. For some children, you cannot push the challenge too far before the frustration is overwhelming. For others, lack of a challenge may exacerbate their frustration. Complementary to pupil 'frustration' is pupil 'satisfaction'. Haylock (1991: 2) reports how he found, in his research, that low-attaining pupils rarely had the opportunity to experience the satisfaction that mathematical achievement can give. Indeed, for every special need mentioned above, the teacher's challenge is to turn 'frustration' into 'satisfaction' caused by that pupil's own mathematical achievement.

ACKNOWLEDGEMENT

Many thanks to Lesley Thorpe – who, after her PGCE, went to teach mathematics at Minsthorpe Community College, Minsthorpe, South Elmsall, Pontefract, West Yorkshire – for giving me permission to reproduce an extract from her *Materials for Teaching* PGCE assignment, University of Leeds, 2003.

FURTHER READING

Brown, S. (2003) 'Ability – a concept concealing disabling environments'. *Support for Learning* 18(2), 88–90.

This article traces the author's understanding of the notion of ability over a long career and is recommended reading. Also recommended is *Support for Learning*, volume 16, no. 1 (2001). This is a whole issue on mathematics and special needs providing a useful set of papers that give an indication of the range of issues involved in special needs mathematics.

Daniels, H. and Anghileri, J. (1995) *Secondary Mathematics and Special Educational Needs*. London: Cassell.

This book contains substantial background to mathematics teaching and SEN. In several places, the authors have taken a historical perspective towards developments in cultural acceptance of SEN, educational legislation and specific SEN provision, which gives a helpful picture of this important part of teaching practice, particularly in England and Wales. Detailed references are given to others' research, making this a useful reference book.

DfES (2001) *Special Educational Needs Code of Practice*. London: HMSO. Downloadable from http://www.teachernet.gov.uk/_doc/3724/SENCodeOfPractice.pdf

Dowker, A. (2004) *What Works for Children with Mathematical Difficulties*. Downloadable from http://www.dcsf.gov.uk/research/data/uploadfiles/RR554.pdf

Dyson, A. and Millward, A. (2000) *Schools and Special Needs: Issues of Innovation and Inclusion*. London: Paul Chapman.

This book gives a clear introduction to inclusion in contemporary English educational thinking. It has very readable case studies, which give a research-based insight into what aspects of a school facilitate inclusion.

***Equals* (formerly called *Struggle*).**

Equals is a termly magazine, dedicated to mathematics and special needs, published by the Mathematical Association. The majority of the articles are by teachers and others working directly with people with special needs. The articles are short and practical.

Finesilver, C. 'Drawing, modelling and gesture in students' solutions to a Cartesian product problem'. *Educate*. Downloadable from http://www.educatejournal.org/index.php?journal=educate&page=article&op=viewFile&path[]=216&path[]=206

Frederickson, N. and Cline, T. (2002) *Special Educational Needs, Inclusion and Diversity: A Textbook*. Buckingham: Open University Press.

This book contains some useful reference material on legal frameworks, on historical development of special educational needs, on assessment issues and further sources. It is set out as a workbook with exercises for the reader (without any hints or 'answers'). However, the chapter on mathematics is disappointing, as it does not give practical insight or advice for teaching mathematics specifically to pupils with SEN.

Haylock, D. (1991) *Teaching Mathematics to Low Attainers 8–12*. London: Paul Chapman.

This practical book focuses on the 'middle-school' age range, but many of the children's difficulties are also to be met in older pupils. Haylock gives plenty of suggestions for engaging activities many of which are suitable for the entire low-attaining secondary cohort. A particularly useful feature of this book is the detail with which a conceptual problem is analysed, then followed by specific activities offered as a potential remedy.

MATHEMATICS IN CONTEXT

Clare Lee and Robert Ward-Penny

INTRODUCTION

An important part of the role of a mathematics teacher is to present mathematics in a situated way, allowing pupils to 'work on open and closed tasks in a variety of real and abstract contexts that allow them to select the mathematics to use' (QCA, 2007a: 147). Whether you use a context-based question from a textbook, engage in an investigation that lasts for a whole lesson or are asked to deliver a set of 'functional' or 'cross-curricular' lessons, you will frequently find yourself linking concepts and methods from the mathematics curriculum to the 'real world'. Taking this approach to teaching mathematics yields a number of benefits for both the teacher and the learner: it can help pupils to construct their own understanding, promote memory, increase motivation and give a partial answer to the ever-present question of 'Why do we have to do this?'

> The reason for pupils' difficulty is explained not in terms of the conceptual complexity of the subject matter, but in terms of its apparent irrelevance and/or the teacher's inability to present it in a coherent, meaningful way.
>
> (Quilter and Harper, 1988: 127)

However, not all contexts are equally useful or even equally valid for use in the mathematics classroom. There are important philosophical and pedagogical issues that influence how you choose contexts and how pupils come to learn the mathematics embedded within them. This chapter will explore some of those issues and offer you ideas about how you might organise your teaching, so that you can present mathematics in context for the benefit of your pupils.

OBJECTIVES

By the end of this chapter you should be able to:

- reflect upon how contextualised learning is related to many of the aims of mathematics teaching;

- understand that teaching pupils to apply their mathematical knowledge and understanding can benefit them in a broader sense;
- evaluate critically the roles, strengths and weaknesses of different types of contexts;
- employ pedagogical strategies to encourage pupils to learn to apply mathematics;
- understand that contexts constitute a key part of cross-curricular and interdisciplinary working and qualifications.

WHY DO PEOPLE DO MATHEMATICS?

If you are training as a mathematics teacher, you are probably aware of some of the plethora of roles and applications that mathematics has in the twenty-first century. Mathematicians and statisticians are hired in disciplines as diverse as engineering and criminology; their expertise is called upon to map the progress of epidemics, send satellites into space and protect the privacy of e-mails. It is easy to forget that not everyone has this awareness and that sometimes people are ignorant of the influence of mathematics on their everyday lives. In a study of pupils' images of mathematics and mathematicians, Picker and Berry (2000) asked a sample of Year 8 pupils why someone would hire a mathematician. Many answers showed that the pupils had no idea; one response was that 'no one is so stupid as to hire a mathematician!' (p. 71). Those pupils who did suggest answers tended to refer to fairly obvious traditional occupations, such as accounting, teaching and banking.

Mathematics can be thought of as a 'chameleon' (Johnston-Wilder and Lee, 2010) – it fades away against the background of the real world and is sometimes only spotted by those who know what they are looking for. Part of the job of a mathematics teacher, therefore, is to help pupils identify aspects of real-life situations where mathematics is relevant. Using contexts in the classroom clearly forms a large part of this. If you regularly link new concepts to real-life applications, and set aside time for pupils to act as investigative mathematicians and problem-solvers, they will develop their personal capacity for seeing mathematics, and opportunities for using mathematics, in the world around them. In later sections of this chapter, we discuss how pupils can think and act as mathematicians in the classroom and hence take 'ownership' of mathematical ideas.

However, it is important to recognise that different people attach different levels of importance to this goal. In Chapter 1, some of the competing interest groups that influence the mathematics curriculum were examined. Each of these interest groups would have a different perspective on the role and relative importance of contexts (Ernest, 1991). An industrial pragmatist might argue that mathematical skills should be taught in industrial and commercial contexts to help the vocational development of pupils, while a social reformer might argue that contexts should be chosen so as to be contemporary and socially relevant, in order to help pupils develop a critical numeracy with which to understand society. Conversely, an extreme mathematical purist might deny the need for contexts altogether, and it is important to remember that purely abstract mathematics can have a power and attraction of its own. Your own views, ideas and opinions will no doubt influence the contexts you choose in your own teaching.

Task 11.1 **Contexts and consequences**

Imagine that you are about to teach a lesson introducing standard deviation. After teaching the method for calculating the standard deviation, you want to illustrate the technique with a context.

- ▪ What contexts might you choose if you were (a) an industrial pragmatist; (b) a social reformer?
- ▪ How might your choices of contexts influence the way you structure your lesson?
- ▪ Is it possible to integrate both sets of aims into your lesson?
- ▪ In each of these instances, how would you answer the question 'Why are we doing this?'

The fourth interest group described in Chapter 1 was the progressive educators, whose main focus was on the personal development of pupils as individuals. Before we look more closely at some examples of different contexts, consider the concerns of this group and recognise the role that training pupils to use and apply mathematics plays in developing pupils' thinking skills.

SKILLS FOR LEARNING MATHEMATICS IN CONTEXT

When pupils learn mathematics in context, they are developing their understanding of the mathematics they are using or even developing new mathematical thinking skills. By using their current understanding to develop mathematics new to them, they are extending their personal domain of mathematics and hence are acting as mathematicians.

> Pupils participate in mathematics when they intentionally develop new mathematical ways to organise their experience or reflect on the organisation, strategies and concepts that they have already developed. This may consist of a search for patterns and consistency or an attempt to generalise or formalise procedures, make connections within the system and develop logical arguments to use to prove and to share their results.

> (Lee, 2006: 39)

Acting as a mathematician requires that pupils use the thinking skills that mathematicians use. In this section, we will discuss what those skills are.

There is a 'narrow' form of teaching mathematics that we have frequently seen in English mathematics classrooms. In this way of teaching, the teacher demonstrates a method or a procedure and the pupils attempt to reproduce this procedure over and over again in order to remember a particular mathematical method. This style of teaching has been shown to be ineffective in preparing pupils for the demands of the real world (e.g. Nuñes et al., 1993). However, it is a widespread teaching method in the UK and it is quite likely that you will come across this way of teaching during your school experience or when you start your first job. Indeed you may choose to use this style on occasion, from amongst several others, in order to help pupils learn a particular mathematical method. Research has shown that, when teachers only ever teach in this way, their pupils develop a shallow knowledge and often a dislike of engaging with mathematics (Skemp, 1976; Boaler, 2009; Ofsted, 2008). Many teachers have felt constrained to teach in this way because examinations, such as the GCSE, have tested procedures and mathematical methods rather than the solving of realistic problems – and teachers and their school are judged by Ofsted on the results that their pupils achieve in GCSE mathematics.

So is there an alternative? The answer to this is an unequivocal 'yes'! Another way is to teach mathematics more realistically; some might even say to teach 'real mathematics'.

> Real mathematics involves problem-solving, creating ideas and representations, exploring puzzles, discussing methods and many different ways of working.
>
> (Boaler, 2009: 2)

In her publications, Jo Boaler has shown that it is not an *either/or* situation (see, for example, Boaler, 1997). It is not a matter of *either* enjoying interesting and motivating mathematics lessons *or* passing examinations. In her study, she found that pupils who were taught mathematics in a project-based, 'real-world' way not only achieved higher grades in examinations than those who developed only procedural knowledge, but also held more positive views about mathematics such that many of them wanted to continue to learn mathematics. This real-world approach will inevitably go beyond just using contexts to illustrate new concepts in lessons and begin to include longer, more extended tasks and problems.

The new National Curriculum for KS3 (QCA, 2007a) is framed in a way that requires pupils to learn about mathematics in context. It sets out a number of key concepts that underpin the *study of mathematics*. Concepts are the constituents of thought, and therefore these are the ways of thinking that the National Curriculum recognises as mathematical. It considers that pupils need to understand the following concepts in order to deepen and broaden their knowledge, skills and understanding of mathematics.

1.1 Competence
   a. Applying suitable mathematics accurately within the classroom and beyond.
   b. Communicating mathematics effectively.
   c. Selecting appropriate mathematical tools and methods, including ICT.

1.2 Creativity
   a. Combining understanding, experiences, imagination and reasoning to construct new knowledge.
   b. Using existing mathematical knowledge to create solutions to unfamiliar problems.
   c. Posing questions and developing convincing arguments.

1.3 Applications and implications of mathematics
   a. Knowing that mathematics is a rigorous, coherent discipline.
   b. Understanding that mathematics is used as a tool in a wide range of contexts.
   c. Recognising the rich historical and cultural roots of mathematics.
   d. Engaging in mathematics as an interesting and worthwhile activity.

1.4 Critical understanding

    a.   Knowing that mathematics is essentially abstract and can be used to model, interpret or represent situations.

    b.   Recognising the <u>limitations and scope</u> of a model or representation.

(pp. 140–1)

Pupils cannot learn these key concepts if they are taught mathematics in a narrow way. They learn to apply suitable mathematics by having to choose the appropriate mathematics to solve a problem. Pupils begin to see mathematics as a connected whole when they are asked to be creative and use their imagination and reasoning to combine understanding of various topics and produce a way forward with some mathematics. Pupils will have to use their competence, creativity and critical understanding, as well as apply mathematical understanding, if they are engaged in a realistic scenario where the mathematics comes out of the context. The key concepts set out many of the characteristics of mathematics in context: that mathematics in context goes beyond the classroom; that it requires selecting appropriate tools, combinations of understanding, experiences and reasoning; and that engaging in mathematics is an interesting and worthwhile activity.

    The National Curriculum also specifies the essential skills and processes in mathematics that pupils need to learn to make progress. These are:

1   Representing

2   Analysing

    a.   Use mathematical reasoning

    b.   Use appropriate mathematical procedures

3   Interpreting and evaluating

4   Communicating and reflecting.

All of these processes are important when learning mathematics in a realistic way.

    Representing and Analysing, particularly the use of mathematical procedures, have been part of the curriculum for many years and are important components of understanding, using and controlling mathematics. Processes 3 and 4, and the use of mathematical reasoning, may be used less in a classroom where the emphasis is on practising and memorising procedures and methods, but they lie at the heart of learning mathematics in a realistic way. For example, mathematicians analyse when they use mathematical reasoning to:

- make connections within mathematics;
- use knowledge of related problems;
- visualise and work with dynamic images;
- identify and classify patterns;
- make and begin to justify conjectures and generalisations, considering special cases and counter-examples;
- explore the effects of varying values and look for invariance and covariance;
- take account of feedback and learn from mistakes;
- work logically towards results and solutions, recognising the impact of constraints and assumptions;
- appreciate that there are a number of different techniques that can be used to analyse a situation;

■   reason inductively and deduce.

(QCA, 2007a: 142)

The same can be said of all the other processes detailed in the National Curriculum. Interpreting and evaluating are essential when actually using mathematics; for example, recognising when a particular tool or train of thought is useful and appropriate, and when it is not, or evaluating a solution that has been suggested.

Task 11.2 **Concepts and processes in context**

In the 'equable shapes' investigation, an equable shape has the same numerical value for its perimeter in 'units' as for its area in 'square units'. Try to find an equable rectangle. How about an equable triangle?

When you have spent a short while trying out ideas, look back at the list of processes above and identify how you have used each of them in your brief investigation. Now look back further at the list of key concepts and identify which of these you have used. For example, did you represent the situation in a diagram and then model it algebraically? Did you use your understanding of area and perimeter (and possibly trigonometry) to construct an algebraic relationship and use that to develop a convincing argument?

Do not forget that pupils will need to be taught how to select and apply appropriate mathematical tools, model situations using mathematical representations and communicate effectively. Such skills will not come naturally. Lessons that are planned to allow the pupils to learn and develop these skills may well seem to take some time away from learning mathematics. However, by using mathematics in context, pupils will come to understand that mathematical skills are important and will be in a position to use them to broaden and deepen their understanding of mathematics.

Other authors have considered how professional mathematicians really think and how this can be applied to classroom learning. According to Cuoco *et al.* (1996), there are habits of mind that research mathematicians use in creating and using mathematics outside school. The aim of these habits of mind is to equip pupils to deal with the 'ill-posed and fuzzy problems' that are characteristic of situations in which mathematics is used in the real world. In order to apply mathematics to understand problem situations, mathematicians use the tools of systematising and abstracting and they look for and develop new ways to describe and represent the problems. These habits of mind are:

■   **pattern sniffing** – analysing, researching and categorising all use this mathematical habit of mind;

■   **experimenting** – this can involve recording results, trying very small or very large numbers or varying parameters. Experimenting requires pupils to start playing with a situation until something seems fruitful. This habit of mind also requires a level of scepticism and being reluctant to accept ideas without justification;

■   **describing** – mathematicians use mathematical language to give precise descriptions, invent notation, argue convincingly and write conjectures, frame questions and state opinions;

■ **tinkering** – taking ideas apart and putting them back together to see what happens if something is left out or if the pieces are put back in a different way. These approaches all help to see a way forward when solving a problem;

■ **inventing** – whether coming up with new rules or algorithms for doing things or providing explanations of how things work, inventing can be a way of bringing clarity to a situation;

■ **visualising** – doing things in your head that could be done with the hands or eyes, but also visualising data, relationships, change and calculations. Visualising allows mathematicians to see what happens if … or to move between states;

■ **conjecturing** – predicting behaviour, checking plausibility and justifying ideas;

■ **guessing** – starting with a possible solution and working backwards or just checking your guess. It may be a surprise to see guessing as a mathematical habit of mind, but mathematicians use guessing to uncover new insights and approaches and it is part of developing a good 'feel' for numbers.

(Adapted from Cuoco *et al.*, 1996)

These habits of mind are important when pupils are presented with a problem that uses mathematics in context, whether it is a short stand-alone question or part of a wider investigation. Pupils will have to look at the problem and think hard about ways that might help begin to find a solution. If pupils are told, for example, that real mathematicians experiment, guess, visualise or invent, then this may free pupils from the belief that they should 'remember' the way forward or that there is 'only one right way' to proceed. The notion that there is 'one correct procedure' is, in our experience, common in people learning mathematics. Pupils may need encouragement to tinker with the problem for a few minutes and see if they can describe a useful way forward. Having discussed what the tinkering has revealed, they could be asked to visualise what would happen if they took one course rather than another. Then the pupils could work collaboratively to experiment with ideas that they think might work. Developing and using the habits of mind that mathematicians use will allow pupils the freedom to learn about mathematics in context as well as developing habits that will be useful in many contexts outside the mathematics classroom.

Task 11.3 **Getting into the habit (of mind)**

In this task you are invited to use the habits of mind to structure the way that you work on a problem. Tinker with the investigation for a while, and then make a guess and experiment.

Either return to your work on 'equable shapes' and extend your ideas further, or try the following connection problem:

Four bases sit at the vertices of a square piece of flat land. If they need to be connected together by the minimum amount of road possible, what road layout would you use?

After you have worked on the problem for a while, reflect on the following questions. When does your guess turn into a conjecture? Did you find that your guess was not helpful – if so, what did you do then? Invent a new way of describing what is happening. Does that help you to describe the model you are working with?

The National Curriculum and the habits of mind literature can be summarised in the following list. When learning mathematics pupils need to:

■   have imaginative ideas;
■   ask questions and make conjectures;
■   make mistakes and use them to learn new things;
■   be organised and systematic;
■   substitute and transform, represent and model, do and undo, reason and justify, look for invariance and change;
■   describe, explain and discuss their work;
■   look for patterns;
■   keep going when it is difficult.

Task 11.4 **Rich tasks, rich learning**

Look at some mathematics websites, for example Nrich (nrich.maths.org), to find a problem that requires as many of the above skills as possible, one in which pupils will need to ask questions and be organised and systematic. Look for one that requires doing and undoing or substitution and transforming, as well as reasoning and justifying.

When you have a suitably rich task, think about a class that you might use the task with and consider how you would help them to fully engage with the task.

We hope that you are now convinced that it is a good idea to offer your pupils the opportunity to learn mathematics in context for at least some of the time that they are learning mathematics. But how do you choose the context and how do you know what contexts you are looking for? We will begin to answer these questions in the next section.

STRENGTHS AND WEAKNESSES OF DIFFERENT CONTEXTS

Imagine now that you are planning to teach a lesson that involves parabolas. You think that it might be motivating for pupils if you include an example of how parabolas occur in the 'real world'. There are a large number of possible contexts that involve parabolas, but you decide to choose from the four that are given below:

■   if you throw a tennis ball across the classroom, it traces out a parabola;
■   espionage agencies sometimes use microphones with parabolic reflectors, as the shape of the reflector gathers sound waves from a large area and focuses them onto the receiver;
■   car headlights often use parabolic reflectors to convert the light from one bulb into a wide beam;
■   astronauts are sometimes trained in a plane nicknamed the 'vomit comet', which follows a vertically parabolic flight path to simulate weightlessness.

Which do you think you might choose and why? Each of these contexts has a different set of strengths and weaknesses. The tennis ball context, for example, is easily demonstrated in the classroom and this physicality might appeal to some learners. By throwing the ball at different angles, you might also begin to explore the idea of a family of curves. However, it is not entirely mathematically genuine – in reality, the path will be slightly distorted from a parabolic one due to air resistance.

The second and third contexts are very similar and offer a lot to the teacher who is trying to communicate the special nature of the *focus* of a parabola. The second is perhaps more engaging than the third, but the third is perhaps more familiar. The fourth example is very interesting, but will lie well outside the experiences of most if not all of your pupils. However, it might be a nice exercise for an A-Level Mechanics class to justify why a journey of this nature would simulate weightlessness.

In this particular instance, each of the contexts offers something to the teacher and to the learner. The main concern would be choosing the right contexts for that class at that time and presenting them in an engaging and effective manner. However, some contexts offer little or nothing to the learner and can actually promote negative ideas about mathematics.

Problems with choosing contexts

There are many potential pitfalls to be aware of when using context-based questions to motivate mathematics learning. For instance:

▨   The question contains the correct level of mathematics, but the context is clearly forced and unreal – the situation described would never occur in reality and mathematics would never actually be used in this way. Too many instances of this kind might unintentionally reinforce the idea that school mathematics is not practically useful. Repeatedly asking pupils to 'suspend their disbelief' invites them to consider that mathematics has nothing to do with the real world. It is hard for pupils to conceive why you would need to calculate what fraction of a cinema audience wears glasses, or work out the median age of seven of your friends.

▨   The context may be real and motivating, but the mathematics may be too complicated and so beyond the reach of the pupils. Too many instances of this type of context can reinforce the idea that school mathematics is not real mathematics and that real mathematics is appallingly difficult. For example, while it is true that mathematics can be used to describe the ripples formed when a stone falls into a pond, partial differential equations lie beyond the capacity of most school pupils.

▨   The question contains the correct level of mathematics, and the context is genuine, but the situation described holds no interest for the pupils or lies firmly outside of their culture. One common example found in textbooks is the 'diluting orange squash' question, where, in reality, orange squash is made by estimating and adjusting to personal taste. Too many instances of this type of context can reinforce the idea that school mathematics is for 'other people' – it is the domain of those who never guess!

Sometimes it is useful, and indeed important, to include contexts from outside pupils' current experiences or to show them examples that utilise high-level mathematics to promote an understanding of the wider mathematical community. However, over-use of any one of these types of contexts can lead to problems. One key principle when choosing contexts is to ask yourself: 'To what extent, and in what ways, is this context *genuine* for my pupils?'

Cons and contexts

Textbooks and worksheets are full of contexts which seem to have little grounding in, or bearing on, reality. This kind of question is often typical:

> Adam has half of a pizza. He then gets one third of a pizza. What fraction of a pizza does Adam have now?

In this question, the fact that Adam is dealing with a pizza has no relevance or bearing on either the mathematical process to be used or how the answer should be interpreted. It is a 'con' rather than a context (Ward-Penny, 2010). A more genuine context to motivate the skill of adding fractions would be to calculate the combined resistance of two resistors added in parallel. Although the numbers used might end up being more challenging, using a genuine context avoids reinforcing the meta-message that mathematics is only useful for solving ridiculously contrived problems.

Task 11.5 **Con or context?**

Look at the three questions below. For each question, identify what mathematical topics it is intended to illustrate. Decide whether the situations described are 'cons' or 'contexts'. If you think they are cons, explain why; then try to think of a more genuine context involving the same mathematical topic:

- Emily writes down a set of five numbers: 10, 11, 16, 18 and 20. Work out the mean of Emily's numbers.
- On a Tuesday, a café serves 80 sandwiches and 20 salads. Find the experimental probability that the next person to order will ask for a salad.
- A ladder, with its base 3m from the bottom of a wall, reaches 8m up the wall. How long is the ladder?

Sometimes you will need to simplify the mathematics used in order to introduce a context into a lesson. For example, signal triangulation is often used by teachers to illustrate the idea of loci. A signal with a time-stamp is sent out from a mobile phone. This is received at three different locations on the ground and gives rise to three circles, centred at the receivers, with radii determined by the respective time lapses.

This is a motivating and interesting context – however, it has been simplified. Most GPS positioning uses satellites above the Earth and so the loci involved are actually spheres. This leads to a slightly more complicated intersection model, one which requires a minimum of four satellites. Of course, explaining this to the pupils in a plenary and asking them why four satellites are required is a valuable exercise in itself, but you must be careful to handle situations like this without devaluing classroom mathematics.

Relevance and identification

So far, we have discussed how contexts should involve genuine situations and also use a genuine level of mathematics. However, the most effective contexts are also personally genuine. In a summary of research into motivation, Middleton and Spanias (1999) came to the same conclusion: that while context is really important, it is not enough in itself – both utility and importance are extrinsic motivators. The presentation of mathematics in context must also be structured to provide intrinsic motivations, demonstrating to pupils that the mathematics they are learning is *useful to them*.

This can be the most difficult of the challenges listed so far, and you must be careful not to stereotype your learners. One of us has an old book on the shelf called *Arithmetic for Women's Trades*, with five chapters on: needle trades, photography, cookery, laundry and simple book-keeping! This kind of stereotyping is frowned upon today, but you must be careful not to seek out contexts that fit a narrow perception of what you think your pupils are interested in. Perhaps you could involve them in devising contexts; for example, you might ask them to come into the next lesson with three different situations in which they have seen decimals (see also Shiu, 1988).

Task 11.6 **Getting the wider picture**

We have been discussing the use and abuse of contexts in mathematics lessons, but contexts are used across many other subject areas to motivate and enhance learning.

Identify three or four other curriculum areas in which contexts are used. It will be helpful at this point to speak to teachers in these curriculum areas to discuss with them the following questions.

▨ How do teachers in other subjects ensure that the contexts they use involve genuine situations and require a realistic level of subject knowledge?
▨ How do teachers in other subjects ensure that the contexts they use are identifiable to pupils?

Afterwards, reflect on what was discussed and try to identify any aspects of good practice that you can learn from other curriculum areas and apply in mathematics lessons.

We are not suggesting that *every* context has to be directly linked to the learners' own previous experience; after all, part of the remit of education is to broaden a pupils' range of experiences. However, it is important to ensure that your overall choice of problems develops both intrinsic and extrinsic motivation. Some contexts are interesting just because the mathematics is fun, and successful problem-solving is motivating in itself. For example, consider the problem, 'If you have 36 panels of fence, each 2m long, what is the largest area of pasture you can enclose for sheep?'. It is unlikely that many of the class will own sheep and exactly 36 fence panels, but the accessibility, extendibility and opportunity to play with mathematical techniques such as trigonometry can be rewarding. Although the mathematical context is somewhat forced, the mathematical process of investigation is real and meaningful and can be visualised. There is also the opportunity for linking the result with other instances of extrema in nature; for instance, a soap bubble is a sphere because this shape minimises surface area for a given volume. Nevertheless, we would definitely advise against only ever teaching mathematics through the medium of sheep and fencing!

PROBLEMS WITH USING CONTEXTS IN TEACHING

The challenges above are already very demanding on a teacher. You will not have time during your school placement to ensure that every context is fully genuine and immediately identifiable to the pupils you are teaching. However, this does not negate the need to help pupils become comfortable with utilising their mathematical skills in a variety of contexts. Research suggests that pupils in England have significant difficulty when moving from abstract formal procedures to context-based problems (see, for example, Anghileri *et al.*, 2002). This is a gap that needs to be addressed if we want pupils to achieve true mastery of the syllabus.

Nevertheless, there are a number of additional cognitive problems associated with using contexts in teaching. One of the most important is teaching children to discern the level of realism that a question asks for. One frequently discussed example is that of the 'lift problem'. Suppose a lift can carry up to 16 people. If 292 people need to go up in the lift, how many times must the lift go up?

At first glance, this appears to be a simple division problem, using the fact that $292 \div 16 = 18.25$. To finish, a pupil must interpret the result in the context of the 'real world' and round the answer up to 19 trips. However, the pupil must ignore the real world when formulating her or his method: we are asked to believe that the people arrive at the building in such a way that the lift is always full; that no-one tires of waiting for 19 trips and takes the stairs; that everyone knows of the '16 person' rule and obeys it, even if they are in a rush...the amount of reality is finely tuned by the examiner, and this has led writers such as Cooper and Dunne (2000) and Gerofsky (2003) to describe the art of answering such questions as a game. What is even more concerning is the fact that Cooper and Dunne go on to suggest that pupils from 'working-class' backgrounds are more likely to fail at this game, drawing inappropriately on their actual experiences when answering a question.

Sometimes the authentic nature of a context can encourage pupils to answer a question *too* authentically, perhaps replacing proportional reasoning with a more simplistic division or estimating wildly to reach an answer that they would be personally satisfied with outside of the classroom. This reflects a certain tension that is often present in lessons between practising and applying, or between emulating the outside world in the classroom and designing an activity that is easily assessed. Managing this tension appropriately for each different class is an important part of teaching mathematics.

Resourcing and managing good contexts

It is beyond the scope of this chapter to furnish you with a large number of high-quality contexts. Equally, it would be inappropriate to end this part of the discussion without some illustrations of what we mean by a good context. One way of resourcing authentic and motivating contexts is to look through academic or professional journals that discuss the teaching of mathematics. It is from one of these journals that we have adapted the following example.

Smith and Thatcher (1991) outline the basics of the mathematics of skid-mark analysis, as used by accident investigators. By plotting the braking distances in the highway code (or using the equations of motion under uniform acceleration), we can arrive at the relationship $k = u^2/s$, where s is the distance travelled by the car in the skid, u is the speed of the car and k is a constant dependant on environmental factors, such as the gradient of the road and the nature of the road surface. To ascertain what speed a driver was travelling at, an investigator will lay down a 'test skid' on the relevant strip of road to help him calculate k. He then measures the skid of the vehicle involved in the accident and uses these values to calculate the speed of the car.

Like many genuine contexts, this scenario offers a lot to the teacher and can be used as either a short example or a longer task. Although it could be utilised as a straightforward 'plug in the numbers' illustration of using a formula, it could easily be extended to help develop some of the habits of mind discussed above. The importance of the parameter k gives rise to the ideas of proportionality and connected variables; furthermore, the whole scenario could lead to a discussion about modelling and its limitations. How convinced are we of our final result? What percentage error would we need to build in to our model to convince a jury to prosecute a speeding driver? What difference might the age or condition of the car make? The level and the depth to which you would discuss these issues would depend on the individual class and we present some ways in which you could manage this discussion in the next section.

Other examples of good contexts we have recently come across include a use of a first-order differential equation to model dieting (Toumasis, 2004), a discussion of the maths and physics present in Formula One racing (Hudson, 2009) and a use of geometric series and recurrence relations to model drug levels in the body (Elgin, 2008). However, these are merely three amongst hundreds and we encourage you to start your career by gathering contexts from peers and colleagues in the schools you visit, and consider joining a subject association to facilitate further sharing (see Chapter 14 for more details). We also recommend that you visit the Bowland Maths website (bowland-maths.org.uk) and review the material for learning mathematics in context there.

TEACHING MATHEMATICS IN CONTEXT

In this section we will discuss the pedagogy that allows pupils to learn 'mathematics in context'. We will look at an approach to teaching that uses the open-ended nature of exploration in order to motivate and engage pupils, thereby allowing them to develop their mathematics in a realistic way. The choice of task will be vital.

We have discussed the need for tasks to allow the pupils to get involved in the mathematics of a situation, exercise real choice about how to proceed and have an outcome that is tangible. Effective tasks of this kind do not have to be investigations that last several lessons, but they should require pupils, for at least part of each lesson, to act and think in ways that mathematicians do – to inquire, ask questions and solve problems. Such tasks can help pupils to make sense of why they are learning mathematical methods and to understand how the mathematical ideas that they learn are related to one another and to real contexts. The mathematics that pupils engage in should require them to think mathematically and to represent that thinking in various ways, making links between different areas of mathematics. Therefore it is a good idea if, over time, pupils engage with tasks that require them to:

- have imaginative ideas;
- ask questions;
- make choices;
- make mistakes and use these errors to learn new things;
- be organised and systematic;
- substitute and transform, look for patterns, represent and model, do and undo, reason and justify, look for invariance and change;
- make links and connections;
- describe, explain and discuss their work;
- keep going when it is difficult;
- present a solution or an outcome.

Some teachers motivate their pupils by explaining that, when they work in these ways, they are learning to be a mathematician. While many people treat mathematics as though it were an unarguable truth, a set of facts that came into being without human agency, it is important to recognise that mathematics can, with validity, be considered, in part, as a socially negotiated set of practices. This means that when pupils reason and justify, substitute and transform, or engage in other mathematical processes, they are developing more mathematics and are therefore acting as mathematicians. Encouraging pupils to see themselves as part of the community of mathematicians – a community made up of those who use, develop and control mathematics – will allow them to feel part of something bigger and to see that they can take ownership of mathematics.

As we have seen, selecting a task is important and requires a great deal of thought. However, once the task has been found, the pupils must work in ways that require them to think as mathematicians and support their own thinking in these ways. Classrooms where this approach is used are often organised so that the pupils sit and work in groups, but this is not the only way. It is also true to say that having the tables arranged so that the pupils sit in groups does not automatically mean that the pupils will work 'collaboratively'.

Although mathematics is often viewed as an individual endeavour, this is usually not the case for 'real mathematicians'. Leone Burton (1999) interviewed over 70 research mathematicians and found that they usually preferred to work collaboratively. They stated that working collaboratively allowed them to learn from each other's work, increase the overall quality of their ideas and share the 'euphoria' of a problem solved. Therefore classrooms where the pupils are experiencing real mathematics should expect pupils to collaborate. Collaboration, of course, does not preclude thinking individually from time to time or discussing and working in pairs. Pupils will need to learn to give one another time to think so that well-thought-out ideas are contributed to the group for criticism in order to improve the overall quality of the final outcome.

What it means to work collaboratively

Truly collaborative discussion is rare in mathematics classrooms (Ofsted, 2008), but it is essential if the pupils are going to work together to solve mathematical problems in a realistic way. Both Alexander (2006) and Mercer (1995, 2000) have written extensively about collaborative discussion. Putting their ideas together, discussion that promotes learning is:

■ *collective* – tasks are addressed together, neither in isolation, nor competitively: the object is for all to learn from the discussion;

■ *reciprocal* – the participants listen to one another, share ideas and deliberately examine alternative viewpoints;

■ *cumulative* – participants build on their own and each other's ideas and chain them into coherent lines of thinking and enquiry;

■ *supportive* – participants articulate their ideas freely without fear of embarrassment over 'wrong' answers, and they challenge and help one another in order to reach a common understanding;

■ *exploratory* – participants explore and elaborate each other's reasoning; challenges are offered and justified;

■ *purposeful* – there is a clear reason for the talk and an agreement between the participants has to be reached.

In classrooms, you may find that some pupils dominate discussions and others find it hard to get a word in. Your pupils may need to be taught how to take part in discussions that promote everyone's learning. In order to promote effective discussions, many teachers have found it useful to set out ground rules for discussions. Ground rules explain exactly what is expected of each person and give guidance about how to talk together profitably.

Task 11.7 **Standing on firm ground**

Prepare a list of 'ground rules for discussion'; you could aim for about six rules. You may find this task easier to complete in discussion with a friend or colleague. Reflect on why this may be.

Asking questions – who asks the questions?

You will probably have noted already that teachers ask a great number of questions during their working day. When the pupils are working collaboratively, the way that questions are used will need thought. As a teacher, you will want to know what the pupils are doing and if they need any particular help or ideas. However, if the pupils are working together and are developing some mathematical ideas, then disturbing their train of thought may be counter-productive. Therefore teachers must ask the right question at the right time. Reflect on these two questions about your own learning:

■ When you are working hard on a piece of complicated mathematics, how do you respond to someone asking how you are getting on?

■ When you are 'stuck', do you want to know the answer or would you prefer to be asked a question that prompts your thinking? And if you do just want to know the answer, which option will help you learn most?

It is sometimes a good idea to ask the groups to work together for about ten minutes trying to understand the problem that has been set and deciding if they have any questions. Make sure that you neither ask nor answer questions during this time. The intention is for pupils to be working together and seeking ideas, not asking you for ideas. If they ask a question, just say, 'that's a good question, write that down'. Use the time to listen to what the pupils are saying and think about any information or interventions that they might need. After ten minutes, hold a mini-plenary and ask the pupils for the questions that they have come up with. Some of these may be organisational and straightforward to answer; others you may want to answer because you think the pupils will need that input, but there will be others still that you suggest they use to guide their own work and enquiry. Suggesting that the pupils come up with questions is part of the 'mathematics in context' way of working. Real mathematicians ask questions and seek answers.

When asking the pupils to work collaboratively, teachers should not encourage the pupils to ask them questions during the discussion phase. Pupils need to be helped to know that they can find answers and, using thought, reflection and discussion with peers, come up with good ways forward to finding a solution. If the teacher answers every question, the pupils rely on the teacher to tell them 'the right way' and their own ideas lose value. Allow and encourage the pupils to pool and explore their ideas by actively encouraging them to find answers for their own questions.

At some stage during the lesson or sequence of lessons, you may decide that you need to ask questions to reassure yourself that the pupils are making progress with their learning. It is a good idea to plan these questions carefully so that they elicit the information that you want. It is also a good idea to give pupils time to think of an answer. If you have demanded that the pupils work in groups to seek their own solutions, you should have time to observe the class actively, listening in on conversations and seeing what the pupils are doing. You can use these observations to frame your questions. Each time you think of a question, write it on the board; then, a few minutes before you want to hold a plenary, you can ask the pupils to look at the questions and be ready with an answer. The plenary could then consist of pupils offering their considered answers, which will give both the teacher and the pupils themselves a great deal of information about how their learning is proceeding.

However, some pupils are used to the idea that, at the first sign of things getting difficult, they are to put up their hand to ask, sometimes just to reassure themselves. In this case you may decide to ban 'hands up' completely, so that they have to think hard before asking for the teacher's or someone else's help. Traffic-light cards can be useful here. Tell the groups that a green card means everything is going well and they do not need any assistance from the teacher, amber means that they have a question they would like to ask but it will wait, and red means they have question and it is urgent. The teacher then looks at the cards and decides where her or his time is best spent. The teacher decides who to go to; he or she is not summoned by the pupils.

Keeping going when it is difficult – perseverance

Teaching pupils to persevere and keep going when things are difficult can be really hard. If pupils are used to being told what to do at every step and asking for help when they feel things are a little difficult, then they will find realistic work very difficult. It can be useful to stage the length of time that pupils are left to their own devices, holding frequent plenaries where progress is discussed as a class and ideas and reassurance are shared. As the pupils get more familiar with this way of working, and begin to develop their own systems and strategies for dealing with problems, then the length of time they are asked to keep going can be extended. Pupils can be trained to persevere, but expecting them to do so straight away without any help can be a recipe for disaster.

Another helpful approach is to discuss as a class what to do when you get 'stuck'. Part of this discussion should emphasise that being 'stuck' is an honourable state to be in (Mason *et al.*, 1982: 49). It indicates that you have moved beyond your comfort zone and are challenging yourself. However, thinking 'I'm stuck so I will stop' is not honourable. Different approaches work for different people: for example, try to explain to yourself why you are stuck and then to a friend, look up the mathematics that you are stuck over in a book, look at some examples and try to apply them to what you want, draw a diagram, and so on. Ensuring that the class has lots of ideas to try before asking the teacher will help them become more self-reliant; it will also free the teacher to deal with the kinds of problems that really need 'professional' help.

Justifying reasoning – how do you learn to do it?

> One of the most important parts of being mathematical is an action called reasoning. This involves explaining why something makes sense and how the different parts of a mathematical solution lead on from one another.
>
> (Boaler, 2009: 43)

Justifying reasoning means finding a convincing argument to explain why the patterns you find must hold for all cases of a problem. Consequently, generalising and justifying 'mutually influence one another' (Ellis, 2007: 225). In fact, justifying and generalising seem to be a two-way process. Learning mathematics in an environment where pupils are required to provide justifications for their reasoning that make sense to other pupils, and can be explained, will promote conjectures about generalisations as a matter of course. When pupils are asked to justify their reasoning, they will make conjectures and question the usefulness of those conjectures, thereby establishing a generalisation. It therefore makes sense that pupils' ability to justify has been linked with the ability to reason algebraically (Reid, 2002).

But how do you learn to justify reasoning? Many pupils find justifying and generalising very difficult. Pupils can find it difficult both to recognise a general statement and to create one (see Knuth and Elliott, 1998); therefore, they will first need to learn to recognise general statements and to begin to create their own. Modelling the process for them will be important as well. For example, consider using the 'jugs problem':

> Can you measure out 4 litres of water using a 3-litre and a 5-litre jug?
> What other volumes can you measure out?
> Can you get all whole-number litre values?
> What if the jugs were 3 litres and 6 litres? What if they were x litres and y litres?

It would probably be a good idea to let the pupils 'tinker' with the problem first and then collect ideas. Pupils can usually recognise which ideas and statements are more 'mathematical' in nature and, therefore, the discussion can model ways of generalising and justifying, thereby helping pupils to recognise what they are aiming for. Sometimes, the pupils can make no headway at all with such tasks and then, as a teacher, you might supply a few statements, some of which are good justifications and some of which contain flaws. Discovering the flaws will provoke a lively discussion in most classes, as well as providing good models for how the pupils can justify their own ideas.

Requiring the pupils to explain their reasoning publicly is another way to help them learn to be able to justify their reasoning. Mercer (2000) suggests that an important aspect of working collaboratively is to insist that all members of a group have to agree on the outcome. In coming to an agreement on a solution to a realistic mathematical task, all pupils will have to explain and justify their ideas within a group. Knowing that the outcomes from their group discussions will need to be explained to the rest of the class will further focus the pupils' minds on explaining carefully and clearly, thereby moving towards generalisation. The audience for the presentations of these ideas should be asked to question any lack of clarity and try to 'pick holes' in any argument. Pupils will often try to be kind to one another and say 'well, you tried'. Becoming successful at learning mathematics requires clarity of expression and valid arguments. Therefore it will be important to stress to the class that they are helping one another to become better at mathematics by questioning and finding flaws. You could also point out that the audience will become better mathematicians if they reflect on and question others' justifications and consider how convincing they are.

Motivation for working in this way

Working realistically with mathematics is motivating. Pupils begin to see how mathematics is present in the real world, they 'get their eye in' and can see the 'chameleon' hiding against the background. Therefore they begin to know that it is important to be able to use and control mathematical ideas.

Mathematics in the real world is 'fuzzy' and is never posed in the careful way of a standard textbook problem. It is hard to see what particular mathematical skill will be needed to untangle the problem at hand and sometimes even the most mathematically literate people need to find a textbook to help them remember a topic or procedure they think they will need to work out an answer to a problem. One answer may well be better (simpler, quicker, more intuitive, more economical of resources, …) than another when using mathematics in the real world, but it is unlikely to be the only correct one. Therefore helping pupils to learn ways of thinking that will enable them to select from a range of mathematical skills, and find out if that works, is more realistic and more empowering than a narrow, disconnected way of learning mathematics.

Feeling empowered is a motivating force. Pupils who successfully come up with a solution, which they have researched, tried out, struggled with and explained to others, begin to know that they can use, apply and control mathematics. Mathematics is no longer a mystifying set of unconnected facts that they have to remember, but rather a set of tools that can be looked up and used to unlock important ideas and work towards a different reality. The pupils themselves will be empowered to mystify people with figures or to use quantitative data to provide evidence of mishandling of funds or resources. They have powerful tools at their fingertips and they can use them. Who would not be motivated?

SUMMARY AND KEY POINTS

Hopefully, this chapter has convinced you of some of the many benefits that contextualised mathematics offers the learner, both in terms of motivation and in developing a secure level of mathematical know-how that will serve them outside school. However, it has also reflected on many of the benefits that teaching mathematics in context offers to the teacher. It is often one of the greatest opportunities you will have to 'sell' your subject to the pupils and even to remind yourself of why you value mathematics so highly. Although integrating contexts can be a demanding or even a daunting process, the long-term benefits are considerable.

Some of those benefits will come from learning to think mathematically and developing mathematical habits of mind (Cuoco *et al.*, 1996). Mathematicians may seem to be mysterious figures to the average pupil, who may have no idea what a mathematician does. Learning about the kind of work that mathematicians engage in will be important for pupils, but so will them learning to act as mathematicians. Learning to work collaboratively, to explore, make choices, solve problems, recognise that mistakes are valuable in learning and, above all, to keep going when things seem difficult are all valuable life skills; they also give pupils partial ownership over mathematics. Pupils who know they can develop, use and control mathematical ideas are more likely to want to continue to learn more mathematics. In addition to this, the current educational climate in England appears to be stressing the value of cross-curricular learning more and more. You may have encountered this already in your placement schools in the form of special days or initiatives, or qualifications such as 'functional mathematics' or the 14–19 diplomas, which are discussed elsewhere in this book. In each of these cases, the discussions above, about choosing high-quality contexts and organising the classroom to promote authentic learning, are important to bear in mind in your planning and teaching.

Now all that remains is for you to go out and do it. Whether you plan to contextualise a lesson on sequences by looking at mathematical epidemiology or by encouraging pupils to investigate social networking websites through a combination of algebraic and graphical techniques, you have a genuine opportunity to make mathematics relevant, enthuse your pupils and change the question 'Why do we have to do this?' to 'What can we do with this next?'

FURTHER READING

Lee, C. (2006) *Language for Learning Mathematics: Assessment for Learning in Practice.* **Maidenhead: Open University Press.**

> This book contains ideas for increasing the amount of talk that the pupils engage in while learning mathematics and gives reasons why this will increase learning.

Mason, J., Burton, L. and Stacey, K. (1982) *Thinking Mathematically.* **New York: Addison-Wesley.**

> Although this book was published in 1982, it is still relevant today and a new edition is imminent at the time of writing. If pupils are to see the relevance of mathematics, first they must know how to think mathematically.

Mercer, N. (2000) *Words and Minds: How We Use Language to Think.* **Abingdon: Routledge.**

> This book will help you know why pupils need to be taught to work collaboratively and use mathematical language and expressions in order to use mathematics in a realistic context.

Ward-Penny, R. (2010) 'Con or context?', *Mathematics in School,* **39(1), 10–12.**

> How real can a real context really be? Make sure that your pupils do not think that mathematics is just a con.

GETTING THE WHOLE PICTURE

John Westwell and Clare Lee

INTRODUCTION

As a mathematics teacher, much of your attention will, of course, centre on teaching mathematics within mathematics lessons. However, it is also important that you consider your broader responsibilities as a teacher more generally. The new National Curriculum (QCA, 2007a) places a statutory responsibility upon schools in England to provide a broad and balanced curriculum that enables all young people to become:

- *successful learners* who enjoy learning, make progress and achieve;
- *confident individuals* who are able to live safe, healthy and fulfilling lives;
- *responsible citizens* who make a positive contribution to society.

It is clear from these requirements that your role as a teacher is much broader than solely assisting the mental development of pupils within the field of mathematics. In this chapter, we will consider what these responsibilities mean in terms of your contribution to the whole curriculum and how your actions in the mathematics classroom can contribute to an individual pupil's personal development as a successful learner, a confident individual and a responsible citizen.

As you start on your teaching career, you may consider that it is enough for you to concentrate on developing pupils' mathematical knowledge, skills and understanding. To take this view, though, is to miss opportunities that arise from taking whole-curriculum and whole-person perspectives. If you address the broader aspects of your role, then the personal qualities and attitudes that support pupils' learning of mathematics may be fostered, at the same time as benefiting their learning of mathematics.

OBJECTIVES

By the end of this chapter you should be able to:

- understand better your role as a mathematics teacher in contributing to the whole curriculum;

- appreciate both the opportunities and difficulties presented by developing cross-curricular ways of working;
- be more aware of your responsibility to contribute to the personal development of your pupils;
- plan more effectively for teaching that addresses the development of pupils as confident individuals and responsible citizens.

THE WHOLE CURRICULUM

Although the secondary school curriculum has traditionally been organised into subjects, with their own slots on the timetable, there has long been recognition that the curriculum is much more than a series of discrete learning experiences. Consequently, there have been attempts over the years to emphasise the *whole* curriculum. For example, when the England and Wales National Curriculum was first introduced, the National Curriculum Council (NCC, 1990) published guidance in a series of papers linked to this issue. The revised National Curriculum (QCA, 2007a) states that cross-curriculum dimensions:

> provide important unifying areas of learning that help young people make sense of the world and give education relevance and authenticity. Dimensions can add a richness and relevance to the curriculum experience of young people. They can provide a focus for work within and between subjects and across the curriculum as a whole, including the routines, events and ethos of the school. ('What are dimensions?' section)

The seven cross-curriculum dimensions defined in the National Curriculum in England are:

- identity and cultural diversity;
- healthy lifestyles;
- community participation;
- enterprise;
- global dimension and sustainable development;
- technology and the media;
- creativity and critical thinking.

Some of these dimensions will, at first glance, seem to be of more relevance to you than others as you teach mathematics, but they all have a clear part to play in educating pupils. It is therefore important that in planning what and how you teach, you remain aware of the requirement to ensure that these dimensions pervade your lessons. It is also true to say that in incorporating these dimensions in your planning, you can make the mathematics that you teach more engaging and interesting. This will, in turn, ensure that pupils' whole-curriculum experience has a positive effect on their attitudes towards mathematics and therefore lead to more successful learners.

Attitudes towards mathematics

One of your aims as a mathematics teacher is likely to be that your pupils develop positive attitudes towards mathematics. Not only can this support more effective and successful learning, but it is also a valid objective in its own right. There have been various official descriptions of attitudes to be fostered and encouraged, including:

- fascination with the subject;
- interest and motivation;
- pleasure and enjoyment from mathematical activities;
- appreciation of the power, purpose and relevance of mathematics;
- satisfaction derived from a sense of achievement;
- confidence in an ability to do mathematics at an appropriate level.

(DES, 1985: 25)

When thinking about attitudes to mathematics, it is also important to think about developing mathematical habits of mind (see Chapter 11), in order to help pupils to see themselves as successful learners of mathematics. A recent Ofsted report on mathematics teaching considered that 'good' teaching was demonstrated when:

- pupils exude enjoyment and involvement in the lesson;
- teachers ensure all pupils participate actively in whole-class activity, such as through using mini-whiteboards in ways which involve all, or partner discussions;
- respect is conveyed for pupils' contributions so that many offer right and wrong comments;
- pupils naturally listen to and respond to each other's comments showing engagement with them.

(Ofsted, 2008: 6)

Ofsted is therefore looking for pupils with good attitudes towards mathematics who enjoy their lessons, participate actively, and respect, listen and respond to one another. These are challenging objectives, all the more so when you consider that every experience that pupils have of learning or using mathematics will, to some degree, shape their attitudes.

> During every mathematics lesson a child is not only learning, or failing to learn, mathematics as a result of the work he [or she] is doing but is also developing his [or her] attitude towards mathematics. In every mathematics lesson his [or her] teacher is conveying, even if unconsciously, a message about mathematics that will influence his [or her] attitude. Once attitudes have been formed, they can be very persistent and difficult to change. Positive attitudes assist the learning of mathematics; negative attitudes not only inhibit learning but [...] very often persist into adult life and affect choice of job.
>
> (DES, 1982: para. 345)

It is essential, therefore, that you pay attention to your pupils' mathematical experience, not only in mathematics lessons but right across the curriculum. Pupils who have a positive attitude will be more prepared to use their mathematics across the curriculum. Involving yourself in the way that mathematics is used across the curriculum will help to ensure that the good attitudes developed in your classroom are not undone by the teaching pupils receive in other subject areas.

Links with other subjects

A good way to start developing a whole-curriculum perspective is to think about the links that mathematics has with other subjects. Establishing a professional dialogue with a colleague who teaches another subject will help develop a mutual understanding of the links that exist between your respective subjects. As a result, your colleague will learn more about the mathematics curriculum, how it is taught and the difficulties that pupils may have with it. You, in turn, will learn more about how and when mathematics is used in the other subject, when it might be helpful to introduce your pupils to particular topics and uncover genuine contexts for mathematics that you could use in your own teaching. It is, of course, also important to establish how mathematics lessons can contribute to the learning of your colleague's subjects as well.

Having developed this greater understanding of the links between the subjects, which is in itself a worthwhile objective, it is possible to go further and plan some lessons collaboratively. This could lead to:

◼ some lessons in the other subject that build on the links with mathematics;
◼ some lessons in mathematics that build on the links with the other subject;
◼ some coordinated lessons in both subjects that have a related focus.

The benefit for pupils of such collaboration is that they have greater opportunity to practise using their knowledge, skills and understanding, and to develop greater appreciation of the 'power, purpose and relevance of mathematics'.

Task 12.1 **Measure audit**

The purpose of this task is to investigate pupils' experience of measuring across the curriculum and to produce a report making recommendations to the mathematics department. Investigate the following questions by talking to as many different subject teachers as is feasible:

◼ What sort of measures do pupils use within the subject, e.g. time, capacity, weight etc.?
◼ What units are normally used for the different measures?
◼ How much practical measuring do pupils do?
◼ What measuring instruments do they use?
◼ Are they required to estimate measurements at all?
◼ At what stages do the pupils first use the different measures?

Also, find out how the mathematics department currently addresses the 'measures' strand through their schemes of work. Write a summary of the results of your investigations. Also make written recommendations to the department regarding:

◼ the stage at which certain measures should be addressed;
◼ the balance of time spent on different sorts of measures;
◼ which conversions between measures may be important and how they can be taught in a way connected to the uses that will be made of them in other subjects;
◼ the kind of practical measuring experiences pupils have in other subjects and how they can be built upon in mathematics lessons.

Despite the obvious benefits in establishing good links with other subjects, this kind of connected teaching has rarely been developed to any great extent in schools. It is clear that there are some significant barriers to overcome. The most serious hindrance to progress is 'lack of time'. Most mathematics teachers recognise the potential for cross-curricular links but find it difficult to organise enough time for establishing them effectively with their colleagues. Cross-curricular work rarely takes top priority, mainly because of the strong subject area culture that exists in many secondary schools. School leaders are increasingly encouraged to challenge this culture and actively support coordinated planning so that pupils start to experience the kind of learning that is set out by the National Curriculum. Schools will be developing working policies in this area and you could seek to be an active participant in making such policies effective and putting them into practice.

Mathematics across the curriculum

There is a clear intention from government bodies that mathematical knowledge, understanding and skills should be both used and learned across the whole curriculum. The National Curriculum requires that pupils be offered cross-curricular opportunities as an integral part of their learning in Key Stage 3. These opportunities should be designed to enhance pupils' engagement with the concepts, processes and content of the mathematics curriculum. The QCA (2007a) says that the mathematics curriculum should be recognised as extending to other subjects and to contexts beyond the school.

The curriculum should provide opportunities for pupils to work on problems that arise in other subjects and in contexts beyond the school:

> *Other subjects:* For example, representing and analysing data in geography, using formulas and relationships in science, understanding number structure and currency exchange in modern foreign languages, measuring and making accurate constructions in design and technology, and managing money in economic wellbeing and financial capability.
> *Contexts beyond the school:* For example, conducting a survey into consumer habits, planning a holiday budget, designing a product, and measuring for home improvements. Mathematical skills contribute to financial capability and to other aspects of preparation for adult life. (p. 147)

This focus is not new. In 2001, schools were advised to focus on numeracy across the curriculum using training materials that were published by the KS3 National Strategy. Advice in the mathematics framework document stated:

> Mathematics contributes to and draws from many subjects and aspects of the curriculum. You can help pupils to appreciate the importance of mathematics in their lives by making these links explicit. [...] Mathematical skills can be consolidated and enhanced when pupils have opportunities to apply them across the curriculum.

> (DfEE, 2001a: 23)

Although these materials did not receive the same attention in many schools as the *Literacy across the Curriculum* materials published earlier, they did highlight the necessity for learning mathematics to be seen as a whole-school issue. However, as mathematics is regarded as a particularly difficult subject by many people, some of your non-mathematical colleagues may need a great deal of support before they develop sufficient confidence to see themselves as teachers of mathematics. Where the senior leadership team recognise the need to view teaching mathematics as a whole-school activity, it is much more likely that pupils will be able to recognise and experience mathematics across the curriculum.

Task 12.2 **Examining cross-curricular mathematics**

Given the greater attention currently being placed on cross-curricular working, your school may have been making progress in this area. In this task, you are to explore what your school is doing to address this whole curriculum issue. In particular, investigate:

▪ whether there is a written policy, what it contains and how it was produced;
▪ what sort of whole-school training on cross-curricular work in general has happened recently;
▪ whether a working group exists within the school to continue developing the policy;
▪ what contribution the mathematics department has made to work in this area.

If the school has not been doing anything to address the issue specifically, investigate:

▪ whether there are plans to do anything;
▪ what barriers there have been to developing policy and actions;
▪ what role the mathematics department expects to play in any developments.

Record in your reflective journal key lessons that emerge from your investigation.

The 14–19 diplomas are starting to be widely used in schools and their specifications emphasise that, whatever you are studying, there is likely to be a mathematical element to it. Students taking any diploma also have to study 'functional mathematics'. The QCA functional skills standards are available to all learners from Key Stage 3 upwards (see Chapter 13). The standards state that learners should build, develop and consolidate skills that can be applied and transferred to a range of contexts, both within and beyond the mathematics classroom. The focus is on securing skills that can be used in learning, work and everyday life. Teachers will need to focus on applying mathematical learning by creating problem-solving opportunities, using tasks that require pupils to think for themselves, and selecting which functional mathematical skills are required in a particular context.

Schools will need to decide if their pupils will build and develop their functional mathematical skills in mathematics lessons alone or across the curriculum. The aim of the specification is that pupils will have opportunities to apply functional skills to a range of purposeful contexts, which are perhaps more usefully provided in a cross-curricular way of working. However, teaching mathematics across the curriculum means that schools will need to make decisions about who will decide when a pupil has mastered the appropriate level of functional mathematics and is ready to be entered for summative assessment.

For the majority of pupils, the teaching and development of functional mathematics will become an integral part of the mathematics curriculum at Key Stages 3 and 4. Within mathematics lessons, pupils will need opportunities to apply their skills to a range of topics relevant to life and work. However, pupils will need to understand where there are opportunities for them to transfer the skills they have developed by developing links to other aspects of the curriculum. Functional skills will be assessed as part of the revised GCSE mathematics specification from 2010 for first award in 2012; however, there is likely to be a stand alone qualification for students studying diplomas beyond statutory school age.

Learning across the curriculum

In the previous subsection, you have seen that developing links with other subjects has implications for your mathematics teaching. However, as well as thinking about subject links, you also need to be aware of the Personal, Learning and Thinking Skills (PLTS), which are also part of the National Curriculum. There are six groups of PLTS:

- independent enquirers;
- creative thinkers;
- reflective learners;
- team workers;
- self-managers;
- effective participants.

The PLTS also have to sit alongside the *cross-curriculum dimensions*, which include: *identity and cultural diversity, healthy lifestyles, community participation, enterprise, global dimension and sustainable development, technology and the media* and *creativity and critical thinking*. All teachers have a shared responsibility for developing pupils' skills in these areas. Just as there were difficulties in developing numeracy across the curriculum, establishing whole-school policies for other cross-curricular skills and dimensions also presents complex problems. Different schools can, consequently, be at quite different stages of development.

There are sources of advice for mathematics teachers, though. For example, the Nuffield website contains case studies of the ways that schools have sought to introduce the cross-curricular dimensions across their curriculum. Schools probably will have made most progress addressing literacy across the curriculum and you may find that specific approaches have been implemented by the mathematics department. In order to address the cross-curricular skills and dimensions within your teaching, you will need to take them into account when you plan your teaching. For example, you may need to consider for example:

- what discussion will take place in the lesson (teamworkers, creative thinking, effective participants and community participation);
- how the development of mathematics in different cultures can become part of mathematics lessons (independent enquirers, self-managers and identity and cultural diversity);
- what resources pupils may use (creative thinking and technology and media);
- what sorts of activities and questions you will use (creativity and critical thinking skills, reflective learners, teamworkers, community participation);

■ what pair/group work will be expected (teamworkers, self-managers, enterprise and community participation);

■ how pupils will be encouraged to reflect on the effectiveness of their learning (reflective learners and creative and critical thinking);

■ introducing a global dimension, for example, by using 'Water Availability' from bowlandmaths.org.uk (*global dimension and sustainable development*, healthy lifestyles, creative thinkers and teamworkers).

Some mathematics teachers have long recognised the value of addressing these personal learning and thinking skills (as well as cross-curricular dimensions) within their teaching. They have devised resources and tasks that have both enriched pupils' mathematical experience and developed their knowledge and understanding in the field being considered. Some of this work has been written up and can act as a stimulus for other teachers (see, for example, the NCETM website or bowlandsmaths.org). Organisations that have an interest in promoting the place of certain themes within the curriculum can also be good sources for ideas and resources. For example, the Worldwide Fund for Nature (WWF, 1990) has published a book on mathematics and environmental education. More recently, Amnesty International has published a resource book linking human rights with mathematics education (Wright, 1999). However, resources are not always available for some of the themes. For example, if the careers education and guidance theme is to be addressed successfully, then some research work may need to be undertaken.

While the curriculum continues to be framed by tight subject boundaries, there will always be areas of study that do not fit neatly into the domain of single subjects. For example, healthy lifestyles and enterprise should be part of every pupils' education, but there is no single subject where this can be adequately addressed. Perhaps the most significant change in this area has been with citizenship education. This is no longer just a desirable cross-curricular theme; it is a statutory part of the National Curriculum in England.

Task 12.3 **What use is mathematics?**

For many pupils, there seems to be little connection between the mathematics they study at school and their future working life. In this task you are asked to plan and teach a lesson or a series of lessons that draw upon the experience of someone who uses mathematics in their work. Preparation will need to begin some time in advance of the lesson.

Begin by establishing contact with someone who you consider uses mathematics in her or his work. This should not be as hard as many people might think; try not to go for bank managers or accountants; rather, choose such professions as engineers, plumbers, electricians and farmers, all of whom make extensive use of mathematics. Recently, I had the tracking on my car checked by laser equipment and the motor engineer measured angles in degrees and minutes and converted those measurements into rotations of an adjusting bolt. Discuss together how mathematics is used in the context of the person's job and consider together how this could be presented to pupils. Plan a lesson that involves:

■ a description of your contact's work;

■ opportunity for pupils to find out more about your contact's career;

> ■ explanation of the way that mathematics is used within the work;
> ■ a task that simulates the kind of mathematical work done in context by your contact.
>
> This sort of lesson is significantly enhanced by having your contact person play a full part, and companies are likely to have a positive reaction to a joint approach for a short release from work to attend the school, but there is still value in the approach if this proves not to be possible.
>
> After the lesson, evaluate it by finding out and reflecting on how both your contact and your pupils found the lesson and considering what would improve similar lessons in the future.

Finally, the case for the mathematics teacher taking whole-curriculum issues seriously is put strongly by the mathematics educator Brian Hudson:

> I would argue for a whole-school approach to environmental education and regard my role as a teacher as involving the education of the whole child. In adopting such an approach, I would expect that I would be more likely to achieve my objectives as a mathematics teacher given the greater level of interest, motivation and understanding on the part of the pupils. At the same time, I would be contributing to their personal development and helping prepare them for their future role as citizens in an increasingly complex and interdependent world. (1994: 124)

THE WHOLE PERSON

As pupils move from primary to secondary school, they experience a major shift in the way their learning is organised. From having had essentially just one teacher, who was responsible for their all-round education, they now have many teachers for many different subjects: the unit of structural organisation becomes the subject as much as the class. Schools try to support pupils through this transition by assigning them a tutor, who is intended to offer the pupils the pastoral care that they need. However, pupils spend the large majority of their time with distinct subject teachers. What is their role in seeing the pupil develop as a whole person? This section examines this question from the point of view of the mathematics teacher.

Personal development

There is general acceptance that schools must address the personal development of their pupils. This is shown by schools acknowledging the importance of establishing a supportive ethos and by the provision of Personal, Health and Social Education (PHSE or variations) courses. Since the 1988 Education Reform Act, schools and curriculum bodies have given much more attention to how all teachers can contribute to the personal development of their pupils. Although the 1944 Education Act had also referred to these aspects of education, schools had not been held to account for their general curricular provision in this area. This changed significantly with the 1992 Education (Schools) Act, which saw the birth of Ofsted and required registered inspectors to report on the development of pupils within the schools they inspected. Beyond these curricular and inspection requirements, the Core Standards for Qualified Teacher Status (QTS) in England require all teachers to:

> understand how children and young people develop and how the progress, rate of development and well-being of learners are affected by a range of developmental, social, religious, ethnic, cultural and linguistic influences.

(C18, TDA, 2007)

Personal development is the means by which all young people are supported in their spiritual, moral, physical, emotional, cultural and intellectual development according to their needs and regardless of their social and/or economic backgrounds. Personal development promotes pupils' well-being and enables them to develop as healthy, enterprising and responsible citizens in society. Although personal development can be thought to be the responsibility of the PHSE tutor or the form tutor, in secondary schools it has to be everyone's responsibility.

Mathematics offers a unique contribution to personal development because of its focus on systematic and logical thinking, reasoning, problem-solving, persistence, and so on. It can contribute to the personal development of pupils as much as, if not more than, every other curriculum area. There has been a long tradition within mathematics education that recognises the contribution that mathematics can make in developing pupils' personal qualities. HMI (DES, 1985) made explicit the qualities it believed should be encouraged through mathematics education, including: being imaginative, creative, flexible, systematic, independent in thought and action, cooperative and persistent (p. 24). Plainly, though, these qualities do not develop as a matter of course: 'To achieve success in each aspect it is essential that the classroom approaches are designed so as to foster its development' (p. 25). Personal development now means planning lessons that enable each pupil to develop in the five areas of the *Every Child Matters* (*ECM*) outcomes. This means that pupils must be helped to develop their mathematical abilities in order to:

- Enjoy and achieve – for example, enjoyment can stem from the creative and investigative aspects of mathematics, from developing mathematical ways of perceiving the world and recognising underlying structures and connections between mathematical ideas.
- Be healthy – for example, mathematics enables pupils to understand the numerical data related to becoming and staying healthy. Monitoring nutritional intake, blood sugar levels and cardiovascular health are all examples where mathematics assists understanding and can lead to making healthy decisions.
- Achieve economic well-being – for example, an understanding of mathematics, and confidence in using a variety of mathematical skills, are both key to young people's ability to play their part in modern society. The skills of reasoning with numbers, interpreting graphs and diagrams, and communicating mathematical information are vital in enabling individuals to make sound economic decisions in their daily lives.
- Make a positive contribution – for example, having confidence and capability in mathematics allows pupils to develop their ability to contribute to arguments using logic, data and generalisations with increasing precision. This, in turn, allows pupils to take a greater part in a democratic society.

When evaluating the effectiveness of lessons, you should consider the impact of your teaching approaches on the development of the pupils' personal qualities alongside the mathematical learning.

Task 12.4 **Observing qualities and attitudes**

For this task, observe a mathematics lesson and consider the impact on the pupils' attitudes towards mathematics and the development of their personal qualities. Prepare an observation sheet that lists positive attitudes towards mathematics (see earlier section) and the personal qualities described in this section. During the lesson record examples of:

■ pupils displaying positive attitudes;
■ pupils displaying negative attitudes;
■ pupils exhibiting positive personal qualities;
■ the teacher actively encouraging positive personal qualities.

After the lesson, write up your observations in your journal and reflect upon the impact on the lesson. In particular, consider how the teacher might have done things differently in order to have had a greater impact on the development of the pupils' qualities and attitudes. Finally, record in your journal the attitudes and qualities that you will aim to foster within your teaching.

Personal development and the cross-curricular dimension

There is, therefore, a responsibility for you as a mathematics teacher, as with other issues addressed in this chapter, to consider the implications for your curriculum planning and classroom practice of incorporating the PLTS, the *ECM* outcomes and the cross-curricular dimensions. Luckily, despite being separately laid out, all three of these aspects of the National Curricular link together when thinking about developing the whole person. Rather than trying to develop tight definitions of these different aspects of teaching, it is perhaps easiest to approach the area by considering some examples of mathematics teaching that demonstrate the wide range of opportunities open to the teacher. These opportunities will be based in the National Curriculum's cross-curriculum dimensions.

IDENTITY AND CULTURAL DIVERSITY

For some mathematics teachers, the area of *identity and cultural diversity* is the most problematic of the aspects of personal development. They associate it with ethnicity or religion and believe it to have no place within mathematics lessons. However, this perspective suggests both a restricted view of cultural diversity and a limited understanding of the nature and history of mathematics.

It can be helpful to consider two ideas when considering your role in the cultural development of your pupils. One is helping pupils to become more aware of and appreciate their own culture and the culture of the society within which they live. The second is helping pupils to understand more about the diversity of cultures that exist both in their own nation and around the world, whilst encouraging them to show respect towards people of these different cultures.

A useful approach to incorporating identity and cultural diversity in mathematics teaching recognises, within the history of mathematics, examples of people who, through exploring ideas within mathematics, have also gained insight into broader areas. Indeed, biographies of mathematicians will sometimes illustrate how they had quite diverse motivations for studying the subject. This aspect of mathematics is now part of the National Curriculum but, depending on how you decide to use such material, you could ask the pupils to develop their skills as independent enquirers, self-managers and reflective learners, while using technology and the media and engaging in creative and critical thinking.

In order to engage with your responsibility in teaching identity and cultural diversity, it is important to recognise mathematics as part of culture. Paul Ernest (1991) suggests that:

> Mathematics is part of human culture, and the mathematics of each culture serves its own unique purposes, and is equally valuable. Consequently, school mathematics should acknowledge the diverse cultural and historical origins and purposes of mathematics, and the real contributions of all, including women and non-European countries. (p. 265)

For some mathematics teachers, this may mean that they must learn a new history of mathematics, which offers more than the traditional Eurocentric perspective, so that they can acknowledge the key role of many cultures in the shaping of today's mathematics. George Joseph's (2010) valuable work tracing some non-European roots of mathematics provides a helpful and thorough introduction to this field.

For many pupils, however, mathematics may almost seem to be *a*cultural – a body of knowledge with no historical or cultural roots. Sadly, this can also be the case for many mathematics graduates. Indeed, you may need to start to build up your own knowledge in this area. It is worth investigating the cultural roots of some aspect of the current mathematics curriculum and considering how your research might enrich the teaching of that topic. By introducing pupils to the social and cultural roots of mathematics, their beliefs about the nature of the subject will begin to change.

The Charis Project and Bowland Maths (www.bowlandmaths.org) deliberately set out to develop resources that can promote pupils' understanding of *identity and cultural diversity* across the curriculum. In the introduction to the mathematics resources (Charis Project, 1997), the editors highlight three approaches that the writers used in producing the materials. The first approach takes advantage of the wide range of human situations in which mathematics has been developed and applied. Consequently, it is possible to choose contexts that allow pupils both to work mathematically and to reflect on cultural diversity issues that emerge from the context. For example, one unit uses a range of mortality statistics to develop pupils' skills in applying probability theory, whilst, at the same time, allowing them to consider their own mortality and attitudes to life and death. An example of a field that crosses over from mathematics to other domains is our understanding of truth; for example, exploring the truth of a series of statements about prime numbers or about 'how risky life is'. Pupils investigate the validity of different statements and consider how they might prove or disprove them. They are then encouraged to reflect on how, in general, they come to accept statements as true and how much they value seeking truth. Working as a team to investigate what such statistics mean, and to present well-formulated ideas to the rest of the class, would also demand the PLTS of teamworkers and creativity.

It can also be useful to recognise how mathematics has been used to model and understand the universe. By working on such models, the pupils will also have opportunity to develop a sense of wonder at the world around them. For example, the field of fractals, while inspiring in its own right, still only offers a limited model of an even more wonderful world. However, when using any of these approaches, your teaching methods or pedagogy will make a difference to how much the pupils get out of the ideas – see Chapter 12 for a discussion of the pedagogical implications of using realistic mathematical contexts. By using a variety of contexts for mathematical learning, giving the pupils opportunities both for personal reflection and group discussion and teamwork, or by asking them to produce a variety of outcomes – poster, presentation, video, radio programme, leaflet, and so on – over time your pupils will be able to develop in all areas of the PLTS.

Mathematics educator Derek Woodrow (1989) warns against a tokenistic approach in this area:

> Care must [...] be taken not to introduce such topics as marginal and trivial activities since this can imply a dismissive view of other societies and values. The same problem relates to the inclusion of historical information. (p. 231)

As well as doing your own research in the field, there are many resources available that you will find helpful. Shan and Bailey's (1991) book and Dodd's (1991) resource book are good examples.

A further aspect of the cultural research that you need to do as a mathematics teacher is to learn more about the cultures of the pupils in your lessons. This will help you to be more alert to opportunities to acknowledge pupils' cultures within your teaching. Indeed, the knowledge that pupils bring from their cultures can act as starting points for a range of mathematical topics. For example, different traditions of geometric design or different ways of calculating may emerge in a culturally rich classroom.

In talking about pupils' culture, it is, however, important to realise that this is not just at the level of ethnic identity. It is also about your pupils' everyday experiences of life. For example, the pupil who works on the market stall, the pupil whose hobby is flying model aeroplanes and the pupil who attends a dance class outside school each bring experiences to the classroom that can contribute to a whole group's mathematical development. However, as well as trying to acknowledge your pupils' cultures in this way, you also need to check that the everyday resources you use do not give a hidden message about the real value placed upon the pupils' cultures.

Community participation

There are two principal ways in which you can promote the development of your pupils as responsible citizens and teamworkers within mathematics lessons. The first is through considering your classroom as a community of people who inevitably encounter ethical issues as you work together. As a mathematics teacher, it is your responsibility to establish a culture in your classroom that promotes effective learning. A fundamental aspect of this is how people relate to each other. This includes teacher–pupil relationships and pupil–pupil relationships. You will no doubt have clear and valued beliefs about the way in which you want people to work together and to treat each other in your classroom. In communicating your values and your expectations to pupils, you are contributing to developing their ability to contribute effectively in any community by presenting a particular set of coherent ethical principles.

You will soon realise, however, if you did not already know, that the simple presentation of ethical values does not mean that your pupils will automatically come to share or adopt these values. Even if they do, they will not necessarily behave in accordance with them. Consequently, you will have to handle situations where pupils have behaved in a way that you believe is ethically unacceptable. Such situations are key opportunities for developing the ability to participate in communities beyond school because they provide opportunity to encourage pupils, either as individuals or as a group, to reflect. Sometimes this is difficult to do in the heat of the moment and so a more extended reflection might be kept back until the end of the lesson. The other side of the coin in this area is to be realistic about your own actions. Sometimes you will behave in ways that are not consistent with your values and so it may be appropriate to acknowledge this to the class. Pupils often have a very keen sense of fairness and so will most probably pick up your inconsistencies if you do not get there before them.

In the same way as a classroom is inevitably a moral domain, it is also a place full of social interaction. This means that mathematics lessons have the potential to support pupils' social development and thus equip them to be team workers and effective participants, and to participate in communities. For example, the mathematics classroom can be a place where pupils learn to:

- work collaboratively in teams;
- both present and listen to ideas and arguments;
- tolerate and appreciate differences in people.

However, it can also be a place where none of this happens. It is your responsibility to make it happen. You may hear mathematics teachers say, 'I can't do all that collaborative, interactive stuff; the pupils just haven't got the social skills'. This is, essentially, abdicating responsibility; it is as though the teacher is saying, 'Let somebody else develop them socially and then, perhaps, I might attempt more ambitious teaching approaches'. However, as with many of the issues raised in this chapter, by abdicating responsibility, teachers are also missing out on opportunities to enhance their pupils' *mathematical* development. The more that we come to understand about the importance of social interaction and communication skills in the process of learning, the more important it becomes for the mathematics teacher to pay attention to the social domain.

Assuming, then, that you accept and, indeed, value your role in promoting the social development of your pupils, what implications does this have for your planning, teaching and assessment? One issue that you should reflect upon when planning is the extent to which you are providing pupils with the opportunity to use and develop their social skills. For example, if in your lessons there is little opportunity for your pupils to interact, then obviously there will be less scope for social development. Instead, over time, you need to plan your lessons so that you make increasing demands upon the pupils' social skills. Indeed, it can be helpful to view this as a structured training or induction programme for your pupils.

Within the lessons, you need to make explicit what you expect of the pupils. Sometimes this may require you to indicate the type of social interaction that you are looking for from the pupils. For example, you might show how different pupils can take on different roles within groups or you might offer phrases that pupils can use when they disagree with each other's ideas. As the lesson progresses, as well as monitoring your pupils' mathematical progress, you can also be assessing and offering feedback on the extent to which they are meeting your stated expectations. The end of the lesson provides an opportunity both for reflection and for further feedback on how well the pupils have demonstrated the social interaction that you have planned to develop. You may also use this time to suggest targets to pupils for future development.

This use of presentation of an argument is part of an important tradition within mathematics and can be particularly seen in the history of statistics. For example, Florence Nightingale developed and used statistical techniques to campaign politically for better medical conditions. As with work on identity and cultural diversity, there are implications for your teaching methods. Giving pupils an opportunity to debate the issues they encounter is essential if any significant development is to occur. They should also be given the opportunity to respond meaningfully to the issue if they feel strongly about it. All of this means that there is the need for sensitivity on your part as you begin to open up what can be quite controversial issues.

Global dimension and sustainable development

Promoting a global dimension in mathematics lessons can be closely related to the subject, and significant moral issues can be raised through your choice of contexts. For example, a resource produced by the Development Education Centre in Dorset contains a unit built around the issue of refugees (DEED, 1993). If you decide to use this resource, or one like it, your pupils will employ statistics to explore the position of refugees and address the way they are treated by our society. The World Bank produces materials that will help you and your pupils explore the often complex yet intriguing social, economic and environmental issues of sustainable development (http://www.worldbank.org/depweb/index.html). Other organisations have developed resources to help pupils and their teachers understand about the global dimension and sustainable development: for example, the Oxfam website contains resources with a mathematical bias about water for all and the world food crisis. There is also an activity in Bowland Maths that asks pupils to use mathematics to consider building a school out of plastic bottles. This activity requires some serious mathematical thinking and reasoning while also providing the basis for a discussion of what sustainable development really is. All of these topics provide pupils with opportunities to use their mathematics to engage with issues of justice in society.

Of course, global development is so much better tackled in conjunction with other curriculum areas within the school. Your school could become a 'Fairtrade' school. Recruiting the RE department, the technology department and the geography department to work with you on a project about fair trade immediately places the mathematics in an appropriate context and gives a real reason for pupils to put their mathematical skills and understanding to use.

Task 12.5 **Reading resources critically**

It should be clear from this chapter that if you are to take seriously your responsibility for the personal development of your pupils, then there are implications both for the resources you use and the teaching methods you employ.

For this task, you need to choose one of the key resources used by the teachers in your school. You should then critically analyse it by bringing the following questions to it:

- What images, if any, are presented by the resource of the different cultures that exist in British society and particularly among the pupils in your school?
- How much opportunity does the resource provide for pupils to engage with the cultural and historical roots of the mathematics they are studying?
- What contexts are used within the resource to provide opportunity for discussion and reflection?
- How much does the resource suggest tasks that require pupils to work collaboratively and learn through social interaction?

Write a short report, either in your reflective journal or for presentation to a mathematics department meeting, evaluating the strengths and weaknesses of the resource in these four areas and identifying what supplementary resources might be needed if the personal development of pupils is to be fostered effectively in their mathematics lessons.

SUMMARY AND KEY POINTS

You have a responsibility as a mathematics teacher that extends beyond just developing your pupils' mathematical knowledge, understanding and skills. You have a part to play in supporting their development in a range of cross-curricular skills, as well as supporting your colleagues as they use mathematics in teaching their subjects. You are also responsible for supporting pupils in their personal development, which includes cross-curricular dimensions, personal learning and thinking skills, and the *Every Child Matters* outcomes, which means you have a responsibility to recognise both the whole curriculum and the whole pupil in your teaching. If you are to teach mathematics in a way that addresses effectively both the whole person and the whole curriculum, you will need to examine the resources and methods you use critically. However, one of the benefits from adopting such an approach is that your pupils will be likely to develop more positive attitudes to learning mathematics and, consequently, learn more mathematics and want to continue to learn mathematics beyond school.

FURTHER READING

Bowland Maths http://www.bowlandmaths.org.uk/

The Bowland Maths materials look very different from most mathematics teaching materials. They consist of innovative case-study problems designed to develop thinking, reasoning and problem-solving skills. Each case study is different, but all provide pupils and teachers with problems that are fun and engaging, while also offering a rich mathematical experience. Bowland Maths also includes professional development materials to help teachers develop the skills needed for the case studies and for the new programme of study.

Charis Project (1997) *Charis Mathematics, Units 1–9 and Units 10–19*. Nottingham: Stapleford Centre.

These two sets of resources, produced by the Charis Project mathematics team, offer a helpful introduction to approaches for promoting spiritual and moral development within mathematics lessons. The units cover a wide range of contexts and KS4 mathematical content. The approaches illustrated by the materials should help you to develop your own tasks for this aspect of your teaching.

Hudson, B. (1994) 'Environmental issues in the mathematics classroom', in Selinger, M. (ed.), *Teaching Mathematics*. London: Routledge, pp. 113–25.
Brian Hudson's chapter provides a helpful introduction to the importance of having a whole-curriculum perspective in teaching mathematics. He illustrates, through using the example of environmental issues, how pupils can be encouraged to appreciate the importance of mathematics for society.

Ofsted (2008) *Mathematics: Understanding the Score* (070863). London: Office for Standards in Education.
A study of the current state of teaching in mathematics, detailing what is going wrong and giving specific and, to some, surprising details about what Ofsted views as good teaching.

Shan, S. and Bailey, P. (1991) *Multiple Factors: Classroom Mathematics for Equality and Justice*. Stoke: Trentham Books.
This book offers an excellent introduction to the role that mathematics teaching can play in both the moral and cultural development of pupils. The authors illustrate how particular groups in society can be disadvantaged by certain teaching methods and resources. They go on to offer a whole range of ideas and sources that will help you to both challenge injustice and increase cultural understanding within your lessons.

Winter, J. (2001) 'Personal, spiritual, moral, social and cultural issues in teaching mathematics', in Gates, P. (ed.), *Issues in Mathematics Teaching*. London: RoutledgeFalmer, pp. 197–213.
Jan Winter's chapter discusses each of these elements in her title, in terms of what they mean in the context of teaching mathematics, and offers some strategies for the classroom. In so doing, she places mathematics teaching more closely at the centre of children's spiritual, moral, social, cultural and personal education than it currently lies.

TEACHING MATHEMATICS POST-16

Geoff Wake

INTRODUCTION

At the time of writing, education in England and Wales is compulsory up to age 16, but as you read this chapter this may have changed, as it is planned that from 2013 all young people in England will be required to continue in education or training to age 17, and from 2015 to age 18. However, the National Curriculum and the mathematics programmes of study for the different Key Stages will continue to define mathematics teaching and learning for pupils up to age 16 and the GCSE will remain as a very important milestone. In some ways, the planned changes to raise the age limit for participation in education is a mere technicality, as already almost all young people continue in education of some form or another, and, as you may discover, many of these will be involved in mathematics education in some way. For some students this study may take the form of 'traditional' qualifications with which you are familiar; for example, those who have been successful at GCSE may go on to take an AS and A-Level in mathematics, and those who struggled may well be looking to improve their GCSE grade. On the other hand, other students may be taking a range of mathematics qualifications with which you are, as yet, unfamiliar. In colleges, more mature students may join 16–19-year-old pupils in learning specific areas of mathematics that they feel will be of help to them.

Teaching mathematics to these post-16 students with a wide range of different needs and demands will offer you a whole new range of challenges and delights. First of all, the goals of those you teach will be much more diverse than those of pupils up to age 16. There is a very wide range of possibilities open to post-16 students when choosing their study programmes and you will need to know about and understand this provision and, in particular, the range of mathematics qualifications that is available. Not only will you need to make sure that you are completely familiar with any mathematics specifications you will teach, but also you must gear your style of teaching to students who are more mature. Some of these may even be older than you are and you may find you are expected to teach in different settings, such as drop-in workshops.

What about the delights? On the whole, almost all your students will be there because they want or need to do some mathematics, and if you are able to offer them the course that best suits their needs they should flourish. Over recent years, considerable thought has been given to provision of mathematics outside of the traditional academic route of GCSE followed by AS and A-Level and you may find some of the newer approaches to teaching and learning for these recently developed courses provide you with insight into teaching and learning mathematics in general.

OBJECTIVES

By the end of this chapter you should:

■   be aware of current thinking about the post-16 curriculum and how this might develop in the near future and long-term;

■   be aware of the different needs of post-16 students and where and how these may be met;

■   be able to look for and evaluate different modes of teaching used post-16;

■   be aware of how to prepare to teach a new topic for students post-16;

■   have an awareness of the potential of ICT in teaching mathematics post-16 and some of the issues surrounding the use of technology in assessment.

BACKGROUND: 14–19 PATHWAYS

You will probably be well aware of the importance of mathematics in the school curriculum – it is considered one of the core subjects at school alongside English and, to a lesser extent, science. It is important, both for individuals and the school/college, that students attain the highest grade possible at GCSE in mathematics, as results in the subject have become increasingly important in performance measures that are used to provide school 'league tables' by which schools and colleges are judged. You might like to consider why such importance has been invested in mathematics, both nationally and more widely across the world, as evidenced by international comparative studies such as PISA (the Programme for International Student Assessment – see www.pisa.gc.ca/what_pisa.shtml). For industrialised nations, such as England and Wales, it is considered desirable to have a well-educated workforce in terms of basic skills such as literacy and numeracy, but particularly in mathematics and science, so as to sustain their economies. This is recognised at the highest levels of government and, consequently, mathematics education often has a higher profile than that of any other discipline. The influential report, *SET for Success* (Roberts, 2002), for example, prepared for the Treasury, pointed to the vital contribution that mathematics makes in many areas of economic activity and how, over the previous two decades or so, the numbers studying the subject to more advanced levels has been in steady decline.

    The recognition that mathematics is, therefore, crucial in the education of school pupils and, in many circumstances, older workers led to a further investigation and report into the teaching of mathematics post-14; an inquiry that was led by Professor Adrian Smith who published his findings in the report *Making Mathematics Count* (DfES, 2004a). The findings of this report were central in informing developments in mathematics education in England in the latter part of the decade up to 2010, and particularly for the 14–19 age group about which it reported: 'It is clear that the overwhelming majority of respondents to the Inquiry no longer regard current mathematics curricula, assessment and qualifications as fit for purpose' (p. 6). It was recommended, therefore, therefore that a range of possible different pathway models should be explored that might better serve the needs of students in this age range, by maintaining long-established and -respected qualifications such as GCSE and AS/A-Level, but possibly redesigning them, as well as developing new qualifications. At the time of writing, in 2010, the work on pathway developments is still underway and decisions about structural changes to existing qualifications and the introduction of new qualifications have still to be taken. Later in this chapter you will have an opportunity to explore the outcomes of this work that are in operation at the moment you are about to enter the teaching profession, but before doing so, the next section introduces a framework that might help you think about different aspects of knowledge that, as a teacher, you will require to function effectively in your professional life.

KNOWLEDGE FOR TEACHING

In 1986, Lee Shulman made explicit that proficiency with subject knowledge was only one part of the knowledge required for effective teaching. He introduced the notion of 'pedagogical content knowledge' – knowledge that bridges the content knowledge of one's subject and the practice of teaching. (As you develop as a teacher, you might like to think of how your knowledge of mathematics develops and changes as you begin to work with pupils.) More recently, a research team in the United States has attempted to gain a better and more structured understanding of knowledge for teaching. Its analysis of many hours of videos of teachers working in classrooms has led it to suggest a number of categories that are summarised by Figure 13.1. This image draws attention to the two major categories of 'subject knowledge' and 'pedagogic content knowledge', each of which is split into three further sub-categories.

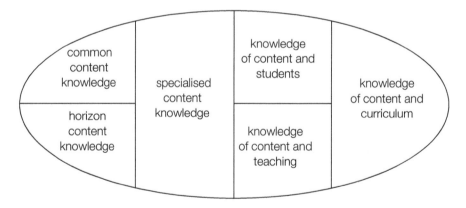

▨ **Figure 13.1** Categories of knowledge for teaching
Source: Ball *et al.*, (2008). Reprinted by permission of Sage Publications

In relation to subject knowledge, Ball *et al.* (2008) identify three sub-categories:

(i)   *common* content knowledge: that is, mathematical knowledge and skills used in settings other than teaching;

(ii) *specialized* content knowledge: that is, mathematical knowledge and skills that are specific to teaching. Such knowledge requires deep understanding of mathematical concepts (and common misconceptions) such that teachers can engage with ways in which learners can be supported to develop understanding rather than just knowing a single procedure to solve a problem;

(iii) *horizon* content knowledge: that is an awareness of how mathematical topics are related over the span of mathematics included in the curriculum. It may be considered as comprising a detailed overview of mathematics and its interconnections.

Additionally, in categorising pedagogic content knowledge, they identify a further three sub-domains:

(iv) knowledge of content and curriculum: that is, knowledge about how mathematics has been structured in the curriculum: for example, how it has been grouped, the prominence given to meta-processes such as proof, modelling, and so on, as well as how it is structured by resources such as textbooks;

(v) knowledge of content and teaching: that is, knowledge that is specifically related to how to organise mathematics. so that it is most likely to be understandable to learners: for example, which examples to use to illustrate a particular topic and the order in which to use them;

(vi) knowledge of content and students: that is knowledge about particular students and how, as a teacher, you might motivate and support their learning.

Task 13.1 **Reflecting on the knowledge you use in your teaching**

Reflect briefly on the structure proposed by Ball and colleagues in relation to your developing knowledge as a teacher, before reading much further.

Think about a lesson you have either taught or observed recently and try to identify and make notes in your journal on the different aspects of teacher knowledge in these different sub-domains that were important in the lesson. You could use a copy of the diagram as a way to organise your thoughts.

Throughout the rest of this chapter, you will have opportunities to consider the subject knowledge you need to develop in each sub-category in order to become an effective teacher of post-16 mathematics.

QUALIFICATIONS: TYPES AND LEVELS

In this and the next section, you will focus on developing *knowledge of content and curriculum*.

When pupils reach the age of 16, and thus come to the end of their National Curriculum experience, they have important choices to make about their future in relation to further study/training and future work. The possible programmes of study available are many; you will have made these very choices yourself, and at this point you may like to consider what options, other than those you eventually chose, were open to you. What other qualifications could you have taken and where would they have led? To develop your knowledge of content and curriculum, you need to understand the qualifications structure in general, as well as mathematics qualifications in particular.

In broad terms, we can consider qualifications as falling into one of three types: general, vocationally related, or occupational. Up to age 16, as pupils in schools follow the National Curriculum towards GCSE, they may only have experience of qualifications in the 'general' category, although some may have studied vocational subjects in areas such as business, leisure and tourism, and so on. After they have completed Year 11, pupils can, at 16, choose to continue their studies within the general category, either resitting some GCSEs or progressing to AS and full A-Level qualifications. However, they also have the possibility of choosing from the many other qualifications that exist in the other two categories. In the next section of this chapter you will consider the important role that mathematics has to play in a range of qualifications, including those where mathematics may be less visible and may appear, at first sight, not so important.

Because of the wide range of qualifications available, a number of frameworks at national level have evolved that attempt to ensure some understanding of qualification equivalence in general terms by introducing notions of levels. Such frameworks undergo development from time to time and you will have an opportunity to explore their current state of play in the second task in this chapter. However, the levels of the main school qualifications have been fixed for some time: high grades at GCSE (C–A*) are at level 2, lower grades at GCSE are at level 1 and AS/A-Level qualifications are at level 3. Recent versions of frameworks at a national level have been designed to allow comparability across Europe and to take account of the amount of time that is expected to be spent on studying such qualifications.

Task 13.2 **Exploring qualifications frameworks**

Use the internet to locate the latest versions of the national qualifications framework (this was called the Qualifications and Credit Framework in 2010). Ensure that you understand its structure by deciding where:

▪ qualifications you have obtained yourself would be located, including those at levels above level 3;
▪ qualifications you have met recently in schools and colleges would be located;
▪ a range of vocationally related and occupational qualifications would be placed.

Qualifications at the same level are judged to have some degree of equivalence. Find out what you can about this from official sources. In doing so, consider how courses of different size (in terms of the amount of study time they require) are given different credit.

You may wish to discuss your findings with other student teachers and your mentors.

MATHEMATICS AND QUALIFICATIONS POST-16

As already suggested, mathematics has a complex role to play across the range of qualifications available to post-16 students. As well as having a number of well-established qualifications to consider, such as GCSE and AS/A-Level, there are a number of newer qualifications that have been developed resulting from the need for pathways as proposed by the Smith Inquiry. For example, there are new qualifications in functional skills. In this section, you will consider these qualifications in a little detail.

AS and A-Level mathematics

In September 2000, A-Level examinations, along with other aspects of the general education curriculum, were reformulated in all subjects: these changes were known as Curriculum 2000. The major change was that all A-Levels became modular, with a first set of modules expected to be examined, in the main, after one year of study, giving rise to an AS (Advanced Subsidiary) qualification. To continue on to achieve a full A-Level qualification in any subject, students then study further modules (designated as A2 modules).

It was the intention that these changes would result in students taking five subjects at AS Level before concentrating on three A-Levels, thus broadening the programme of study for many. In reality, most students have found the workload associated with four AS Levels sufficiently challenging.

Although each awarding body (in England, these are AQA, Edexcel and OCR) can offer its own AS and A-Level in mathematics, there is an agreed common 'core' of pure mathematics at both AS and A-Level around which each awarding body's specification should be designed. Beyond this core of pure mathematics, there is the possibility for students to study some 'applied mathematics'. At the time of writing, it is not clear how much flexibility will be allowed in new A-Levels to be taught from September 2012. However, there has been an increasing amount of control exercised over the design of A-Level mathematics qualifications in the recent past in order that all students can be considered likely to have covered the same material, which is something that universities consider helpful.

A proportion of those studying A-Level mathematics take this further by studying AS or A-Level further mathematics, which is offered by each of the awarding bodies. Although the numbers studying this are relatively low, they increased quite rapidly recently due to the work of the Further Mathematics Support Network that allows schools and colleges to cope with small numbers or even individual students who wish to pursue AS or A-Level further mathematics. This support has included access to tuition and online resources and also professional development for teachers unfamiliar with mathematics teaching at this level. You should take some time to find out what support the Further Mathematics Support Network offers (http://www.furthermaths.org.uk/index.php).

Task 13.3 **Exploring the structure of AS/A-Level mathematics and further mathematics**

From the three awarding body (AQA, EdExcel, OCR) websites (for addresses see Appendix 2), download versions of the AS/A-Level specifications in mathematics and further mathematics they are offering for teaching from the forthcoming September.

Using these mathematics and further mathematics specifications, compare and contrast the structure of the AS and A-Level awards across the three awarding bodies, identifying what is the same and what is different. To assist you, draw up a table to organise the details you uncover, including the contribution that each module makes to the overall award, the use of technology allowed, length of examination paper, and so on.

Highlight any differences that you find.

What implications, if any, do you consider there are for schools and colleges?

You may wish to discuss your findings with other student teachers and your mentors.

Task 13.4 **Using examination specifications and papers**

The aim of this task is that you develop some understanding of the relationships between an AS/A-Level specification, the examination papers and any published teaching materials.

You will need a specification for one AS/A-Level module from one of the awarding bodies, at least one past examination paper and its mark scheme, the examiners' report for the paper and an appropriate A-Level textbook. If you are in a school or college where students study AS/A-Level mathematics, this may be straightforward; if not, you will need to obtain the materials from one of the awarding bodies. These are often available at an awarding body's website (for addresses, see Appendix 2).

Look through the examination paper and write down the topics you think each question is assessing. Match these with the content in the specification for the module. Is there a close match? Does the examination cover all, or most, of the topics in the module's specification? Find suitable chapters in the textbook. Do they enable you to cover the topics in sufficient depth to answer the questions?

Does the specification give enough detail to work from?

Look at the comments in the examiner's report. Can you understand why students might make the mistakes discussed? Think of ways of helping students to avoid losing marks in these ways.

Discuss your findings with other student teachers and your mentors.

General Certificate of Secondary Education (GCSE)

While this is essentially a qualification for the end of Key Stage 4, some post-16 students will not have achieved a high-enough grade for their own purposes or career ambitions and will be looking to improve their performance. This is not easy. Many students will come to your classes feeling that they have failed at mathematics. You will find that you need many different strategies when teaching GCSE resit classes compared to a first run-through with pupils in Years 10 and 11 – you will need to develop your *knowledge of content and students.* Colleges in such situations may, in addition to timetabled classes, use a combination of an individual learning plan and workshop provision with each student undergoing some form of initial diagnostic assessment, allowing support to be tailored to individual needs. Students can then seek help in the mathematics workshop where staff can work with them using a range of targeted resources.

More usually, especially in 11–18 schools, students are class-taught in the same way as at Key Stage 4. This can succeed where students only require more practice to improve their examination technique, but unless handled sensitively it can reinforce the students' sense of alienation. Whatever the teaching strategy, it is important for students to see improvement in their learning as the course progresses.

It may be that other newer qualifications may be more appropriate and motivating for these students. However, the status of GCSE is such that it is often difficult for students to consider anything else. For example, a high grade (C–A*) in GCSE mathematics is a requirement for entry to the teaching profession, and although some qualifications might be deemed 'equivalent', there is a lot of pressure for students to ensure they have an appropriate GCSE grade.

Task 13.5 **Diagnosing where help is needed**

Imagine you are about to start teaching a new group of GCSE resit students. They are taking a one-year course to improve their grades to a C or above.

Choose a suitable GCSE specification and study the content and some sample papers. These can be downloaded from the awarding bodies' websites (see Appendix 2 for the web addresses). Devise a questionnaire and/or test that will help you diagnose the weaknesses of your students at the beginning of the course. How can you discover where students need help without reinforcing their feelings of inadequacy?

Try your questionnaire or test on some of your fellow student teachers (those not training to teach mathematics). Use the responses to consider how you would devise a programme of study for one of the students.

During your school or college experience, study the structure of the GCSE resit provision. Ask the teacher responsible for his or her evaluation of its strengths and weaknesses.

If possible, talk to some students on the resit course to get their perspective.

Mathematics support for other qualifications and students' programmes of study

As you might expect, mathematics has an important role to play in supporting students' other areas of study and qualifications. For example:

■ students studying AS/A-Level in psychology and geography who need to use some statistical ideas beyond those met at Key Stage 4;
■ science students (particularly those studying physics) who need to apply mathematics in solving problems;

▪ students following a range of vocationally related courses (such as business students) who may need to use a range of statistical ideas.

Schools and colleges have always tried to make provision for students in the first two categories, perhaps running courses such as 'maths for scientists'. Particularly if you work in a college, you may find that you are asked to assist students in the last of these categories, i.e. those following vocational qualifications who may have a mathematics unit as part of their overall programme of study. However, because the mathematics that is part of these qualifications is often so closely integrated with the course of study (e.g. engineering), these classes are frequently taught by specialists in that field. Even in such cases, if you work in a college's drop-in support workshop, you may find yourself working with students and mathematics in very different ways from those with which you may be more familiar. There will be a need for you to develop many aspects of your knowledge for teaching, particularly your *pedagogic content knowledge.* You will need to learn about new curriculum specifications and structures relating to mathematics in support of these students' particular needs, whilst also having a general understanding of their programmes.

Qualifications in the vocational category seem to undergo development and change on a very regular basis. It has proven impossible to date to put in place a system of such qualifications that have the status of, and respect accorded to, GCSEs and AS/A-Levels. However, it should be apparent that there is, and always will be, a need for vocational qualifications for this phase of education and, consequently, there will always be a need for mathematics teaching that supports them. An important part of the pathways work that emanated from the Smith Report looked at developing the Free-Standing Mathematics Qualifications (FSMQs) at levels 1, 2 and 3 with just this need in mind. Again, at the time of writing, it is not clear how these will be structured as part of the post-16 mathematics qualification provision, but it does seem likely that they will have an important role to play. Such qualifications seem particularly important if we are to meet the needs of employers better in relation to the mathematical competence of workers. We could move to a position where almost all post-16 students study some mathematics as part of their programme, something that would bring us into line with other industrialised nations.

In the next task, you will have an opportunity to explore the mathematics qualification provision that might support students taking vocationally orientated programmes of study.

Task 13.6 **Mathematics in vocationally related courses**

Choose a current vocationally related qualification, for example in an area such as engineering, leisure and tourism or business. You will find specifications available on awarding body websites. Look though the specification and identify possibilities where students will have to use mathematical skills to assist them with their studies. Explore whether this fact is highlighted in some way in the specification. It may be that additional advice is given elsewhere on a government agency or examination board website. Explore this possibility also.

Consider how you might structure your teaching differently to support these students with their learning of this mathematics compared with how you usually teach. What knowledge for teaching do you need to develop to support the learning of such students?

Task 13.7 **Qualifications to support alternative pathways**

Free-Standing Mathematics Qualifications (FSMQs) were designed to provide a modular structure of support for students on programmes of study that include general and/or vocationally related courses without other mathematics provision. They therefore allow the development of alternative pathways to that of GCSE followed by AS and A-Levels in mathematics.

During the pathways developments, combining FSMQs at levels 1 and 2 to give an overarching GCSE in Use of Mathematics and at level 3 combining FSMQs to give an AS and A-Level in Use of Mathematics were both explored. At the time of writing, it was not clear whether, or in what form, these qualifications would survive.

Explore the role of FSMQs in the current provision of mathematics qualifications. You will need to search the awarding body websites (see Appendix 2), and for an overview, maybe the website of the government agencies for qualifications and curriculum.

How do these qualifications organise mathematics differently to other qualifications? How is this likely to appeal to students?

Find out if FSMQs can be combined in different ways, at levels 1, 2 and 3, to give an overarching qualification, and find out how colleges and schools are using these alternative qualifications.

Discuss your findings with other student teachers and your mentors.

Functional skills in mathematics

Functional skills in mathematics, English and ICT are the latest manifestation of an attempt to ensure that all school-leavers have a level of competence in these three key areas. Earlier attempts to achieve this have seen 'Core Skills' and 'Key Skills' being defined in each of these three important areas, but as you might surmise, these earlier attempts have not been particularly successful and it remains to be seen how functional mathematics will fare. Although, as a qualification, 'functional mathematics', like its predecessors, may prove difficult to establish in the curriculum, it is likely that you will agree that all students should be functional with their mathematics in the way expressed in this statement from the Qualifications and Curriculum Development Agency:

> Individuals with functional mathematics skills understand a range of mathematical concepts and know how and when to use them. They:
>
> ■ have the confidence and capability to use mathematics to solve increasingly complex problems;
> ■ are able to use a range of tools, including ICT as appropriate;
> ■ possess the analytical and reasoning skills needed to draw conclusions, justify how these conclusions are reached and identify errors or inconsistencies;
> ■ are able to validate and interpret results, judging the limits of the validity and using the results effectively and efficiently.
>
> (http://curriculum.qcda.gov.uk/key-stages-3-and-4/skills/functionalskills/
> index.aspx#page4_a)

At the start of the pathways developments, it was considered that students should sit a separate examination in functional mathematics at GCSE, but although this requirement was scrapped, the underpinning ideas have informed developments of GCSE overall, with questions in GCSEs adopting more of a 'functional' flavour. However, separate assessments for functional mathematics will be used with a range of students in post-16 settings and you may need to become familiar with their requirements.

It is planned that functional skills qualifications will eventually replace adult numeracy qualifications such as entry-level qualifications in numeracy (skills for life), for which many adult learners are currently awarded a certificate. Depending on how well-established functional skills qualifications are at the time you are reading this chapter, you might want to explore what qualifications exist for adults in numeracy/mathematics at entry level (you should have identified this level when exploring qualifications frameworks earlier). If you are working as a mathematics teacher in an FE college, it is possible that you will be asked to contribute to the teaching of adults on such courses. This may present a considerable challenge, as such learners often have very low self-esteem with regard to their mathematical abilities: you will certainly have to consider developing your *knowledge of content and students*.

Important issues to consider if you are asked to teach students functional skills are those that surround 'transfer' or application of mathematical knowledge from one area of study to another. This is recognised as being problematic, but it is at the very heart of what *functionality* is about. There are a number of different opinions about how students can develop their understanding so that they can successfully apply mathematics: do you teach the required knowledge, skills and understanding and then give examples of how these can be applied, or do you teach them through applications from the outset? You may like to consider, at this point, how you would go about this difficult task.

Particularly pertinent to problems of transfer of mathematics is research in the area of situated cognition and recent research about mathematics in workplaces, which highlight how it is possible to become mathematically competent while working in one particular context, but how transfer into other contexts can remain problematic (Lave, 1988; Hoyles *et al.*, 2010; Williams and Wake 2007). Finally, in relation to functionality, you may also like to think about how confident *you* will be at applying mathematics in a wide range of contexts.

Task 13.8 **When is mathematics 'functional'?**

From one of the awarding bodies' websites, download the functional mathematics specifications and a sample assessment paper (with its mark scheme if this is available).

Explore these from the point of view of considering how they promote functionality.

Identify in the specification how mathematical content and process skills are made explicit. How much prominence is given to process skills? How much prominence is given to mathematical content?

Choose a question from the assessment paper – do it, and try to identify the process skills required. Use the mark scheme to identify where marks are awarded to process skills (and which skills). Repeat this for a number of questions. What conclusions can you draw?

> Reflect on how the *knowledge of content and curriculum* you are beginning to develop raises issues for other knowledge for teaching you need to develop.
>
> You may wish to discuss the needs you have identified with colleagues and your mentor.

Advanced Extension Awards

Advanced Extension Awards, designed to challenge the most able A-Level students, were introduced in 2002, replacing Special Papers, and will remain available, in mathematics only, until at least 2013. They are based on the subject criteria for A-Level and consist of a single three-hour exam in which the use of calculators is not allowed, with success leading to a Merit or Distinction grade.

You might like to consider the aims of the qualification set out below in the context of your response to the example question given in Figure 13.2.

> The AEA in mathematics aims to provide a sense of achievement and a stimulating mathematical challenge through:
>
> ■ encouraging students to use what they have been taught;
> ■ encouraging students to think beyond what they have been taught;
> ■ encouraging students to develop confidence, stamina and fluency in working through unfamiliar and/or unstructured problems that might demand multi-step analysis or the exploration of different possibilities;
> ■ building chains of logical reasoning and using concepts of proof;
> ■ testing critical thinking and the critical evaluation of a mathematical argument;
> ■ rewarding elegance, clarity and insight in the solution of mathematical problems.

---

4. A curve C has equation $y = f(x)$ with $f'(x) > 0$. The x-coordinate of the point P on the curve is a. The tangent and the normal to C are drawn at P. The tangent cuts the x-axis at the point A and the normal cuts the x-axis at the point B.

   (a) Show that the area of $\triangle APB$ is

   $$\frac{1}{2}[f(a)]^2\left(\frac{[f'(a)]^2 + 1}{f'(a)}\right)$$ (8)

   (b) Given that $f(x) = e^{5x}$ and the area of $\triangle APB$ is e^{5a}, find and simplify the exact value of a. (4)

■ **Figure 13.2** Example of an AEA mathematics question
Source: Edexcel

INSTITUTIONS CATERING FOR POST-16 STUDENTS

In general, post-16 students can pursue their studies in three types of institution:

■ 11–18 schools, either in the state or independent sector;
■ sixth-form colleges;
■ colleges of further education (FE).

The first two cater mainly for students wishing to take general academic qualifications, while colleges of FE offer a wider range of vocationally related and occupational qualifications together with some general qualifications. Most students at 11–18 schools and sixth-form colleges will be attending full time and, although they may have part-time jobs, these will usually not be related to their studies. Colleges of further education will have similar students, as well as others who may be attending part time, with students possibly having a job related to the course they are taking, or they may be trying to gain new qualifications to allow them to change career. You may be surprised to learn that a little less than 30 per cent of all 17-year-olds in England were in full-time study in schools in 2008, whereas almost 35 per cent were in full-time study in FE and sixth-form colleges, with an additional 5.5 per cent studying part time in such colleges.

While the choice of institution will be a matter for each student, you should be able to offer advice to your pupils. Therefore, you should be aware of the breadth of courses available in mathematics and other subjects that schools and colleges offer.

Task 13.9 **The diversity of provision**

Find out about courses at your local college of further education, sixth-form college and at a school that offers post-16 mathematics. Find details from the internet or call each one and ask for details of the mathematics courses they are offering as well as their general brochure.

■ At whom does the information appear to be targeted?
■ What does each institution see as their specific strengths?
■ Compare the teaching provision at each for A-Level mathematics. How do they differ in entry requirements, teaching time, style of teaching?
■ Make a table showing the variety of courses available at each of the institutions.
■ What advice could you give to a student trying to decide where to study for A-Levels or vocationally related qualifications?
■ Look at the profile of what the mathematics department offers in each institution. Does this tell you anything about what it might be like to work within these institutions?
■ Discuss your findings with other student teachers and your mentor.

THE NATURE OF STUDENTS POST-16

When teaching post-16 in any institution, your students may range in age from 17 to 77! (particularly if you are teaching in an FE college) and will expect to be treated as adults. (This is why we have used the term 'student' throughout this chapter in contrast to 'pupil', which is used elsewhere in this book.) Many of the approaches you use to teach certain topics and the classroom strategies you use with younger students may be inappropriate with these more mature students. You will have to develop additional pedagogic content knowledge in the area of *knowledge of content and students*. For example, one of the most difficult tasks in teaching in this sector is to encourage your students to take responsibility for their own learning. Students who have just left school, in particular, will probably be used to having their learning planned for them and they will be used to a teacher directing them closely – many will want to continue in this way. It is vital, however, that your students are helped to set goals and timetables for their own learning. The dividing line between this minimal guiding and leaving them to drift along is a very fine one.

Modular courses may help to overcome some difficulties by allowing the results from early modules to provide feedback and motivation. The student who has failed to plan successfully for the first module exam can learn from his or her mistakes and hopefully improve before too much harm is done. However, modular courses also have the drawback that some students rely on the fact that exams can be repeated, and hence fall further and further behind. This can distort your teaching programme, as these students will expect to receive help on earlier modules that others have passed.

The first few weeks in an FE or sixth-form college can be extremely demanding for both you and your students. They are likely to have come from a wide range of backgrounds and schools, and your first task will be to make sure that you do not start teaching at a totally inappropriate level, whatever the course.

A-Level mathematics is a difficult course for many students and the drop-out rate in the first few weeks from this and other post-16 mathematics courses is often high. Your A-Level students may range from those with a grade C at GCSE to those with a grade A*. The difference in content previously covered by these two groups is potentially large and the confidence of students will probably also vary considerably. It is likely that you will find that your students' mastery of algebra is very variable, and consequently it may be tempting to start the A-Level course with a few weeks of solid algebraic techniques. However, you should think very carefully before embarking on such a programme. You need to consider carefully how to merge the learning of new and interesting mathematics with the revision of the techniques that your students should have already mastered. The idea is to ensure that your students are motivated by learning something new and do not lose confidence by constantly being faced with ideas that they found difficult at GCSE.

One way to do this may be by running two modules at the same time, one pure and one applied, giving students the opportunity to develop algebraic skills relatively slowly in each module. Equally, you must not allow those students who have already covered much of the early work to become bored, perhaps encouraging such students to study for an AS Level in further mathematics.

TEACHING STYLES

Teaching post-16 students rather than younger pupils will not reduce the need for careful lesson planning. Sometimes college timetables are organised so that your teaching will occur in large chunks. It is quite common to find a session of two-and-a-half hours for a mathematics class. This means that you may only see your group once or twice a week, so a badly planned lesson can mean that a week's teaching has vanished unprofitably.

As well as considering the content you will include in lessons, you need to consider teaching and learning styles. While whole-class teaching is often appropriate post-16, it must not be taken to mean a diet of lecturing from the front. Such lecturing may enable you to get through the material, but it may be at the expense of students' understanding. The principles discussed in Chapter 4 are still relevant here and it is desirable to use a variety of teaching styles: teaching from the front, teacher-led discussion, group work, example and practice, practical work, investigations, and so on. However, you need to integrate these techniques carefully if they are to be effective.

It is worth considering the following extract from an Ofsted (2006) report that evaluated mathematics provision for 14–19-year-olds. It points to factors that acted against high achievement:

> Many teachers had a good personal knowledge of mathematical techniques but a restricted range of teaching strategies: demonstration, followed by practice of standard procedures, predominated. The teachers were effective in showing students what to do but mathematics became an apparently endless series of algorithms for them rather than a coherent and interconnected body of knowledge. The result was that lessons did not develop sufficiently the students' ability to reason and discover solutions for themselves. (para. 19)

You may also like to think carefully about the following extracts from a range of Ofsted reports of mathematics departments in schools and colleges highlighting good practice in post-16 mathematics teaching. Consider how recent practice in post-16 teaching of mathematics you have observed corresponds with what is highlighted here.

■ Staff working together as a team have designed a well-structured package of informative handouts and assignments. Homework is set regularly and marked promptly and thoroughly. Teachers provide clear, accurate and energetic exposition of mathematical theory. Students make effective use of graphic calculators to explore the behaviour of mathematical functions. They undertake investigations and work well in groups. In all the lessons seen, there was an excellent working relationship between staff and students.

■ In mechanics, the study of theory is well supported by practical experiment ensuring students develop a good conceptual understanding.

■ Students work well in small groups. Sometimes, they present each group's solutions to problems to the rest of the class.

■ In the best lessons, teachers share the objectives of the lessons with students, who know exactly what they have to do, and work well individually or together on difficult tasks.

■ Some teachers, particularly in lessons for adults, are adept at managing lesson time well, ensure a 'crisp' start to lessons and enable all students to make appropriate progress.

One way of engaging students with the mathematics they need to learn is to use tasks that they can work on together. A good starting place to consider how you might do this in post-16 teaching is the resource *Improving Learning in Mathematics*, which was developed to support better approaches to teaching and learning in the post-16 sector. This multimedia resource builds on successful practice to explore more active ways of learning that involve group work, discussion and open questioning so that learners gain in confidence and learn to think mathematically. The task below will give you a flavour of what the resource offers and Malcolm Swan's (2006) book, *Collaborative Learning in Mathematics: A Challenge to Our Beliefs and Practices,* explains the research and design principles that informed the design of the materials and the approaches they hope to promote.

Task 13.10 **Supporting group work at A-Level**

Look at the task sheet in Appendix 6. This is just part of an activity supplied in the resource *Improving Learning in Mathematics* (you can find out more about this at the National Centre for Excellence in Teaching Mathematics [NCETM] website: https://www.ncetm.org.uk/resources/1442

Work with a group of fellow students to complete the task.

As a group consider all the mathematics you were required to use – make some brief notes of the mathematical understanding that was required.

Discuss the advantages and disadvantages of using such a task compared with working through a practice exercise from a textbook.

Reflect on how the use of such tasks require you to develop your knowledge for teaching. Share your thoughts as a group.

PREPARING TO TEACH A TOPIC

Almost every post-16 student you will teach will be working towards an examination that is important to them. It is likely that you will be following a scheme of work that has been developed very carefully to ensure that students will have access to all of the material they need to cover in preparation for this examination. You will need to work with this scheme of work, together with the subject specification, the recommended text and other resources to prepare for your lessons. Before you start to teach the course, look through the specification and highlight any areas where you are unsure of the mathematics.

Work through the relevant examples and exercises in the textbook. It is important that you do this. Remember that textbooks are notorious for mistakes in their answers, and it can be dispiriting to get a different answer from the one in the back of the book, whether you are a student or a teacher. Highlight those areas that you think are not well explained. Get help from a fellow teacher if you need to, but remember to make notes on what problems you had and how the answers were explained to you. Once you have dealt with the areas of mathematics that you are unsure of, you can start to prepare to teach effectively.

Write down the content that you need to cover in each lesson. Look for links with content that students have already mastered. Helping your students see their mathematical knowledge as a coherent whole, rather than them learning it as a series of unrelated topics, will enable them to become more confident. One way you might go about organising your teaching of a lesson (or sequence of lessons) is to consider what a student needs to *know*, what *skills* they need and what mathematical concepts they need to *understand*, in order to be able to answer the questions or engage in the activities you will ask them to do. Having a clear view of the *knowledge*, *skills* and *understanding* you are asking of students should assist you when you come to think through the structure of your lessons and the learning tasks you use. Figure 13.3 gives an example of the type of analysis you might carry out.

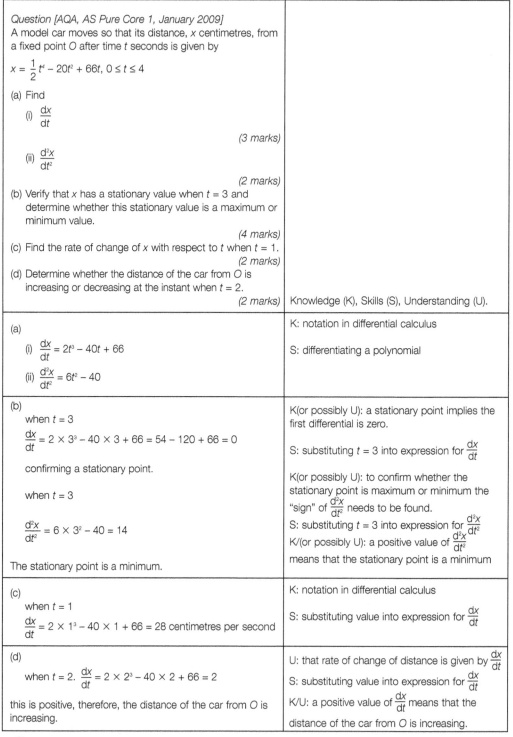

	Knowledge (K), Skills (S), Understanding (U).

Question [AQA, AS Pure Core 1, January 2009]
A model car moves so that its distance, x centimetres, from a fixed point O after time t seconds is given by
 	
$x = \frac{1}{2}t^4 - 20t^2 + 66t,\ 0 \le t \le 4$
 	
(a) Find
   (i) $\frac{dx}{dt}$
                               (3 marks)
   (ii) $\frac{d^2x}{dt^2}$
                               (2 marks)
(b) Verify that x has a stationary value when $t = 3$ and determine whether this stationary value is a maximum or minimum value.
                               (4 marks)
(c) Find the rate of change of x with respect to t when $t = 1$.
                               (2 marks)
(d) Determine whether the distance of the car from O is increasing or decreasing at the instant when $t = 2$.
                               (2 marks)	

(a)
 	
   (i) $\frac{dx}{dt} = 2t^3 - 40t + 66$
 	
   (ii) $\frac{d^2x}{dt^2} = 6t^2 - 40$
	K: notation in differential calculus
	
	S: differentiating a polynomial

(b)
   when $t = 3$
 	
   $\frac{dx}{dt} = 2 \times 3^3 - 40 \times 3 + 66 = 54 - 120 + 66 = 0$
 	
   confirming a stationary point.
 	
   when $t = 3$
 	
   $\frac{d^2x}{dt^2} = 6 \times 3^2 - 40 = 14$
 	
   The stationary point is a minimum.
	K(or possibly U): a stationary point implies the first differential is zero.
	
	S: substituting $t = 3$ into expression for $\frac{dx}{dt}$
	
	K(or possibly U): to confirm whether the stationary point is maximum or minimum the "sign" of $\frac{d^2x}{dt^2}$ needs to be found.
	S: substituting $t = 3$ into expression for $\frac{d^2x}{dt^2}$
	K/(or possibly U): a positive value of $\frac{d^2x}{dt^2}$ means that the stationary point is a minimum

(c)
   when $t = 1$
 	
   $\frac{dx}{dt} = 2 \times 1^3 - 40 \times 1 + 66 = 28$ centimetres per second
	K: notation in differential calculus
	
	S: substituting value into expression for $\frac{dx}{dt}$

(d)
   when $t = 2$. $\frac{dx}{dt} = 2 \times 2^3 - 40 \times 2 + 66 = 2$
 	
   this is positive, therefore, the distance of the car from O is increasing.
	U: that rate of change of distance is given by $\frac{dx}{dt}$
	S: substituting value into expression for $\frac{dx}{dt}$
	K/U: a positive value of $\frac{dx}{dt}$ means that the distance of the car from O is increasing.

▨ **Figure 13.3** Knowledge, skills and understanding required to solve an AS Level question
Source: Edexcel AS Level Pure 1 paper (June, 2001)

Analysing the knowledge, skills and understanding required of your students in this way allows you to identify what you have to teach. Your task now is to develop your lessons in a way that will allow students to learn all these things. Perhaps the most difficult problem is to devise engaging lessons that focus on understanding: how, for example, do you support students developing a graphical visualisation of quadratic functions that is related to significant features, such as maximum/minimum points and roots? One way is to devise tasks that students explore using technology (see the next section and Task 13.12).

Task 13.11 **Five-minute explanations**

Prepare a five-minute *explanation* of each of these key 'facts' of A-Level mathematics:

- a quadratic $ax^2 + bx + c = 0$ can have no, one, or two real roots;
- the 'completed square' form of a quadratic function can be used to find the coordinates of its maximum or minimum point;
- the derivative of a function gives its gradient;
- integration evaluates the area 'under' the graph of a function;
- turning points of functions can be found where their derivatives are zero;
- at a local maximum point, the second derivative of a function is negative;
- the nature of the geometric transformation of the graph of $y = f(x)$ produced by $y = af(x)$ and $y = f(ax)$;
- the laws of logarithms.

Try out your explanations either with some AS/A-Level students or other student teachers. Reflect carefully on your, and their, experience.

THE USE OF ICT IN POST-16 MATHEMATICS

One question that always seems to arouse a great deal of controversy is to what extent students should be allowed to use calculators and computer software in mathematics (see also Chapter 9 and Johnston-Wilder and Pimm, 2004). In many courses, your students will be expected to be able to use such technology effectively and to decide whether its use is appropriate or not. They will also have to develop strategies to cope when such technology is not available.

You might like to consider where you stand in relation to this question by considering some of the uses to which graphic calculators may be put. Before you make up your mind, consider some of the uses highlighted in Figure 13.4.

You may have already used graphic calculators with pupils at Key Stages 3 or 4. However, the powerful facilities of the graphic calculator are particularly suited to mathematics at Advanced level. Not only do they allow you to carry out complex calculations, as illustrated in Figure 13.4, but they also allow students to have another way available for developing important mathematical concepts. To gain some understanding of this, carry out the next task.

Evaluating derived functions Here finding $\dfrac{dy}{dx}$ at $x = 1$, where $y = 12x^2$. This can be evaluated using a single command or, alternatively, first shown graphically and then found.	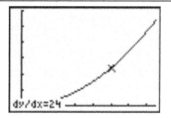
Evaluating definite integrals Here $\int_{3}^{5} x^3 \, dx$ is evaluated using a single command. Alternatively, $y = x^3$ is graphed and then $\int_{0}^{5} x^3 \, dx$ is evaluated and shown graphically.	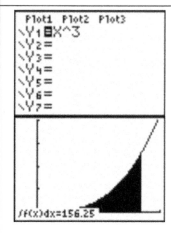
Calculating probabilities associated with the normal distribution Here the probability that a ten-year-old boy has a height less than 150 cm is calculated assuming that the height of the population is normally distributed with mean 141.8 cm and standard deviation 5.51 cm.	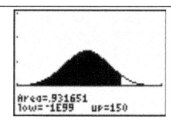

▪ **Figure 13.4** Some uses of graphic calculators at Advanced level

---

Task 13.12 **Exploring advanced mathematics with a graphic calculator**

The aim of this task is to provide you with an opportunity to explore some of the facilities of a graphic calculator, while thinking about how you might use one in your teaching of a mathematical topic at AS/A-Level.

You will need a graphic calculator. Although there is a wide range of graphic calculators available, each having a somewhat different way of operating, they all allow you to perform a similar range of operations, such as plotting graphs, tracing along functions or zooming in on a significant feature of the graph of a function.

Explore how you can consider a function as transformation of the basic function of its type. For example, how can $g(x) = (x + 1)^2 + 2$ be considered as a translation of the function $f(x) = x^2$?

Do this systematically by considering how:

■ f(x) + a is related to f(x);
■ f(x + a) is related to f(x);
■ af(x) is related to f(x);
■ f(ax) is related to f(x).

Use a function such as f(x) = x² or f(x) = 2x. Systematically vary the value of a (e.g. take a = 1, 2, 3, etc.). The series of graphic calculator screen shots in Figure 13.5 suggest how you might go about doing this.

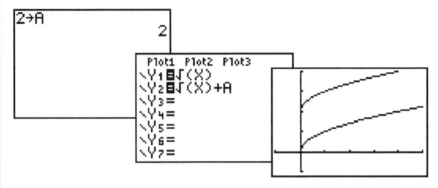

■ **Figure 13.5** Exploring transformations of functions using a graphic calculator

The variety of different types of calculator your students bring to your class may cause problems when you want to make use of this technology in your teaching. You need to be familiar with the kinds of facilities available on a graphic calculator and to think about their role in teaching.

There are also, of course, many powerful software packages that can be used to do mathematics: a challenge for you is to use them effectively in your teaching, particularly to assist students in their development of important concepts. For example, you may like to consider your own understanding of differentiation. Now take a careful look at the two diagrams in Figure 13.6. These have been developed using the powerful, graph-plotting package *Autograph.*

The first of these shows a graph of the function f(x) = sin(x). The package can be set up to draw this function slowly, so that students can see y being plotted as x increases. This is perhaps much more effective than drawing the graph so quickly that it appears as a ready-made picture. The next screen shows how a tangent is dynamically drawn at 'each' point of the function and the value of its gradient plotted giving rise to 'the gradient function' or derived function. Again, the package plots this slowly, so students can appreciate what is happening. The plotting can be paused where the gradient is zero and you can use this to highlight the relationship between significant features of a function and its derivative.

It is perhaps impossible here to give you a sense of the potential power of such software used as a tool for teaching and learning. You really need to try the software for

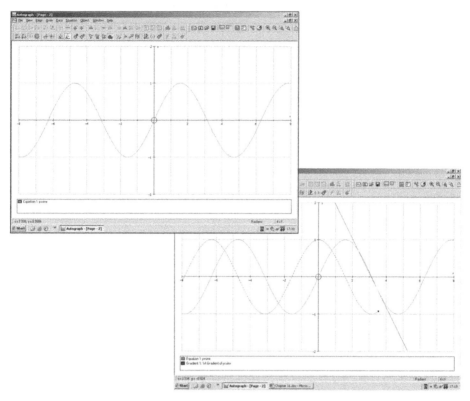

■ **Figure 13.6** Exploring the gradient function of $y = \sin(x)$ using *Autograph*

yourself to gain an appreciation of the full potential that it offers. You may be surprised to learn that such ideas and uses of technology in mathematics were first promoted only in the early to mid-1980s (by David Tall).

REFLECTING ON THE PAST: LOOKING TO THE FUTURE?

In reading this chapter, you have probably realised that little seems fixed for very long in the post-16 sector. On a number of occasions throughout the chapter, the phrase 'at the time of writing' has been used and it has been suggested that by the time you read the chapter the situation is likely to have changed. Even the detailed structure of GCSEs and A-Levels were unsettled when the chapter was written, and these are possibly the most settled of all parts of the English education system. Much less well established are vocationally related qualifications, and over the past 20 years or so these seem to have undergone a constant process of change. What does seem certain, however, is that mathematics will continue to play an important role in the education of many, if not all, in the post-16 sector, allowing the potential for a range of different and challenging teaching roles for mathematics specialists.

In the Smith Inquiry report (DfES, 2004a), there was recognition that the available qualifications, curriculum and assessment structures that then existed did not provide suitable pathways for students, and different alternatives were discussed and have subsequently been explored. Fundamental to this debate is the question of whether there should be a single pathway that students follow at different rates, or whether there could or should be a number of different pathways that vary in content, level of difficulty and level of abstraction of the mathematics studied. The former approach meets demands for equity, that all students should have equal access to all mathematics, whereas the latter route recognises the likelihood of students having different needs and suggests that their experience of mathematics could be tailored (or restricted) to their needs.

This is a question that has been exercising the minds of those responsible for the design of curriculum structures and qualifications in the period following the Smith report, but is also one that curriculum managers in schools and colleges have to tackle when deciding how to organise provision for the students they recruit. Task 13.13 provides an opportunity for you to consider some of these issues and where you stand on them in more detail. In doing so, you will be prompted to think back to your own, specific, experience of mathematics education, in order to consider the expanded view you will be developing as you work towards entering the teaching profession and think about the future shape of mathematics education for post-16 students.

Task 13.13 **A new mathematics curriculum**

In this task, you are asked to consider pathways models that might provide a suitable mathematics curriculum for post-14 students.

You will need a copy of the Smith report, and you should read the end of Chapter 4 (paras 4.42–4.62 inclusive). This will allow you to have an overview of some possible models for different pathways that students could follow in mathematics. In the light of your reading and your developing knowledge of the current 14–19 qualifications in mathematics, consider the following questions:

■ Where do you stand on whether there should be a single or multiple pathways to study mathematics post-14? How do you justify your position?

■ What would you include in a course entitled 'Mathematical literacy' at each level?

■ Which of the models presented as illustrative and for discussion in the report would allow teachers to be most innovative in developing their teaching and learning? Why do you believe this to be the case?

■ Which model best caters for the mathematically most able and which for the mathematically least able?

■ Can each of the models satisfy the general principles (identified in paragraph 4.43) to which they should conform?

How does the emerging curriculum structure support (or not) your thinking about pathways? If possible, discuss your thinking within a group including other student teachers and your mentor.

Finally, to conclude the chapter, two tasks are proposed to prompt you to explore some of the issues that underpin what has been discussed here in greater depth. The first of these is far removed from your personal involvement, something which is considered in detail in the second.

The first of these final tasks suggests that you question who controls the curriculum that you have been considering. The same question, of course, can be asked of the National Curriculum. Where does the National Curriculum come from? Why is it the way it is?

The second task returns to the framework that was introduced at the beginning of the chapter to structure the knowledge required for teaching mathematics. This framework and the different sub-domains have been referred to at various points throughout the chapter and, as a final conclusion to the chapter, you are asked to reflect on the knowledge that you require to develop to become a teacher of mathematics for post-16 students.

Task 13.14 **Whose mathematics is it anyway?**

This chapter has introduced many issues in relation to the structure of mathematics education provision for post-16 students. How has this structure been determined? Because mathematics has a special role to play as both a discipline worthy of study in its own right and a support of other disciplines across the sciences and social sciences, there are many stakeholders or interest groups who want to have a say, if not control, the structure and nature of the mathematics we teach and which students learn.

Ernest (2000), in a discussion of different interest groups' attempts to influence the introduction of the National Curriculum, identified five categories (expanding and renaming some of the four discussed in Chapter 1 of this book):

1   **Industrial trainers**: requiring basic mathematical skills and numeracy;
2   **Technological pragmatists**: requiring basic skills and learning to solve practical problems with mathematics;
3   **Old humanist mathematicians**: requiring understanding and capability in advanced mathematics, with some appreciation of mathematics;
4   **Progressive educators**: requiring confidence building, creativity and self-expression through mathematics;
5   **Public educators**: requiring empowerment of learners as critical and mathematically literate citizens in society.

Ernest suggested that the first three groups managed to shape the emerging definition of school mathematics, with the fourth group having to be satisfied with the inclusion of the 'using and applying' strand, which has struggled until recently to establish its place in the classroom.

Use the Ernest article and the interest groups he identifies with the emerging picture of mathematics post-16 to analyse who has been able to exercise influence and control over the curriculum. You may want to read literature in relation to policy and systemic change more widely. Ernest, P. (2000) 'Why teach mathematics?', in White, J. and Bramall, S. (eds), *Why Learn Maths?* London University Institute of Education, pp. 1–14. Available at: http://people.exeter.ac.uk/PErnest/why.htm

Task 13.15 **Developing knowledge for teaching**

This chapter has introduced an empirically derived framework based on observation of teacher practice in classrooms that identifies sub-categories of knowledge for teaching mathematics. This framework expands in some detail Shulman's idea of pedagogic content knowledge, identifying various categories of knowledge that teachers are observed to draw upon in their classroom interactions with students.

Read fully the paper by Ball *et al.* (2008) and reflect on the extent to which this allows you to bring some structure to identify your own needs in relation to teaching mathematics post-16.

Video the teaching of a post-16 mathematics lesson. This could be of any group of students in relation to any post-16 mathematics qualification. Ideally, you may wish to work with videos of more than one lesson with students on different courses.

Analyse the lesson(s) using the Ball *et al.* framework. Are there categories of teacher knowledge that you can observe (either explicitly or implicitly) that are not accounted for by the framework? You may wish to inform your thinking by reading about teacher knowledge more widely.

SUMMARY AND KEY POINTS

The role of the mathematics teacher of post-16 students is complex:

■ you will need to be aware of the wide range of possibilities open to students in their studies and the various mathematics courses that they can follow;
■ you will have to be confident with a wide variety of mathematical content ranging from basic numeracy to advanced mathematical concepts;
■ students come from very diverse backgrounds and past experiences;
■ you will need to consider how you can use a wide range of teaching styles to ensure students engage fully with their mathematics;
■ incorporating the technology of graphic calculators and computers in your teaching and student learning will likely provide you with a challenge;
■ changes are likely, both in the near future and long term, to post-16 qualifications in general and to mathematics qualifications and courses in particular.

While you will have to work within all these constraints and challenges and have a complete mastery of the mathematics needed, the experience can be particularly rewarding.

FURTHER READING

Ball, D., Thames, M. and Phelps, G. (2008) 'Content knowledge for teaching: what makes it special?'. *Journal of Teacher Education* **59(5)**, 389–407.
This paper explores knowledge for teaching and has been used to set a framework around which you might structure your understanding of what you might be expected to know to become a successful teacher of post-16 students. It builds on the seminal work of Lee Shulman who first explored pedagogic content knowledge.

DfES (2004) *Making Mathematics Count*. London: HMSO.

This major report (the Smith report) into the teaching of mathematics post-14 is essential reading for mathematics teachers who wish to be well-informed about the full range of issues pertinent to their teaching of this age group. Chapter 3 is particularly useful for student teachers wishing to have a complete overview of mathematics qualifications available to post-16 students. The report is available from the DfES and from the following website: www.mathsinquiry.org.uk/report/index.html

Ernest, P. (2000) 'Why teach mathematics?', in White, J. and Bramall, S. (eds) *Why Learn Maths?* London University Institute of Education, pp. 1–14. (Available online at http://people.exeter.ac.uk/PErnest/why.htm)

In this chapter, Paul Ernest explored some underlying issues of importance to the design of the National Curriculum by considering why we should teach mathematics. As part of his reflections, he considers who controls the curriculum, thereby giving some insight into why it is the way it is.

Noyes, A. (2009) 'Participation in mathematics: what is the problem?'. *Improving Schools*, 12(3), 277–288.

This article deals with participation in post-compulsory mathematics education and the author argues that 'the central problem is neither that of devising an economically motivated strategy for increasing student numbers nor simply raising the level of mathematical capability attained. Rather, the central problem is about *what* mathematics to teach, *how* and *why*?'.

Tikly, C. and Wolf, A. (2000) *The Maths We Need Now: Demands, Deficits and Remedies*. University of London Institute of Education.

This readable collection of papers contains a number of chapters (e.g. 1, 2, 3, 4 and 5) that are pertinent to understanding some of the issues relevant to mathematics teachers who teach post-16 students. Issues raised include how we do not prepare students adequately in the UK, in terms of their mathematics education, for study in higher education.

PROFESSIONAL DEVELOPMENT

Gill Hatch and Clare Lee

INTRODUCTION

Initial training for teaching is the beginning of a process of lifelong learning. Successful teachers of secondary mathematics develop and adapt their practice both in the context within which they operate, with regard to their own growing knowledge, and of an awareness of what mathematics can most usefully be taught and how pupils learn mathematics. Professional development as a teacher starts from the moment you start thinking about entering the profession. Getting a post at a school where you are going to be actively encouraged to make use of your strengths and which will help you develop other areas of your practice is the next step in the process.

Classroom teaching used to be quite an isolated activity, with professional development manifested by a course provided by an external organisation, for example the local authority. Nowadays, there is a much greater recognition of the potential for professional development that comes about through contact with other teachers and their experiences, for example an Advanced Skills Teacher or colleagues in your own department. Many schools have recognised the value of working together to develop practice through coaching or mentoring schemes. Much can also be gained indirectly through reading what other teachers have written in professional journals, e.g. *Mathematics Teaching* (from the ATM) or *Mathematics in School* (from the MA), or through videotapes of practice, both informal in school and more formal, through, for example, the NCETM or *Teachers TV*. Working with other teachers will enable you to gain new ideas and insights and also to obtain personal support and sympathetic, yet constructively critical, feedback.

The purpose of this chapter is to help you to find effective sources for support at the beginning of your teaching career and to identify your particular needs for further professional development and how you might satisfy them as your career progresses.

OBJECTIVES

By the end of this chapter you should:

- be aware of the particular strengths you offer to a school and a department, as well as your priorities for early professional development;
- be able to make use of this awareness in identifying and applying for suitable posts;

■ be ready to take advantage of the induction opportunities in your first post;

■ be aware of a range of sources for continuing professional development including coaching and mentoring.

FINDING THE RIGHT POST

Your development as a mathematics teacher will get off to the best start if you become part of a supportive department in a post whose demands are well-matched to your own existing qualities as a teacher, but is one which, nevertheless, offers challenges and opportunities for gaining new competence.

When thinking about applying for a post, it is a good idea to first think about what you bring to the profession of teaching mathematics. There is an increasing trend for posts available in September to be advertised as early as January, as it can be problematic for schools to secure a full quota of mathematics teachers in some areas. Therefore, you may find yourself trying to complete an application form before you have completed even half of your course. This can be difficult, but remembering why you decided to train as teacher will help you, as well as thinking about lessons you have taught that went well and why you enjoyed them. Remember, you will have many strengths to bring to teaching, so make sure that you record them on your application form. It may be worth accessing the Career Entry and Development Profile (CEDP) pack produced by the TDA (Training and Development Agency for Schools; www.tda.gov.uk/, still available at the time of writing) and complete a career entry profile. Filling in the CEDP means that you will have to ask yourself the kinds of questions that you will need to answer on an actual job application form.

Before you apply for any posts, consider what type of schools and mathematics departments you might be suited to and, most importantly, wish to teach in. Schools that cater for secondary pupils vary in many ways; some obvious, others less so. You will have got to know quite a lot about the particular schools in which you have trained, but how much do you know about other secondary schools in the neighbourhood and in other parts of the country? What features are you looking for in your first teaching position? Would you like it to be similar to your training school or are you looking for different challenges and opportunities?

It is easy to find out factual information about schools, such as the number on the roll, the age range catered for, whether the school has a sixth form, whether it is mixed- or single-sex, comprehensive or selective, religious or secular, rural, suburban or inner-city. Some of these aspects may be important to you, others may be immaterial; you will need to think about whether there is a particular characteristic that appeals to you strongly or one which you wish to avoid.

Possibly even more important than any of the above, however, is the ethos of the school and, in particular, of the mathematics department. Whilst you may get clues about ethos from hearsay reports or reading the school prospectus or website, you can only really find out about it by spending time in the department, talking with and observing teachers and pupils, separately and together. It is important to discover school policy on interpersonal issues: for example, equal opportunities, bullying or partnership with parents, and how such policies are implemented in practice. What does the mathematics department state as its aims and how do members of the mathematics department view these aims? What approaches are used in teaching mathematics and what resources are available? What is the department's attitude to using Information Technology and how does that align with yours? What sort of atmosphere prevails in the classes and how do pupils respond to what is on offer? What provision is made for professional development of staff?

You will only get answers to these questions when you visit the school. Consequently, if the school offers the opportunity of an informal visit prior to the interview, it would be a good idea to take up that offer. However, do not forget that, even though the visit is informal, it provides a chance to make an impression. Therefore, if you like the school, you will want the impression you make to be a good one.

Task 14.1 **Characteristics of teaching posts**

Make a list of the characteristics that a mathematics teaching post might have. You might do this in three columns, according to characteristics you regard as essential in the post you hope for, those characteristics that you feel are desirable and those that would be counter-indications for you.

Compare your list with your own strengths as a teacher and see if you want to modify your aspirations and, hence, aspects of your list.

Obviously, you will need to spend time on your application, as this is where you make the first impression on a school and its staff and governors. A well-presented letter, which shows how you meet the essential and desirable aspects of the post as specified in the application details, along with some examples to back up the statements, will be your best route to gaining an interview. A clear, well-laid-out curriculum vitae (CV) will also help the school assess if you are the person they wish to interview. Equally, a scruffy letter or application form accompanied by an out-of-date CV will create a bad impression and may well filter you out of the selection process. Schools may ask that letters are handwritten, although they will normally accept a word-processed letter. CVs must always be word-processed, which also means that you can easily keep your CV up-to-date. Many schools and local authorities now encourage you to apply online or at least provide electronic application forms that you can fill in clearly and carefully. When using online forms, do not forget to check spelling and punctuation carefully, as many templates do not automatically 'spellcheck'. Hence mistakes can be missed. It is just as important to present yourself as well as possible in an online form as it is when sending in an application form accompanied by a well-presented covering letter and CV.

As you compose your application, consider what a school is likely to want to know about you. This will be a two-way process; you will want to know about the school and department ethos and the school will want to know how well you will fit into *their* community. The school will be interested in your personal qualities and your attitudes and approaches to mathematics teaching. It is important to be honest, but you will have many good qualities, so make sure that you highlight them. At an interview, you may be asked questions that encourage you to demonstrate your personal qualities, in order to allow you to make them evident. For example, a popular interview question is to invite you to describe two mathematics lessons you have given, one of which went well and one which did not work out as you had planned, and then to give an account of what you learned from *each* of these situations. It pays to think ahead and to anticipate how you would answer such a question. You can also expect to be asked questions about some aspect of recent government educational initiatives. There will also, of course, be many questions about your specific background and experience and how it relates to the post they are advertising. Would you, for example, be able to undertake A-Level teaching or work with children with particular special educational needs? Are you familiar with a particular software package? Any such matters should be indicated on your CV and it is reasonable to refer to this in an interview, but also to take the opportunity to elaborate on your experience and interests.

Once you have prepared your CV, you will be ready to begin searching for a suitable post. The major source of advertisements for teaching posts is still the national press, notably the *Times Educational Supplement* and the education section in *The Guardian*. However, there are many online sources, in particular the online job sections for the two newspapers previously mentioned. If you are interested in a particular school, or you are limited to specific geographical areas, it is worth looking at the school or local authority's website. Schools will often notify Higher Education Institutions in their area when they have vacancies, so make sure you know where these are posted in your institution. Many websites will allow you to sign up for e-mail alerts when positions matching your specification become available, which can help make sure that you do not miss that ideal job.

Once you have found an advertisement for a post that seems to be suitable for you, and submitted an application that has gained you a place on the shortlist, the next stage is the actual interview. As well as the mental preparation that you went through as you compiled your application, it can be very helpful to try out your interview skills on a critical friend. Consider who might help you to rehearse likely scenarios and who will give you honest criticism and constructive advice. If you find a friend who is willing to help, arrange a time and place where you can have your practice interview undisturbed, and let your mock interviewer be the first to know the outcome of the real thing, especially if it is a cause for celebration. Do not to be too downhearted if you are not offered a post; schools are looking for a particular set of characteristics, some of which will not appear on the advertisement. They are developing their own team and if someone else seems to them to fit in better, then that person is more likely to get the post. It is worth thinking through your performance at interview and trying to improve the way you presented yourself and the way you answered the questions. But sometimes it is just the case that someone else fitted in more with their ideas or requirements.

THE FIRST YEAR OF TEACHING

Some of the main influences on the way you teach mathematics, especially at the beginning of your career, are the people you have seen teaching. This includes teachers who have taught you mathematics in the past, as well as people you have worked with recently. You may be unaware of the most positive influences, precisely because when you witnessed them your attention was on the mathematics not the person, whereas you may have vivid recollections of practice you definitely do not wish to emulate. When you are about to take the first step of your career as a mathematics teacher, it is a good moment to reflect on the kind of mathematics teacher you want to be and to decide to work on this vision from the beginning.

Task 14.2 **Significant memories**

Think about salient moments from your own experience of mathematics teaching – as learner, observer or teacher. Returning to what you wrote in response to the first task of Chapter 1 might prove interesting here. Recall a teacher who made a vivid impression on you. Try to describe an incident that captures what you remember. Reflect and analyse what it was about the actions of the teacher that made the impression so vivid.

Now picture yourself acting as teacher to someone working on some mathematics where you were surprised, pleasantly or unpleasantly, by the result. Reflect on what caused the surprise.

Now consider what sort of teacher you want to be. Use both of the above incidents and your other experiences to help you decide how you want to act towards learners and the way that you want to present mathematics. Write a letter to yourself to open at the end of your first year of teaching, to help you keep to your ideals and principles.

Support during your NQT year

As part of your teaching practice, you will have had someone who was appointed as your mentor. In your first year as a newly qualified teacher (NQT), there are usually opportunities for the mentoring process to continue as you work together on your Career Entry and Development Profile. Making the most of this opportunity will help you to develop more quickly as an effective teacher. Therefore, it is a good idea to ask who will be acting as your mentor when you visit the school. It is best if this person is not your head of department; it could even be someone from a different department in a small school. The object of appointing a mentor is to make sure that there is someone who has a supportive and challenging role but does not have line-management responsibilities for you. The mentoring relationship is changed if the person is also required to make formal reports on or judgements about your work. Having a mentor who is not your head of department will probably mean that you have two people to go to for help and support and who are challenging you to be the best you can be. Having a mentor who is not your head of department will also mean that you know who to go to if issues occur with either person.

Setting up a mentoring contract can be useful. Although it may seem overly formal at the start of what you hope will be a friendly and supportive relationship. Setting up the type of contract set out below can help to contend with expectations on both sides. If you do not like the idea of a contract, then think about this table as 'a few questions that need answering right at the start'.

A mentoring contract

Your local authority (LA) will have a policy and framework that you can take advantage of for supporting NQTs; this often includes a series of meetings for all new teachers in your area. If your first post is in an LA school, you will have automatic access to this programme and will receive information about it. The school itself will almost certainly

▪ **Table 14.1** A mentoring contract

Decision	Possible answers might be …	Comment
The purpose of the mentoring?	To provide support and challenge during your first year as a teacher or in a new school.	It is vital to discuss what exactly the purpose of the contract is. Mentoring should be more than having a nice little chat from time to time.
What kinds of support and challenge does the mentor expect to give?	Keeping an eye on events that are coming up and helping prepare you for them, e.g. parents evenings, activity week. Someone who is not your line manager with whom you can discuss any issues or ideas. Someone who can observe your lessons and can highlight what you are doing well and offer general ideas and specific suggestions for development. Help with identifying CPD needs and accessing provision, especially request for cover forms.	The next two questions are important – by setting out expectations, both the mentor's and yours, you begin to see how you can work together profitably. The contract should be mutually beneficial. A new teacher will gain a great deal from interacting with someone more experienced in the school or department. The more experienced colleague gains as well; sometimes it is an affirmation that she or he has valuable knowledge to share. But sometimes colleagues see the flaws in accepted systems or ways of working because they see them through new eyes.
What do you as a new teacher expect from your mentor?	Someone to ask who explicitly says that there is no such thing as a silly question. If you need to ask something, you would like to feel comfortable in asking. Help with understanding the systems and deadlines in school, e.g. writing reports, accessing data systems. Support when things seem to be difficult. Ideas when you are tired and seem to have run out of your own. Challenge to keep you striving to be the best teacher you can be.	
How often will you meet? When and where will you meet? For how long?	Weekly after school for the first half-term and less often but regularly thereafter. Meeting in a private room not a classroom where you might be disturbed. Meeting for half an hour during first term, possibly for longer when the meetings are less frequent.	Setting out exactly where, when and how long may seem too formal. It is not. If you do not organise this, and put it in diaries, meetings may well not happen and the relationship will not build as it should. There is the potential for problems that could have been sorted out to become big issues. A private room will be important, you need to be able to talk about whatever is on your mind.

■ **Table 14.1** continued

Decision	Possible answers might be ...	Comment
Who will be responsible for scheduling our meetings?	The mentor – but open to requests.	
What will be the ground rules for your discussions?	Confidentiality, openness, candour, truthfulness, etc.	
If problems arise, how will they be resolved?	The head of department sets up the mentoring partnership, so any problems within it can be referred to her by either party.	You hope you will get on well with your mentor. but if you do not, for whatever reason, you must know whom to talk to.
Initial focus of meetings:	• the school behaviour policy and implementing it consistently; • using the school's IT system as part of teaching; • motivating and interesting ideas for teaching.	Set out an initial focus and revise those foci at each meeting. This allows the mentor to prepare ideas and things like system permissions. The meetings become purposeful and effective.

also have its own induction programme of meetings. Some of these meetings will be for all teachers who have recently come to the school and others will be for NQTs specifically and may include any trainee teachers who are in the school. Schools think carefully about what they want their new staff to know about the school and what ideas they want them to discuss and form a view about. Therefore, these meetings are an important part of developing as a teacher and becoming part of the community of the school.

Local higher education institutions (HEIs) also provide courses for NQTs and other practising teachers that lead to a Masters level qualification, possibly building on the credits that you gained as part of your PGCE training. These courses will offer an opportunity to meet teachers from a wide range of backgrounds and are known to add significantly to your development as a teacher.

Task 14.3 **Getting support as an NQT**

Find out what support your school or LA, Specialist Schools and Academies Trust or HEI offer for NQTs.

DEVELOPING AS A TEACHER

Teaching can be a stressful occupation. Some aspects of stress reduce with experience, while others may come about because of the need to cope with continual change. The subtitle of Guy Claxton's (1989) book, *Being a Teacher*, is 'Coping with change and stress'. In it he argues that finding one's own scope for controlling change and working on being the kind of teacher one aspires to be is an essential component of coping with stress. Although his book is addressed to all teachers, secondary teachers of mathematics will find much in it that can help them to plan and control their professional development.

Even when you no longer have the formal support of a mentor, colleagues can be a key source of support and professional development. You may be able to arrange to spend occasional lessons observing a willing colleague teach, or your department or school may encourage formal co-coaching agreements. If you want to take part in co-coaching (which is an excellent opportunity to develop your practice), it is important to agree beforehand how this will be organised and, as with the mentoring agreement detailed previously, you will want to agree on various aspects. Co-coaching implies a more equal relationship between the participants, and the object of the agreement is for both of you to develop some aspect of teaching. Therefore, an agreement should be reached about exactly what it is that you will each focus on developing. It could be something like questioning, improving the attainment of boys or using more practical ideas in teaching mathematics.

Almost certainly, you will agree to work together in planning and teaching lessons, putting into practice the ideas for change that you have decided might work. You may decide to observe one another's lessons, team-teach some of the lessons or videotape your own lessons and work together to evaluate them. Therefore, you will need to agree to spend at least three lessons on this co-coaching project and at least one of the coaching pair will need to be released from their normal lesson at some point. Consequently, before embarking on a co-coaching episode, you will need the agreement of the senior leadership team. The three lessons will likely include a planning session, the taught lesson and a further lesson to evaluate the planned lesson and to decide on what has been learned as a result of the co-coaching.

Having a critical friend is beneficial in many walks of life, and teaching is no exception. Even when no formal mentoring or co-coaching arrangement is on offer, you can seek out a colleague who is willing to be your critical friend, perhaps on a mutual basis. Such a mutual arrangement is sometimes referred to as *co-mentoring* (Jaworski and Watson, 1994). In the long term, you will probably also seek to develop what Jaworski and Watson call an 'inner mentor'.

In-service courses and events

All schools set aside some time for 'in-house' professional development. In your first post you will find out how the programme for this is organised in your school. Some of the time is likely to be spent on whole-school issues; at other times, the mathematics department will work together on issues they have identified for themselves. At first, you may wish to listen to your colleagues and discover the way in which the department works together, but be ready for the opportunity to take a more active role, perhaps by preparing and leading some aspect of a planned INSET session.

There will also be local courses and INSET sessions available for teachers from a range of schools, perhaps organised by the LA or through meetings arranged by some other agency or group: for example, your local branches of the Mathematics Association, the Association of Teachers of Mathematics, or the NCETM. It is important that any courses you take fit in with your own priorities for professional development and those for your department. Although you might see a course that really interests you, the school will only fund you to go on that course if it fits in with previously identified development plans.

Task 14.4 **Matching courses with development plans**

Obtain the school development plan and find the section that indicates the development plans for the mathematics department. Using your list from Task 14.3 and any other CPD courses you can find, for example on the NCETM website, identify those courses that develop the areas identified in the school development plans. Which of these fit in with your own plans?

Many PGCE courses now carry with them course credits at the Masters level. There is, at the time of writing, a commitment for everyone in the teaching profession to hold a Masters level qualification, and therefore many courses are being developed to allow teachers to gain this qualification. Usually, universities set a time within which existing credits must be used, but this is often up to five years, so there is no rush to take such courses. You may choose to use Masters level courses to focus on improving your knowledge about leadership or other general education issues or about mathematics education or some combination. What courses you choose will depend on your own particular interests. You may find a local institution that offers part-time or full-time higher degrees or a distance-taught course (such as those offered by the Open University) might have practical advantages, according to your situation.

Eventually, you might choose to go on for a doctorate. As well as being of intrinsic interest, a higher degree will enhance your eligibility for a variety of senior posts and you can choose the topics you work on according to your longer-term ambitions.

There are often small bursaries available for those teachers that would like collaboratively to research an area of mathematics practice. These are currently available from the NCETM. A small-scale, action-research project in collaboration with others can provide a useful way to develop professionally and can, if you choose, be linked with gaining credit for a Masters degree at a higher education institute.

Meeting other mathematics teachers

The Association of Teachers of Mathematics (ATM) and the Mathematical Association (MA) were both mentioned in Chapter 1, and various of their publications have been referred to throughout this book. Both of these associations have websites that give information about membership, local branches, publications and other activities of the association. Their website addresses are: http://www.atm.org.uk/ (ATM) and http://www.m-a.org.uk/ (MA). From the websites, you will be able to discover whether there is a local branch of one or other group in your area. Going to a local branch meeting can be a useful way of meeting other mathematics teachers as well as finding out about the services these organisations offer and seeing some of their publications before deciding whether to become a member of the national organisation. Both offer reduced subscriptions to student teachers and NQTs, so it is worthwhile investigating them as early as possible, so as to take advantage of any special offers.

Task 14.5 **Meeting other maths teachers**

Find out what local opportunities there are, both formal and informal, for associating with other teachers of mathematics and working together on issues of mutual need and interest.

Both the ATM and the MA hold their annual conferences during the Easter holidays and both hold occasional day conferences, usually on Saturdays, focused on particular issues of current concern. Again, it is worth finding out at an early stage whether there is any local funding that could provide financial support for attending such a conference.

Other organisations that hold one-day conferences in various parts of the country may also offer agendas that appeal to you. Three such are the Gender and Mathematics Association (GAMMA), the British Society for the History of Mathematics (BSHM) and the British Society for Research into Learning Mathematics (BSRLM). Contact details for these groups are given in Appendix 2.

Journals and books

The professional associations are an excellent source of publications for teachers of mathematics. Both the Association of Teachers of Mathematics and the Mathematical Association publish journals:

■   *Mathematics Teaching and Micromath* (ATM), which appears quarterly, has articles and reviews on a wide range of issues relevant to all mathematics classrooms.
■   *Mathematics in Schools* (MA) is classroom-focused and published five times a year.
■   *Mathematical Gazette* (MA) is a quarterly journal in which most articles deal directly with mathematics itself rather than the teaching of it. These can be a rich source relevant to sixth-form teaching.

Both associations have a range of other publications for teachers, including physical materials, software and posters for classrooms, as well as books and pamphlets. Reading what others, including classroom teachers, have written, trying out some of the ideas and perhaps contributing a letter of feedback to the journal are all ways of working on your own ideas about teaching and developing your 'inner mentor'. After a while this can lead to writing up your reflections on some teaching ideas or experiences of your own and submitting them to a journal.

There are a number of books about mathematics teaching available from bookshops and through libraries, some of which are single- or joint-authored, while others are edited collections of readings. Among those you may find useful as a beginning teacher are:

Backhouse *et al.* (1992), Costello (1991), Johnston-Wilder and Pimm (2004), Lee (2006), Pimm (1988), Pimm and Love (1991) or Selinger (1994). Two other books, which have been around a little longer but which have attained almost classical status as sources of teaching ideas, are *Notes on Mathematics for Children* by members of the ATM (reissued 1985) and *Starting Points* (Banwell *et al.*, 1986).

DEVELOPING AS A MATHEMATICIAN

An important way of creating a classroom atmosphere conducive to the learning of mathematics is for pupils to be taught by teachers who themselves are engaged, and are seen to be engaged, in the process of *doing* mathematics. An example of someone 'being a mathematician' helps learners to form a picture of what that means and gives them some strategies to emulate.

Some teachers choose to undertake personal study of mathematics as direct professional development. The quotation below is from the writing of a teacher who chose to do just that.

> Reflections on my own learning gradually moved away from describing the personal significance of particular incidents and started to address the question of how these events informed my understanding of the processes of learning mathematics.
>
> Although demanding, the process of trying to put mathematical ideas into words had been crucial to forming insights into ways of thinking. By listening to others, I became aware of the differences in representation and language which supported or obscured our individual understandings. I realised how much I had assumed and how little I really knew about the children I taught.
>
> (Hatch and Shiu, 1997: 167)

School-based in-service sessions devoted to doing mathematics together as a department can also be invigorating, as well as casting light on how pupils learn. A publication that is suitable for initiating mathematical activity, either by an individual or a department, is *Learning and Doing Mathematics* (Mason, 1988 – see Further Reading).

A frequent (and motivating) starting point for personal mathematical activity is the need to teach a topic for the first time or even to teach a topic you have not previously studied. Sometimes, the first stage is to find a textbook to develop your own understanding of the topic; at other times, finding a fruitful teaching approach to traditionally awkward topics is more pressing. The Centre for Mathematics Education at the Open University produces a series of booklets for teachers who wanted to *update* their own mathematics. The Project Update site (http://labspace.open.ac.uk/course/view.php?id=4780) provides free access to these materials, which offer a general way of analysing a mathematical topic before teaching it, as well as providing specific teaching ideas on the teaching of angle, ratio and probability. The companion pack, *Developing Own Thinking*, deals with some very general ideas underpinning large areas of mathematics.

Another useful book is *Adapting and Extending Secondary Mathematics Activities* (Prestage and Perks, 2001). This book looks at many ways in which standard school mathematical tasks can be modified to produce pupil tasks that are significantly more interesting and challenging. It can be very helpful when you are looking for ways to encourage your pupils to think for themselves.

Another aspect of developing as a mathematician is finding out about the different media through which a topic can be introduced – especially, perhaps, through use of calculators and computers. Visually exciting demonstrations can be found for many mathematical ideas on *Teachers TV*, *YouTube* and on the ATM website. It is worth exploring what is on offer to help you show how interesting and engaging mathematics can be. Doing some personal work on, for example, graphic calculators (see Galpin and Graham, 2005) or exploring specific software packages, such as *Cabri-Géomètre* or *The Geometer's Sketchpad*, can be doubly beneficial. Electronic whiteboards add an extra dimension to what can be done with computer packages and videotape, as well as offering a new recording environment.

Task 14.6 **Unsure about an area of maths?**

Identify a particular area of mathematics you feel apprehensive about teaching. This might be a particular topic or it might be an approach using some unfamiliar technology. List possible sources of help and information such as colleagues, resources within school, material from books or journals or via the internet. Draft a brief plan for working on the topic that includes an assessment of the time you might spend on it. What is it you feel you want or need to know?

CAREER DEVELOPMENT

To end this chapter, spend a few minutes looking ahead and envisaging how you would like your career as a mathematics teacher to develop. What do you hope to be doing in five years' time and what formal qualifications are there that might help you achieve your ambitions?

In the last few years, it has been recognised that it is important to provide some form of career development that offers teachers promotion while allowing them to retain their classroom role. In this way, able teachers are not lost from the classroom into administrative or other roles. There is a system by which teachers can be recognised as advanced skills teachers (ASTs). These are teachers who have been externally assessed and recognised as having excellent classroom practice. They are given additional payment and increased non-contact time in order to share their skills with other teachers in their own and other schools. You can find more about the AST scheme on the Teachernet website (http://www.teachernet.gov.uk/professionaldevelopment/ast/). If you see excellence in your own curriculum area, rather than management, as being the way you wish your career to develop, you may wish to explore such a role.

As you gain experience in your profession, you may want to explore becoming a Chartered Mathematics Teacher (CMathTeach). This designation aims to identify those teachers who are at the forefront of the profession and encapsulates standards of professional excellence across mathematics teaching in the twenty-first century. Therefore, it will be a requirement for ASTs in mathematics. It will benchmark you at the same level as a chartered mathematician, chartered scientist, chartered engineer and so on. To apply for the CMathTeach designation, individuals must be a member of at least one of the mathematics education organisations and also satisfy certain requirements in the following four areas: Pedagogy, Mathematics, Experience, and Continuing Professional Development. Further details can be found at: http://www.ima.org.uk/cmathteach/index.html

A more conventional role is that of subject head of department. The holder of this post is still very involved in classroom work, but also takes on developmental and administrative responsibility for coordinating mathematics teaching within a school. Another school-based role that appeals to many teachers is that of mentor for student teachers. Mentor training is often available when a mentor is appointed and is normally provided by the institution or partnership that places student teachers in the school.

SUMMARY AND KEY POINTS

Now you are ready to start on your career as a secondary mathematics teacher. What you learn about teaching and learning mathematics over next few years, and what your pupils learn about mathematics, will depend on what you have already learned, the new experiences you have and the use you make of them. As a maturing professional, you have the opportunity and the responsibility to make choices about those experiences. The more interested you become in how you operate as a teacher, the more interesting and rewarding your teaching will be.

FURTHER READING

Claxton, G. (1989) *Being a Teacher*. London: Cassell.
This book is about how to be a successful schoolteacher in a time of uncertainty, change, increased pressure and conflicting demands. It explores the scope that individuals have for staying positive and how they can deal with the pressures in the most effective way.

Mason, J. (1988) *Learning and Doing Mathematics*. York: QED Books.
This book focuses attention on fundamental processes of mathematical thinking. It turns out that these are neither new (you already know how to employ them, but you may not always do so when appropriate), nor are they restricted to doing mathematical problems. The same processes are involved in both *doing* and *learning* mathematics.

MA (1995) *Starting as a Secondary Mathematics Teacher*. Leicester: The Mathematical Association.
Whatever your route into mathematics teaching, this booklet offers advice from making the first application through to the interview and your first year as that all-important NQT. As the authors acknowledge, at the time of writing the rules and regulations were constantly changing, and indeed they are still changing, but do not worry – the goal posts keep moving for all teachers.

Prestage, S. and Perks, P. (2001) *Adapting and Extending Secondary Mathematics Activities: New Tasks for Old*. London: David Fulton.
This book is invaluable for finding ways both to enliven and to deepen the tasks you set for pupils. The authors look at various ways of doing this and the book has a down-to-earth approach that inspires confidence in making the attempt.

TDA (2003, and onwards) *Career Entry and Development Profile Pack*. London: Training and Development Agency.
Since 1998, all providers of initial teacher training are required to provide newly-qualified teachers with a TDA Career Entry Profile. The purpose of the profile is to convey a summary of information about new teachers' strengths and priorities for their further professional development. It includes a pro forma guide for recording the targets and action plan for the induction period, as agreed between the school and the NQT. The career entry pack changes somewhat in format from year to year. It was renamed Career Entry and Development Profile in 2003 (www.tda.gov.uk/teachers/induction/cedp.aspx).

APPENDIX 1
GLOSSARY OF
TERMS

All items with * appear in the list of useful addresses in Appendix 2.

AAIA	Association for Acheivement and Improvement through Assessment
ACCAC*	Awdurdod Cymwysterau, Cwricwlwm ac Asesu Cymru Qualifications, Curriculum and Assessment Authority for Wales
ACME*	Advisory Committee on Mathematics Education
ADD	attention deficit disorder
ADHD	attention deficit and hyperactivity disorder
AEA	advanced extension awards
AEN	additional educational needs
AfL	Assessment for Learning
ALIS	A-Level information system
AoN	Application of Number (04/09)
APP	Assessing Pupils' Progress materials published by the National Strategies and QCDA.
APU	Assessment of Performance Unit was established in 1975, within the DES, to provide information about general levels of performance of pupils in schools, and how these change over time. In 1989 this function became part of the Schools Examination and Assessment Council (SEAC).
AQA*	Assessment and Qualifications Alliance
AS	Advanced Subsidiary examination
ASD	autistic spectrum disorder
AST	advanced skills teacher
AT	attainment target
ATM*	Association of Teachers of Mathematics
AVA	audio-visual aids
Basic skills	literacy, numeracy and ICT for all pupils
BCME	British Congress in Mathematics Education
Becta*	British Educational Communications and Technology Agency
BSHM*	British Society for the History of Mathematics
BSRLM*	British Society for Research into Learning Mathematics
BTEC	Business and Technician Education Council

CAME*   Cognitive Acceleration in Mathematics Education project
CARN*   Collaborative Action Research Network
CCEA   Council for the Curriculum Examinations & Assessment in Northern Ireland
CMathTeach   chartered teacher of mathematics
Cockcroft Report   DES (1982) *Mathematics Counts*. Report of the Committee of Inquiry into the Teaching of Mathematics in Schools, chaired by W.H. Cockcroft
Core skills   Application of Number, Communication, Information Technology, Improving Own Learning and Performance, Working with Others, Problem-solving, also known as Key Skills
DCELLS   Department for Children, Education, Lifelong Learning and Skills (Wales)
DCSF   Department for Children, Schools and Families
DENI*   Department of Education for Northern Ireland
DES   Department for Education and Science (became DFE)
DFE   Department for Education (became DfEE)
DfEE   Department for Education and Employment (became DfES)
DfES*   Department for Education and Skills (became DCSF)
Equals   journal, published by the MA, containing articles about mathematics and SEN – a resource for those working to ensure that all pupils will benefit from mathematics
FSMQ   Freestanding mathematics qualification
GAIM   Graded Assessment in Mathematics
GAMMA*   The Gender and Mathematics Association
GCSE   General Certificate of Secondary Education
GNVQ   General National Vocational Qualification
HIMED   History in Mathematics Education
HMI   Her Majesty's Inspector(ate)
HMSO   Her Majesty's Stationery Office
IB   International Baccalaureate®
ICME   International Congress in Mathematics Education
ICT   Information and Communication Technology
IMA*   Institute of Mathematics and its Applications
IT   information technology
ITT   initial teacher training
JMC   Joint Mathematical Council of the United Kingdom
Key skills   Application of Number, Communication, Information Technology, Improving Own Learning and Performance, Working with Others, Problem-solving, also known as Core Skills
KS   Key Stage
LA   local authority
LEA   local education authority (became LA)
LMS*   London Mathematical Society
LMS   Local Management of Schools
LTS   Learning and Teaching Scotland, which publishes the Curriculum for Excellence for the Scottish government
MA*   Mathematical Association

Mathematics in Schools	journal produced for mathematics teachers by the MA
Micromath	journal that used to be produced for mathematics teachers by ATM
MT	*Mathematics Teaching*, a journal produced for mathematics teachers by the ATM
MTi	*Mathematics Teaching Interactive*, an online journal produced for mathematics teachers by the ATM
NAMA	National Association of Mathematics Advisers
NANAMIC	National Association of Numeracy and Mathematics in Colleges
NC	National Curriculum in England
NCC	National Curriculum Council, merged with SEAC in 1993 to form SCAA
NCET	National Council for Educational Technology, became Becta
NCETM*	National Centre for Excellence in Teaching Mathematics
NCTM*	National Council for Teachers of Mathematics, an association for teachers of mathematics, based in the United States, with members across north America.
NCVQ	National Council for Vocational Qualifications (see QCA)
NFER*	National Foundation for Educational Research
NICCEA	Northern Ireland Council for the Curriculum, Examinations and Assessment
NQT	newly qualified teacher (a teacher in their first year of teaching)
NNS	National Numeracy Strategy for KS1 and 2 in England
NS	National Strategy for KS3 mathematics in England
OCR*	Oxford and Cambridge Regional
Ofsted	Office for Standards in Education
OHMCI	Estyn Her Majestys Inspectorate for Education and Training in Wales
OU	Open University
Ofqual*	Office of Qualifications and Examinations Regulator
PLTS	Personal, Learning and Thinking Skills as defined in the NC (QCA, 2007)
RSS*	Royal Statistical Society
PGCE	Postgraduate Certificate in Education
PoS	programme of study
QCA*	Qualifications and Curriculum Authority, 1997–2010, brought together the work of NCVQ and SCAA, with additional powers, to provide overview of curriculum, assessment and qualifications from preschool to higher vocational levels
QCDA*	Qualifications and Curriculum Development Authority (replaced QCA from 2010)
QTS	qualified teacher status
RS	Royal Society
RSS*	Royal Statistical Society
SATs	Standard Assessment Tests
SoAs	Statements of Attainment
SCAA	Schools Curriculum and Assessment Authority, 1993–1997
SCITT	School-centred Initial Teacher Training

SEAC	School Examination and Assessment Authority (1988–1993) merged with NCC to form SCAA
SEED*	Scottish Executive Education Department
SEN	special educational needs
SENCO	special educational needs coordinator
SOED	Scottish Office Education Department (became SEED in 1999, on devolution)
SMP	School Mathematics Project
SQA	Scottish Qualifications Authority
TES	*Times Educational Supplement*
TGAT	Task Group on Assessment and Testing
TDA	Teacher Development Agency
TTA*	Teacher Training Agency (became TDA)
WO	Welsh Office (became Wales Office, 1999)
WOED*	Wales Office Education Department

See also http://www.nfer.ac.uk/emie/content.asp?id_content=363

APPENDIX 2
SOURCES AND
RESOURCES

USEFUL ADDRESSES

Advisory Committee on Mathematics Education (ACME)
The Royal Society
6–9 Carlton House Terrace
London SW1Y 5AG
020 7451 2571
www.royalsoc.ac.uk/acme/index.htm

Assessment and Qualification Alliance (AQA)
Stag Hill House
Guildford GU2 7XJ
01483 566506
www.aqa.org.uk

The Association of Teachers of Mathematics (ATM)
Unit 7, Prime Industrial Park
Shaftesbury Street
Derby DE23 8YB
01332 346599
www.atm.org.uk

Awdurdod Cymwysterau, Cwricwlwm ac Asesu Cymru
Qualifications, Curriculum and Assessment Authority for Wales (ACCAC)
Castle Buildings
Womanby Street
Cardiff CF1 9SX
029 2037 5400
www.accac.org.uk

Becta
Milburn High Road
Science Park
Coventry CV4 7JJ

01203 416669
www.becta.org.uk

BSHM
June Barrow-Green
Faculty of Mathematics and Computing
The Open University
Walton Hall
Milton Keynes MK7 6AA
www.dcs.warwick.ac.uk/bshm

BSRLM
www.bsrlm.org.uk

CAME
http://www.kcl.ac.uk/schools/sspp/education/research/projects/came.html

Collaborative Action Research Network (CARN)
www.did.stu.mmu.ac.uk/carn

Chartwell-Yorke
114 High Street
Belmont
Bolton BL7 8AL
01204 811001
www.chartwellyorke.co.uk

Department for Education and Skills
Sanctuary Buildings
Great Smith Street
London SW1P 3BT
020 7925 5000
www.dfes.gov.uk

Department of Education for Northern Ireland
Rathgael House
Balloo Road
Bangor
Co. Down BT19 7PR
028 9127 9279
www.deni.gov.uk

Edexcel
Stewart House
32 Russell Square
London WC1B 5DN
0870 240 9800
www.edexcel.org.uk

GAMMA
c/o ATM

Government Statistical Service
www.statistics.gov.uk

Institute of Mathematics and its Applications (IMA)
Catherine Richards House
16 Nelson Street
Southend-on-Sea
Essex SS1 1EF
01702 354020
www.ima.org.uk

London Mathematics Society (LMS)
Burlington House
Piccadilly
London W1V 0NL
020 7637 3686
www.lms.ac.uk

The Mathematical Association (MA)
259 London Road
Leicester LE2 3BF
0116 221 0013
www.m-a.org.uk

NCETM
www.ncetm.org.uk

NCTM
www.nctm.org

National Foundation for Educational Research (NFER)
The Mere
Upton Park
Slough SL1 2DQ
01753 574123
www.nfer.ac.uk

nfer-Nelson
414 Chiswick High Rd
London W4 5TF
0845 602 1937
www.nfer-nelson.co.uk

NRich Online Maths Club
nrich.maths.org.uk

OCR
www.ocr.org.uk .

Ofqual
www.ofqual.gov.uk/

Open University Centre for Mathematics Education
The Open University
Walton Hall
Milton Keynes MK7 6AA
01908 653550
cme.open.ac.uk

Oxford Educational Supplies Ltd
Weston Business Park
Weston on the Green
Oxfordshire OX25 3SX
01869 344500
www.oxford-educational.co.uk

Pearson Publishing
01223 350555
www.pearsonpublishing.co.uk/education/

QED Books
Pentagon Place
195B Berkhamsted Road
Chesham
Bucks HP5 3AP
0345 402275
www.qedgriffin.com

The Royal Statistical Society (RSS)
12 Errol Street
London EC1Y 8LX
0171 638 8998
www.rss.org.uk

Scottish Executive Education Department (SEED)
Victoria Quay
Leith
Edinburgh EH6 6QQ
0131 556 8400
www.scotland.gov.uk

The SMILE Centre
108a Lancaster Rd
London W11 1QS

020 7598 4841
smilemathematics.co.uk

Tarquin Publications
Stradbroke
Diss
Norfolk IP21 5JP
01379 384 218
www.tarquin-books.demon.co.uk

Teacher Training Agency (TTA)
www.useyourheadteach.gov.uk/ .

Texas Instruments
education.ti.com/educationportal

Wales Office Education Department
National Assembly for Wales
Cathays Park
Cardiff CF1 3NQ
029 2082 3207
www.wales.gov.uk/
www.learning.wales.gov.uk/

JOURNALS

Mathematics in Schools (MiS). Produced by the Mathematical Association (MA) for members five times a year, this professional journal publishes articles on a wide range of topics connected with teaching and learning the mathematics curriculum. It is aimed at teachers of mathematics, especially those who teach the 7–16 age range. Contact address is via the MA office, listed in the previous section.

Mathematics Teaching (MT). This is one of two professional journals about the teaching and learning of mathematics produced by the Association of Teachers of Mathematics (ATM), the other being *Micromath*. Launched in 1955, *MT* is now a well-established and widely read quarterly. The journal covers a broad range of topics that relate to the practice of teaching mathematics at all levels. Contact address is via the ATM office, listed in the previous section.

MTi. This is the second (online) of two ATM professional journals, which first appeared in 2009. It is a journal about learning and teaching mathematics using new technology, with articles and overviews by specialists and classroom practitioners (who are at times the same). Contact address is via the ATM office, listed in the previous section.

WEBSITES

There is a great range and variety of websites in mathematics education. We have given some sites throughout the book, but these may go out of date. Up-to-date versions can be found at the website we have made to go with this book: see cme.open.ac.uk/QTS

APPENDIX 3
MAKING CLOSED
TASKS OPEN

Some examples of the ways in which 'closed' tasks can be modified to make them 'open' are shown in Table A3.1. These are taken from page D7 of the Mathematics National Curriculum Non-Statutory Guidance (NCC, 1989). See also Prestage and Perks (2001) and Mason and Johnston-Wilder (2004b).

■ **Table A3.1** Samples of modified tasks

Closed task	Modified task
$2 + 6 - 3 =$	What numbers can you make from 2, 3 and 6?
$3 \times 5 =$	Make up some questions whose answer is 15
Find the value of x 9, 4, x°	Investigate what the sine button on a calculator does
Continue this sequence: 1, 2, 4	Discuss how the sequence 1, 2, 4 . . . might continue
Find the area of this triangle	Construct some triangles with the same areas as this one
What do we call a five-sided shape?	What shapes/configurations can you make with five lines?
Play a particular board game	Design a board game for four people using a dice and counters
Draw the graphs of 1) $y = 3x + 5$ 2) $y = 2x - 5$ 3) $y = 6 - x$	Investigate the graphs of $y = ax + b$ for different values of a and b
Copy and complete this addition table:	Investigate the possible ways of completing this table:

Copy and complete this addition table:

+	4	7
2		
6		

Investigate the possible ways of completing this table:

	3	4
	7	

Source: NCC, 1989: D7

APPENDIX 4 STARTING WITH ICT: PRACTICALITIES FOR BEGINNERS

In this appendix, an introductory description is offered for the tools discussed in Chapter 9: calculators, spreadsheets, graph plotters, graphic calculators, dynamic geometry packages, programming languages such as Logo, CD-ROMs and the internet. The first level, 'acquainted', represents having met and used the tool enough to know what it is. This appendix will tell you what the tool is and how to get started.

You will make most progress if you have personal access to the technology with which you need to teach. If, in addition, you see technology as a logico-mathematical environment, new to you, in which you are operating as a mathematician, those many frustrations you encounter will be tackled in a way that will enhance your teaching. Remember to give yourself time to learn a new package – like a new language, ICT skills develop over time, with practice.

GENERAL

We suggest you start by contacting Chartwell-Yorke (see Appendix 2 for contact details) and asking for a copy of the latest catalogue 'Mathematics and ICT'. They will send you a CD-ROM with demonstration copies of software mentioned in this book. We suggest you acquire a personal computer if at all possible, to give you access to software and hardware at the times when you are most receptive to spending some time working with software. We suggest you have your own scientific calculator and access to a graphic calculator.

CALCULATORS

You may already be familiar with calculators. If not, the most important thing to watch out for is the logic that the calculator uses in its calculations. It is important to check that you (and the pupils) are working with a scientific calculator rather than an 'arithmetic' calculator, such as those used in many building societies.

To check, try calculating $2 + 3 \times 4$. An arithmetic calculator will respond with 20, whereas a scientific calculator will do the multiplication first.

Do not expect to be able to operate any modern calculator at short notice as small variations can be confusing at first. Do expect to model mathematical problem-solving behaviour if a pupil has a problem with a model with which you are unfamiliar.

SPREADSHEETS

A spreadsheet is an electronic table, which offers an algebraic environment in an accessible format. Cells are labelled by their row and column. The figure below shows cell B1 highlighted: the symbol for multiplication is '*'; from B1 the formula '=A1 times three' has been 'filled down' to all the cells below. The result is part of the three-times table.

B1		=A1*3

	A	B	C
1	1	3	
2	2	6	
3	3	9	
4	4	12	
5	5	15	
6	6	18	
7	7	21	
8	8	24	
9	9	27	
10	10	30	
11			
12			

■ **Figure A4.1** A spreadsheet

Most computers these days come with a spreadsheet built in. The spreadsheet Excel, published by Microsoft, is widely available in schools and colleges in Britain, both on Mac and PC computers, and it is an industry standard. However, any equivalent spreadsheet with a graphing facility, such as Gnumeric, which is a free spreadsheet program, will do similar things, very often in a similar way. There are probably spreadsheets available on computers in any library available to you.

A spreadsheet can be a tool for generating and exploring simulated data. The random number generator can be used to set up simulations of random processes. The simulated data is easily formatted and, after manipulation in Excel, it can easily be exported to other packages. Use the spreadsheet to generate lottery numbers.

The random number generator is one of a wide range of functions that can be pasted into a sheet from a built-in library.

If you start working with macros, a form of programming with a spreadsheet, you will be able to set up sheets to explore families of functions, and to use animated graphs to explore what happens when you change the values of the parameters.

On a lighter note, pupils enjoy changing the presentation of the spreadsheet, for example the font size, the column width and the row height, as in the Figure A4.2.

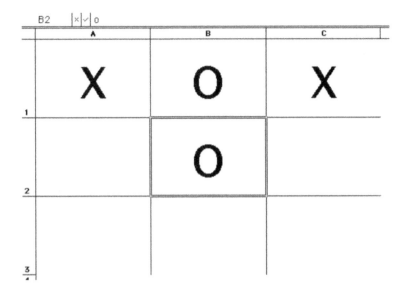

■ **Figure A4.2** Altering the presentation of a spreadsheet

Further reading

Mathsnet, The A–Z of spreadsheets (http://www.mathsnet.net/a2zofssheets.html).

GRAPH PLOTTERS

Software for plotting graphs of functions allows you to:

■   manipulate graphs;
■   solve equations graphically, by estimating, then 'zooming in' on, a point of inter-section;
■   study relationships, by superimposing graphical representations and by changing scale.

Recent packages also include the means to study transformation geometry. In some graph plotters (for example, in version 3 of *Omnigraph*), you are also able to drag a point on a curve and watch the equation change.

Your school may use, for example, *Omnigraph*, *Autograph* or a free online graph plotter such as Maths Online available from www.univie.ac.at/future.media/moe/onlinewerkzeuge.html

Further reading

Mathsnet, Graphs (http://www.mathsnet.net/graphs.html).

GRAPHIC CALCULATORS

A graphic calculator is a calculator with a big screen, which enables the user to draw graphs, zoom in and out, and experiment. Many come with options of function, polar, or parametric graphs. It is also possible to tabulate functions and to explore sequences. Once you get started, much more becomes possible.

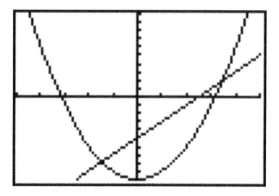

▨ **Figure A4.3** A graphic calculator screen

The Casio 7000g was one of the earliest graphic calculators. Then Texas Instruments brought out the TI-81, which many people found easier to use because it employed a system of menus. The Casio equivalent was the 7700g. Both of these had a friendly starting section in the manual. There is now a wide range to choose from. You will be able to borrow a graphic calculator if you do not want to buy one yet. Either your school may be able to loan you one, or Texas Instruments run a loan programme. Contact TI or Oxford Educational Supplies. If you are an absolute beginner, try the new series of books by Alan Graham and Barry Galpin, which go with the TI-83, available from Oxford Educational Supplies. If you decide to buy your own, it is cheaper to buy from an educational supplier such as Oxford Educational Supplies than from a high-street shop. Work through the Getting Started section of the manual.

Further reading

Mathsnet, Calculators (http://www.mathsnet.net/graphcal/graphiccalcs.html).

DYNAMIC GEOMETRY PACKAGES

Dynamic geometry software has points, lines and circles as basic objects, and allows constructions such as the mid point between two points. So, for example, in the figure below, two points are made, then a line segment is drawn between them; two circles are then constructed using the original points as centre and radius point for one and vice versa for the second. Finally, a third point is identified as a point of intersection. A triangle is constructed using the three points. As either of the two original points are moved around, the diagram changes, but the triangle stays equilateral.

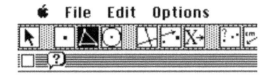

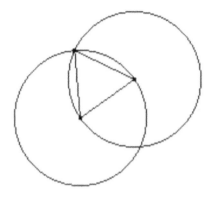

■ **Figure A4.4** Dynamic geometry

There are two main products used in schools, *Cabri-Géomètre* and *The Geometer's Sketchpad*, and if you have no funds, a freeware one called *GeoGebra*. ATM sells a short 'Getting Started' guide to each of these. You can obtain a trial copy of your chosen dynamic geometry package either by contacting a supplier or by downloading from the internet.

Further reading

Mathsnet, Interactive (http://www.mathsnet.net/interactive.html).

PROGRAMMING LANGUAGES

Logo is 'the name for a philosophy of education and for a continuously evolving family of computer languages that aid its realisation' (Abelson and di Sessa, 1980: 412). Papert (1980) has written an inspiring account of the thinking behind Logo. As there are various implementations available you will need to be aware of variations.

The fundamental idea is that the pupil is instructing a turtle to move and construct geometric objects, or trajectories. So, for example, if the turtle was told:

```
Forward 40
Right 90
Forward 40
Right 90
Forward 40
Right 90
Forward 40
```

it would draw a square. From this simple beginning, modelling of topics such as Newtonian motion, 3D coordinates and even general relativity (Abelson and di Sessa, 1980) are possible but there are many steps in between. Perhaps the most interesting feature of the Logo languages is that they support recursion.

A copy of MSW Logo can be downloaded from the internet. For example, there is a Windows version at http://www.softronix.com/logo.html Experiment a little before you start Chapter 9.

Further reading

Mathsnet, Logo (http://www.mathsnet.net/logo.html).

THE INTERNET AND CDROMS

If you do not yet know anything at all about the internet, take the opportunity to visit a library, either your school library or a public one, and ask the librarian to show you. The vast majority of children have internet access, through school, home and internet cafés. Many online lists of useful sites exist. One example that has been set up for teachers of mathematics who are new to the internet is *Teaching Secondary Mathematics with ICT*. To access this site, start by typing in http://cme.open.ac.uk and then point and click to follow the link. The links are usually represented by underlined text as you can see in Figure A4.5.

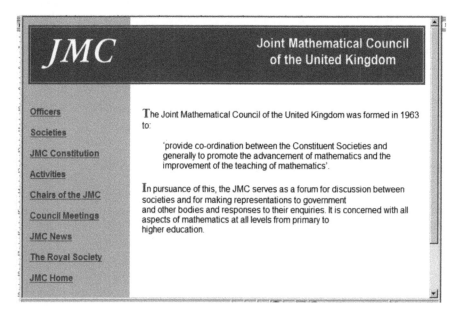

■ **Figure A4.5** JMC website (http://www.jmcuk.org.uk)

APPENDIX 5
PRACTICAL TASK:
ROLLING BALLS

ROLLING ALONG

You have to investigate the motion of a ball as it rolls along a horizontal track.

You will need: a large table; a hard, smooth ball; a short ramp; some track and a tape measure or a couple of metre rules; three wooden blocks; some stopwatches; some Blu-Tack

Set up the apparatus as shown in Figure A5.1:

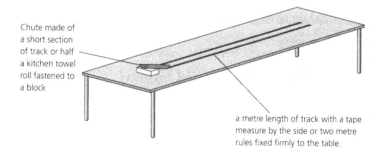

Chute made of a short section of track or half a kitchen towel roll fastened to a block

a metre length of track with a tape measure by the side or two metre rules fixed firmly to the table.

■ **Figure A5.1** Apparatus needed for the ball-rolling task

Release the ball near the top of the ramp so that it rolls nearly to the end of the track before stopping. (Release it from lower down the slope if it goes straight off the end of the track.) Mark your release point by fixing a small block above the ball. Release the ball several times. How fast is it going? Make some predictions.

Now start your measurements. Place a small block on the track 40 cm from the bottom of the chute. Release the ball from the marker on the chute and measure the time taken from the bottom of the chute to the block. Repeat this several times and take an average. What sort of average should you take?

Move the block to 70 cm and repeat, then go to 90 cm and finally allow the ball to come to rest. Fill in the table.

Average time taken from bottom of chute (secs):	....	....	....	......	....
Distance travelled from bottom of chute (m):	0.4	0.5	0.7	0.9	....

Enter the data in your graphic calculator and try to fit a function to it. (It should go through (0,0). Why?)

Differentiate your function to get the velocity of the ball. What does this tell you about the motion? You may need to change your function if what it tells you about the motion is patently wrong.

You should now be able to calculate the acceleration of the ball and hence the force acting on it. Placing blocks under the table legs nearest the end of the track will enable you to investigate the motion of a ball rolling up and down a slope.

GENERAL NOTES ON ANY PRACTICAL INVESTIGATION

Practicals can be used in two ways. The first is as a means of validating theory you have already learnt. The second is to build up a picture of a real-life situation. This can be explained by subsequent learnt theory. You must learn how to record and analyse data and interpret your results.

Experimental technique

Experimental technique is important in any practical. The following notes may help you when investigating motion.

ACCURACY

What sources of inaccuracy are there? For instance, in measuring time, do the errors due to your reaction time at the beginning and end of the run cancel each other out? Stopwatches are difficult to use for times less that 0.6 s. Consider the use of a mean or median in choosiing which measurement to use in your analysis.

REPEATABILITY AND CONSISTENCY

The data collected *must* be obtainable by other experimenters at other times. It is also important that the experiment is consistent, especially if you are using different runs to collect a set of measurements. You are assuming that the same thing happens each time you start the experiment and so you can interrupt the run at different points.

When rolling a ball down a slope, for example, it must be released from exactly the same point each time, and also it must roll smoothly down the track without bouncing from side to side. The following points may help with timing:

1   Have a few dummy runs to get yourself familiar with the stopwatch.
2   Call out '3,2,1,Go!' as you start.
3   An audible signal at the end of a run will mean your reaction time errors are minimised.

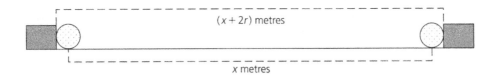

Make sure you measure the distance travelled carefully. You will be modelling the ball as a point source. In reality, you must allow for its radius.

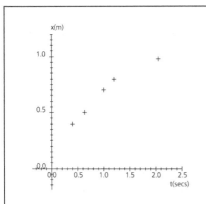

Figure A5.2 Allowing for radius when measuring distance

A student carried out the practical and recorded her results and calculations. Read them carefully and then follow them using your own data.

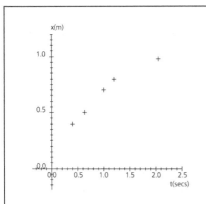

1   I set up the practical and collected some data. I repeated each measurement five times and took the median value.
I got the following data points (0, 0), (0.4, 0.4), (0.61, 0.5), (1.01, 0.7), (1.19, 0.8), (2.06, 0.98) and plotted them on my graphic calculator.
(I plotted time on the horizontal so I could differentiate to get the velocity.)
The ball stopped at 98 cm.

Figure A5.3 Plotted points on a graphic calculator

2   I tried to fit a function to the data. As the graph must pass through the point (0, 0), a straight line was not appropriate. There seemed to be two possibilities; these were:

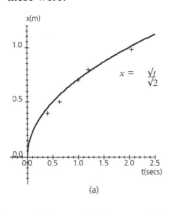

$$x = \frac{\sqrt{t}}{\sqrt{2}}$$

(a)

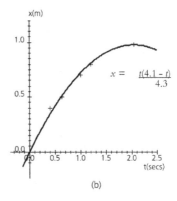

$$x = \frac{t(4.1 - t)}{4.3}$$

(b)

Figure A5.4a and b Two possible curved graph lines

The velocity of the ball is given by the slope of the curve. I differentiated both functions to get the slope.

For $x = \dfrac{\sqrt{t}}{\sqrt{2}} = \dfrac{\sqrt{2}}{2}\, t^{0.5}$

$v = \dfrac{\sqrt{2}}{4}\, t^{0.5}$

The slope when $t = 0$ is infinitely great, i.e. the velocity is greater than the speed of light. Hardly likely.

Also the slope is never zero so the ball never stops moving. Again this was not what happened so the graph is not a good model of the motion.

For $x = \dfrac{t(4.1 - t)}{4.3}$

This differentiates to give $v = 0.953 - 0.465t$.

The slope when $t = 0$ is about 0.9 i.e. the speed is around 1 m s⁻¹.

Also when $t = 2.05$ the speed is zero. Admittedly after this the ball appears to go backwards but this only showed me that the model only holds between $t = 0$ and $t = 2.05$.

On the whole this seems to fit what actually happened rather well.

3 To find the acceleration and the force I used the model $x = t\,(4.1 - t)/4.3$, $v = 0.953 - 0.465\, t$

The acceleration of the ball is $^{dv}/_{dt}$ or -0.465 ms⁻².

The mass of the ball is 40 grams.

Thus the force acting on the rolling ball would appear to be around is 0.02 Newtons.

I didn't join the points up with straight lines because that would mean the ball appears to speed up and slow down in jerks.

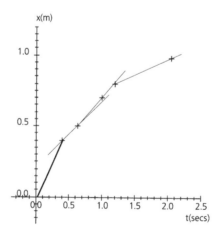

Figure A5.5 The rejected straight-line graph

APPENDIX 6
GROUP ACTIVITY

A13 Simplifying logarithmic expressions: Card set B – Odd one out

This example is taken from the pack 'Improving Learning in Mathematics', published in 2005 by the Department for Education and Skills Standards Unit (see Swan, 2005). You can find out more about this resource at the National Centre for Excellence in Teaching Mathematics (NCETM) website: https://www.ncetm.org.uk/resources

Teacher instructions

Give learners the cards below, cut into horizontal strips. You could give the strips out one at a time or all together. Ask learners, working in pairs, to identify which is the odd one out in each strip. When they have done this, they should write in the blank space as many expressions as they can think of that are equivalent to the odd one out. Discuss some of the possibilities by asking learners to suggest an equivalent expression and then explain why it is equivalent.

$\log_2 8$	$\log_3 9$	$\log_4 64$	
$\log_2 0.5$	$\log_4 0.25$	$\log_8 0.5$	
$\log_2 8^3$	$\log_2 4^4$	$\log_2 2^9$	
$\log_2 x^6$	$\log_2 x^2 + \log_2 x^3$	$\log_2 x^3 + \log_2 x^4$	
$-2 \log_2 x$	$\log_2 \frac{1}{x^2}$	$\log_2 \sqrt{x}$	

REFERENCES

Abelson, H. and di Sessa, A. (1980) *Turtle Geometry*, Cambridge, MA: MIT Press.

ACME (2007) ACME response to QCA's Secondary Curriculum Review (see p. 3 of http://www.acme-uk.org/downloaddoc.asp?id=44)

Adhami, M., Johnson, D. and Shayer, M. (2007) *Thinking Maths,* rev. edn. Oxford: Heinemann.

Ahmed, A. (1987) *Better Mathematics*. London: HMSO.

Ainley, J. (1987) 'Telling questions', *Mathematics Teaching*, 118, 24–26.

Ainley, J., Bills, L. and Wilson, K. (2005) 'Designing spreadsheet-based tasks for purposeful algebra', *International Journal of Computers for Mathematical Learning*, 10(3), 191–215.

Albers, D. (1986) 'Paul Halmos', in Albers, D. and Alexanderson, G. (eds) *Mathematical People: Profiles and Interviews*, Cambridge, MA: Birkhäuser, pp. 119–32.

Alexander, R. (2006) *Towards Dialogic Teaching*, York: Dialogos.

Anghileri, J., Beishuizen, M. and van Putten, K. (2002) 'From informal strategies to structured procedures: mind the gap!', *Educational Studies in Mathematics*, 49(2), 149–70.

APU (1986) *Decimals Assessment at Age 11 and 15*. Slough: National Foundation for Educational Research.

ARG (1999*) Assessment for Learning: Beyond the Black Box.* (Available as a pdf from: www.qca.org.uk/ages3-14/afl/294.html)

Ashcraft, M. (1995) 'Cognitive psychology and simple arithmetic: a review and summary of new directions', in Butterworth, B. (ed.) *Mathematical Cognition*. Hove: Psychology Press, pp. 3–34.

Ashcraft, M. (2002) 'Math anxiety: personal, educational, and cognitive consequences', *Current Directions in Psychological Science*, 11(5), 181–5.

Askew, M., Bliss, J. and Macrae, S. (1995) 'Scaffolding in mathematics, science and technology', in Murphy, P., Selinger, M., Bourne, J. and Briggs, M. (eds), *Subject Learning in the Primary Curriculum: Issues in English, Science, and Mathematics*, London: Routledge, pp. 209–217.

Askew, M. and Wiliam, D. (1995) *Recent Research in Mathematics Education 5–16*, London: HMSO.

ATM (1985) *Notes on Mathematics for Children*, Derby: The Association of Teachers of Mathematics.

ATM (1993a) *Talking Maths, Talking Languages*. Derby: The Association of Teachers of Mathematics.

ATM (1993b) *Using and Applying Mathematics*. Derby: The Association of Teachers of Mathematics.

Backhouse, J., Haggarty, L., Pirie, S. and Stratton, J. (1992) *Improving the Learning of Mathematics*. London: Cassell.

Ball, D., Thames, M. and Phelps, G. (2008) 'Content knowledge for teaching: what makes it special?', *Journal of Teacher Education*, 59(5), 389–407.

Banwell, C., Saunders, K. and Tahta, D. (1986) *Starting Points for Teaching Mathematics in Middle and Secondary Schools*. Diss: Tarquin Publications.

Barham, J. and Bishop, A. (1991) 'Mathematics and the deaf child', in Durkin, K. and Shire, B. (eds) *Language in Mathematical Education: Research and Practice*. Buckingham: Open University Press, pp. 179–87.

Barton, B. (2008) *The Language of Mathematics: Telling Mathematical Tales*. New York, NY: Springer.

Becta (2003) *Key Stage 3 Maths Inset Pack*, Coventry: British Educational and Communications Technology Agency. (See also: www.ictadvice.org.uk/index.php?section=tl&cat=001002007&rid=3569)

Becta (2009) *Secondary Mathematics with ICT: A Pupil's Entitlement to ICT in Secondary Mathematics*, Coventry: British Educational and Communications Technology Agency.

Black, P., Harrison, C., Lee, C., Marshall, B. and Wiliam, D. (2002) *Working inside the Black Box: Assessment for Learning in the Classroom*, London: NFER-Nelson.

Black, P., Harrison, C., Lee, C., Marshall, B. and Wiliam, D. (2003) *Assessment for Learning: Putting It into Practice*. Maidenhead: Open University Press.

Black, P. and Wiliam, D. (1998) *Inside the Black Box*. London: King's College. (www.kcl.ac.uk/depsta/education/publications/blackbox.html or as a pdf from: www.qca.org.uk/ages3-14/afl/294.html)

Blair, H., Dimbleby, B., Loughran, B., Taylor, I. and Vallance, J. (1983) 'A Birmingham maths trail', *Mathematics in School*, 12(4), 14–15.

Boaler, J. (1997) *Experiencing School Mathematics: Teaching Styles, Sex and Setting*, Buckingham: Open University Press.

Boaler, J. (2009) *The Elephant in the Classroom: Helping Children Learn and Love Maths*. London: Souvenir Press.

Boaler, J. and Greeno, J. (2000) 'Identity, agency and knowing in mathematics worlds', in Boaler, J. (ed.) *Multiple Perspectives on Mathematics Teaching and Learning*. Westport, CT: Ablex.

Bold, B. (1982) *Famous Problems of Geometry and How to Solve Them*. New York: Dover.

Borasi, R. (1992) *Learning Mathematics through Inquiry*. Portsmouth, NH: Heinemann.

Boyd, W. (1973) *Emile for Today*. London: Heinemann.

Brown, M. (1981) 'Place value and decimals', in Hart, K. (ed.) *Children's Understanding of Mathematics: 11–16*. London: John Murray, pp. 48–65.

Brown, M., Brown, P. and Bibby, T. (2008) '"I would rather die": reasons given by 16-year-olds for not continuing their study of mathematics', *Research in Mathematics Education*, 10(1), 3–18.

Brown, S. (2003) 'Ability – a concept concealing disabling environments', *Support for Learning*, 18(2), 88–90.

Budge, D. (1997) 'Boost to morale on maths and science', *The Times Educational Supplement*, 4239, 26 September, p. 1a.

Burton, L. (1999) 'The practices of mathematicians: what do they tell us about coming to know mathematics?', *Educational Studies in Mathematics*, 37(2), 121–43.

Butler, R. (1988) 'Enhancing and undermining intrinsic motivation', *British Journal of Educational Psychology*, 58(1), 1–14.

Butt, G. (2008) *Lesson Planning*, 3rd edn. London: Continuum.

Callinan, J. (1992) 'Mathematics and physical disabilities', *Struggle*, 34, 17–19.

Capel, S., Leask, M. and Turner, T. (eds) (1995) *Learning to Teach in the Secondary School: A Companion to School Experience*. London: Routledge.

Capel, S., Leask, M. and Turner, T. (eds) (2009) *Learning to Teach in the Secondary School: A Companion to School Experience*, 5th edn. London: Routledge.

CCEA (2010) *Northern Ireland Curriculum*. Belfast: Council for the Curriculum, Examinations and Assessment.

Charis Project (1997) *Charis Mathematics, Units 1–9 and Units 10–19*. Nottingham: Stapleford Centre.

REFERENCES ▨ ▨ ▨ ■

Cheng, Y., Payne, J. and Witherspoon, S. (1995) *Science and Mathematics in Full-time Education after 16*. London: Department for Education and Employment.

Chinn, S. and Ashcroft, J. (1993) *Mathematics for Dyslexics*, London: Whurr Publishing.

Clark-Jeavons, A. (2004) 'Developing the use of the interactive whiteboard in the secondary mathematics classroom', in Johnston-Wilder, S. and Pimm, D. (eds) *Teaching Secondary Mathematics with ICT*. Maidenhead: Open University Press.

Clarke, S. (2005) *Formative Assessment in the Secondary Classroom*, London: HodderMurray.

Claxton, G. (1989) *Being a Teacher: Coping with Change and Stress*, London: Cassell.

Cocker, M., Critcher, H., Stevens, W. and Rigby, J. (1996) 'Starting a secondary school maths club', *Mathematics in School*, 25(5), 33–6.

Connolly, P. and Vilardi, T. (eds) (1989) *Writing to Learn Mathematics and Science*. New York: Teachers College Press.

Cooper, B. (1985) *Renegotiating Secondary School Mathematics*. Barcombe: Falmer Press.

Cooper, B. (1994) 'Secondary mathematics education in England: recent changes and their historical context', in Selinger, M. (ed.) *Teaching Mathematics*. London: Routledge, pp. 5–26.

Cooper, B. and Dunne, M. (2000) *Assessing Children's Mathematical Knowledge*, Buckingham: Open University Press.

Cornwall, J. (1997) *Access to Learning for Pupils with Disabilities*. London: David Fulton.

Costello, J. (1991) *Teaching and Learning Mathematics 11–16*. London: Routledge.

Coxeter, H. (1961) *Introduction to Geometry*. New York: Wiley.

Cresswell, M. and Gubb, J. (1987) *The Second International Mathematics Study in England and Wales* (International Studies in Pupils Performance Series). Slough: NFER-Nelson.

Cuoco, A., Goldenberg, E. and Mark, J. (1996) 'Habits of mind: an organizing principle for mathematics curricula', *Journal of Mathematical Behaviour*, 15(4), 375–402.

Dadd, T. (1998) 'Mathematics eNRICHment activities'. *Micromath*, 14(2), 35–40.

Daniels, H. and Anghileri, J. (1995) *Secondary Mathematics and Special Educational Needs*. London: Cassell.

Daniels, H., Visser, J., Cole, T. and de Reybekill, N. (1999) 'Emotional and behavioural difficulties in mainstream schools', *DfES Research Brief* no. 90 (www.dfes.gov.uk/sen/documents/RB90.doc).

Davis, P. and Hersh, R. (1986) *The Mathematical Experience*. Harmondsworth: Penguin.

DCELLS (2008) *The National Curriculum for Wales*. Cardiff: Department for Children, Education, Lifelong Learning and Skills, Welsh Assembly Government.

DCSF (2008) *The Standards Site* (http://nationalstrategies.standards.dcsf.gov.uk/app).

de Villiers, M. (1994) 'The role and function of a hierarchical classification of quadrilaterals', *For the Learning of Mathematics*, 14(1), 11–18.

DEED (1993) *Summing up the World*, available from DEED, Kingsleigh School, Hadow Road, Bournemouth, BH10 5HS.

DES (1982) *Mathematics Counts*. Report of the Committee of Inquiry into the Teaching of Mathematics in Schools, chaired by W. H. Cockcroft (The Cockcroft Report). London: HMSO.

DES (1985) *Mathematics from 5 to 16*, Curriculum Matters 3. London: HMSO.

DES/WO (1987) *National Curriculum Task Group on Assessment and Testing* (TGAT). London: HMSO.

DES/WO (1989) *Mathematics in the National Curriculum*. London: HMSO.

DES/WO (1991) *Mathematics in the National Curriculum*. London: HMSO.

DfEE (1998) *Teaching: High Status, High Standards*. Circular 4/98, London: Department for Education and Employment.

DfEE (1999a) *Mathematics: the National Curriculum in England*. London: HMSO.

DfEE (1999b) *National Numeracy Strategy: Framework for Teaching Mathematics from Reception to Year 6*. London: Department for Education and Employment.

DfEE (2000) *Mathematical Vocabulary Book*. London: Department for Education and

Employment, available at: http://nationalstrategies.standards.dcsf.gov.uk/node/84996 (accessed April 2010).

DfEE (2001a) *Key Stage 3 National Strategy – Framework for Teaching Mathematics: Years 7, 8 and 9*. London: Department for Education and Employment.

DfEE (2001b) *Guide to the Framework*, published by National Strategies (http://www.counton.org/resources/ks3framework/).

DfEE (2001c) *Guide to the Framework*, published by National Strategies (http://www.counton.org/resources/ks3framework/ accessed 27 January 2010).

DfES (2000) *The National Numeracy Strategy: Mathematical Vocabulary*. London: Department for Education and Skills.

DfES (2001) *Special Educational Needs Code of Practice*, London: HMSO. (Downloadable from: http://www.teachernet.gov.uk/_doc/3724/SENCodeOfPractice.pdf)

DfES (2004a) *Making Mathematics Count*. London: HMSO.

DfES (2004b) *Pedagogy and Practice: Teaching and Learning in Secondary Schools, Unit 1: Structuring Learning*. London: Department for Education and Skills.

DfES (2005) Wave 3 Mathematics, Primary National Strategy, London: HMSO. (Downloadable from http://nationalstrategies.standards.dcsf.gov.uk/primary/publications/inclusion/wave3pack)

Dickson, L., Brown, M. and Gibson, O. (1984) *Children Learning Mathematics*. London: Cassell.

Dodd, P. (1991) *Mathematics from Around the World, a Multicultural Resource Book*, available from 73, Beech Grove, Whitley Bay, Tyne and Wear, NE26 3PL (Tel: 01912 525892).

Dörfler, W. and McLone, R. (1986) 'Mathematics as a school subject', in Christiansen, B., Howson, G. and Otte, M. (eds) *Perspectives on Mathematics Education*. Dordrecht, Holland, D. Reidel, pp. 49–97.

Dowker, A. (2004) *What Works for Children with Mathematical Difficulties*. (Downloadable from http://www.dcsf.gov.uk/research/data/uploadfiles/RR554.pdf)

Dowker, A. (2005) *Individual Differences in Arithmetic*. London: Taylor and Francis.

Dweck, C. (2006) *Mindset: The New Psychology of Success*. New York: Random House.

Dyson, A. and Millward, A. (2000) *Schools and Special Needs: Issues of Innovation and Inclusion*. London: Paul Chapman.

Eagle, R. (1995) *Exploring Mathematics through History*. Cambridge: Cambridge University Press.

Earl, L., Watson, N., Levin, B., Leithwood, K., Fullan, M. and Torrance, N. with Jantzi, D., Mascall, B. and Volante, L. (2003) *Watching and Learning: Final Report of the External Evaluation of England's National Literacy and Numeracy Strategies*. Toronto, ON: OISE/UT.

Elgin, D. (2008) 'Drugs in the body', *Mathematics in School*, 37(4), 2–3.

Ellis, A. (2007) 'Connection between generalising and justifying', *Journal for Research in Mathematics Education*, 38(3), 194–229.

Entwistle, N. (2000) 'Promoting deep learning through teaching and assessment: conceptual frameworks and educational contexts'. Paper presented at the Teaching and Learning Research Programme Conference, Leicester, November. Retrieved 14 April 2010 from http://www.tlrp.org/acadpub/Entwistle2000.pdf

Ernest, P. (1991) *The Philosophy of Mathematics Education*. Basingstoke: Falmer Press.

Ernest, P. (2000) 'Why teach mathematics?', in White, J. and Bramall, S. (eds) *Why Learn Maths?* London University Institute of Education, pp. 1–14. (Available online at http://people.exeter.ac.uk/PErnest/why.htm)

Fairbrother, R. (1995) 'Pupils as learners', in Fairbrother, R., Black, P. and Gill, P. (eds) *Teachers Assessing Pupils: Lessons from Science Classrooms*. Hatfield: Association for Science Education, pp. 105–24.

Finesilver, C. (2009) 'Drawing, modelling and gesture in students' solutions to a Cartesian product problem', *Educate*, Special issue, December, pp. 21–36 (http://www.educatejournal.org/index.php?journal=educate&page=article&op=viewFile&path[]=216&path[]=206).

Finkelstein, E. and Samsonov, P. (2007) *PowerPoint for Teachers: Dynamic Presentations and Interactive Classroom Projects*. San Francisco, CA: Jossey Bass.

REFERENCES ▤ ▤ ▤ ■

Finzer, W. and Bennett, D. (1995) 'From drawing to construction with *Geometer's Sketchpad*', *Mathematics Teacher*, 88(5), 428–31.

Fontana, D. and Fernandes, M. (1994) 'Improvements in mathematics performance as a consequence of self-assessment in Portuguese primary school pupils', *British Journal of Educational Psychology*, 64(3), 407–17.

Foster, C. (2008) *Variety in Mathematics Lessons*, Derby: Association of Teachers of Mathematics.

Frederickson, N. and Cline, T. (2002) *Special Educational Needs, Inclusion and Diversity: A Textbook*. Buckingham: Open University Press.

Frederickson, J. and White, B. (1997) 'Reflective assessment of students' research within an inquiry-based middle school science curriculum', Paper presented at the annual meeting of the American Educational Research Association, Chicago, IL.

French, D. (2006) *Resource Pack for Assessment for Learning in Mathematics*. Leicester: The Mathematical Association.

Gage, J. (2005) *How to Use an Interactive Whiteboard Really Effectively in Your Secondary Classroom*. London: David Fulton.

Galloway, D., Leo, E., Rogers, C. and Armstrong, D. (1996) 'Maladaptive motivational style: the role of domain specific task demand in English and mathematics', *British Journal of Educational Psychology*, 66(2), 197–207.

Galpin, B. and Graham, A. (2005) *First Lessons with Graphics Calculators*. Corby: A+B Books.

Gammon, A. (2002) *Key Stage 3 Mathematics: A Guide for Teachers*. London: Beam.

Gates, P. (2002) 'Issues of equity in mathematics education: defining the problem, seeking solutions', in Haggarty, L. (ed.) *Teaching Mathematics in Secondary Schools: A Reader*. London: RoutledgeFalmer, pp. 211–28.

Gerofsky, S. (2003) *A Man Left Albuquerque Heading East: Word Problems as Genre in Mathematics Education*, New York: Peter Lang.

Ginsburg, H. (1981) 'The clinical interview in psychological research on mathematical thinking: aims, rationales, techniques', *For the Learning of Mathematics*, 1(3), 4–11.

Gormas, J. (1998) *Developing Mathematical Power: The Transformation of a High School Mathematics Teacher*, Unpublished PhD thesis, East Lansing, MI: Michigan State University.

Goulding, M. (2002a) 'Cognitive acceleration in mathematics education: teachers' views', *Evaluation and Research in Education*, 16(2), 104–19.

Goulding, M. (2002b) 'Do teachers understand the theory behind CAME?', in Goodchild, S. (ed.) *Proceedings of the British Society for Research into Learning Mathematics*, 22(1), 25–30.

Goulding, M. (2002c) 'Developing thinking in mathematics', in Haggarty, L. (ed.) *Aspects of Teaching Secondary Mathematics*. London: RoutledgeFalmer with the Open University.

Graham, A. (1996) 'Open calculator challenge', *Micromath*, 12(3), 14–15.

Graham, A. (2006) *Developing Thinking in Statistics*, London: Paul Chapman Publishing.

Graham, A. and Duke, R. (2010) *An Applet for the Teacher: Mathematics for the Imagination*, St Albans: Tarquin Publications.

Gray, E. and Tall, D. (1994) 'Duality, ambiguity, and flexibility: a "proceptual" view of simple arithmetic', *Journal for Research in Mathematics Education*, 25(2), 116–140.

Griffiths, H. and Howson, G. (1974) *Mathematics, Society and Curricula*. Cambridge: Cambridge University Press.

Haddon, M. (2003) *The Curious Incident of the Dog in the Night-Time*. London: Cape.

Hanna, G. (1989) 'Mathematics achievement of girls and boys in grade eight: results from twenty countries', *Educational Studies in Mathematics*, 20(2), 225–32.

Hardy, G. (1940) *A Mathematician's Apology*, Cambridge: Cambridge University Press.

Harnasz, C. (1993) 'Do you need to know how it works?', in Selinger, M. (ed.) *Teaching Mathematics*. London: Routledge, pp. 137–44.

Harris, J. (1995) *Presentation Skills for Teachers*. London: Routledge.

Hart, K. (ed.) (1981) *Children's Understanding of Mathematics: 11–16*. London: John Murray.

Hatch, G. and Shiu, C. (1997) 'Teachers research through their own mathematics learning', in Zack, V., Mousley, J. and Breen, C. (eds), *Developing Practice: Teachers' Inquiry and Educational Change*, Deakin, Victoria: Centre for Studies in Mathematics, Science and Environmental Education, Deakin University, pp. 159–168.

Haylock, D. (1982) 'The mathematics of a dud calculator'. *Mathematics Teaching*, 101, 15–16.

Haylock, D. (1991) *Teaching Mathematics to Low Attainers 8–12*, London: Paul Chapman Publishing.

Haynes, A. (2007) *100 Ideas for Lesson Planning*. London: Continuum.

Healy, L., Hoelzl, R., Hoyles, C. and Noss, R. (1994) 'Messing up', *Micromath*, 10(1), 14–16.

Hersh, R. (1979) 'Some proposals for reviving the philosophy of mathematics', *Advances in Mathematics*, 31(1), 31–50.

Hersh, R. (1998) *What Is Mathematics, Really?* London: Vintage.

Hewitt, D. (2004) 'Thinking numerically: structured number', in Johnston-Wilder, S. and Pimm, D. (eds), *Teaching Secondary Mathematics with ICT*. Buckingham: Open University Press, pp. 43–61.

Hoare, C. (1990) 'The invisible Japanese calculator'. *Mathematics Teaching*, 131, 12–14.

Hodgen, J. and Wiliam, D. (2006) *Mathematics Inside the Black Box*. Slough: NFER-Nelson.

Hodgen, J., Küchemann, D., Brown, M. and Coe, R. (2008) 'Children's understandings of algebra 30 years on', in *Proceedings of the British Society for Research into Learning Mathematics*, 28(3), 36–41.

Holt, J. (1964) *How Children Fail*. Harmondsworth: Pelican.

Holt, J. (1970) *How Children Learn*. Harmondsworth: Pelican.

Howson, G. (1991) *National Curricula in Mathematics*, Leicester: The Mathematical Association.

Hoyles, C. (1982) 'The pupils' view of mathematics learning'. *Educational Studies in Mathematics*, 13(4), 349–72.

Hoyles, C., Noss, R., Kent, P. and Bakker, A. (2010). *Improving Mathematics at Work: The Need for Techno-mathematical Literacies*. London: Routledge/Taylor & Francis.

Hudson, B. (1994) 'Environmental issues in the mathematics classroom', in Selinger, M. (ed.) *Teaching Mathematics*. London: Routledge, pp. 113–25.

Hudson, J. (2009) 'The mathematics and physics of Formula 1', *Mathematics in School*, 38(4), 7–13.

Inglese, J. (1997) 'Teaching mathematics to pupils with autistic spectrum disorders: exploring possibilities'. *Equals*, 3(2), 18–19.

Isoda, M., Stephens, M., Ohara, Y. and Miyakawa, T. (eds) (2007) *Japanese Lesson Study in Mathematics: Its Impact, Diversity and Potential for Educational Improvement*. Singapore: World Scientific.

James, N. and Mason, J. (1982) 'Towards recording', *Visible Language*, 16(3), 249–58.

Jaworski, B. (1985) 'A poster lesson', *Mathematics Teaching*, 113, 4–5.

Jaworski, B. (1992) 'Mathematics teaching: what is it?', *For the Learning of Mathematicsp*, 12(1), 8–14.

Jaworski, B. and Watson, A. (eds) (1994) *Mentoring in Mathematics Teaching*, Brighton: Falmer Press.

JMC/Royal Society (1997) *Teaching and Learning Algebra Pre-19*. London: The Royal Society.

JMC/Royal Society (2001) *Teaching and Learning Geometry 11–19*. London: The Royal Society.

John, P. (1991) 'A qualitative study of British student teachers' lesson planning perspectives', *Journal of Education for Teaching*, 17(3), 301–20.

John, P. (1993) *Lesson Planning for Teachers*. London: Cassell.

John, P. (1994) 'The integration of research-validated knowledge with practice: lesson planning and the student history teacher', *Cambridge Journal of Education*, 24(1), 33–47.

John, P. (2006) 'Lesson planning and the student teacher: re-thinking the dominant model', *Journal of Curriculum Studies*, 38(4), 483–98.

Johnson, D. (ed.) (1989) *Children's Mathematical Frameworks 8–13: A Study of Classroom Teaching*. Slough: National Foundation for Educational Research.

REFERENCES ▨ ▨ ▧ ▪

Johnson, D. and Millett, A. (eds) (1996) *Implementing the Mathematics National Curriculum*. London: Paul Chapman.

Johnston-Wilder, S. and Lee, C. (2010) 'Mathematical resilience', *Mathematics Teaching*, p. 218.

Johnston-Wilder, S. and Mason, J. (eds) (2006) *Developing Thinking in Geometry*. London: Paul Chapman Publishing.

Johnston-Wilder, S. and Pimm, D. (eds) (2004) *Teaching Secondary Mathematics with ICT*. Buckingham: Open University Press.

Jones, K. (1997) 'Some lessons in mathematics: a comparison of mathematics teaching in Japan and America'. *Mathematics Teaching*, 159, 6–9.

Jones, K., Gutiérrez, Á. and Mariotti, M. A. (2000) Guest editorial, Proof in dynamic geometry environments, PME special issue, *Educational Studies in Mathematics*, 44, 1–3.

Jordan, R. and Powell, S. (1995) *Understanding and Teaching Children with Autism*. Chichester: Wiley.

Joseph, G. (2010) *The Crest of the Peacock: Non-European Roots of Mathematics*, 2nd edn. Princeton, NJ: Princeton University Press.

Katz, V. (2008) *A History of Mathematics*, 3rd edn. New York: HarperCollins.

Kerry, T. (2002) *Learning Objectives, Task Setting and Differentiation*. Cheltenham: Nelson Thornes.

Kerslake, D. (1981) 'Graphs', in Hart, K. (ed.) *Children's Understanding of Mathematics: 11–16*. London: John Murray, pp. 120–136.

Kerslake, D. (1986) *Fractions: Children's Strategies and Errors*. Slough: National Foundation for Educational Research.

Keys, W., Harris, S. and Fernandes, C. (1996) *Third International Mathematics and Science Study: First National Report*. Slough: National Foundation for Educational Research.

Kitchen, A. (1998) 'Using calculators in schools', *Micromath*, 14(2), 25–9.

Kluger, A. and DeNisi, A. (1996) 'The effects of feedback interventions on performance: a historical review, a meta-analysis, and a preliminary feedback intervention theory'. *Psychological Bulletin*, 119(2), 254–84.

Knuth, E. and Elliot, R. (1998) 'Characterising students' understandings of mathematical proof'. *The Mathematics Teacher*, 91(8), 714–17.

Lave, J. (1988) *Cognition in Practice: Mind, Mathematics and Culture*. Cambridge: Cambridge University Press.

Lawson, C. and Lee, C. (1995) 'Numeracy through literacy'. Proceedings of the Joint Conference of the British Society for Research into Learning Mathematics and the Association of Mathematics Education Tutors. Loughborough: BSRLM/AMET, pp. 43–46.

Lee, C. (2006) *Language for Learning Mathematics: Assessment for Learning in Practice*. Maidenhead: Open University Press.

Li, Y., Chen, X. and Kulm, G. (2009) 'Mathematics teachers' practices and thinking in lesson plan development: a case study of teaching fractional division', *ZDM – the International Journal on Mathematics Education*, 41(6), 717–31.

Lorenz, J. (1982) 'On some psychological aspects of mathematics achievement assessment and classroom interaction'. *Educational Studies in Mathematics*, 13(1), 1–19.

MA (1987) *Maths Talk*. Cheltenham: Stanley Thornes.

MA (1992) *Mental Methods in Mathematics: A First Resort*. Leicester: The Mathematical Association.

MA (1995) *Why, What, How? Some Basic Questions for Mathematics Teaching*. Leicester: The Mathematical Association.

Mackrell, K. and Johnston-Wilder, P. (2004) 'Thinking geometrically: dynamic imagery', in Johnston-Wilder, S. and Pimm, D. (eds) *Teaching Secondary Mathematics with ICT*. Buckingham: Open University Press, pp. 81–100.

MacNamara, A. and Roper, T. (1992) 'Unrecorded, unobserved and suppressed attainment: can our pupils do more than we know?' *Mathematics in School*, 21(5), 12–13.

Masingila, J. and de Silva, R. (2001) 'Teaching and learning school mathematics by building on students' out-of-school mathematics practice', in Atweh, B., Forgasz, H. and Nebres, B. (eds) *Sociocultural Research on Mathematics Education: An International Perspective.* Mahwah, NJ: Lawrence Erlbaum, pp. 329–44.

Mason, J. (1988) *Learning and Doing Mathematics.* London: Macmillan Education.

Mason, J., Burton, L. and Stacey, K. (1982) *Thinking Mathematically.* New York: Addison-Wesley.

Mason, J., Graham, A. and Johnston-Wilder, S. (2005) *Developing Thinking in Algebra.* London: Paul Chapman Publishing.

Mason, J. and Johnston-Wilder, S. (2004a) *Fundamental Constructs in Mathematics Education.* London: RoutledgeFalmer.

Mason, J. and Johnston-Wilder, S. (2004b) *Designing and Using Mathematical Tasks.* Milton Keynes: The Open University.

Matthews, M., Hlas, C. and Finken, T. (2009) 'Using lesson study and four-column lesson planning with pre-service teachers'. *The Mathematics Teacher*, 102(7), 504–8.

Mercer, N. (1995) *The Guided Construction of Knowledge.* Clevedon: Multilingual Matters.

Mercer, N. (2000) *Words and Minds: How We Use Language to Think.* Abingdon: Routledge.

Middleton, J. and Spanias, P. (1999) 'Motivation for achievement in mathematics: findings, generalizations and criticisms of the research', *Journal for Research in Mathematics Education*, 30(1), 65–88.

Miller, L. (1992) 'Teacher benefits from using impromptu writing prompts in algebra classes'. *Journal for Research in Mathematics Education*, 23(4), 329–40.

Morgan, C. (1988) *Writing to Learn in Mathematics*, Unpublished MSc. Option Report. London: University of London Institute of Education.

Morris, G. (1986) 'The Bristol maths trail'. *Mathematics Teaching*, 114, 2–3.

Nardi, E. and Steward, S. (2003) 'Is mathematics T.I.R.E.D.? A profile of quiet disaffection in the secondary mathematics classroom', *British Educational Research Journal*, 29(3), 345–67.

NCC (1989) *Mathematics National Curriculum Non-statutory Guidance.* York: National Curriculum Council.

NCC (1990) *The Whole Curriculum.* York: National Curriculum Council.

NCET (1994) *The IT Maths Pack.* Coventry: National Council for Educational Technology.

Nickson, M. (2004) *Teaching and Learning Mathematics: A Teacher's Guide to Recent Research and its Application.* London: Continuum.

Nolder, R. (1991) 'Mixing metaphor and mathematics in the secondary classroom', in Durkin, K. and Shire, B. (eds) *Language in Mathematical Education: Research and Practice.* Buckingham: Open University Press, pp. 105–113.

Noyes, A. (2007) *Rethinking School Mathematics.* London: Paul Chapman Publishing.

Nuñes, T. and Moreno, C. (1997) 'Solving word problems with different ways of representing the task', *Equals*, 3(2), 15–17.

Nuñes, T., Schlieman, A. and Carraher, D. (1993) *Street Mathematics and School Mathematics.* Cambridge: Cambridge University Press.

OECD (2007) *PISA 2006: Science Competencies for Tomorrow's World Executive Summary.* Paris: Organisation for Economic Co-operation and Development.

Ofqual (2009) *GCSE Subject Criteria for Mathematics* (http://www.ofqual.gov.uk/743.aspx).

Ofsted (2003) *The Key Stage 3 Strategy: Evaluation of the Second Year.* London: Office for Standards in Education.

Ofsted (2006) *Evaluating Mathematics Provision for 14–19-year-olds*, London: Office for Standards in Education.

Ofsted (2008) *Mathematics: Understanding the Score* (070063). London: Office for Standards in Education.

Ofsted (2009a) *Mathematics: Understanding the Score: Improving Practice in Mathematics* (Secondary), London: Office for Standards in Education.

Ofsted (2009b) *The Evaluation Schedule for Schools (Guidance and Grade descriptors for*

Inspecting Schools in England from September 2009). Manchester: Office for Standards in Education.

Ofsted (2009c) *Grade Criteria for the Inspection of Initial Teacher Education 2008–11*. London: Office for Standards in Education.

Oldknow, A., Taylor, R. and Tetlow, L. (2010) *Teaching Mathematics Using ICT*, 3rd edn. London: Continuum.

Orton, A. (2004) *Learning Mathematics: Issues, Theory and Classroom Practice*. London: Cassell Education.

Papert, S. (1980) *Mindstorms: Children, Computers and Powerful Ideas*. Brighton: Harvester Press.

Pask, G. (1976) *The Cybernetics of Human Learning and Performance*. London: Hutchinson.

Picker, S. H. and Berry, J. S. (2000) 'Investigating pupils' images of mathematicians', *Educ Stud Math* 43(1), 65–94.

Pimm, D. (1987) *Speaking Mathematically: Communication in Mathematics Classrooms*. London: Routledge and Kegan Paul.

Pimm, D. (ed.) (1988) *Mathematics, Teachers and Children*. London: Hodder and Stoughton.

Pimm, D. (1995) *Symbols and Meanings in School Mathematics*. London: Routledge.

Pimm, D. and Love, E. (eds) (1991) *Teaching and Learning School Mathematics*. London: Hodder and Stoughton.

Pinel, A. (1986) *Mathematical Activity Tiles Handbook: An ATM Discussion Book*. Derby: The Association of Teachers of Mathematics.

Plato (trans. Lee, H., 1987) *The Republic*. Harmondsworth: Penguin.

Portwood, M. (1997) 'Step by step', *Special Children*, 104, 18–20.

Prestage, S. and Perks, P. (2001) *Adapting and Extending Secondary Mathematics Activities: New Tasks for Old*. London: David Fulton.

Pumfrey, E. and Beardon, T. (2002) 'Art and mathematics: mutual enrichment', *Micromath*, 18(2), 21–27.

QCA (2001) *Using Assessment to Raise Achievement in Mathematics*: *Key Stages 1, 2 and 3*. London: Qualifications and Curriculum Authority. (Available from the QCA website: www.qca.org.uk/ages3-14/afl/)

QCA (2007a) *National Curriculum*. London: Qualifications and Curriculum Authority. See http://curriculum.qcda.gov.uk/key-stages-3-and-4/index.aspx

QCA Research Faculty (2007b) *Evaluation of Participation in GCE Mathematics*, Final Report.

Quilter, D. and Harper, E. (1988) 'Why we didn't like mathematics and why we can't do it', *Educational Research*, 30(2), 121–34.

Reid, D. (2002) 'Conjectures and refutation in grade 5 mathematics', *Journal for Research in Mathematics Education*, 33(5), 5–29.

Reynolds, D. (1996) 'The truth, the whole-class truth', *The Times Educational Supplement*, 1471, 7 June, p. 21.

Rich, B. (1993) 'The effect of the use of graphing calculators on classroom presentation', in Burton, L. and Jaworski, B. (eds) *Proceedings of the International Conference on Technology in Mathematics Teaching* (TMT 93). University of Birmingham, p. 556.

Roberts, G. (2002) *SET for Success: The Supply of People with Science, Technology, Engineering and Mathematics Skills*, London: HM Treasury.

Rowe, M. (1974) 'Wait time and rewards as instructional variables: their influence on language, logic and fate control', *Journal of Research in Science Teaching*, 11(4), 81–94.

Rowland, T. (1992) 'Pointing with pronouns'. *For the Learning of Mathematics*, 12(2), 44–48.

Ruddock, G. (1998) *Mathematics in the School Curriculum: An International Perspective* (www.inca.org.uk/pdf/maths_no_intro_98.pdf).

Ruthven, K. (1990) *Personal Technology in the Classroom – the NCET Graphic Calculators in Mathematics Project*. Cambridge: University of Cambridge Department of Education/National Council for Educational Technology.

Sadler, D. (1989) 'Formative assessment and the design of instructional systems', *Instructional Science*, 18(2), 119–44.

Scott-Hodgetts, R. (1986) 'Girls and mathematics: the negative implications of success', in Burton, L. (ed.) *Girls into Maths Can Go*. London: Holt, Rinehart and Winston, pp. 61–76.

Selinger, M. (ed.) (1994) *Teaching Mathematics*. London: Routledge.

Selinger, M. and Baker, L. (1991) *The What, Why, How and When of Mathematics Trails*. Derby: Association of Teachers of Mathematics.

Selkirk, K. (1983a) 'Simulation exercises for the classroom – 4: the Potato beetle', *Mathematics in School*, 12(4), 10–13.

Selkirk, K. (1983b) 'Simulation exercises for the classroom – 5: looking for a home', *Mathematics in School,* 12(5), 26–28.

Sells, L. (1973) *High School Mathematics as the Critical Filter in the Job Market*, Unpublished PhD thesis. Berkeley, CA: University of California.

Sfard, A. (2008) *Thinking as Communicating: Human Development, the Growth of Discourses, and Mathematizing*. Cambridge: Cambridge University Press.

Shan, S. and Bailey, P. (1991) *Multiple Factors: Classroom Mathematics for Equality and Justice*. Stoke: Trentham Books.

Sharp, C., Keys, W. and Benefield, P. (2001) *Homework: A Review of Recent Research*. Slough: National Foundation for Educational Research.

Shayer, M. (1999) 'Cognitive acceleration through science education II: its effects and scope', *International Journal of Science Education*, 21(8), 883–902.

Shayer, M., Johnson, D. and Adhani, M. (1999) 'Does "CAME" work?', in Bill, L. (ed.) *BSRLM Proceedings – June meeting*. Coventry: Mathematics Education Research Centre, University of Warwick, pp. 79–84.

Sherman, J. (1982) 'Mathematics: the critical filter: a look at some residues'. *Psychology of Women Quarterly*, 6(2), 428–44.

Shiu, C. (1988) 'A problem-solving approach to diagnostic assessment', in Pimm, D. (ed.) *Mathematics, Teachers and Children*, London: Hodder and Stoughton.

Shuard, H. and Rothery, A. (eds) (1984) *Children Reading Mathematics*. London: John Murray.

Shulman, L. S. (1986) 'Those who understand: knowledge growth in teaching', *Educational Researcher*, 15(2): 4–14.

Sinclair, J. and Coulthard, M. (1975) *Towards an Analysis of Discourse*. Oxford: Oxford University Press.

Sinclair, N. (2004) 'Mathematics on the internet', in Johnston-Wilder, S. and Pimm, D. (eds) *Teaching Secondary Mathematics with ICT*. Buckingham: Open University Press, pp. 201–14.

Sinclair, N. (2006) *Mathematics and Beauty: Aesthetic Approaches to Teaching Children*. New York: Teachers College Press.

Sinclair, N., Pimm, D. and Higginson, W. (eds) (2006) *Mathematics and the Aesthetic: New Approaches to an Ancient Affinity*. New York: Springer.

Skemp, R. (1976) 'Relational understanding and instrumental understanding'. *Mathematics Teaching*, 77, 20–26.

Smith, J. (2004) 'Developing paired teaching placements', *Educational Action Research*, 12(1), 99–125.

Smith, R. and Thatcher, D. (1991) 'Skidding of cars and quadratic formulae'. *Teaching Mathematics and its Applications*, 10(2), 53–7.

SOED (1991) *Curriculum and Assessment in Scotland, National Guidelines – Mathematics, 5–14*. Edinburgh: Scottish Office.

Sorensen, P., Greenwood, Y., Linden, A. and Watts, R. (2006) *Paired Student Placements in Partnership Schools: A Report to the TTA*. London: Teacher Training Agency (http://partnerships.ttrb.ac.uk/viewarticle2.aspx?contentId=11868).

Standards Unit (2005) *Improving Learning in Mathematics*. Available from:

http://tlp.excellencegateway.org.uk/teachingandlearning/downloads/default.aspx# math_learning (accessed on 28 November 2009).

Stigler, J. W. and Hiebert, J. (1999) *The Teaching Gap: Best Ideas from the World's Teachers for Improving Education in the Classroom*. New York: Free Press.

Stigler, J., Fernandez, C. and Yoshida, M. (1996) 'Traditions of school mathematics in Japanese and American elementary schools', in Steffe, L. *et al.* (eds) *Theories of Mathematical Learning*. Mahwah, NJ: Lawrence Erlbaum Associates, pp. 149–175.

Stigler, J. and Hiebert, J. (1997) 'Understanding and improving classroom mathematics instruction: an overview of the TIMSS video study'. *Phi Delta Kappan*, 79(1), 14–21.

Stubbs, M. (1983) *Language, Schools and Classrooms*, 2nd edn. London: Methuen.

Swan, M. (2005) *Improving Learning in Mathematics: Challenges and Strategies*. London: Department for Education and Skills Standards Unit. (Also available from https://www.ncetm.org.uk/files/224/improving_learning_in_mathematicsi.pdf)

Swan, M. (2006) *Collaborative Learning in Mathematics: A Challenge to Our Beliefs and Practices*. Leicester: National Research and Development Centre for Adult Literacy and Numeracy (NRDC) and the National Institute of Adult Continuing Education (NIACE).

Tahta, D. (1980) *A Boolean Anthology*. Derby: The Association of Teachers of Mathematics.

Tall, D. (1987) *Readings in Mathematics Education: Understanding the Calculus*. Derby: The Association of Teachers of Mathematics.

TDA (2007) *Professional Standards for Teachers*. London: HMSO. (Downloadable from http://www.tda.gov.uk/teachers/professionalstandards.aspx)

Tikly, C. and Wolf, A. (2000) *The Maths We Need Now: Demands, Deficits and Remedies*. University of London Institute of Education.

Toumasis, C. (2004) 'A mathematical diet model', *Teaching Mathematics and its Applications*, 23(4), 165–71.

TTA (1997) *Career Entry Profile Pack*. London: Teacher Training Agency.

TTA (2003a) *Career Entry and Development Profile Pack*. London: Teacher Training Agency.

TTA (2003b) *Qualifying to Teach: Professional Standards for Qualified Teacher Status and Requirements for Initial Teacher Training*. London: Teacher Training Agency.

Tyler, R. (1949) *Basic Principles of Curriculum and Instruction*. Chicago, IL: University of Chicago Press.

Ward-Penny, R. (2010) 'Con or context?' *Mathematics in School*, 39(1), 10–12.

Watson, A. (1994) 'What I do in my classroom', in Selinger, M. (ed.) *Teaching Mathematics*. London: Routledge, pp. 52–62.

Watson, A. (1996) 'Teachers' notions of mathematical ability in their pupils', *Mathematics Education Review*, 8, 27–35.

Watson, A., de Geest, E. and Prestage, S. (2003) *Deep Progress in Mathematics*: *The Improving Attainment in Mathematics Project* (http://www.atm.org.uk/journal/archive/mt187files/ DeepProgressEls.pdf).

Watson, A. and Mason, J. (1998) *Questions and Prompts for Mathematical Thinking*. Derby: The Association of Teachers of Mathematics.

Wells, D. (1991) *The Penguin Dictionary of Curious and Interesting Geometry*. Harmondsworth: Penguin.

Wiliam, D. and Bartholomew, H. (2004) 'It's not which school but which set you're in that matters: the influence of ability grouping practices on student progress in mathematics', *British Educational Research Journal*, 30(2), April.

Williams, D. and Stephens, M. (1992) 'Activity 1: five steps to zero', in Fey, J. and Hirsch, C. (eds) *Calculators in Mathematics Education* (NCTM Yearbook). Reston, VA: National Council of Teachers of Mathematics, pp. 233–4.

Williams, J. S. and Wake, G. D. (2007) 'Black boxes in workplace mathematics'. *Educational Studies in Mathematics*, 64(3), 317–43.

Wilson, P. and Edwards, J. (2009) 'Paired ITE teaching placements: implications for partnership development'. *Proceedings of the British Society for Research into Learning Mathematics*, 29(2), 82–7.

Winter, J. (2001) 'Personal, spiritual, moral, social and cultural issues in teaching mathematics', in Gates, P. (ed.) *Issues in Mathematics Teaching*. London: RoutledgeFalmer, pp. 197–213.

Wood, D. (1998) *How Children Think and Learn*, 2nd edn. Oxford: Basil Blackwell.

Woodrow, D. (1989) 'Multicultural and anti-racist mathematics teaching' in Ernest, P. (ed.), *Mathematics Teaching: The State of the Art*. Lewes: Falmer Press, pp. 229–35.

Wragg, E. (1995) 'Lesson structure', in Anderson, L. (ed.), *International Encyclopaedia of Teaching and Teacher Education*, 2nd edn. Oxford: Pergamon Press, pp. 207–11.

Wragg, E. and Brown, G. (2001) *Questioning in the Secondary School*. London: RoutledgeFalmer.

Wright, P. (ed.) (1999) *The Maths and Human Rights Resource Book: Bringing Human Rights into the Secondary Mathematics Classroom*, London: Amnesty International.

WWF (1990) *Mathematics and Environmental Education*. Godalming: World Wildlife Fund.

Zazkis, R., Liljedahl, P. and Sinclair, N. (2009) 'Lesson play: planning teaching versus teaching planning'. *For the Learning of Mathematics*, 29(1), 39–46.

NAME AND AUTHOR INDEX

SUBJECT INDEX

eBooks – at www.eBookstore.tandf.co.uk

A library at your fingertips!

eBooks are electronic versions of printed books. You can store them on your PC/laptop or browse them online.

They have advantages for anyone needing rapid access to a wide variety of published, copyright information.

eBooks can help your research by enabling you to bookmark chapters, annotate text and use instant searches to find specific words or phrases. Several eBook files would fit on even a small laptop or PDA.

NEW: Save money by eSubscribing: cheap, online access to any eBook for as long as you need it.

Annual subscription packages

We now offer special low-cost bulk subscriptions to packages of eBooks in certain subject areas. These are available to libraries or to individuals.

For more information please contact webmaster.ebooks@tandf.co.uk

We're continually developing the eBook concept, so keep up to date by visiting the website.

www.eBookstore.tandf.co.uk